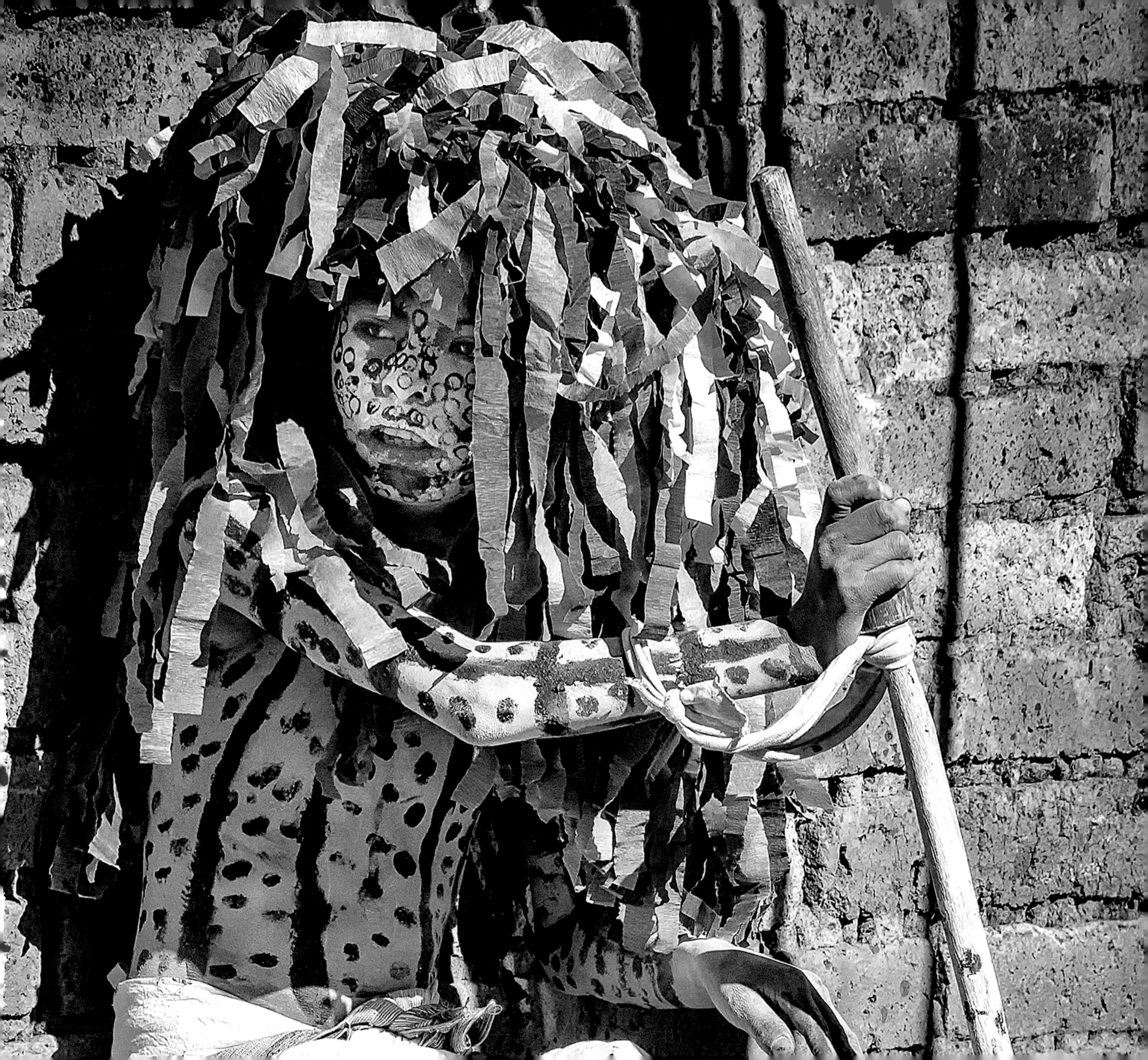

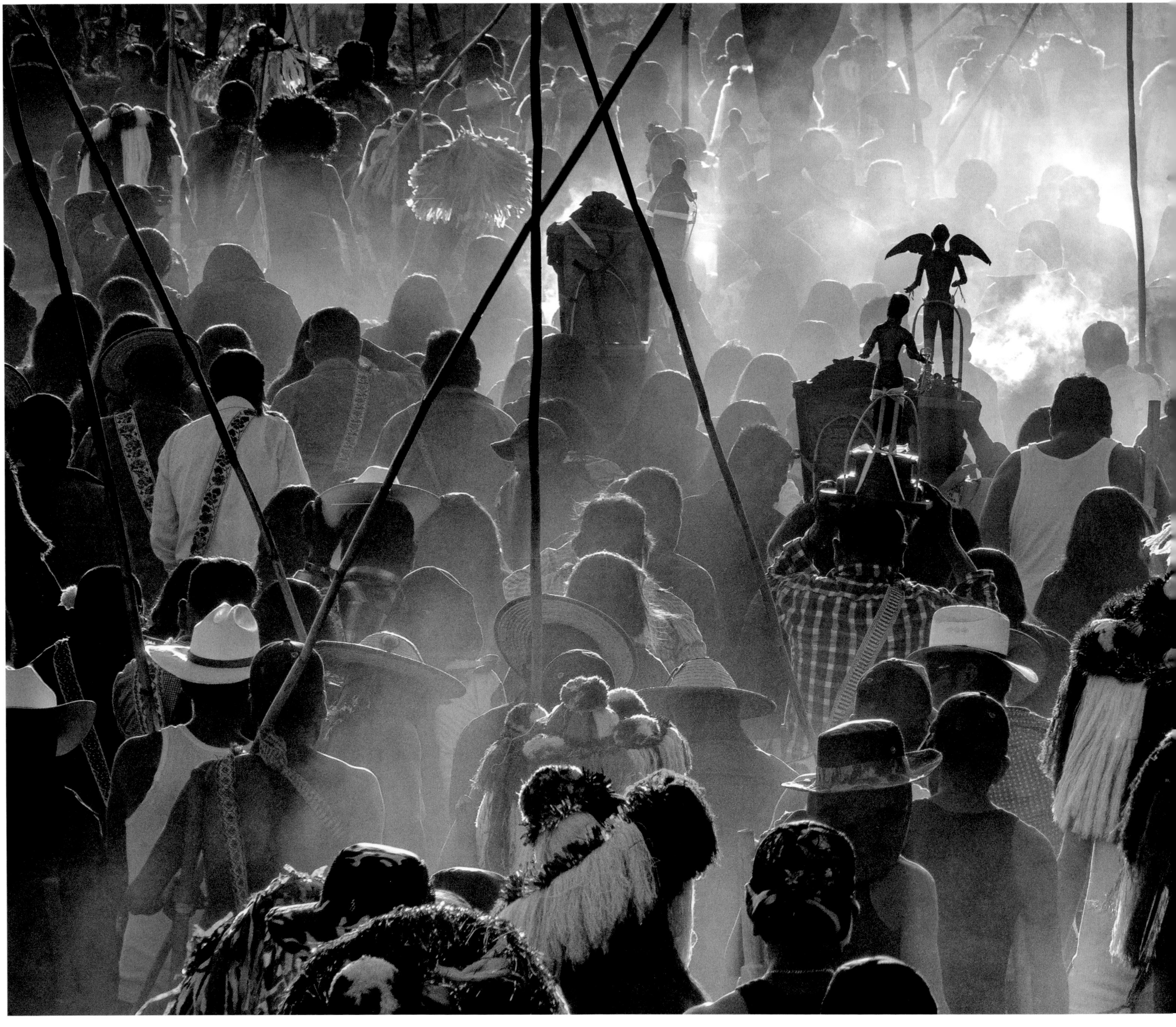

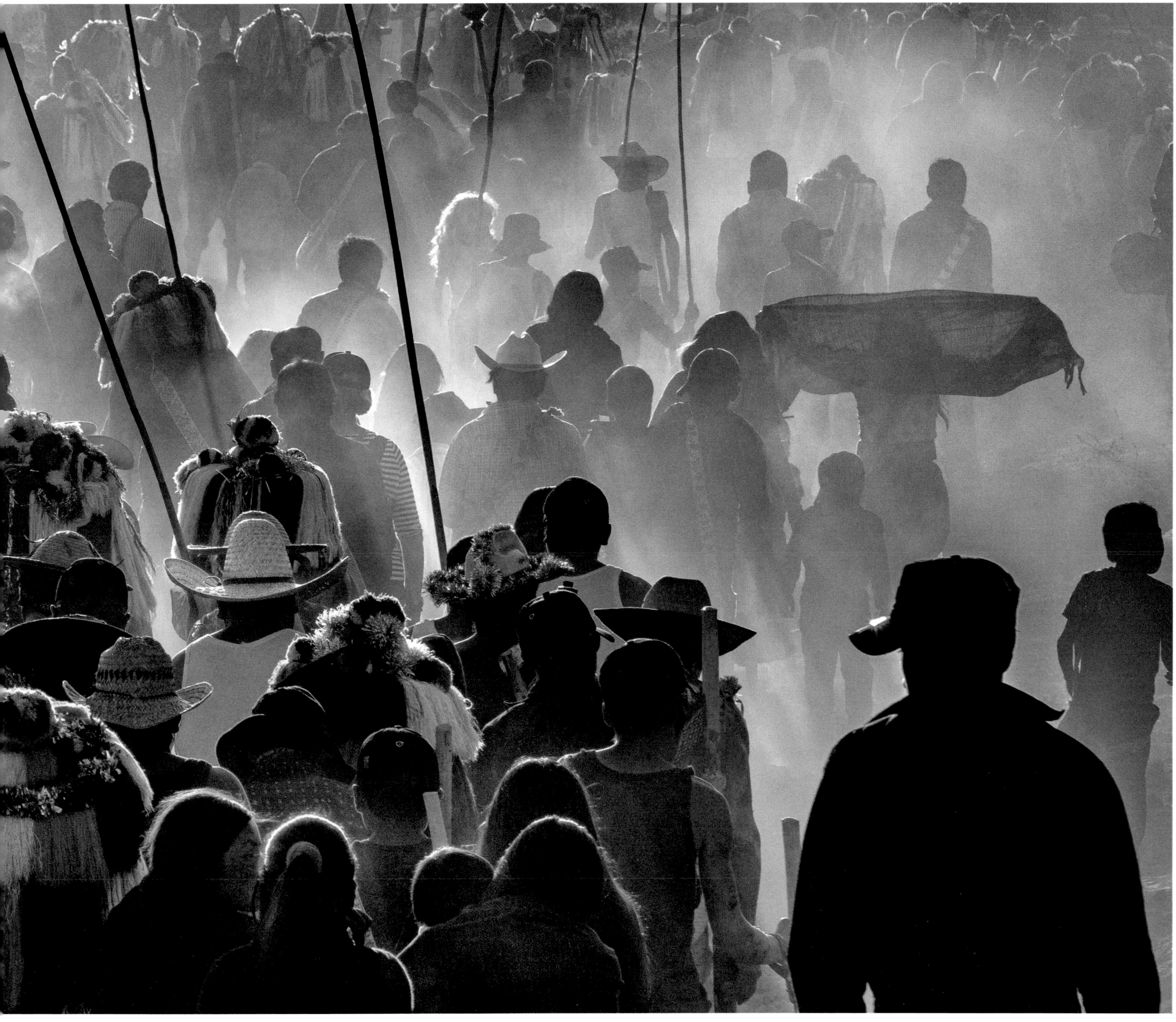

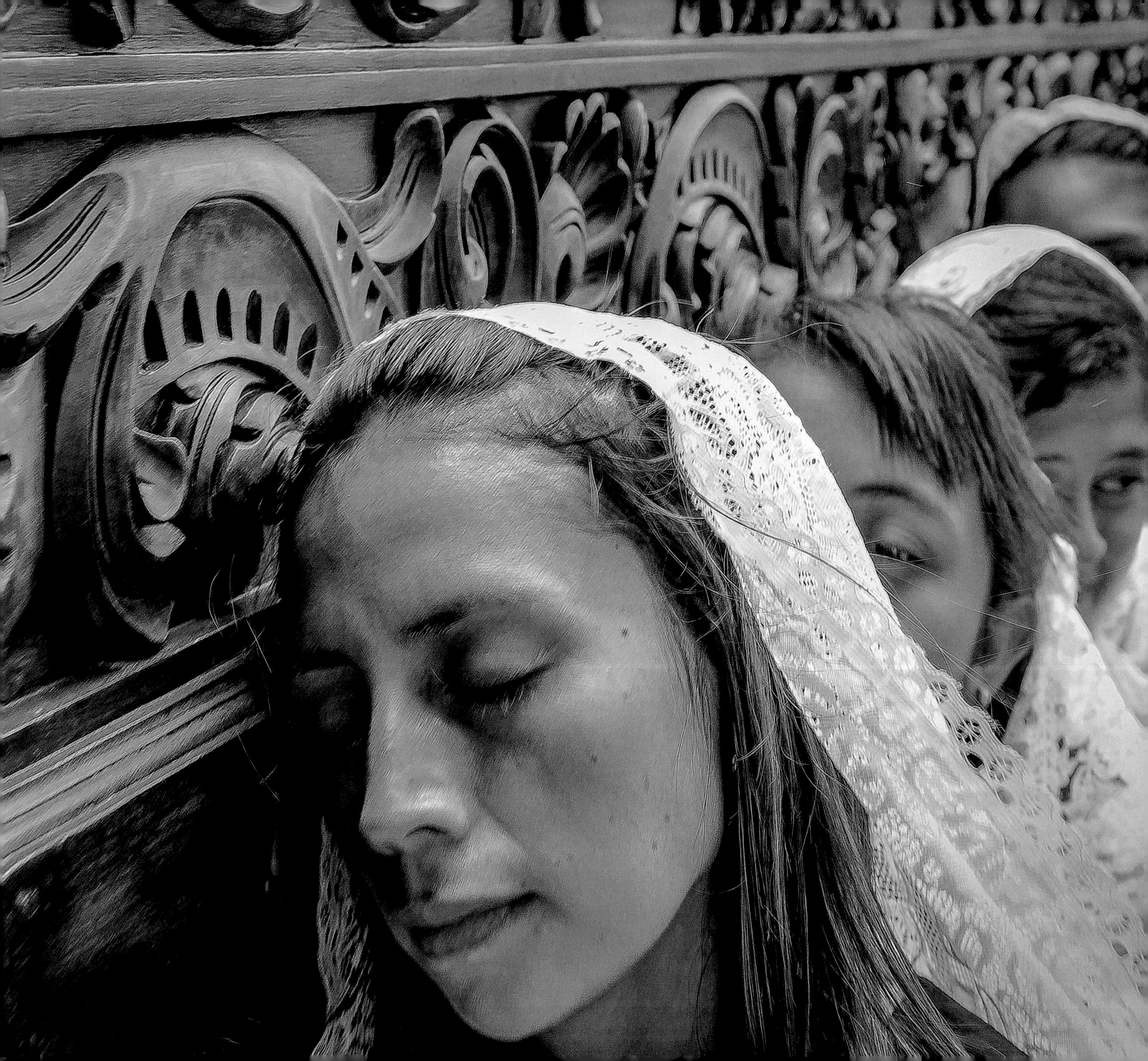

Seasons of Ceremonies

RITES AND RITUALS IN GUATEMALA AND MEXICO

WILLIAM FREJ

Introduction by

Anne Frej

Essays by

Gary H. Gossen

Frine Castillo Badillo & Philip E. Coyle

Nicolasa Chávez

Museum of New Mexico Press
Santa Fe

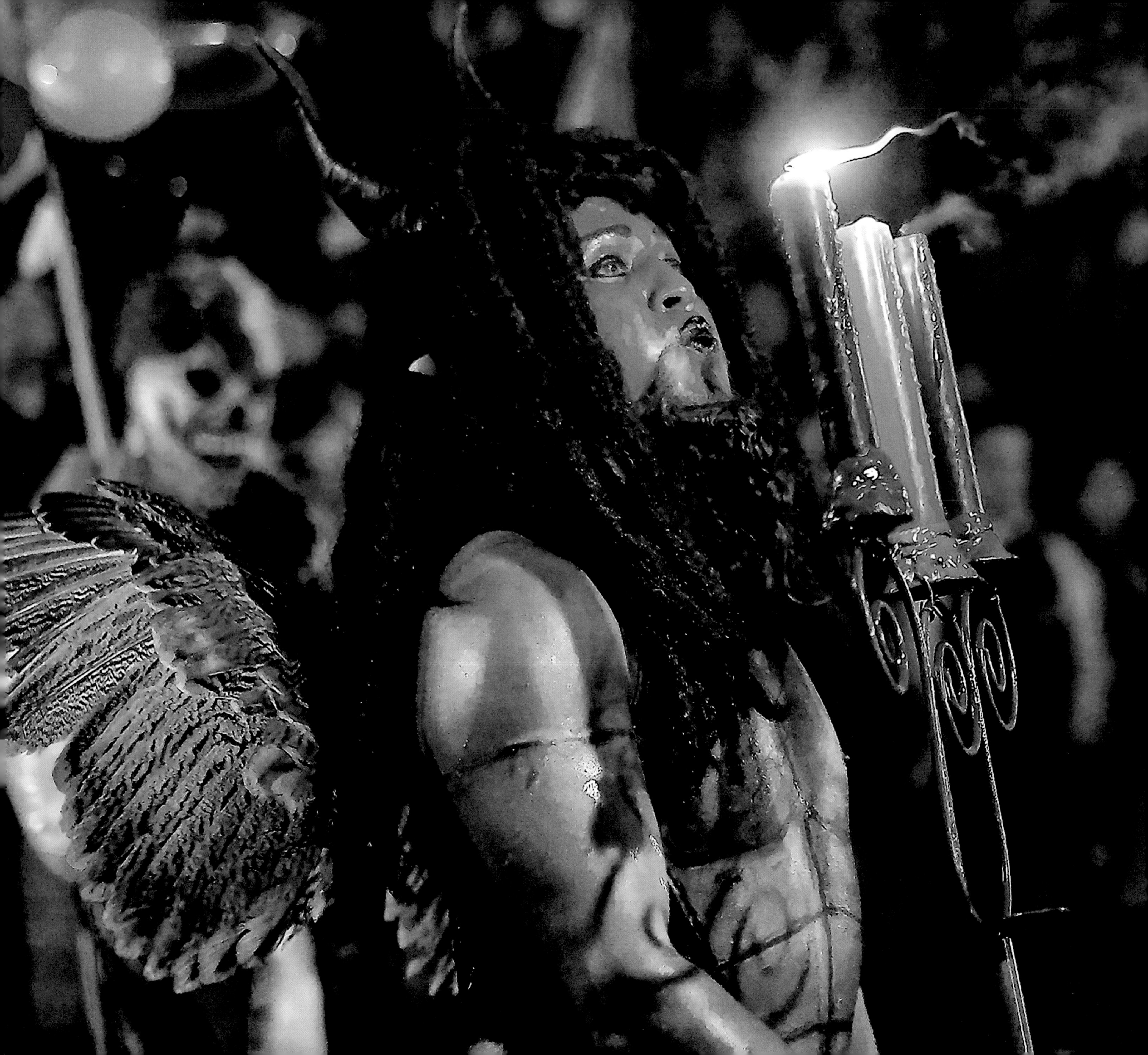

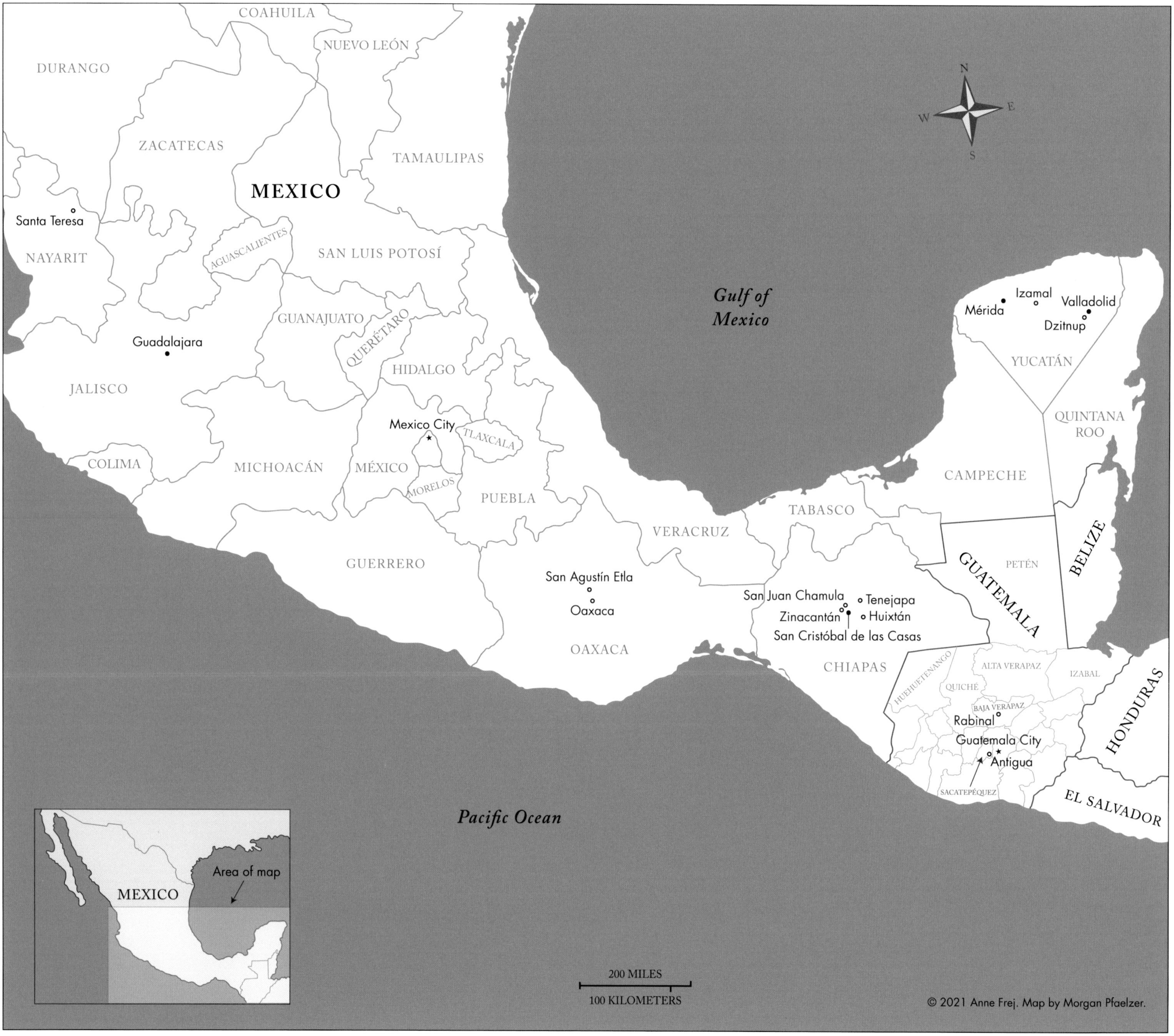
COAHUILA
NUEVO LEÓN
DURANGO
ZACATECAS
TAMAULIPAS
MEXICO
Santa Teresa
NAYARIT
AGUASCALIENTES
SAN LUIS POTOSÍ
Gulf of Mexico
GUANAJUATO
QUERÉTARO
Guadalajara
HIDALGO
JALISCO
Mexico City
TLAXCALA
COLIMA
MICHOACÁN
MÉXICO
MORELOS
PUEBLA
VERACRUZ
GUERRERO
San Agustín Etla
Oaxaca
OAXACA
N
E
W
S
Izamal
Mérida
Valladolid
Dzitnup
YUCATÁN
QUINTANA ROO
CAMPECHE
TABASCO
PETÉN
GUATEMALA
BELIZE
San Juan Chamula
Tenejapa
Zinacantán
Huixtán
San Cristóbal de las Casas
CHIAPAS
HUEHUETENANGO
ALTA VERAPAZ
IZABAL
QUICHÉ
BAJA VERAPAZ
Rabinal
Guatemala City
Antigua
SACATEPÉQUEZ
HONDURAS
EL SALVADOR
Pacific Ocean
Area of map
MEXICO
200 MILES
100 KILOMETERS
© 2021 Anne Frej. Map by Morgan Pfaelzer.

Introduction

ANNE FREJ

THE PHOTOGRAPHS IN THIS BOOK present vignettes from thirteen festivals that are celebrated throughout the year in Mexico and Guatemala. These ceremonies have pre-Columbian origins overlaid with Christian religious practices and holidays introduced by the Spanish colonizers, and are generally arranged around agricultural cycles. Few occur during the peak summer growing season, when everyone is busy tending to their crops, hence our focus on rituals that take place in winter, spring, and fall.

We hope the images gathered here portray the intensity and complexity of these rituals within the context of each community's distinctive traditions and practices. At the most visible, public level, the traditional clothing, dances, and colorful processions grab the viewer's attention. But a look below the surface reveals that these are carefully staged events with profound meaning not only for the participants but for each community.

We attended these ceremonies as respectful outsiders, sometimes with only limited knowledge of what to expect. In every case we were overwhelmed afterward with the desire to know more about what we had just seen and experienced. This book is a result of that desire. As accompaniment to the photographs here, four eminent scholars have contributed essays on three of the celebrations. As essayists Philip E. Coyle and Frine Castillo Badillo suggest, this information offers insights into the belief systems that frame these festivities, allowing us to "move beyond the edge of the plaza." Knowing more about the myths and stories of these communities helps viewers comprehend the sense of the magic that is such an integral part of the events depicted here.

Common beliefs dating back to pre-Columbian times unite many of the people spread throughout Mesoamerica and still provide a foundation for their outlook on the nature of a sacred cosmos and their role in it. In his essay "Religious Traditions of Mesoamerica," Gary H. Gossen describes the early cultural history of a region that spans the area from Central Mexico to Guatemala, Honduras, Belize, El Salvador, and northern Costa Rica. At the time of the Spanish contact with the New World in the 1500s, there were still dozens of ideological power centers overseen by a ruling elite and religious hierarchy representing official religions, while people at the lower levels of society avidly maintained their own local religious traditions. On top of this base rests the legacy of the Spanish conquistadors and the Catholic fathers who followed them into the New World and added a layer of Western religion, resulting in a hybrid of Indigenous and Catholic spiritual practices. The rites and rituals we see today are the expression of this intermingling.

Our visual chronicle of three seasons of ceremonies in Mexico and Guatemala starts in winter, with two feast days devoted to the Virgin Mary. Each of the titles or names given to the Virgin is regarded as a saint in her own right, and each has her own distinctive image and feast day. Our Lady of Izamal is honored on December 10 each year in the town of Izamal, Yucatán, with processions and blessing in the open atrium of the Convent of San Antonio de Padua. The Feast of Our Lady of Guadalupe takes place in towns and villages all over Mexico two days later, on December 12, the anniversary of her appearance in 1531 to Juan Diego, the poor shepherd who witnessed her on a hill outside what is now Mexico City. In the Yucatán, people participate in candlelit processions through city streets and prayers and worship at churches. Young devotees can be seen on streets and highways, riding bicycles or walking with flags bearing the distinctive figure of the Virgin of Guadalupe encircled by sunbeams and standing on a crescent moon.

On Christmas Eve, a unique dance with three characters in wooden masks takes place in the small village of Dzitnup, in central Yucatán. The dance's narrative features Abraham and Isaac battling with the Devil to protect the infant Jesus. This adaptation of a Christian story from the Old Testament recounts a bigger story of good versus evil, as many rituals do.

In Zinacantán and Tenejapa, both in Chiapas, feast day celebrations honoring town patron saints take place in the period before Lent. The Feast of San Sebastián in Zinacantán honors a Christian saint, but it also marks the start of a new year. Events from the town's ancient and historical past are blended together and accompanied by raucous rituals and characters in costume carrying stuffed dead animals. The Feast of San Ildefonso in nearby Tenejapa is a more solemn observance, with the focus on a procession carrying images of the Virgin Mary and San Ildefonso from the church through the streets of the town. More than mere symbolic representations, these saints are beings that must be honored and cared for so that they may bestow favors to the faithful in a reciprocal arrangement and intercede on their behalf with the higher divinities.

The Rabinal Achí is a pre-Hispanic play with music and masked characters that is performed in the small Guatemala highland town of Rabinal. In simple terms, it tells the story of two warring factions, but for the community, it has much deeper meaning related to ways of understanding the world. As in many other Maya communities, this major celebration is timed to coincide with the feast day of the town's Catholic patron saint, San Pablo.

Carnival celebrations in the weeks leading up to the period of Lent—the forty days of fasting, sacrifice, and personal reflection before Easter—are busy times in the mountainous state of Chiapas in Central Mexico. The tradition of Carnival emerged in Europe during the Middle Ages as an antidote to the austerity of Lent and came to the New World during the Spanish Colonial Period. In towns and villages throughout Mexico and Guatemala, Carnival often coincides with other indigenous Maya celebrations that relate to the lost five days in the Maya calendar. Photographs of Carnival in Huixtán and Tenejapa illustrate how communities personalize their celebrations within a common framework.

The Festival of Games in San Juan Chamula takes place over four days before and including Ash Wednesday, the first day of Lent. It's an elaborate presentation with extensive preparations and intense ritual play among a huge cast of characters. In his essay "The Chamula Festival of Games: A Complex Self-Portrait," anthropologist Gary H. Gossen explains how the festival helps the community of Chamula appraise itself and its role in the world by ritually destroying and reconstructing its moral community. Disruptive forces are vanquished, and the Sun/Christ prevails.

The arrival of spring, which corresponds to the spring equinox, around March 20, is a time of rebirth and resurrection. Easter celebrations, which are pegged to the first full moon after this date, take place in Christian communities all over the world. In the colonial city of Antigua, outside Guatemala City, the Holy Week before Easter is marked by processions of wooden palanquins for statues of saints carried by groups of men or women and the creation of beautiful, ephemeral "carpets" of flowers and other natural materials laid on top of city streets.

In the remote village of Santa Teresa, in Nayarit, Mexico, the celebration of Puáaxku jitsé takes place in the week before Easter, but it goes far beyond the Passion Play typically performed around the world during Holy Week. In their essay "The Holy Week of Puáaxku jitsé," Coyle and Castillo explain that ancient belief systems were not easily eradicated by the Spanish, if at all. The annual Puáaxku jitsé rituals create connections between the people of Santa Teresa and the magical natural forces all around to help assure health and well-being. Natural objects, places, and even ritual actors such as the Xumuávika, who are painted black and white and play an important role in the celebration, are not just symbolic representations. They hold an actual life force.

Summer, which begins around June 20 or 21, the date of the summer solstice, is a time of intensive agriculture activities, so there are fewer major celebrations. Fall, which begins on the date of the fall equinox, around September 23, is the season of harvesting crops. All over the world, there are celebrations honoring the dead at the end of October and beginning of November, a time when shorter days lead into winter.

The Day of the Dead—known in Spanish as Día de los Muertos, or just Muertos—is celebrated widely in Latino communities. Nicolasa Chávez's essay "Día de los Muertos: Honoring the Dead" provides historical context for this popular holiday. When the Spanish—who already celebrated All Saints' Day and All Souls' Day—arrived in Mexico, they encountered Indigenous ceremonies honoring the dead. Over time, the practices of these very different cultures blended into the joyous Muertos festivities celebrating lost loved ones that we see today.

Observing these celebrations requires a metaphysical perspective that may be unfamiliar to many of us in modern society. As explained by the essays in this book, deeply held beliefs and worldviews underlie these complex events, which are embarked upon not for enjoyment or even celebration, but as an essential way of creating connections to the natural forces of the universe. The rites and rituals such as the ones illustrated here are manifestations of reality, not mere portrayals or re-enactments of ancient myths. They serve not only to unite communities and celebrate the seasons of the year but, most importantly, to help to ensure harmony and health now and for generations to come.

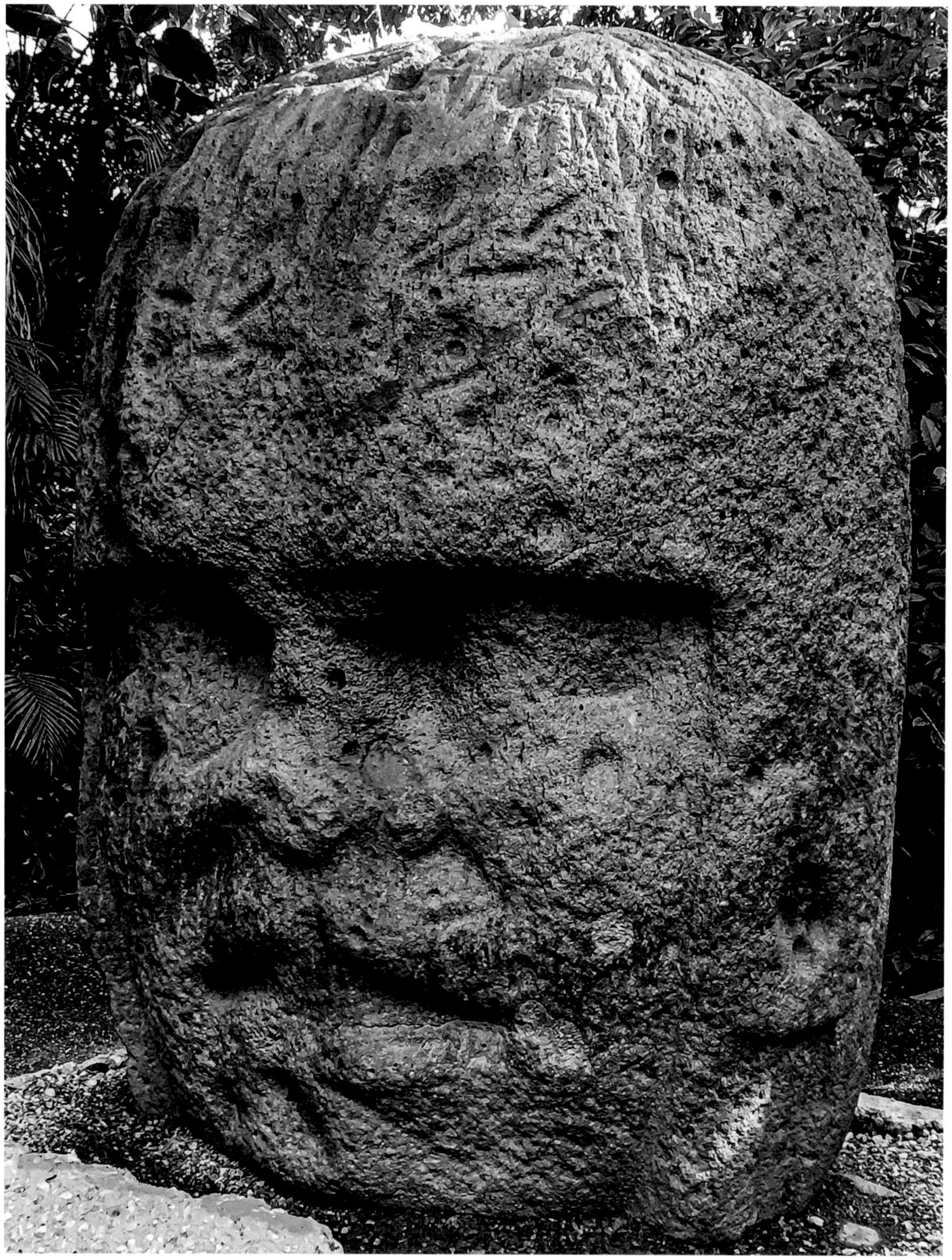

An Olmec stone head found at La Venta, Tabasco, Mexico, and now on display at La Venta Park, Villahermosa, Mexico, 2019 (Anne Frej)

Religious Traditions of Mesoamerica

GARY H. GOSSEN WITH ANNE FREJ

Author's Note: This essay was compiled and edited by Anne Frej from Gary H. Gossen texts, which have been excerpted from *The Legacy of Mesoamerica,* by Robert M. Carmack, Janine L. Gasco, and Gary H. Gossen (Upper Saddle River, NJ: Prentice Hall, 1996) and *Telling Maya Tales* by Gary H. Gossen (New York and London: Routledge, 1999) with permission of the publishers.

The region known by anthropologists and historians as Mesoamerica was characterized by Native American cultures that have shared, with several other regions of the world, the achievement of state-level societies and larger polities such as kingdoms and empires. Several contemporary cultural groups of this region who are heirs of both a pre-Columbian past and Spanish missionization are portrayed in the photographs in this book: the Maya in Yucatán, Chiapas, and the highlands of Guatemala, plus the Náayeri, of Nayarit, and the people of Oaxaca. This essay frames the background of these cultures within the context of greater Mesoamerica.

Cultural History of Mesoamerica

The earliest Americans arrived on the continent as fishers, hunters, and gatherers. They lived in small nomadic bands, and it is assumed that they had spiritual beliefs and practices that were possibly similar to the shamanic traditions that survive today today among the Inuits and other sub-Arctic Indigenous people of North America and among the nomadic hunters and gatherers of Amazonia. It is believed that shamanic belief and supernatural meditation formed a substratum of spirituality in which all Amerindian cultures participated to some degree. Shamanism in its ancient form is thought to have been a highly individualistic and pragmatic form of spirituality, the goal of the religious quest being essentially to ensure human well-being, food supply, and health by interacting with the spirits of animals, plants, geographical features, and deities that were believed to be responsible for hunting, gathering, and fishing resources, as well as human destiny.

Upon the base of thousands of village cultures there evolved, in what is known by archaeologists as the Preclassic or Formative Period (2000 BCE–200 CE), large, composite units of social integration. From the beginning of this period, Mesoamerican religious traditions, like the region itself, began to evolve a distinctive identity. One of the strongest early expressions in the archaeological record suggesting political and social integration above the level of a village culture occurs in the Olmec Style. Originating around 1150 BCE in the Central Gulf Coast of Mexico, this distinctive iconography depicting a baby-faced human jaguar motif seen in colossal stone heads, as well as stone sculptures and ceramics, appears to be associated with a major cult that came to wield considerable political and ideological influence over large parts of Central and Eastern Mexico by the time of Christ.

It was once believed that the Olmec civilization constituted the major foundational culture from which subsequent expressions of Mesoamerican civilization evolved—it was known to be very old and it exhibited most of the essential traits of Mesoamerican culture. There is now increasing evidence that it was not just the Olmec culture but, rather,

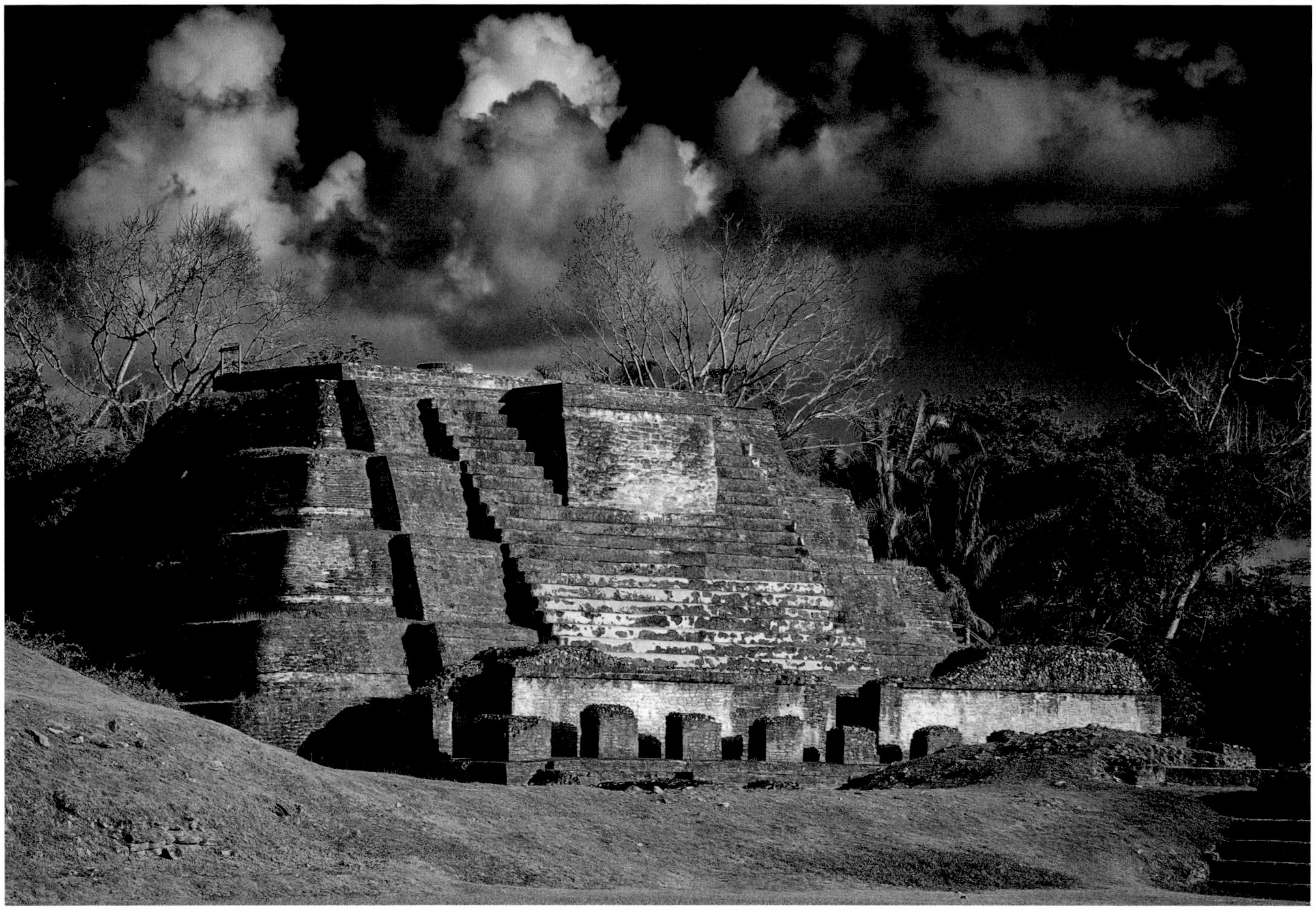

Altun Ha, a Maya city that flourished during the Classic Period, Rockstone Pond, Belize, 2018

several influential Formative Period societies that provided the foundation of Mesoamerican culture. Mesoamerican civilization evolved as the complex product of both the political and economic means to form larger integrated polities and the symbolic forms that rationalized and legitimized the existence of these greater units of integration. Religion clearly ranked as a major political and ideological force in this created universe of meaning in ancient Mesoamerica.

The Classic Period (200–900 CE) was a period of consolidation of theocratic states throughout Mesoamerica, in hundreds of variants stretching from Central Mexico to Honduras. All of the city-states of this period were focused administratively on carefully planned ceremonial centers characterized by monumental religious architecture and elaborate subsidiary structures. They appear to have been ruled by hereditary divine kings who lived surrounded by architectural and artistic expressions of their grandeur. Indeed, through study and interpretation of the great urban centers of this period, it seems clear that their overall spatial design and major structures expressed nothing less than divine cosmograms, or replications of the cosmos.

During the Postclassic phase of the Classic Period (850–1521 CE) many of the major lowland Maya cities were apparently abandoned, but life went on, and the subsequent cultural expressions of all areas of Mesoamerica were extraordinary. The Postclassic Period is the phase of ancient Mesoamerican history that is best known to us, for contact-period Spanish observers and chroniclers actually witnessed and recorded minute details of this world even as they were destroying it in order to create colonial New Spain.

Exploration of Mesoamerica by Spaniards began between 1517 and 1519, as first Hernández de Córdova, then Juan de Grijalva, and finally Hernán Cortés sailed around the Yucatán Peninsula and northward along the Gulf Coast of Mexico. In 1519, while Cortés and his men were camped with the Totonac Indians of Veracruz, they witnessed the arrival of a group of Aztec tax collectors. The Spaniards were astonished by the extreme deference with which the Totonacs served the Aztecs and began to understand—perhaps for the first time—just how politically complex and culturally diverse the newly discovered world of Native peoples really was.

The point was driven home even more forcefully to the Spaniards as they began their history-making journey from the Veracruz coast to the Central Basin of Mexico. At each step along the way they encountered economically richer, culturally more sophisticated, and politically more powerful peoples. Beyond Totonac country, they felt they were entering a different sort of country, one in which the gleaming plastered stone buildings of the towns and fortresses reminded them of Spain itself. The Spaniards were unprepared for what they saw in November 1519, when they finally reached the Basin of Mexico and entered the Aztec capital of Tenochtitlán. There they experienced the pomp, ceremony, and great wealth surrounding Motecuhzoma (also known as Montezuma), the ruler of the Aztec Empire. The Spaniards quickly determined that the Aztec Empire was vast, extending for hundreds of miles in all directions, and that they had seen only a small part of the Mesoamerican world, and that many other kingdoms, large and small, were yet to be explored and subdued. With the fall of Tenochtitlán to the Spaniards in 1521, Cortés began to send his captains on military expeditions from the Basin of Mexico to contact and, if necessary, conquer the diverse peoples and kingdoms of Mesoamerica. In the wake of these events, the region is heir today of the hybrid Spanish and Native American cultural forms that resulted from the Spanish conquest.

At the time of contact, Mesoamerica was the seat of dozens of state theocracies, and it was a sophisticated and cosmopolitan scene. All of these ideological power centers constituted "great traditions" in Robert Redfield's sense of the term,[1] signifying that they represented the official ideological canon of the ruling elite and the associated priesthood that controlled the destinies of millions of people of diverse ethnic and linguistic backgrounds who were forced to live as economic tributaries and dependencies of the urban administrative centers. However, the local village cultures that constituted the peasant peripheries of the theocratic states were themselves bearers of religious customs and beliefs that reflected their own local experiences of memory and practice. Followers of these local religions expressed what Robert Redfield called "little traditions," because they continued to practice highly local spiritual activities even as they had to adapt to larger state demands in terms of their public ceremonial life. Thus, in addition to maintaining obligatory cult affiliations that emanated from the urban centers, precontact Mesoamericans also engaged in local shamanic, ancestral, and agricultural practices.

Indigenous Religious Practice Under Spain

It is reasonable to expect that when the Spanish missionary state decapitated and destroyed the major public foci of pre-Columbian religious practice, obliging local elites to become lay catechists—or, at least, local sponsors—of the new Christian doctrine, they did so in highly diverse ways that were subject to local practice. In effect, Christianity became the new great tradition to which all were required to pay lip service. Little traditions, whose religious practices had been for millennia focused on rituals of home, lineage, and field, did not lose their vitality, though these local foci of religious practice received a new overlay of Christian ideas.

By the end of the sixteenth century, Mesoamerica had been profoundly transformed. New Spain—as Mexico and Central America were called by the Spaniards—was fully established, as one of the two linchpins, along with Peru, of Spain's New World empire. Hundreds of churches sat on or near the ruins of pyramid mounds that had been the foundations of ancient Mexican and Maya structures. In fact, these stone ruins often provided the building materials for the new colonial structures.

The concept of God and associated central doctrines of Christianity did not reach the newly converted in a way that the missionaries expected, for these Christian concepts often merged as a new semantic overlay with what were already, prior to the Spanish conquest, complex, multifaceted ideas. For example, throughout Mesoamerica in the Colonial Period—and even today in thousands of Indigenous communities—Jesus Christ has become one of several manifestations of the ancient Sun God. Similarly, the Virgin Mary has merged with multiple expressions of the ancient Moon Goddess and other female deities. The Christian saints also became associated with various pre-Christian concepts and deities.

The missionary friars of the Catholic mendicant orders had tremendous influence and prestige during the early decades of Spanish rule in Mexico and Guatemala, but it is important to note that Native people played an active role in formulating their own understanding of Christianity and the practices associated with the religion. They interpreted Christianity in terms that were more or less compatible with their own cultures. Also, since Native people had no concept of religion or faith as a clearly defined entity separable from the rest of culture, they did not comprehend what it was that they were supposed to be giving up and taking on.

To the Native people, Christianity appeared as a set of practices, many of which resembled their traditional practices of prayer, offerings, processions, dramas, fasting, and the use of sacred images. It was on these expressive and often collective behaviors that the Native people focused,

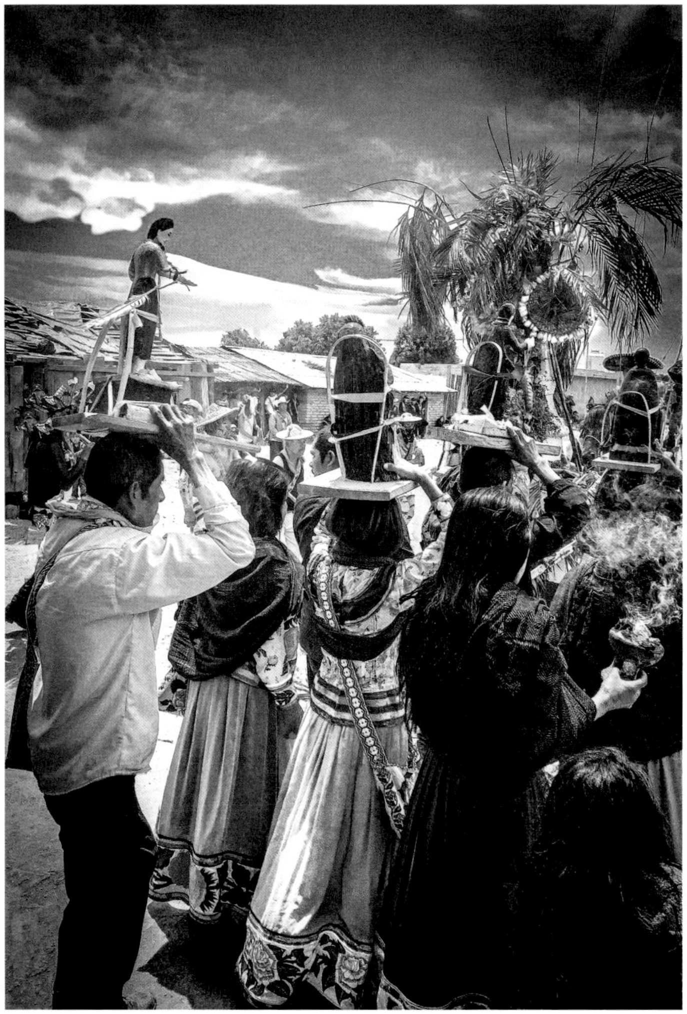

Saints carried on small wood palanquins in procession during the Puáaxku jitsé celebrations, Santa Teresa, Nayarit, Mexico, 2019

sometimes with notable enthusiasm. Christianity proceeded as a process of addition and substitution with the existing repertoire of devotional practices. Over time, new prayers, new images, new songs, new penances, and new festivals were adopted as many of the old practices were abandoned. But there was never a sudden and total substitution of a new faith for an old.

Traditional religion was more a matter of collective community rites and celebrations than of an individualized personal faith. Native spirituality was closely linked to collective experiences involving elaborate ritual rather than to private prayer and contemplation. Over time, Christianity would become, above all, a collective public enterprise associated with community identity—now centered on a patron saint rather than a tutelary divinity.

At the periphery of the distribution of folk Catholic traditions of Hispanic Latin America lie tens of thousands of local religious traditions that belong neither to the pre-Columbian nor to the Christian moral universes. These highly localized spiritual expressions are best understood as unique belief systems. Each community represents an ever-evolving tradition derived from pre-Columbian roots and Hispanic-Catholic missionization.

In general, only the larger Native communities had resident priests. Smaller communities would receive occasional visits from priests who lived in other towns. On these visits the priest would celebrate Mass, baptize new babies, conduct marriage ceremonies, and hear confessions. As a result, the Native people were able to exercise considerable control over their own religious life. Persons from the community handled many day-to-day affairs and also organized community festivals.

With the paucity of clergy necessary to service thousands of Indigenous parishes, Indian lay catechists, often drawn from the old elite classes, were trained in doctrine by the missionaries. They typically received instruction in Spanish and were taught the basic elements of the catechism, with the expectation that they would carry on day-to-day maintenance of the faith in their communities when the the Spanish clergy were not present. Known in Mesoamerica as *sacritanes* (sacristans) and *maestros de capilla* (chapel choir masters), these Indigenous representatives of the Catholic Church were often responsible for assisting with the daily office, for translating prayers and canticles into Native languages, and for serving as the link between local communities with the Church and the Crown.

Religious organization below the occasionally present parish priest (usually a Spaniard or mestizo) and the trusted lay assistants (sacristans and choir masters) consisted of associations of local people who were designated to sponsor and maintain images of saints, to care for their accoutrements and clothing, and to be responsible for paying for annual festivals in their honor. These cult-maintenance groups were vigorously encouraged in Mesoamerica. Typically, the leaders would bear titles such as *mayordomo* (steward) and *alférez* (standard bearer). They received honor and prestige for their contributions to community life and for their sponsorship of particular saints who were identified as being special patrons and protectors of local health, prosperity, and well-being.

With this system in place, religious events and festivals could be conceived and staged, mingling themes from pre-contact beliefs and practices, with relative autonomy. If the cults to the saints—as ubiquitous in the Colonial Period as they are today—served the purpose of mobilizing individual communities in corporate celebration of approved icons, they also functioned to encourage the new forms of Indian Christianity as highly distinct from one another and from creole and mestizo beliefs and practices.

The most important institution in Native religious life was the *cofradía* (religious brotherhood). These voluntary organizations were, and are today, overseen by the Catholic Church, but members have freedom to organize their religious celebrations much as they choose. A small village might have just two or three cofradías, but a larger town might have a dozen, and a city would have several attached to its neighborhood churches. Each would be responsible for the public celebration associated with its designated devotion. For example, a cofradía dedicated to the Passion of Christ would conduct an elaborate procession on Good Friday and act out a dramatization of the Crucifixion.

Catholic saints were regarded as community sponsors and protectors. Under a colonial policy, the name of each town's patron saint was combined with the town's traditional name to yield a composite designation—for example, San Juan Chamula. The relationship between the Native communities and their new Christian patron-deities retained—and still retains today—a contractual character, wherein

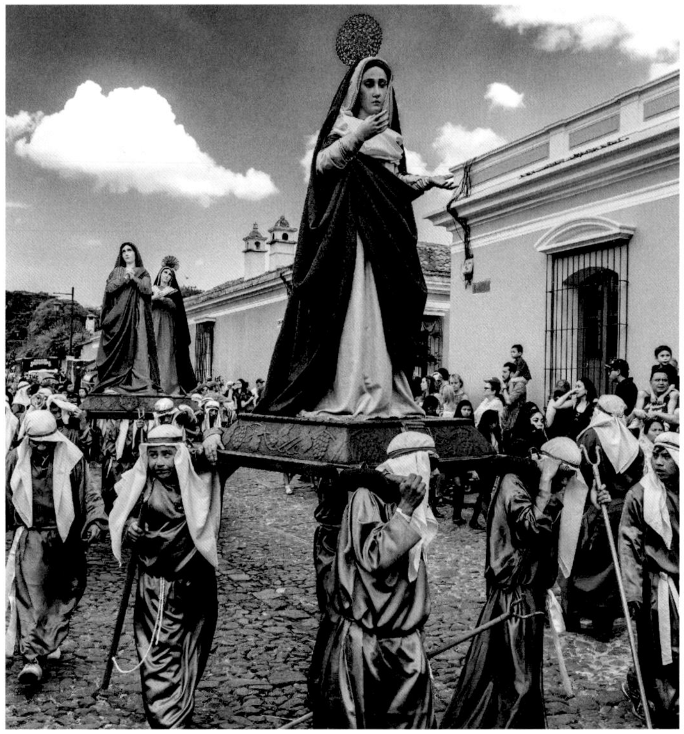

An image of the Blessed Virgin Mary carried in procession during Holy Week, Antigua, Guatemala, 2019

the community provides service in exchange for the saint's protection and support. No reward is bestowed without adequate payment.

Today, the principal saint worshipped throughout Mexico, by Native people and mestizos alike, is Our Lady of Guadalupe, an advocation of the Blessed Virgin Mary. The story of her apparition to a humble Indian is an important national myth, symbolizing the merging of Spanish and Indigenous cultures, under divine sanction, into the Catholic and mestizo nation. After Mexico gained its independence from Spain, this cult began to function as an expression of national identity.

The emphasis on public celebration also shows how easily nonpublic beliefs and practices might continue to express significant pre-Columbian content and ideas. Highly localized precontact rituals and practices associated with the individual life cycle, family, and domestic life could, with relative ease and impunity, persist and successfully coexist with the more prescribed content of public devotion. Agricultural and fertility rituals, along with related beliefs and practices associated with ancestors and deities for rain, wind, and earth, constituted an area in which precontact customs could continue in relative isolation from the vigilance of Spanish Crown authorities. This helps to account for the persistence of hundreds of forms of shamanic curing and divination practices in the modern era.

It is helpful to consider the myriad syncretic forms that evolved in the colonial era as expressing both prescribed uniformity in the structure (if not content and practice) of public devotion and relatively unmonitored domestic and individual religious practice, much of which was veiled discreetly from the vigilance of the Catholic Church. The many expressions of this public-domestic mix of spiritual beliefs and practices are further multiplied by the fact that the linguistic and cultural mosaic of colonial Mesoamerica was, as it is today, enormously diverse.

It is relatively easy to speak of certain themes that unify Mesoamerican spirituality, but it must be noted that there are millions of people for whom these themes do not hold true. In spite of this, generalization is possible about a relatively circumscribed segment of Indian Mesoamerica that is represented by the photographs in this volume.

Core Features of Mesoamerican Spirituality

Six core features of spirituality span the linguistic diversity and ethnic, political, and ecological boundaries of Mesoamerica across several millennia. Because these traits are so widespread and apparently so durable, it is not unreasonable to assert that religion, cosmology, and related symbolic constructions may be among the more important features that unify the Native peoples of the region as a distinctive cultural space, both past and present. The realm of spiritual and religious traditions does not lie far removed from the lives of all contemporary peoples residing in the bounds of the ancient Mesoamerican lands.

The Concept of Individual Co-essences

Perhaps linked to a deep shamanic past, Mesoamerican spiritual traditions throughout the region carry a fundamental commitment to the idea that each individual carries a predestined fate that is expressed by co-essence bestowed at the time of conception. Sometimes merely an abstract destiny, but more often embodied in the person of a deity or an animal or a spirit companion, this co-essence experiences the life journey of the human counterpart through good and ill, often determining in the supernatural world what will befall the individual—power or wealth, sickness or health, early death or a fulfilled life, humility or power.

In both the ancient and modern eras, the co-essence embodies, exalts, and constrains individual power and destiny, for these forces are, in essence, from elsewhere. Since this idea constitutes a conceptual foundation for a kind of predestination, it is not unreasonable to link it with a certain skepticism about the capacity of individuals to make their own way in the world through their own volition.

Cyclical Time as a Sacred Entity

It is clear that sacred, cyclical solar time has held powerful sway in both the ancient and contemporary Mesoamerican universe, whether in its macro form as a four- or five-part grand creation and restoration cycle that constitutes all of history or in its micro form as the metaphor of the day as a minimal cycle of heat, in its calendrical mode, in its astronomical mode, in its ritual mode, or in the smallest nuances of verbal metaphor and poetics. Other natural and cultural cycles—such as the human life cycle, the human gestation cycle, the agricultural cycle, and the festival cycle—are all laced into the daily and annual solar cycles to create a cosmos that places humankind in an inherited, sacred, temporal order that demands human maintenance. This is not a system in which the human will is free to indulge its whims or to innovate in the hope of achieving personal or collective gain. It is a spiral that cannot move forward without contemplating and retracing its past positions and prior forms. The cultures represented in this book exemplify the contemplation of the past as necessarily replicated in the present.

The Structure of the Vertical and Horizontal Cosmos

Both ancient and modern Mesoamerican communities recognize a consistent delimitation of sky, earth, and underworld in the spatial layout of the cosmos, with mediation among these realms as a key intellectual, political, and religious activity. With successful mediation comes power, wisdom, even personal health and community survival. Some variant of this spatial structure, with subunit segmentation and corresponding cardinal directional symbolism, occurs throughout pre-Columbian Mesoamerica and in hundreds of contemporary communities. Shamanism, heroic narratives, key integrating symbols, and deities themselves—particularly Sun, Moon, Jaguar, Wind, Lightning, Earth Lords, Serpents, Jesus Christ, the Virgin Mary, and the saints, even the individual co-essences—all depend for their power and efficacy upon spatial mobility within all or parts of the tripartite vertical cosmos (sky, earth, and underworld) and the related four-part horizontal cosmos. Through the mediation of supernatural forces that traverse this spatio-temporal whole, the individual gains access to, and also is constrained by, the whole.

Conflict as a Creative and Life-Sustaining Force

Conflict is the genesis and precondition for order. What makes the conflict motif peculiarly Mesoamerican is twofold. First, conflict is divinely ordained. Thus, it is primordial, ubiquitous, and easy to rationalize. Second, the parties in the conflicts are often dual aspects of the same supernatural being, social unit, or person. For example, the Passions (ritual personages who sponsor the cult to the Sun/Christ deity in the Chamula Tsotsil ritual of annual renewal) simultaneously represent the pre-cultural forces that helped to kill the Sun/Christ before the First Creation of the mythic era, and function as the policemen who keep order at the festival and defend the sacred symbols of the Sun/Christ's cult.

Complementary Dualism

Mesoamerican ideology accommodates complementary duality easily. Perhaps it has always been so in the ebb and flow of Mesoamerican history, as the little communities of the hinterland absorbed wave after wave of new state ideas and religions that emanated from the urban centers. The issue of duality and subsequent dialogue and conflict between these dual principles is indeed the dynamic force that creates the cosmos in the Maya world, ancient and modern. Not only is this dynamic tension sacred, but it is complementary rather than oppositional, contemporaneous rather than sequential. The pattern of complementary dualism also recalls and illuminates the ubiquitous Mesoamerican custom of addressing ancestors, deities, and ritual personages with a bisexual honorific title—for example, Father-Mother.

The Extraordinary Power of Spoken and Written Language

Throughout the region, Mesoamericans linked language and dialogue to the dawn of consciousness in the creation of the human condition. In time present, as in time past, language—with its wide range of rhetorical, poetic, and musical embellishments—has behaved as a sacred symbol that allows humans to share qualities and communicate with gods. In effect, beautifully executed speech and song are the only substances, with the possible exception of blood, that the human body can produce that are accessible to—and worthy before—divine beings.

A Glimpse of Mesoamerican Spirituality

The photographs in this volume provide a glimpse of the complex expression of Mesoamerican spirituality as it has evolved over five centuries into our time. You, as a reader, are invited to imagine the massive social energy, the roar of fireworks and explosions, the flowing of billows of pine-scented incense, the chants, the drums, the flutes, the replication of the past that is illustrated here in time present.

NOTES

1. Robert Redfield, *The Folk Culture of Yucatan* (Chicago: University of Chicago Press, 1941).

Winter

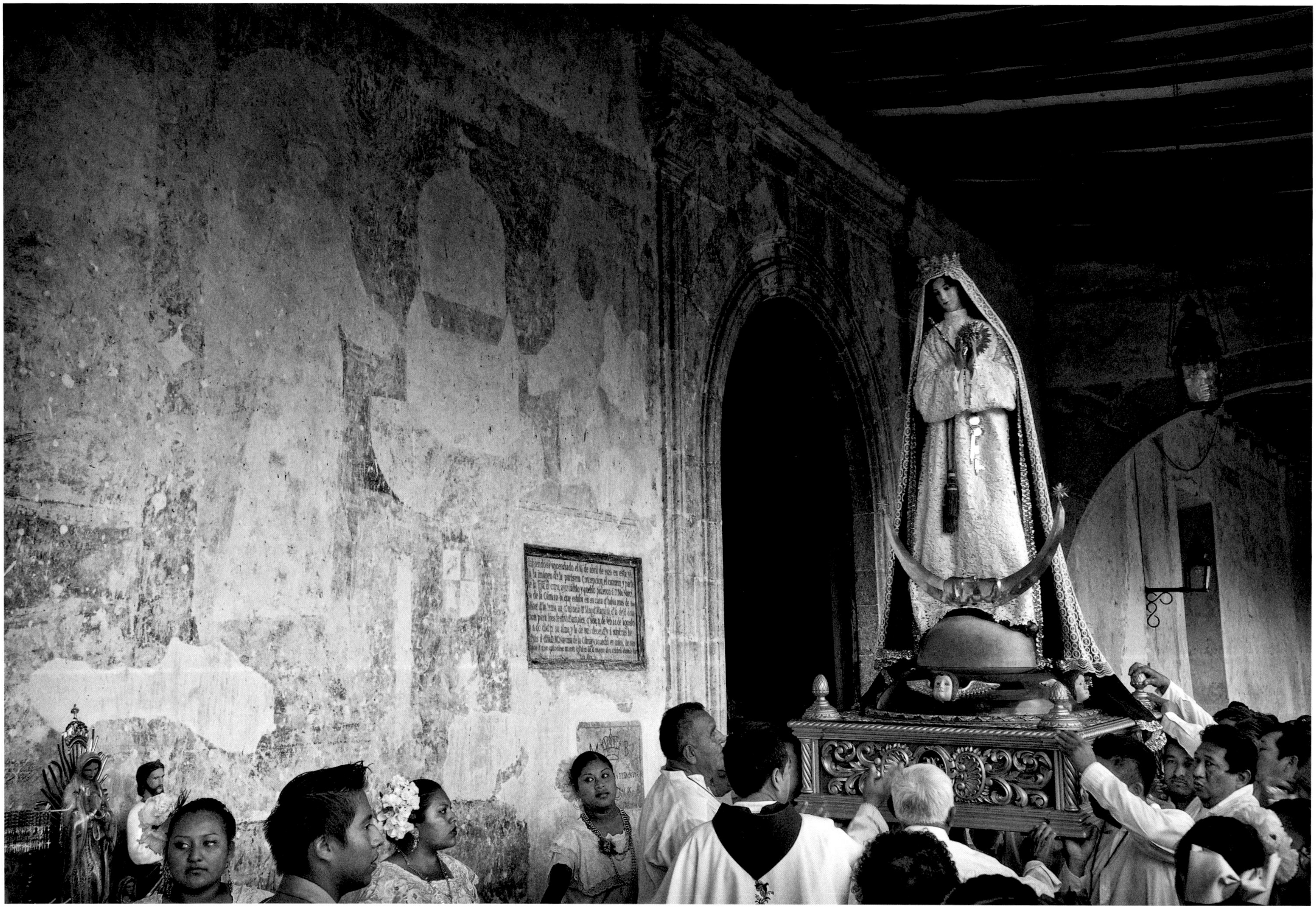

OUR LADY OF IZAMAL CARRIED IN PROCESSION, 2014

Our Lady of Izamal Ceremony and Procession

December 8
Izamal, Yucatán, Mexico

Izamal, a beautiful colonial city situated forty miles from Mérida, the capital of Yucatán state, is one of Mexico's major pilgrimage sites. Because the ancient Maya considered this city to be the home of both Kinich Kak Moo (the manifestation of the Sun God) and Itzamná (the Creator God), religious pilgrims and worshippers have come to Izamal since before 1000 BCE.

In the 1500s, the massive Maya pyramid in the center of what is now Izamal was demolished at the behest of a Franciscan priest, Fray Diego de Landa. In its place—and built using stones from the pyramid—is the complex of the Convent of San Antonio de Padua, which includes a church and monastery (large religious complexes were known as *conventos* in Spanish Colonial times).

In 1560, Fray Landa acquired twin life-size carved wooden statues, commissioned in Guatemala, of the Virgin Mary of the Immaculate Conception. He brought one to a church in Mérida and the other to the convent in Izamal, where soon after devotees attributed many miracles to her presence. These miracles resulted in a growing number of pilgrimages to view the Virgin Mary and participate in processions to honor her.

Over the next four centuries, the Virgin's miracle-making abilities continued to attract devotees. In the 1600s, the end of a yellow fever epidemic was attributed to the Virgin, and in the early 1700s her miraculous powers were believed to end another plague. After this divine intervention, the Virgin was given a new title: Our Lady of Izamal. In 1829, a major fire destroyed the statue of the Virgin in her Izamal sanctuary. Anguished residents of Izamal asked their fellow Yucatecans in Mérida to donate the statue in their possession to their church. It was agreed, and the Virgin was brought by foot procession to Izamal. Since that time, miracles and healings have continued to be noted by believers.

Every year on December 8, Our Lady of Izamal is celebrated through processions, blessings, masses, prayers, and song. Thousands of pilgrims attend these spiritual activities and join the procession, following the Virgin as she is carried on a carved wooden palanquin around the esplanade that encircles the convent's open atrium, the second largest in the world after St. Peter's Square in the Vatican.

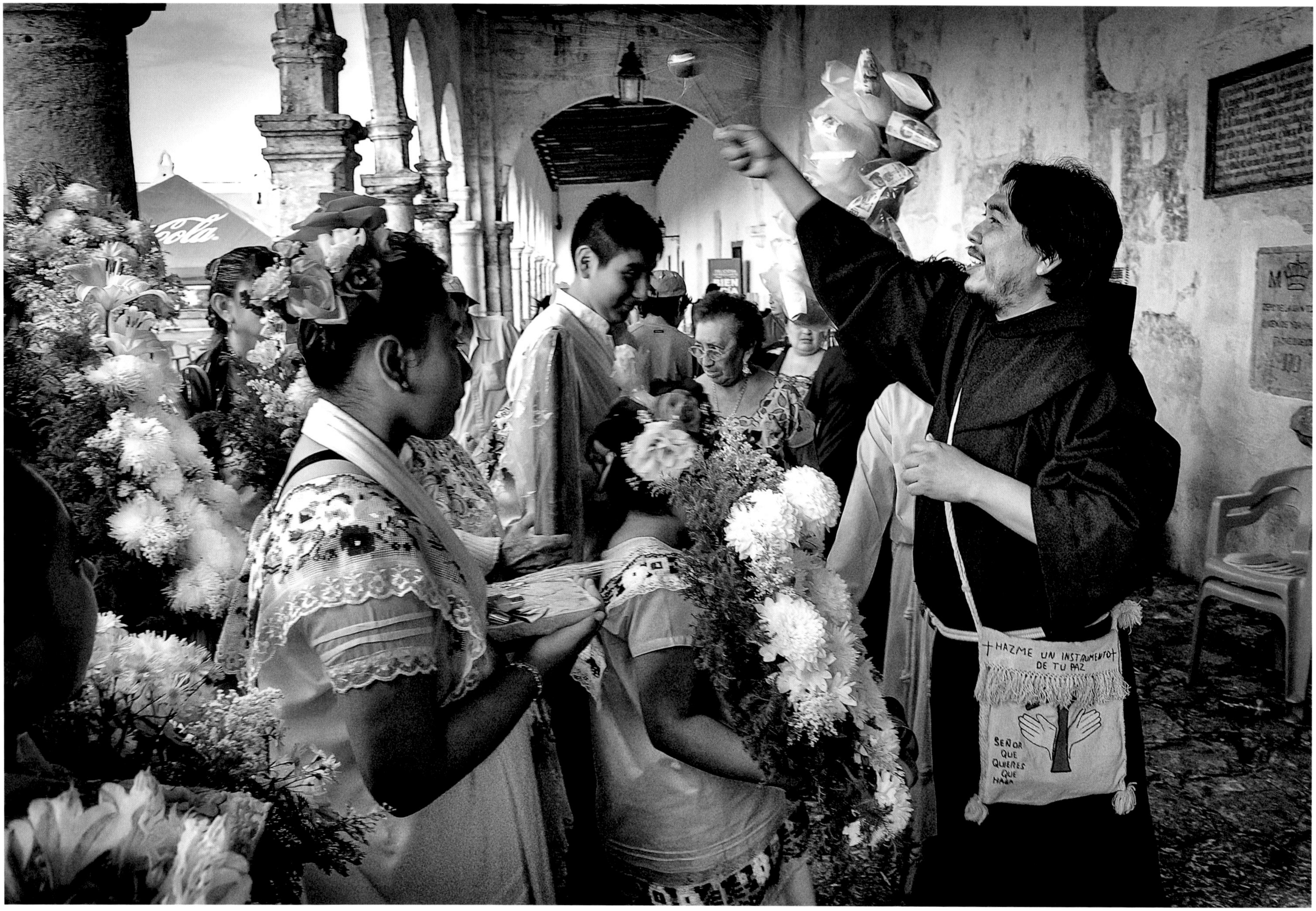

A PRIEST BLESSING DEVOTEES, 2014

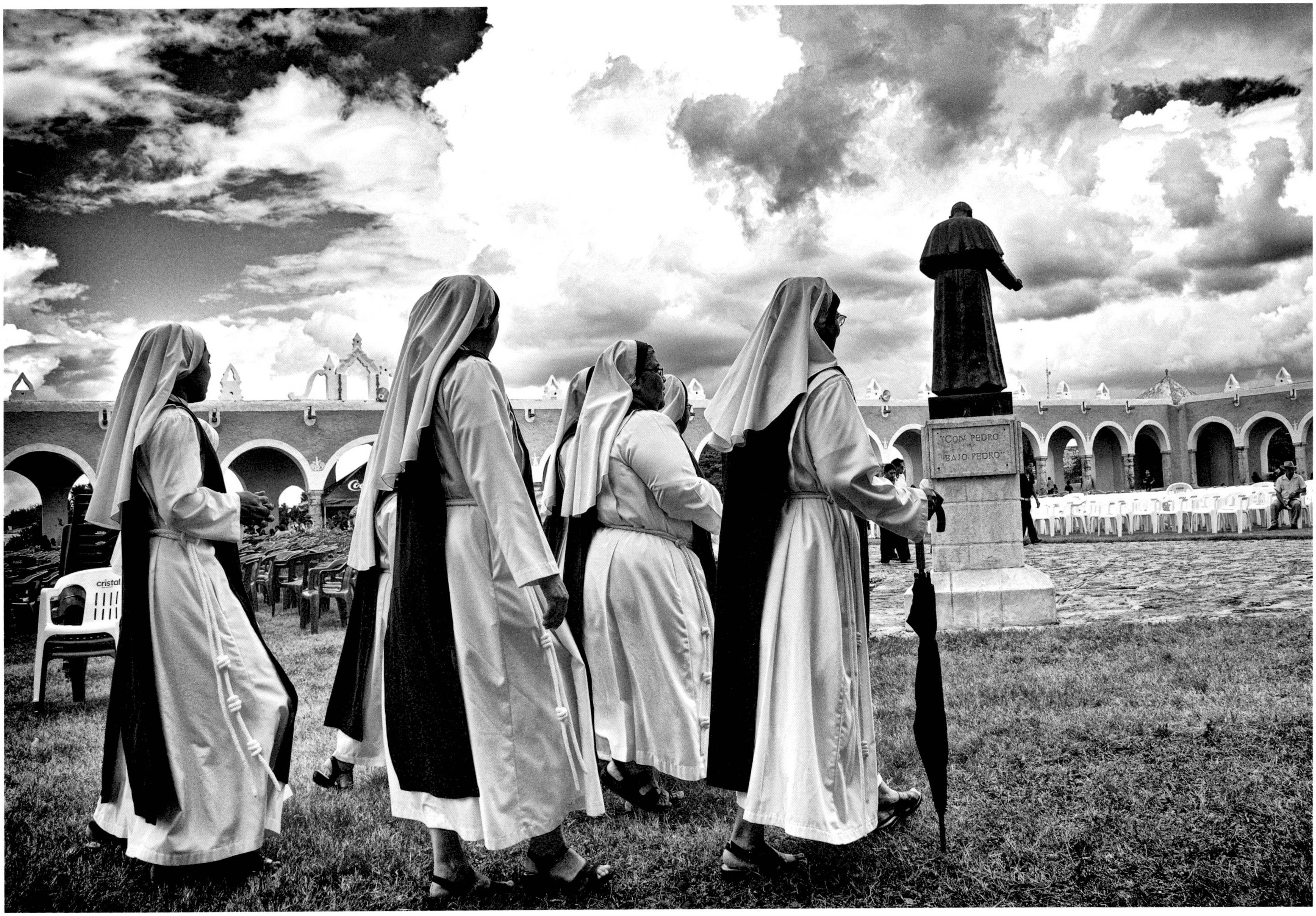

NUNS AWAITING THE START OF THE PROCESSION, 2014

following spreads: YOUNG WOMEN IN THEIR FINEST DRESS, 2014
THE COMMUNITY PAYING TRIBUTE TO OUR LADY OF IZAMAL, 2014

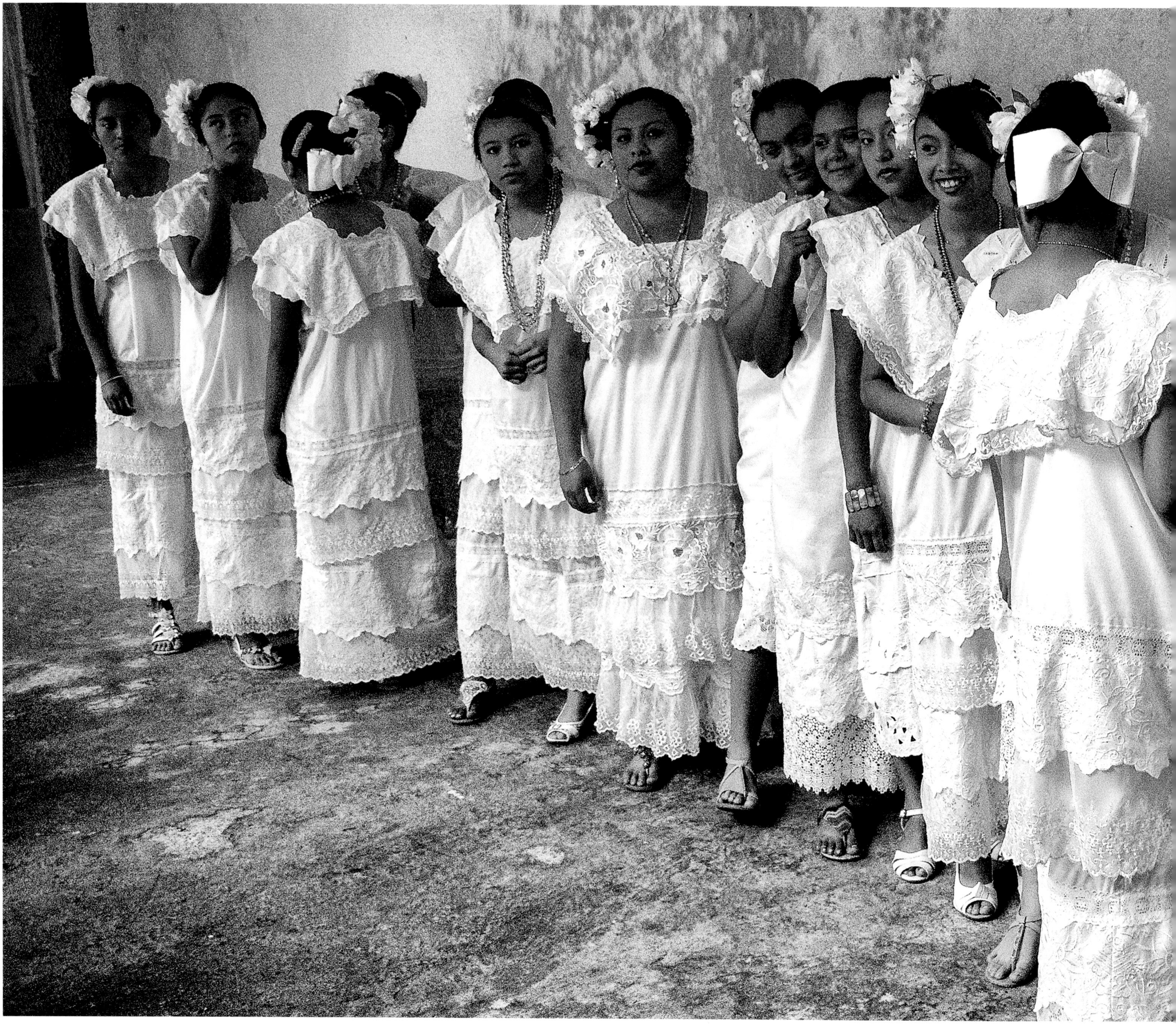

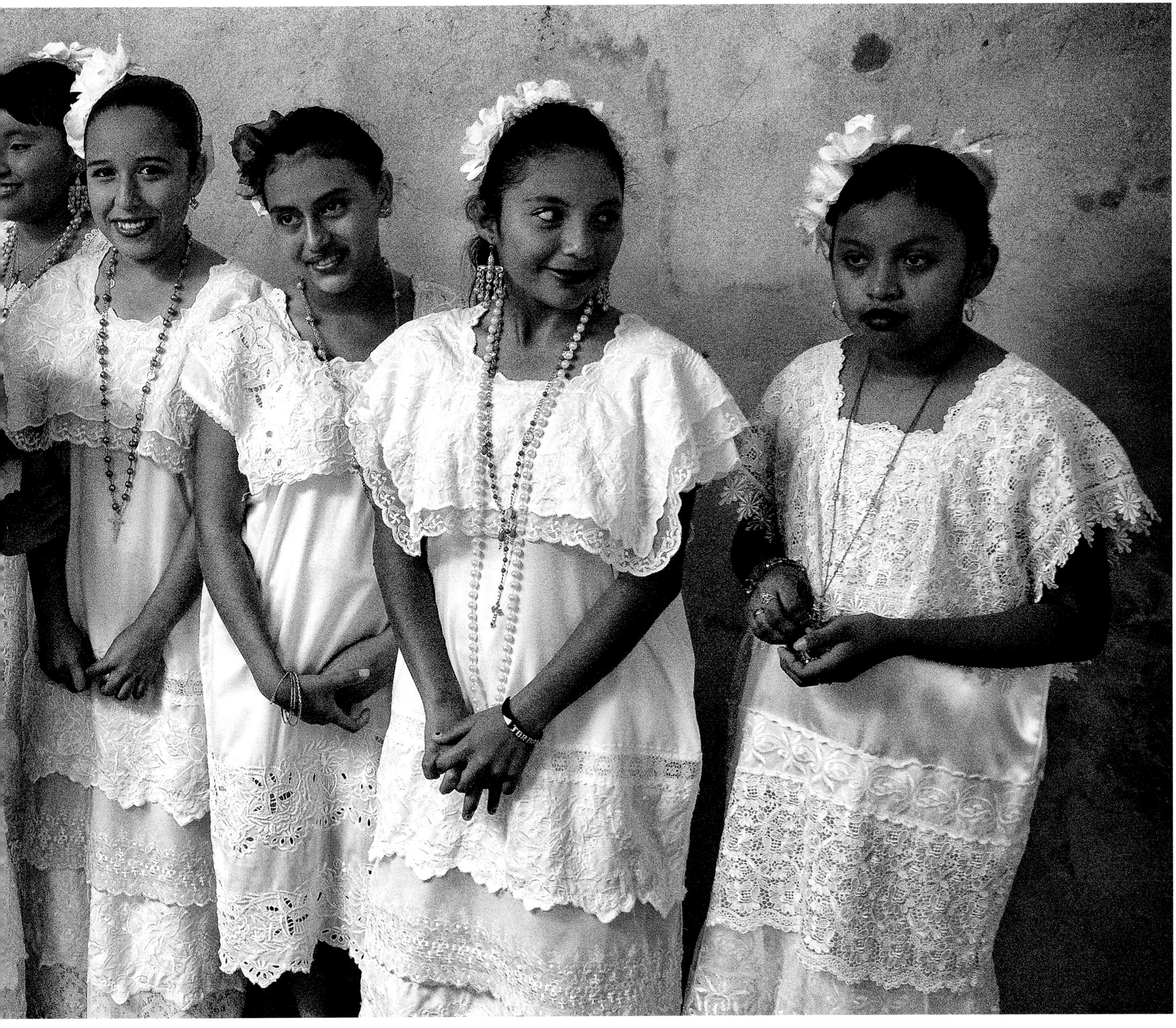

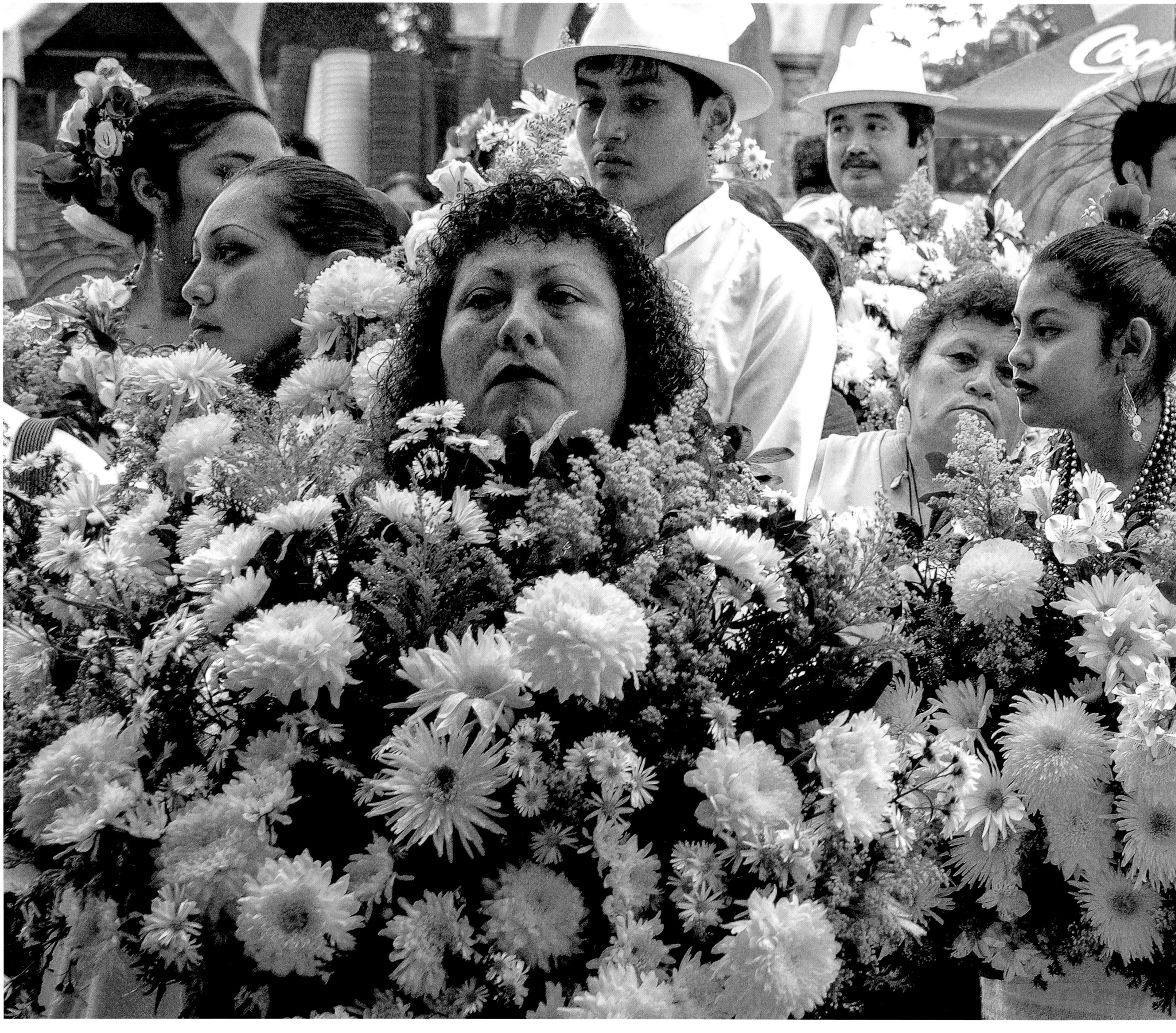

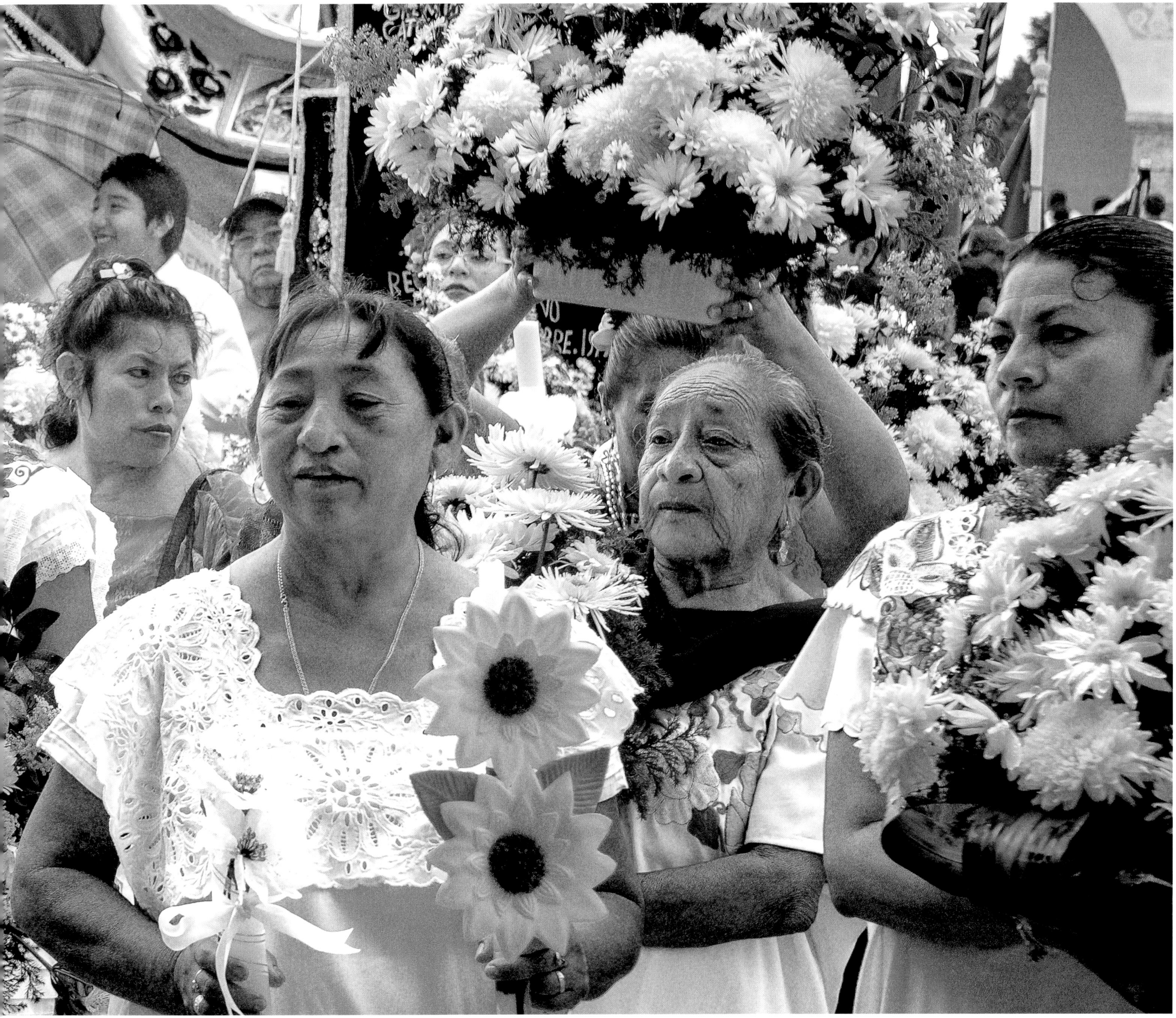

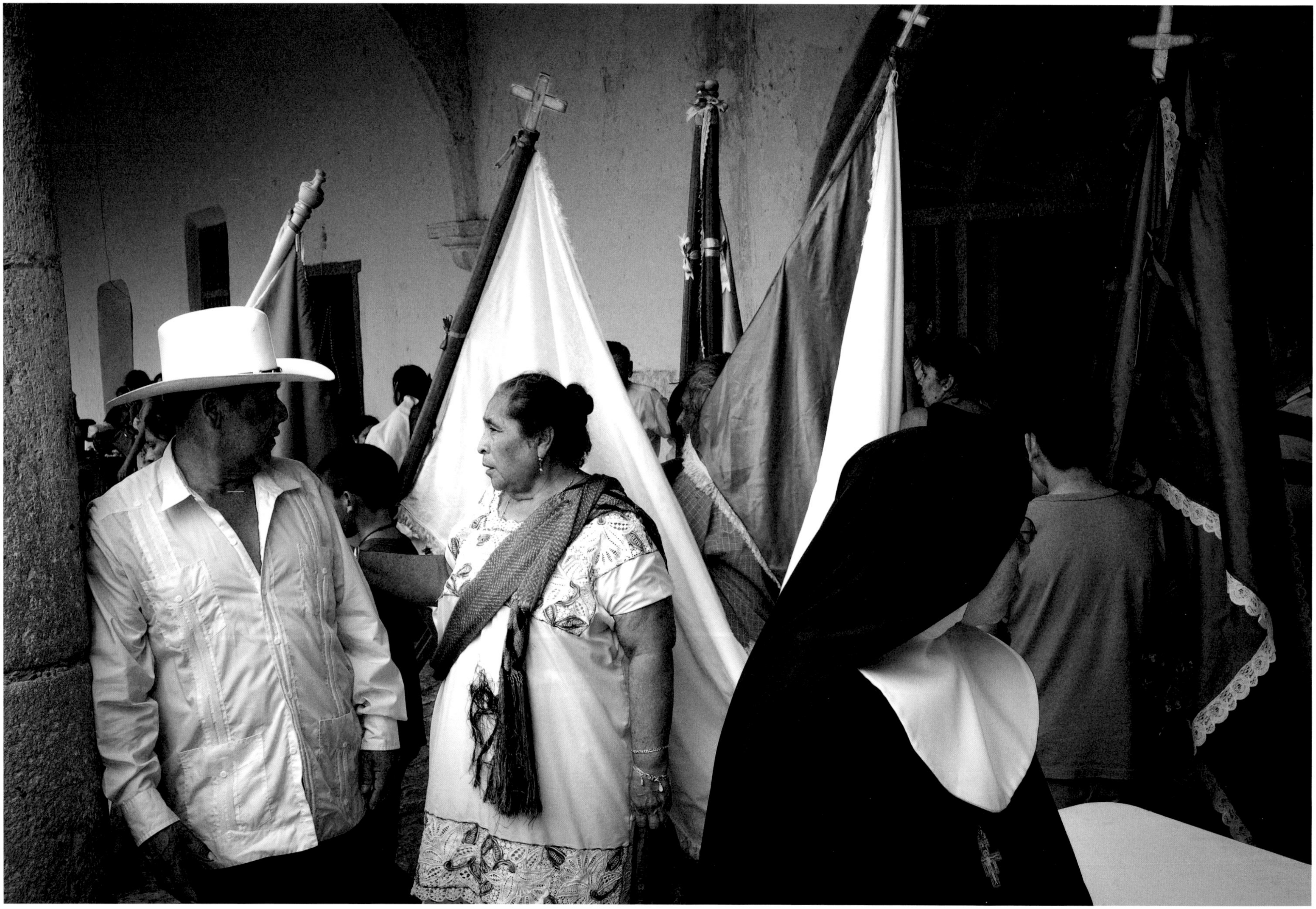

above and opposite: AWAITING THE PROCESSION, 2014

following spread: THE BEGINNING OF THE PROCESSION, 2014

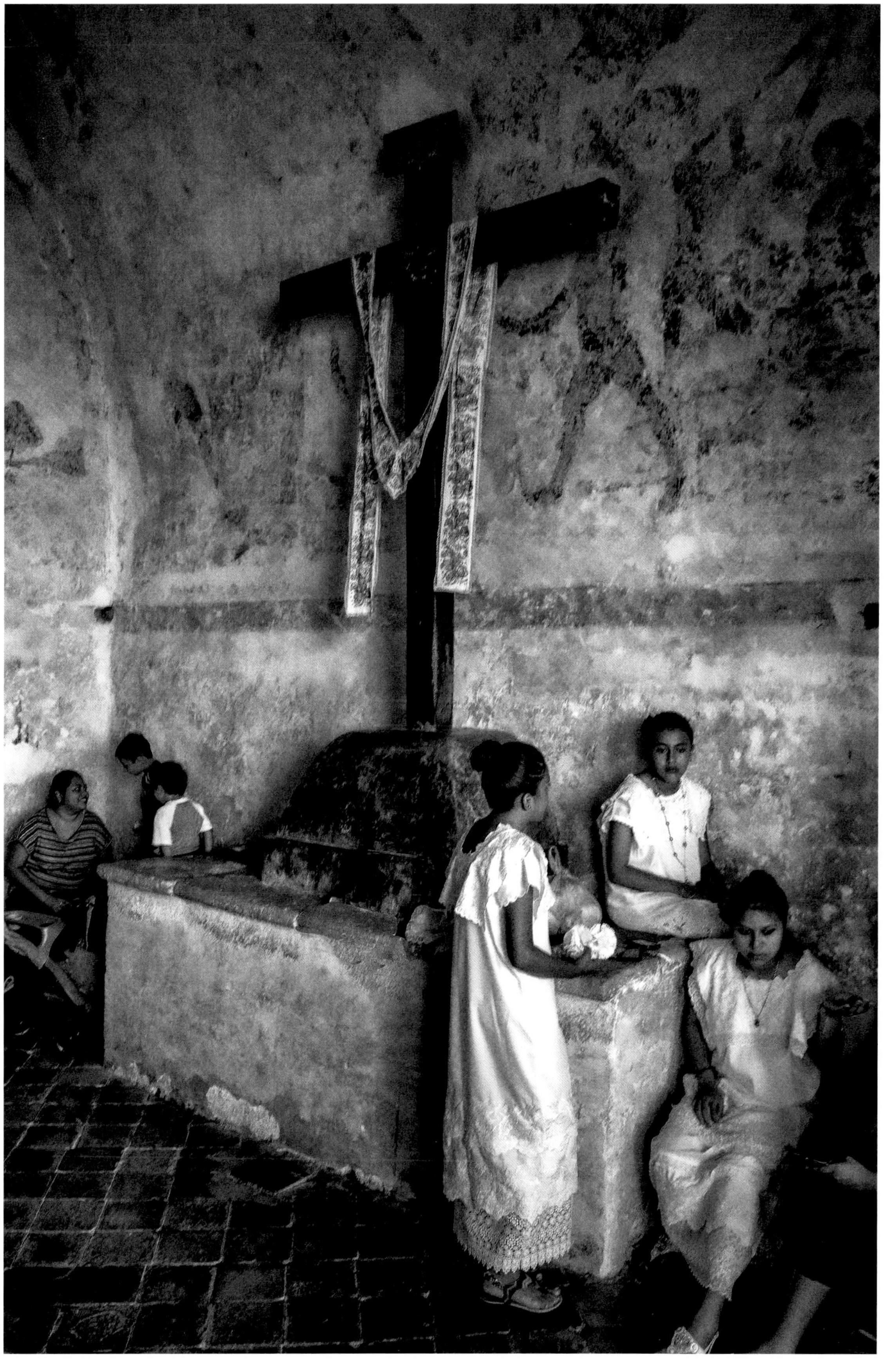

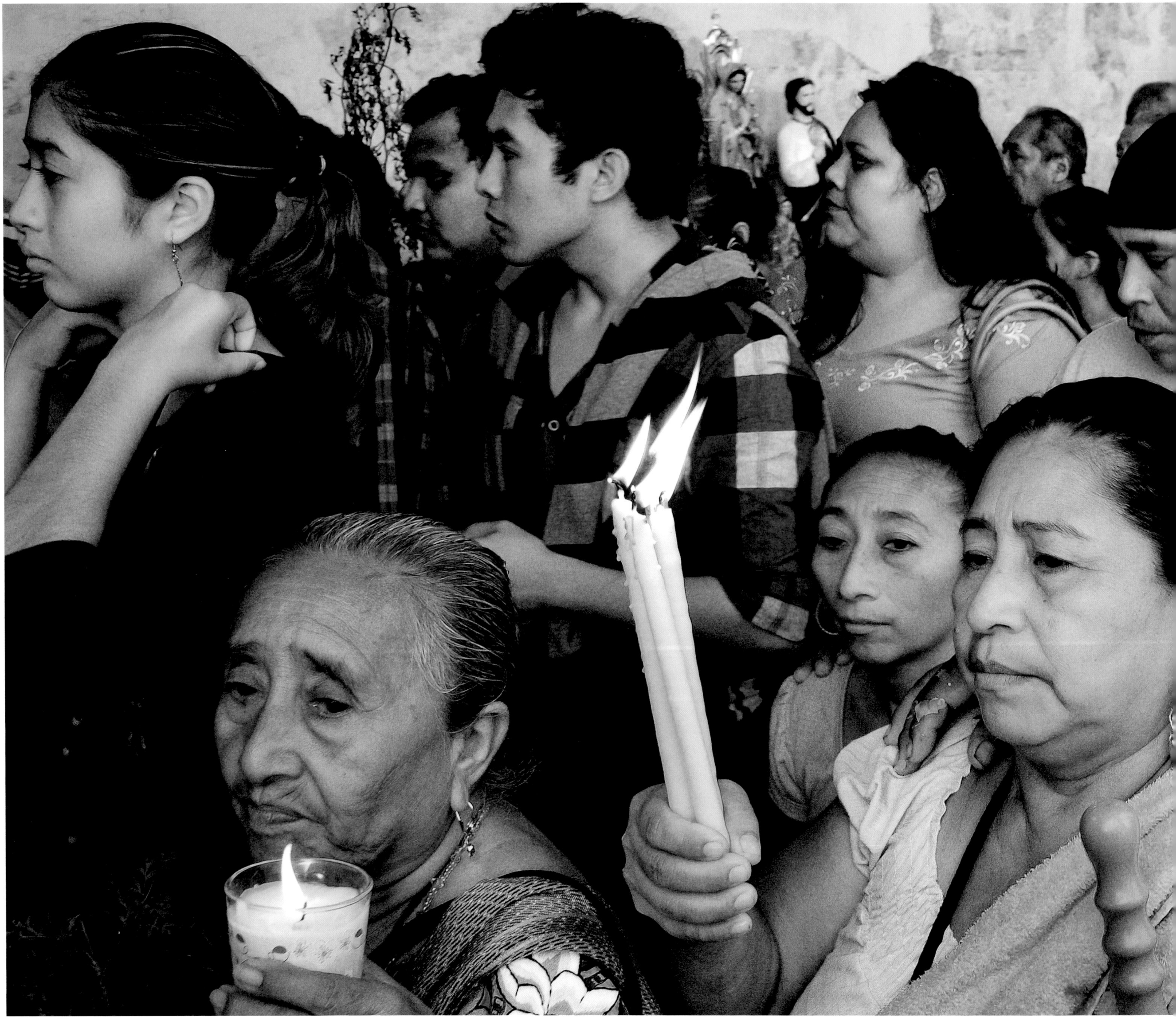

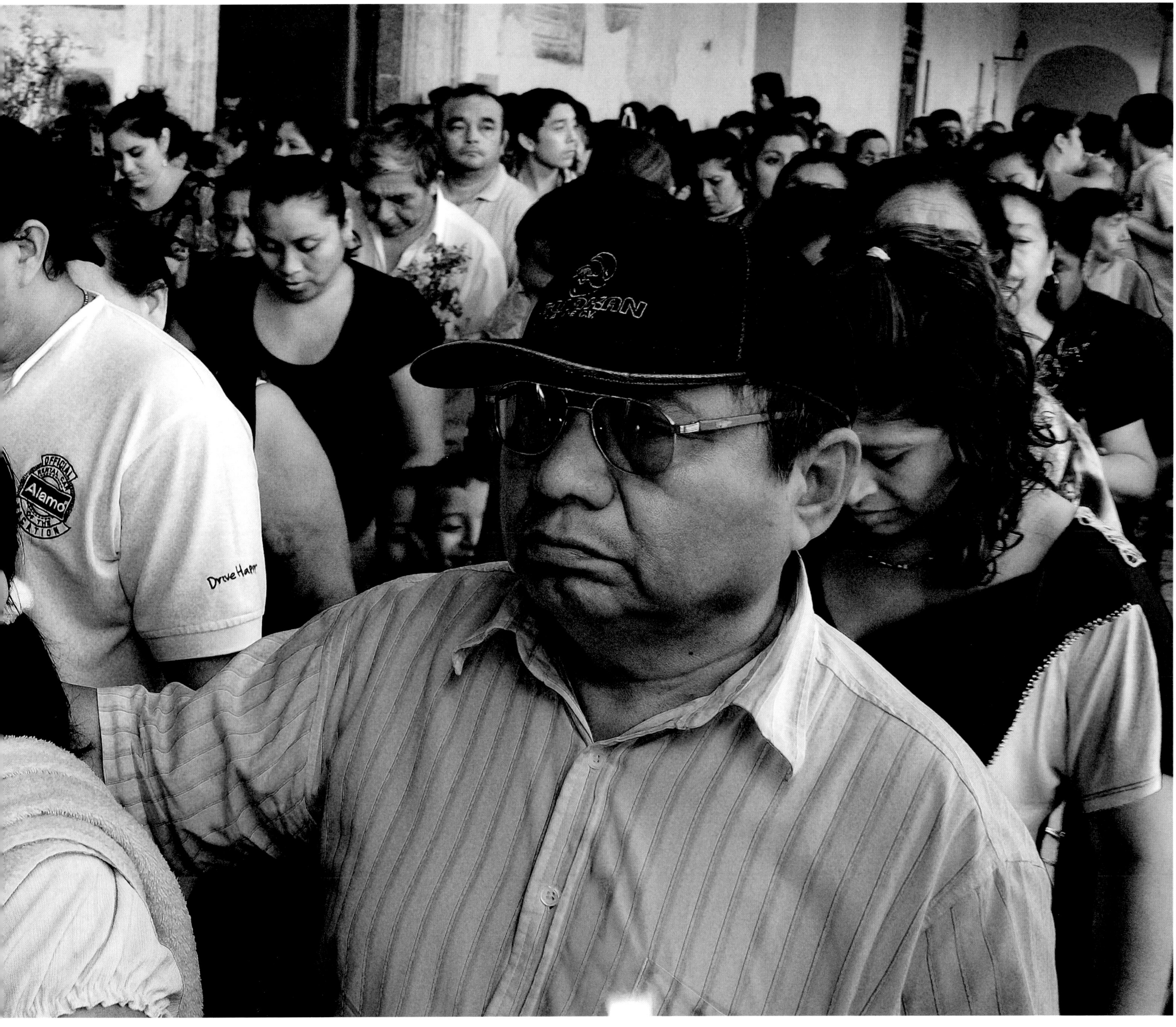
Alamo

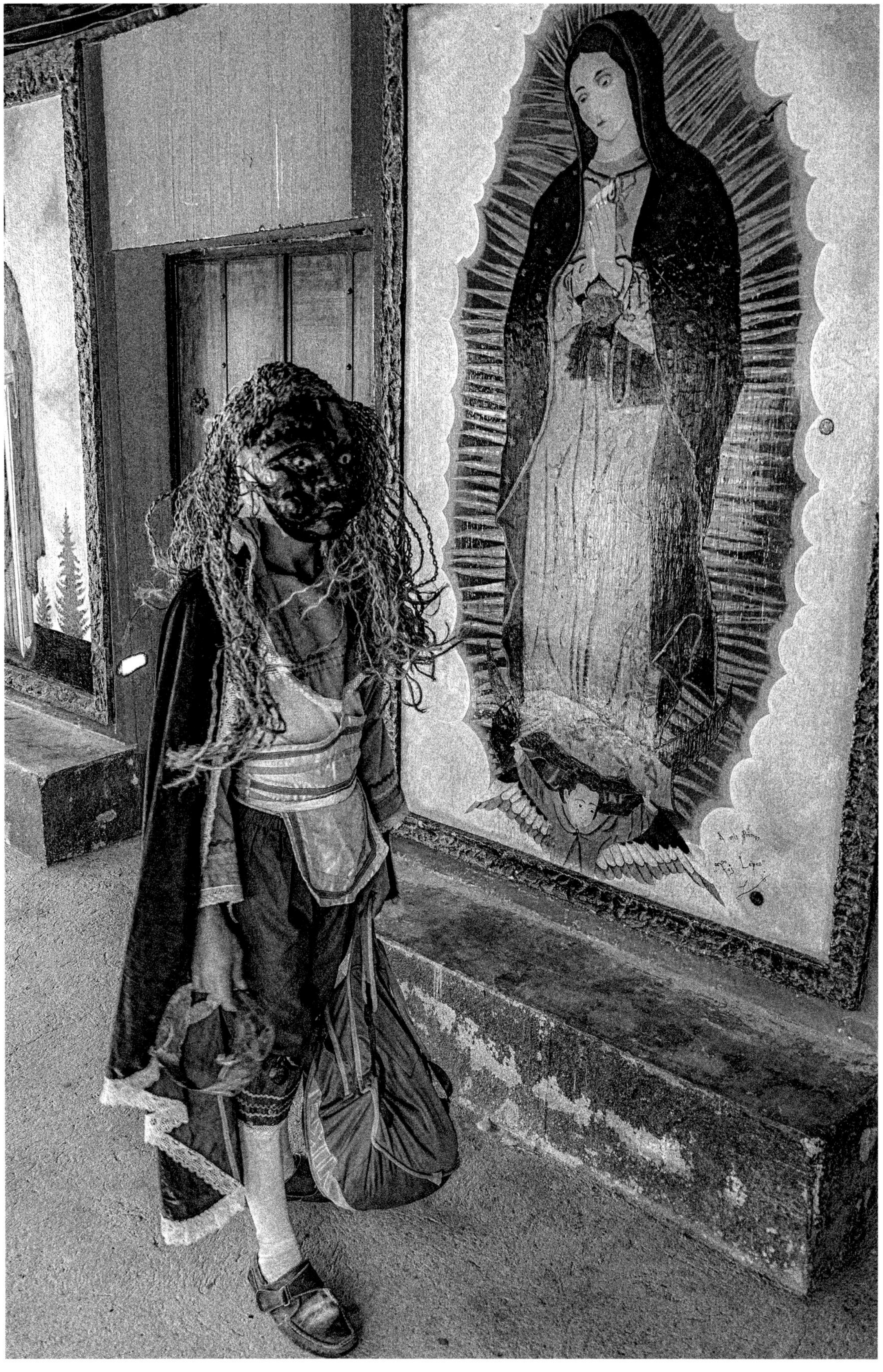

Our Lady of Guadalupe Feast Day

December 12
Yucatán, Mexico & Rabinal, Guatemala

Millions of Mexicans, Guatemalans, and other Latin Americans venerate the Virgin of Guadalupe and celebrate a feast day in her honor on December 12. Her story, which dates back to the sixteenth century, is based in part on the Spanish colonialists' efforts to convert the Indigenous peoples of the New World to Catholicism. As demonstrated throughout colonized Latin America, the Spanish evangelizers used Catholic saints to replace Indigenous gods in the religious conversion process.

According to legends, an Indigenous man named Cuauhtlatohuac, known by his Christian name, Juan Diego, lived in a small village near Mexico City. When Juan Diego walked by a hill called Tepeyac (considered the home of the Earth Mother goddess), a cloud appeared. Within it stood an image of the Virgin Mary, speaking to him in his native Nahuatl language. Juan Diego reported his vision to the Bishop of Mexico City, who asked that the Virgin give Juan Diego another sign. She again appeared to Juan Diego, and this time provided roses for him to carry in his cape to the bishop. On December 12, Juan Diego visited the bishop and opened his cape. To the astonishment of the bishop, roses fell to the ground. The image of the Virgin appeared on the cape where the roses had been, exactly as she had appeared at the hill of Tepeyac.

This story of Our Lady of Guadalupe and her appearance before a humble man on a sacred hill was an important incentive in the conversion of Indigenous people to Christianity. For more than five centuries, Our Lady of Guadalupe has symbolized the merging of Indian and Spanish cultures.

Mexicans have embraced Our Lady of Guadalupe in their daily lives, and devotion to her continues. On October 12, 1945, Pope Pius XII named Our Lady of Guadalupe the Patroness of the Americas. In 2002, Pope John Paul II canonized Juan Diego, making him the first Indigenous American saint.

opposite: DANCER IN RABINAL, 2019

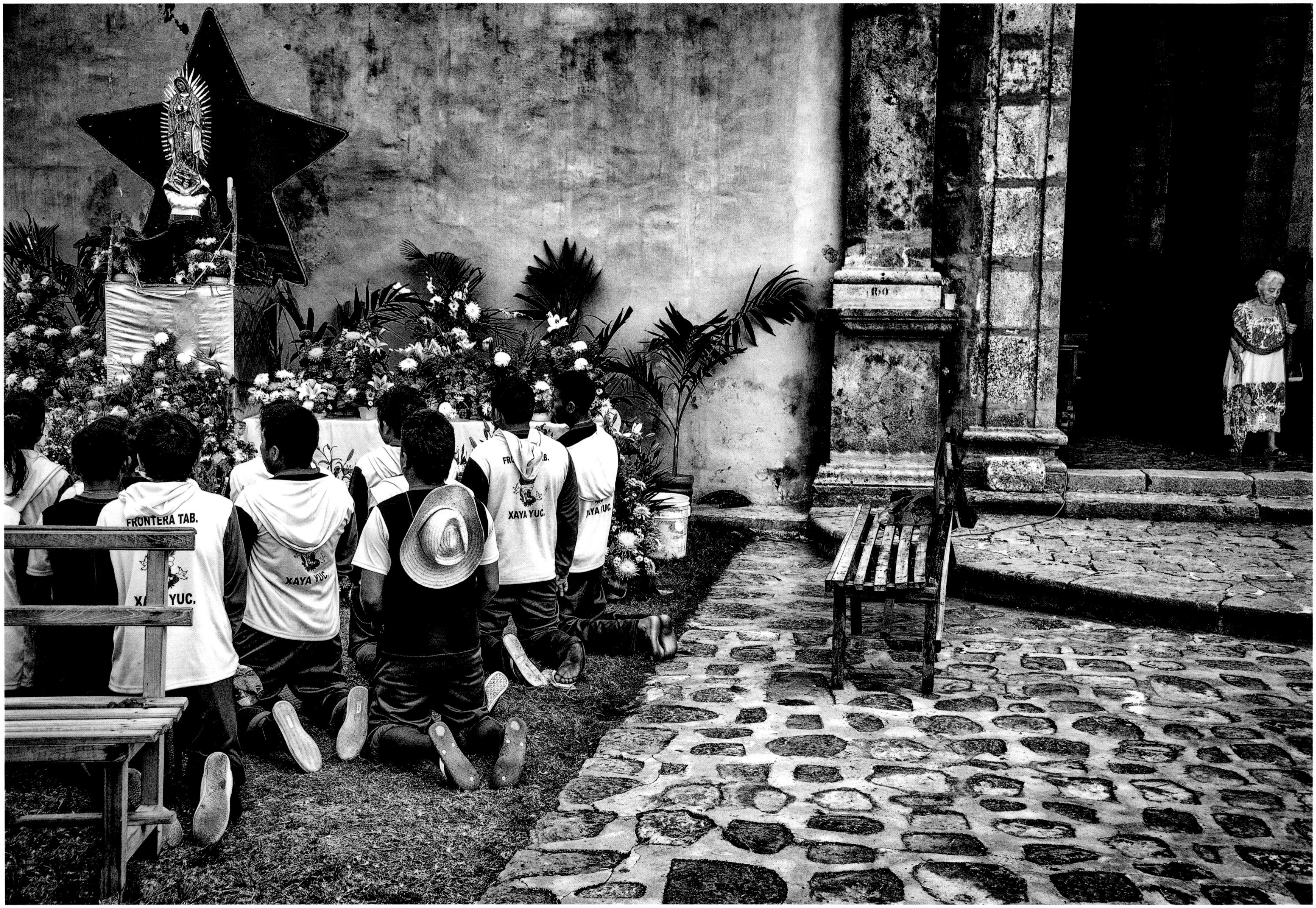

PRAYERS TO OUR LADY OF GUADALUPE IN OXKUTZCAB, 2014

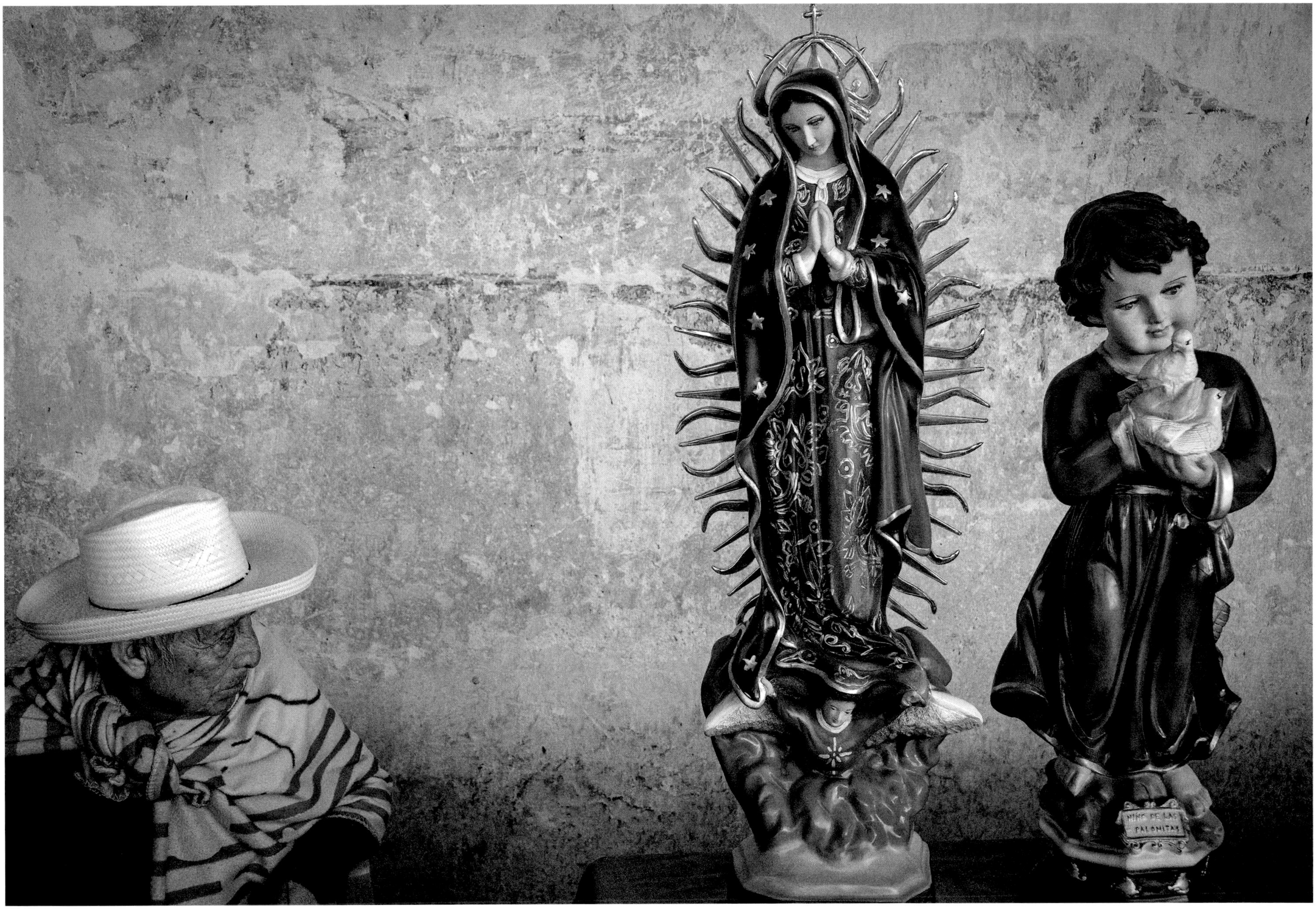

OUR LADY OF GUADALUPE HONORED IN IZAMAL, 2014

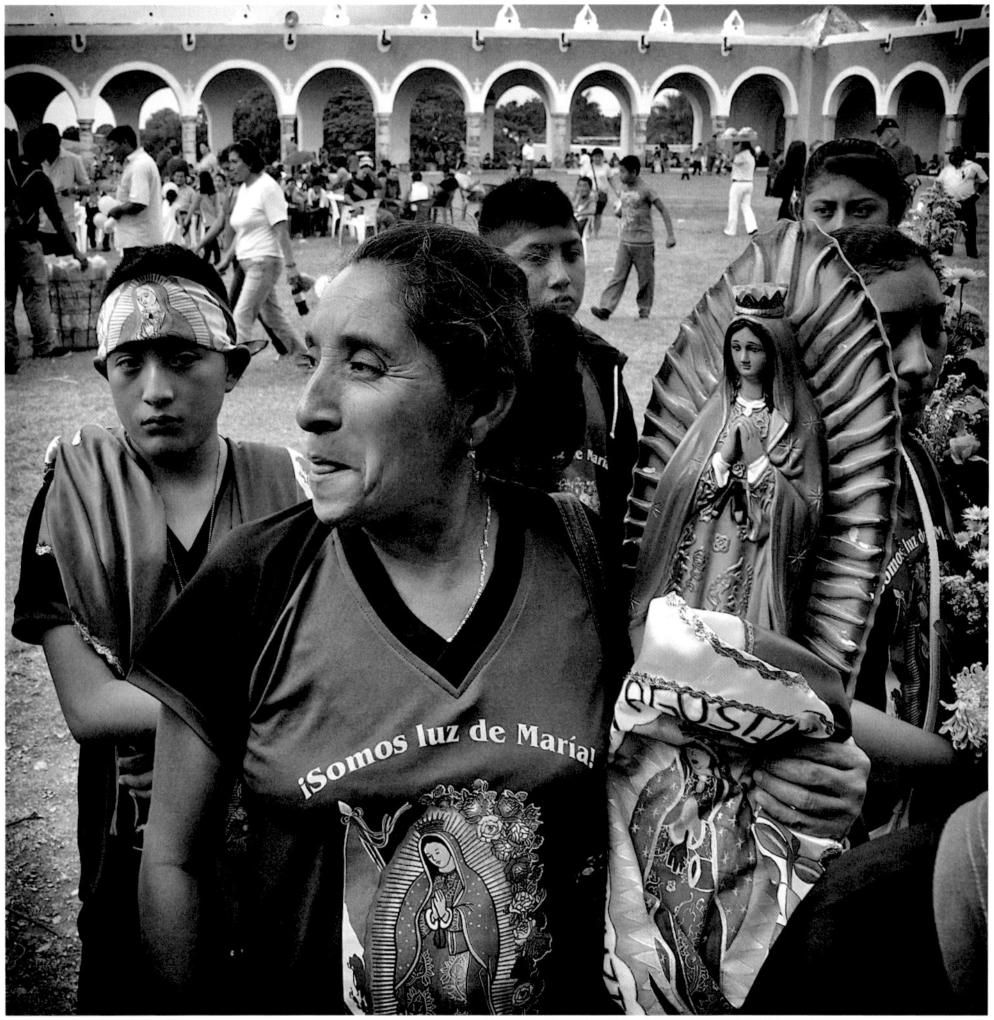

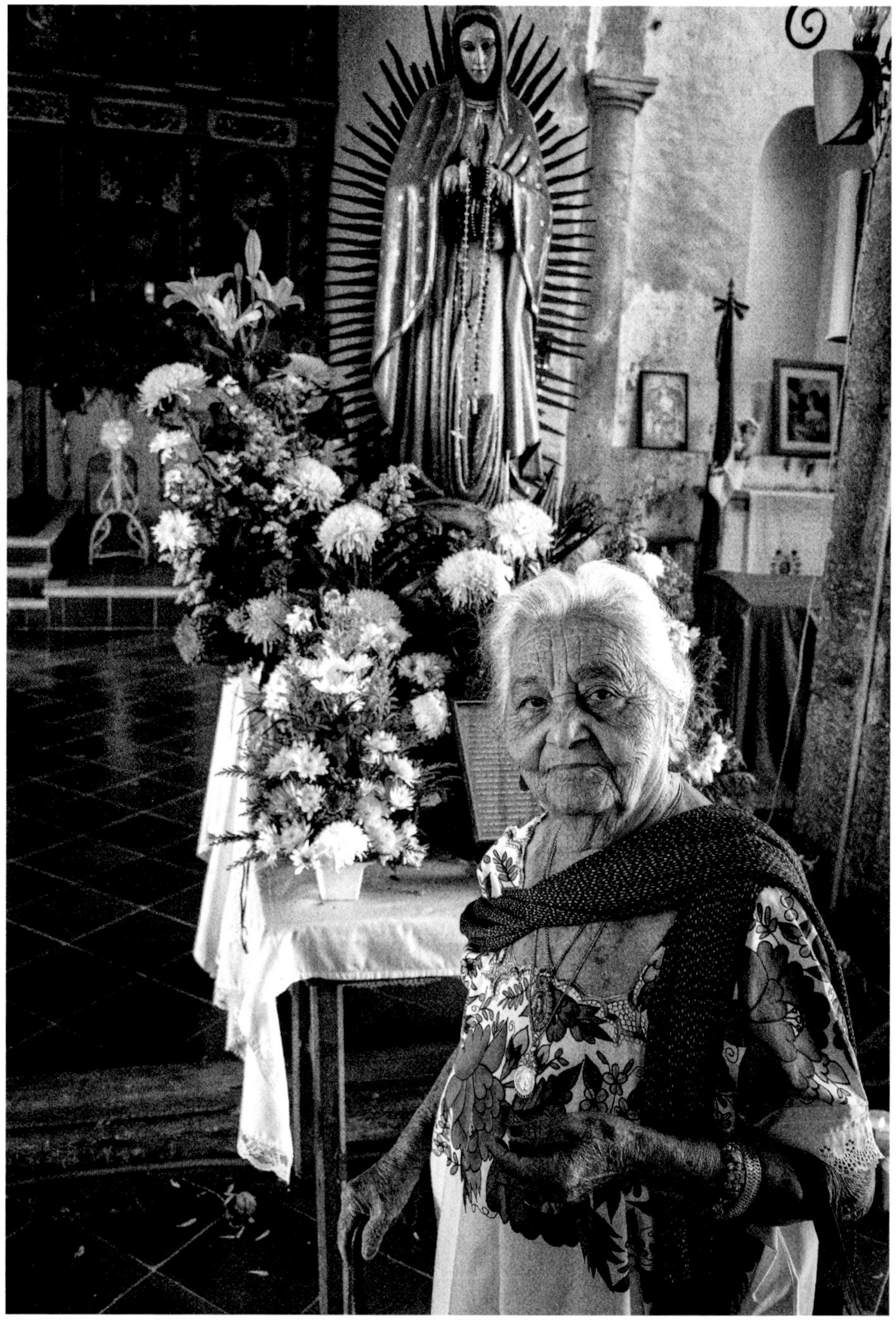

OUR LADY OF GUADALUPE, IZAMAL, 2014
center: THE CHURCH OF SAN FRANCISCO DE ASÍS IN OXKUTZCAB, 2014

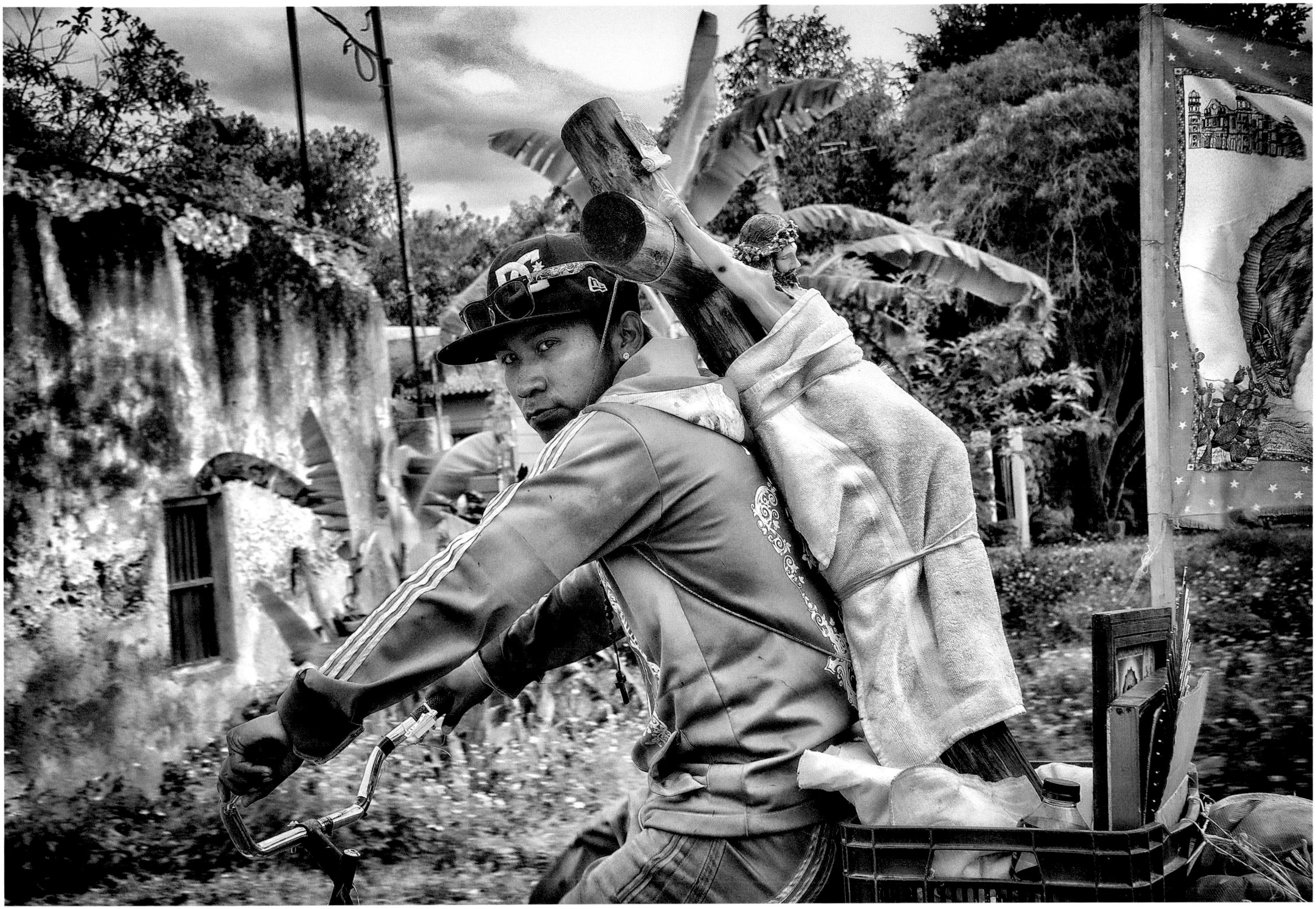

BICYCLE PROCESSION ON FEAST DAY
OF OUR LADY OF GUADALUPE, NEAR MUNA, 2014

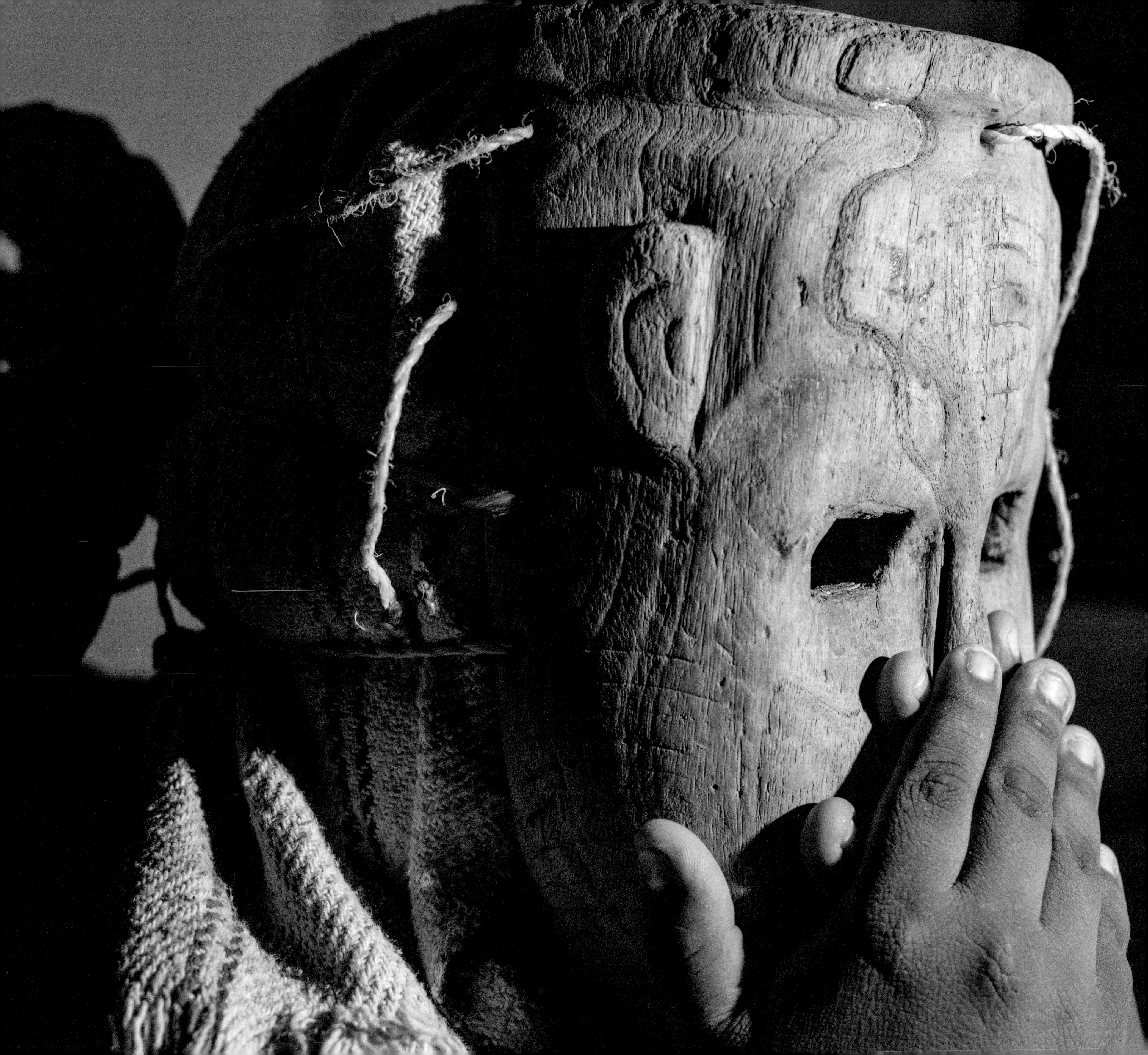

Masked Dance of Abraham and Isaac

December 24
Dzitnup, Yucatán, Mexico

In Dzitnup, a small Maya village near Vallodolid, Yucatán, the Masked Dance of Abraham and Isaac takes place every Christmas Eve. This unique religious performance is reputed to be the only remaining ceremony in the Yucatán in which performers still use wooden masks.

The dance and processions in the church demonstrate the role of Abraham and his son Isaac in protecting the infant Jesus from evil, as represented by the Devil. This local adaptation combines the Christmas story and the Old Testament story of Abraham (who was willing to sacrifice his son Isaac) with pre-Hispanic rituals, illustrating one of the many distinctive ways that Indigenous communities blend elements of their religious history.

The performance is organized by a select group of mayordomos associated with the parish church, which is dedicated to Saint Andrew. As in many indigenous ceremonies and rituals throughout Mexico and Guatemala, the village priest does not officiate during this ceremony days, nor is he present. There are only three dance performers, but the worshippers inside the church play an active role.

At the commencement of the ceremony, a group of women gather inside the parish church to pray and sing Christmas carols in both Spanish and Mayan. The three dancers gather in the church's sacristy and dress as Isaac, Abraham, and the Devil in primitive wooden masks. They then enter the church, which represents the temple of Abraham and Isaac, and the procession of the faithful begins.

The Devil exits to the church plaza, followed by Abraham and Isaac, who battle him with long staffs to symbolically rid evil from the earth. Abraham and Isaac then perform a simple dance, emulating the trot of a horse. Accompanied by a wooden drum, the church bells become a part of the ceremony, in a complex demonstration of dance, sound, and dialogue.

Inside the church, parishioners lift a statue of Jesus from his crib and take up statues of the Virgin Mary, Joseph, and the Three Wise Men. Now joined by Abraham and Isaac, this group of the faithful continues in a procession, making six turns around the central aisle of the church from the door to the altar. After this portion of ceremony ends, festivities continue later, on Christmas morning at homes in the village.

opposite: PREPARING FOR THE MASKED DANCE OF ABRAHAM AND ISAAC, 2017

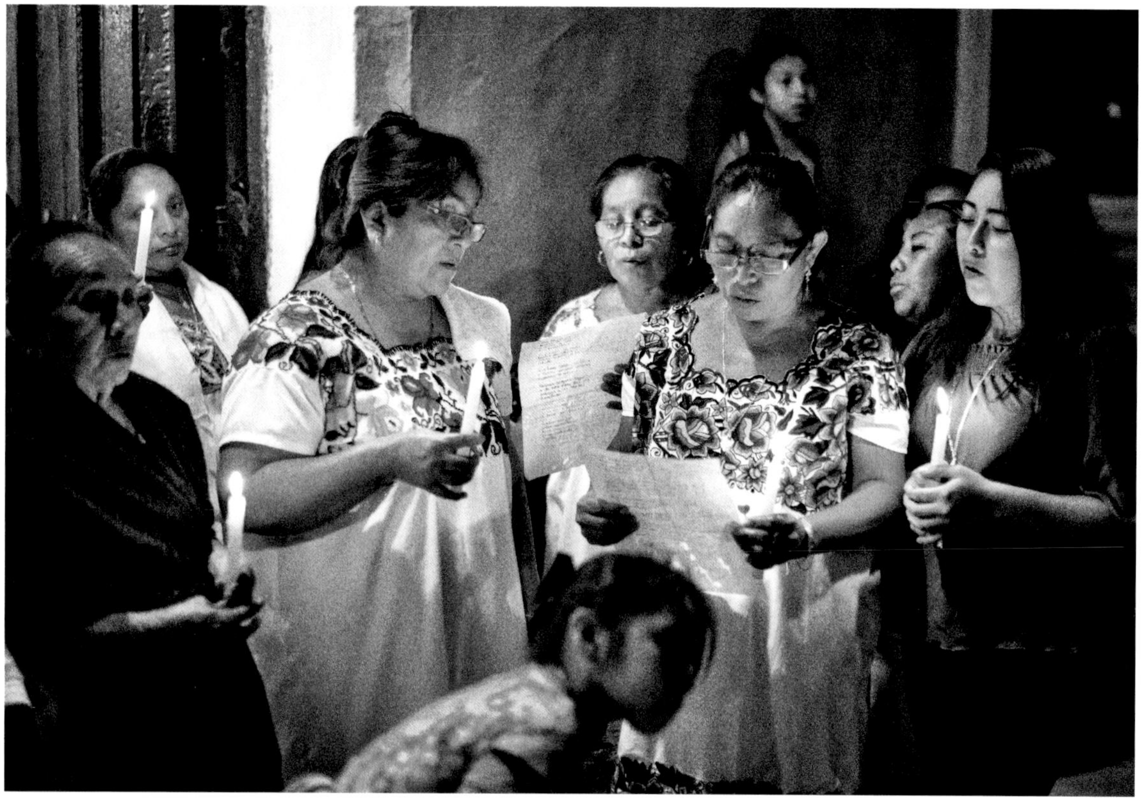

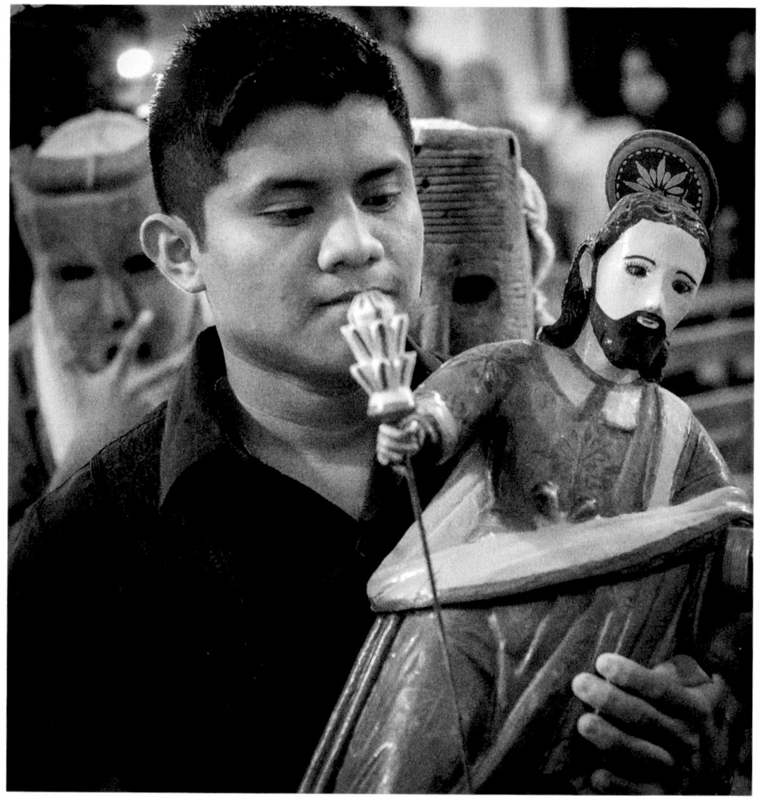

OUTSIDE THE CHURCH ON CHRISTMAS EVE, 2017

center and opposite: PROCESSION OF THE SAINTS INSIDE THE CHURCH, 2017

following spread, left: PREPARING FOR THE MASKED DANCE OF ABRAHAM AND ISAAC, 2017; right: MASKED PERFORMERS, 2017

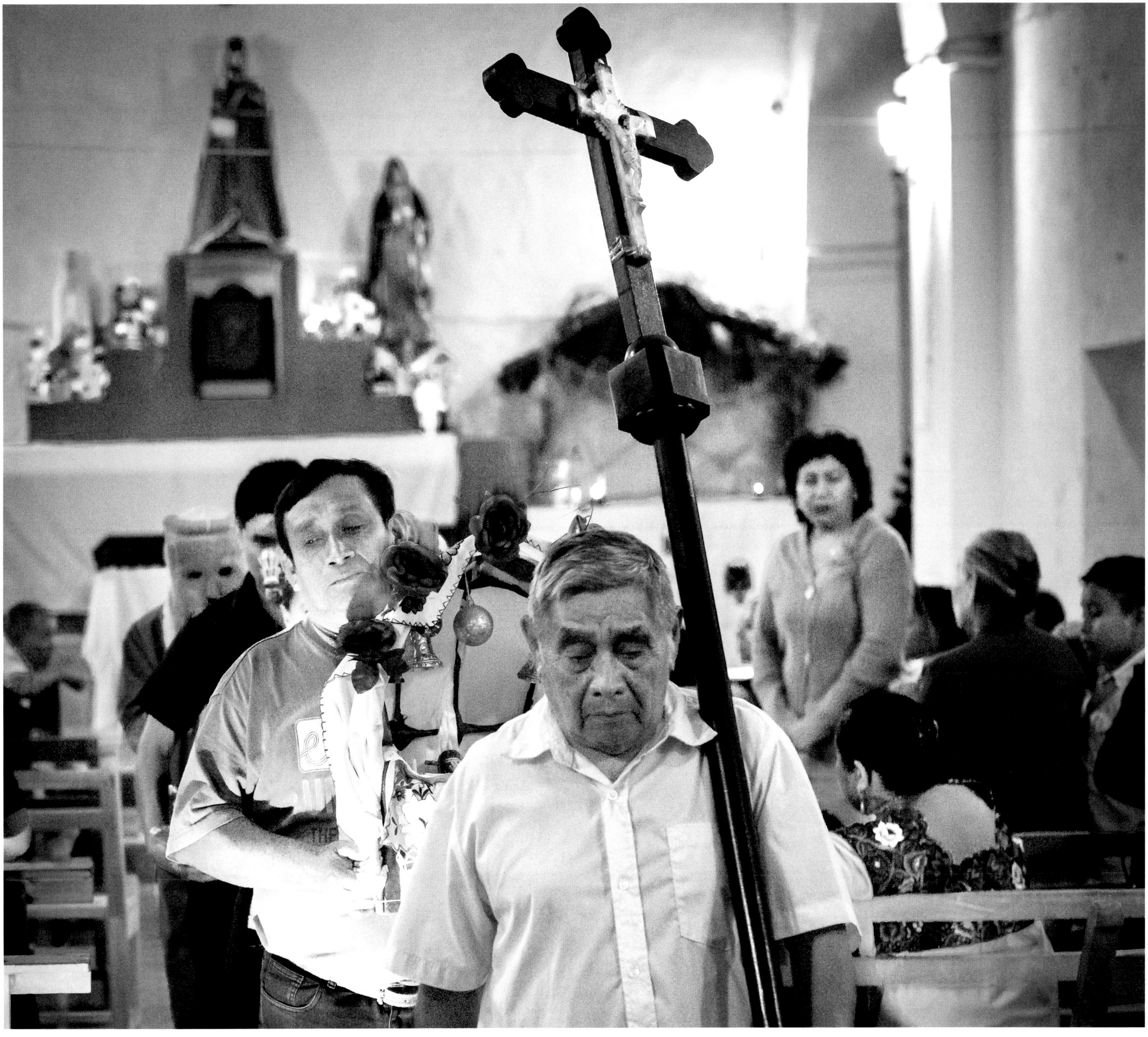

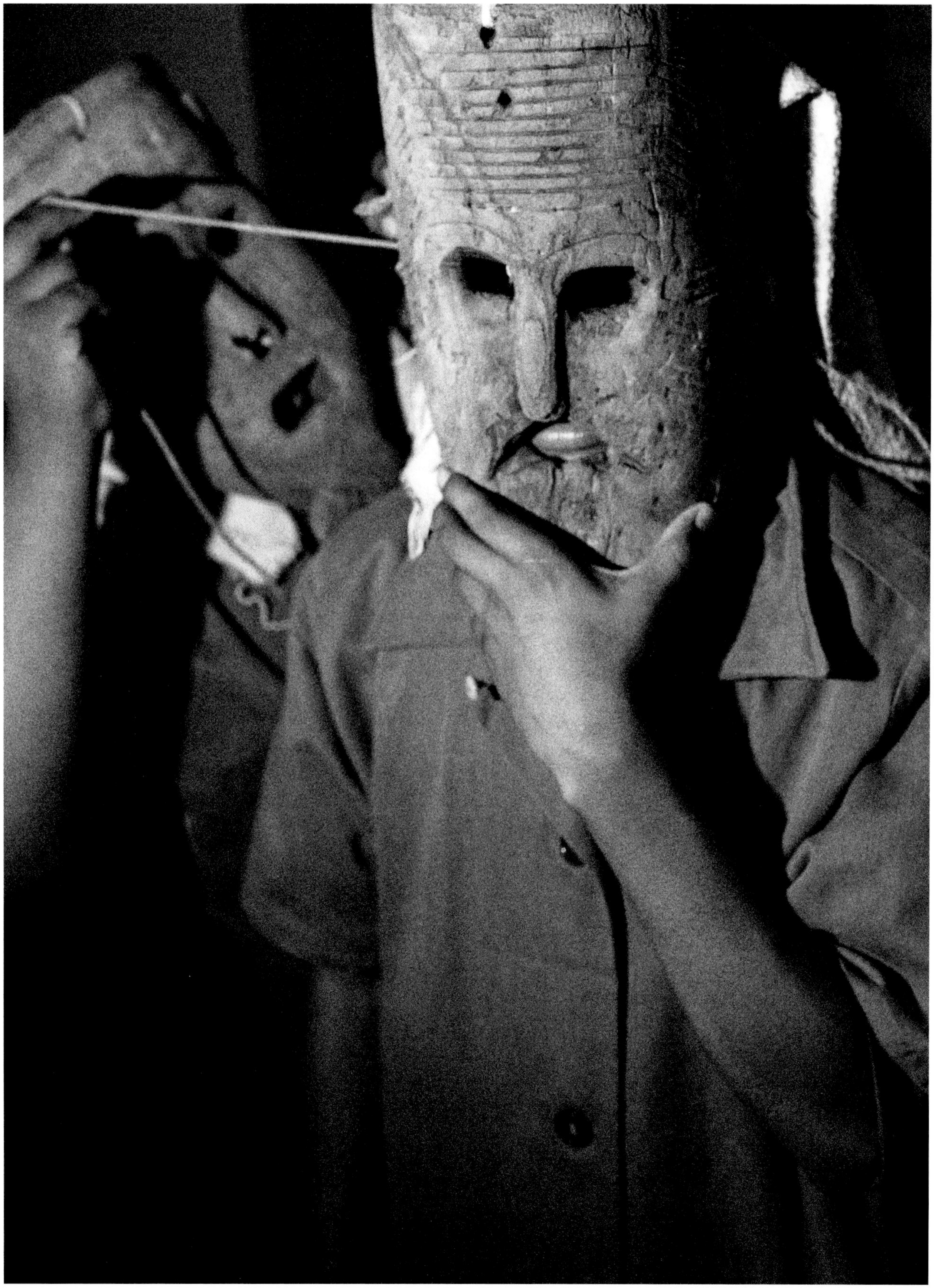

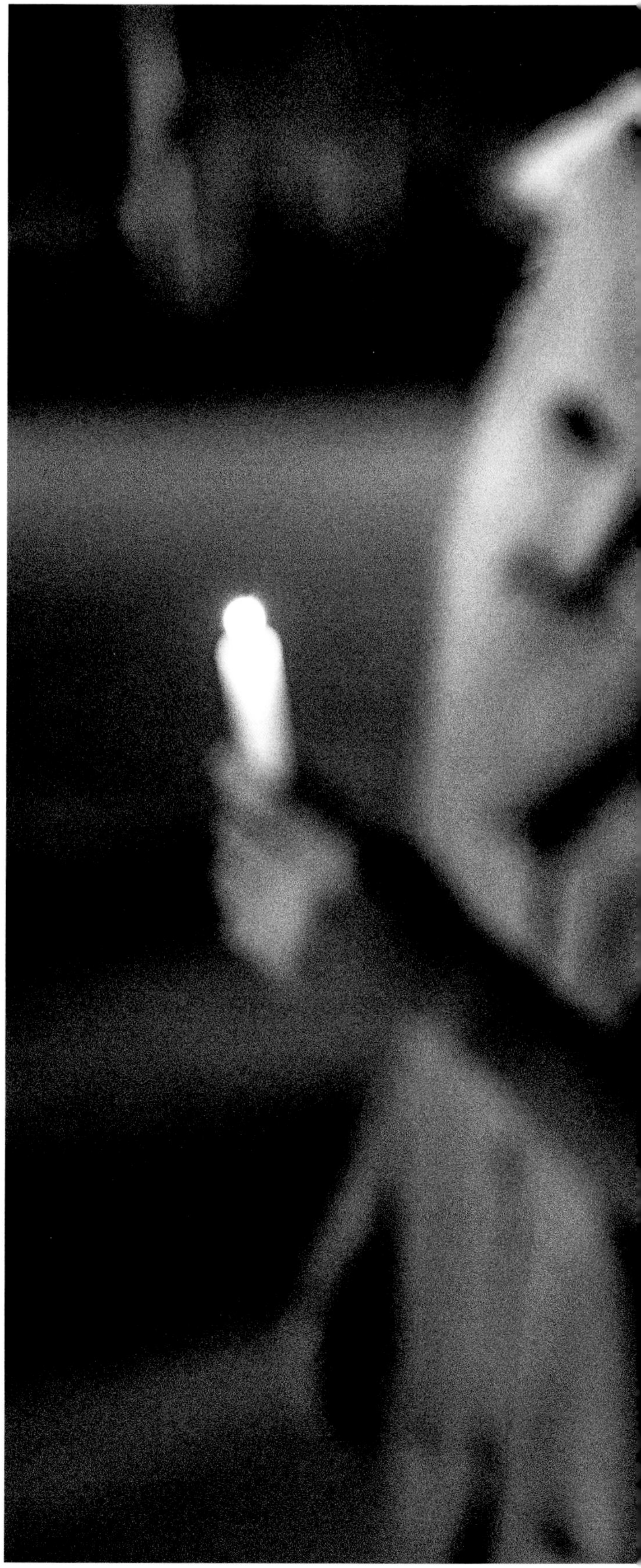

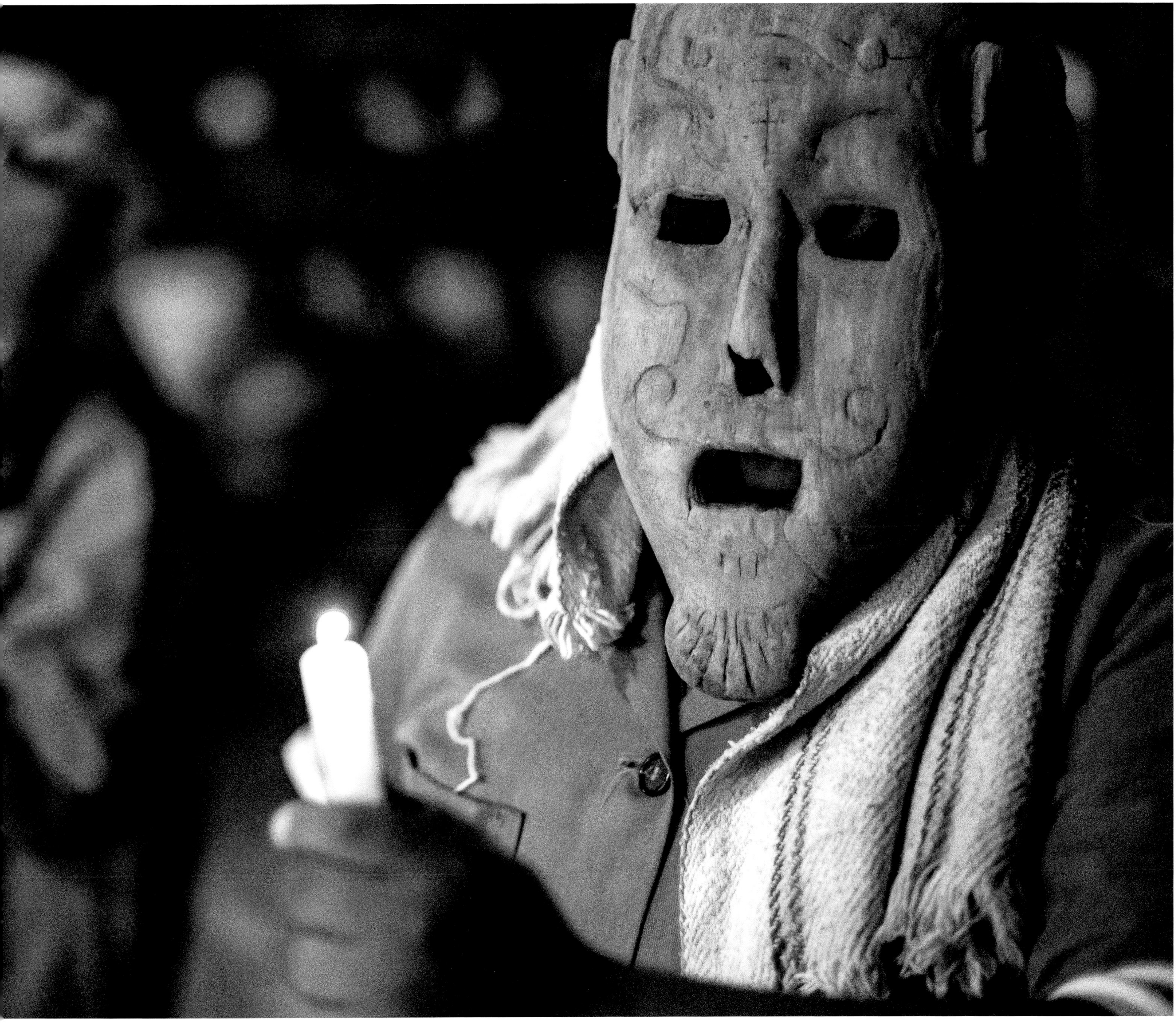

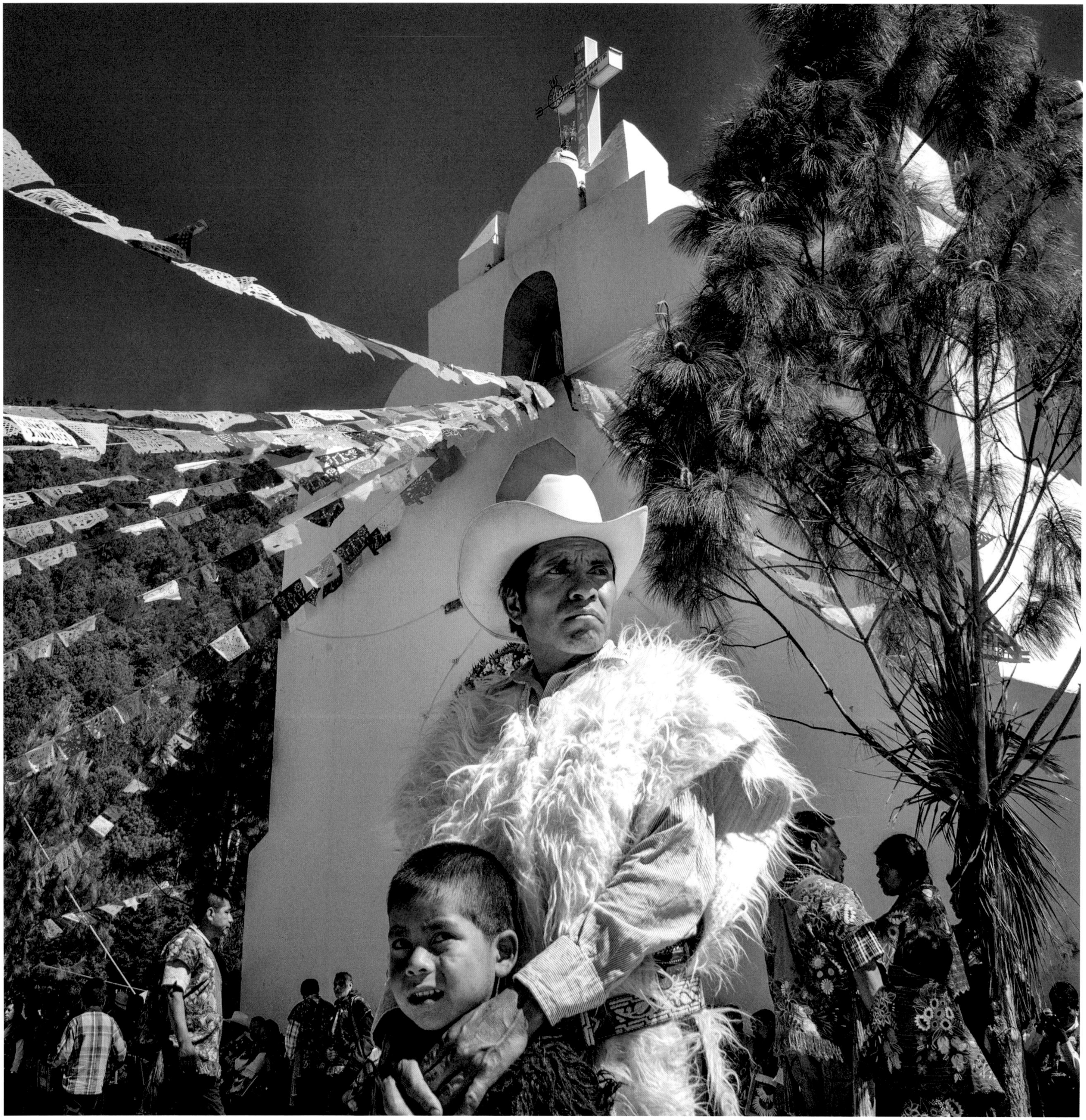

Feast of San Sebastián

January 20
Zinacantán, Chiapas, Mexico

The spectacular nine-day Feast of San Sebastián held in Zinacantán (known officially as San Lorenzo Zinacantán), Chiapas, is much more than a feast day. While it honors the martyred early Christian Saint Sebastian, it also marks the end of an old year and the start of a new one for the Tsotsil Maya residents of this community. Like New Year festivities everywhere, it is a wild and raucous celebration.

The Feast of San Sebastián lasts from January 17 to 25, with the primary celebration held on January 20. Like other festivals throughout Mexico and Guatemala, it integrates indigenous pre-Hispanic traditions with the culture and religion introduced by the Spanish. The Roman persecution of Saint Sebastian, ending in his death for his Christian beliefs, has certain similarities to the persecution and oppression of the Zinacantecos by the Spanish colonialists and may explain why he is honored at this festival. Like other festivals in Chiapas, it combines and condenses the community's long history into common themes.

A wide variety of colorful characters performs ritual tasks throughout the festival. As seen in the roles they play, as well as the costumes they wear, these players replay centuries of history from ancient Maya times through the colonial period and up to today. In addition to the town's mayordomos, performers include the Alcaldes from the previous year, who become Spanish Gentlemen dressed in embroidered red coats, the Regidores (White Heads), and the Lessor Regidores, or Lacandons, an Indigenous group living in Chiapas that the Zinacantecos fought while serving in the Spanish colonial armies. Two prominent character groups are the Alféreces, who dress in one-piece jaguar costumes and carry stuffed dead animals, and the Mayores, also known as Blackmen, whose blackened faces feature eyes and mouths rimmed with white. It is believed these men not only represent African slaves who served in the armies of the Spaniards but also demons and tricksters from the unknown side of the earth.

opposite: FRONT OF THE CHURCH OF SAN SEBASTIÁN, 2015

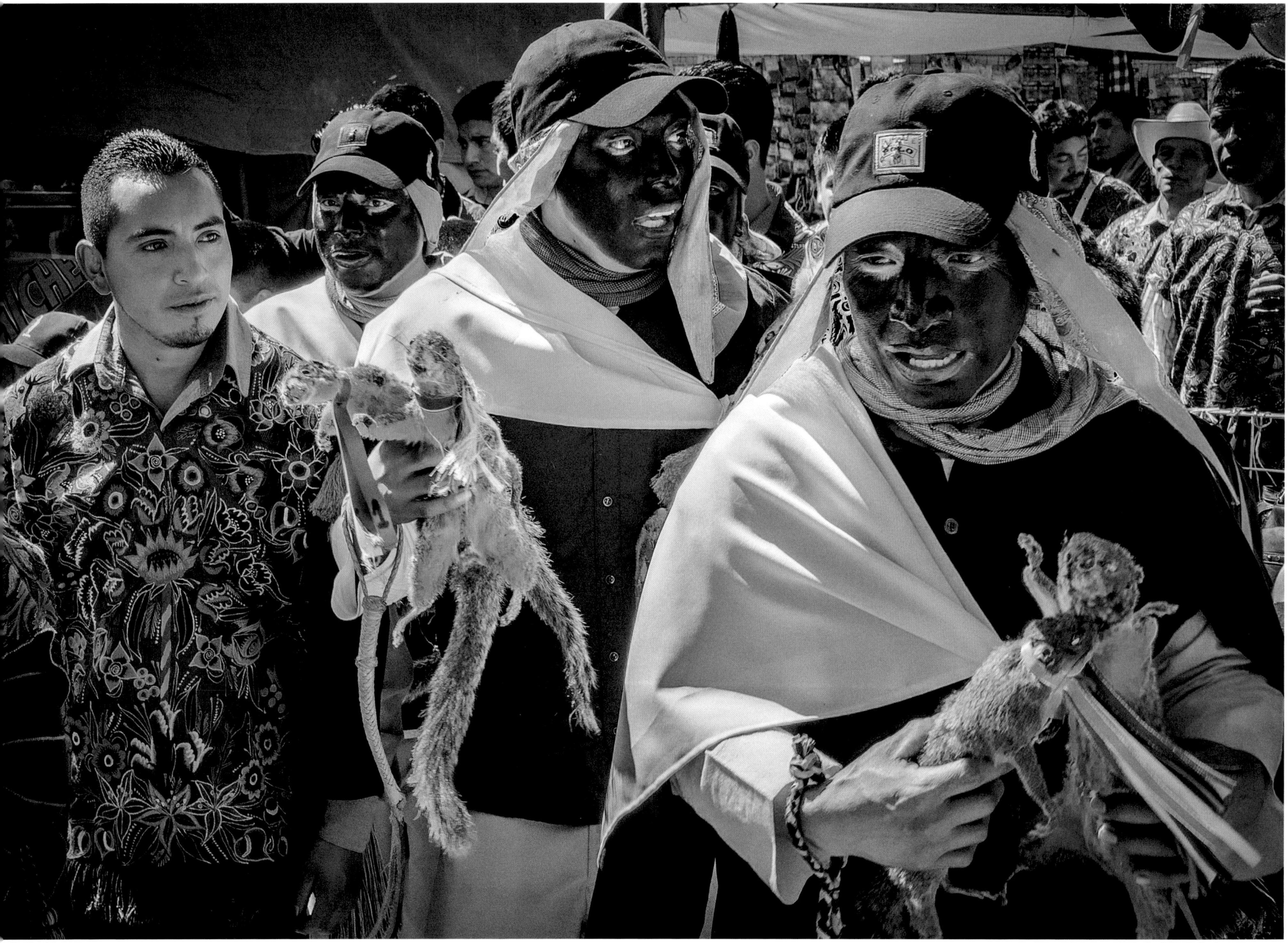

BLACKMEN GATHERING THEIR STUFFED SQUIRRELS, 2015

opposite: TEMPTING A JAGUAR CHARACTER WITH SQUIRRELS, 2015

following spread: JAGUARS DESCENDING FROM THEIR PERCH AND DISTRIBUTING SWEETS, 2015

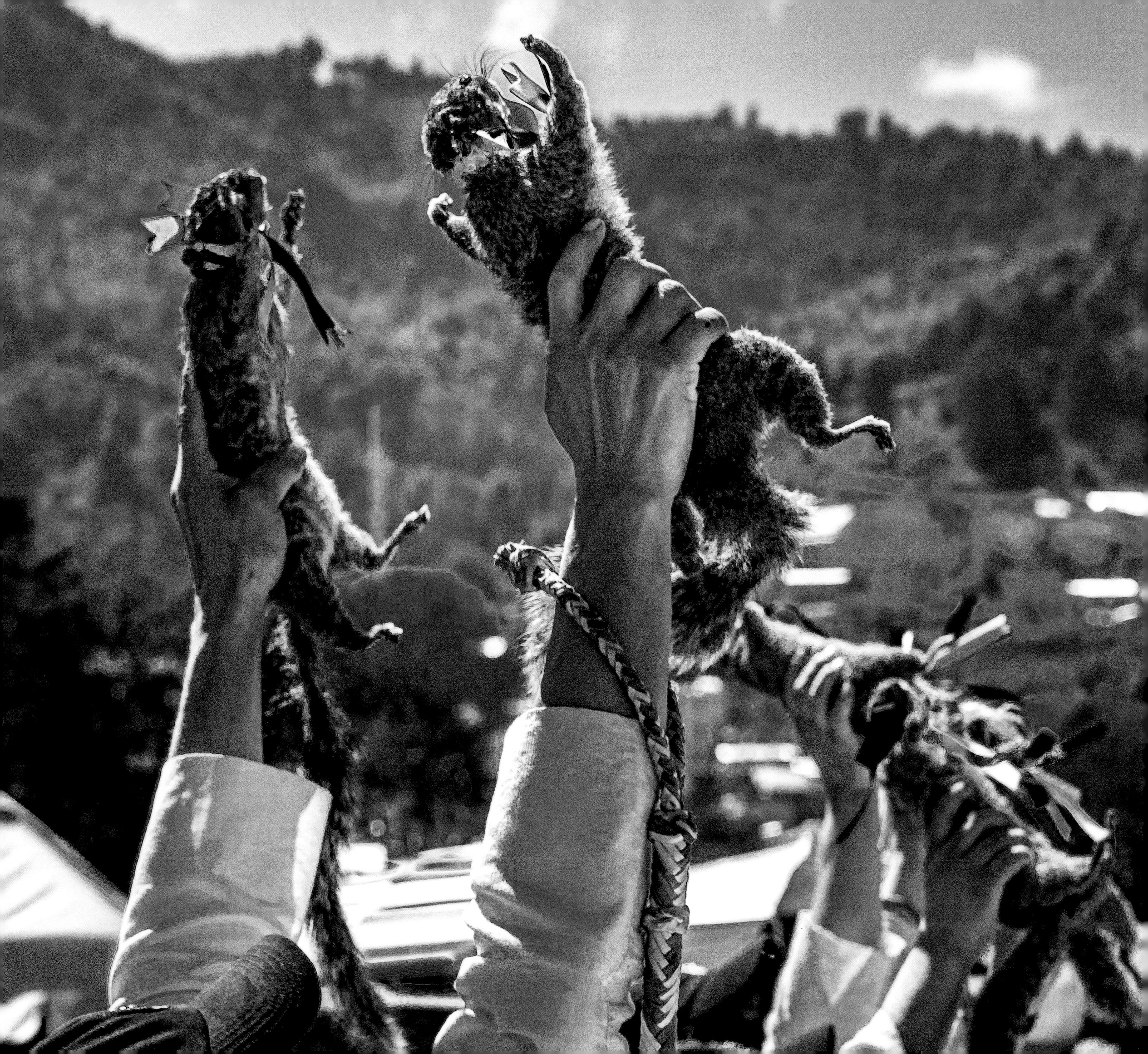

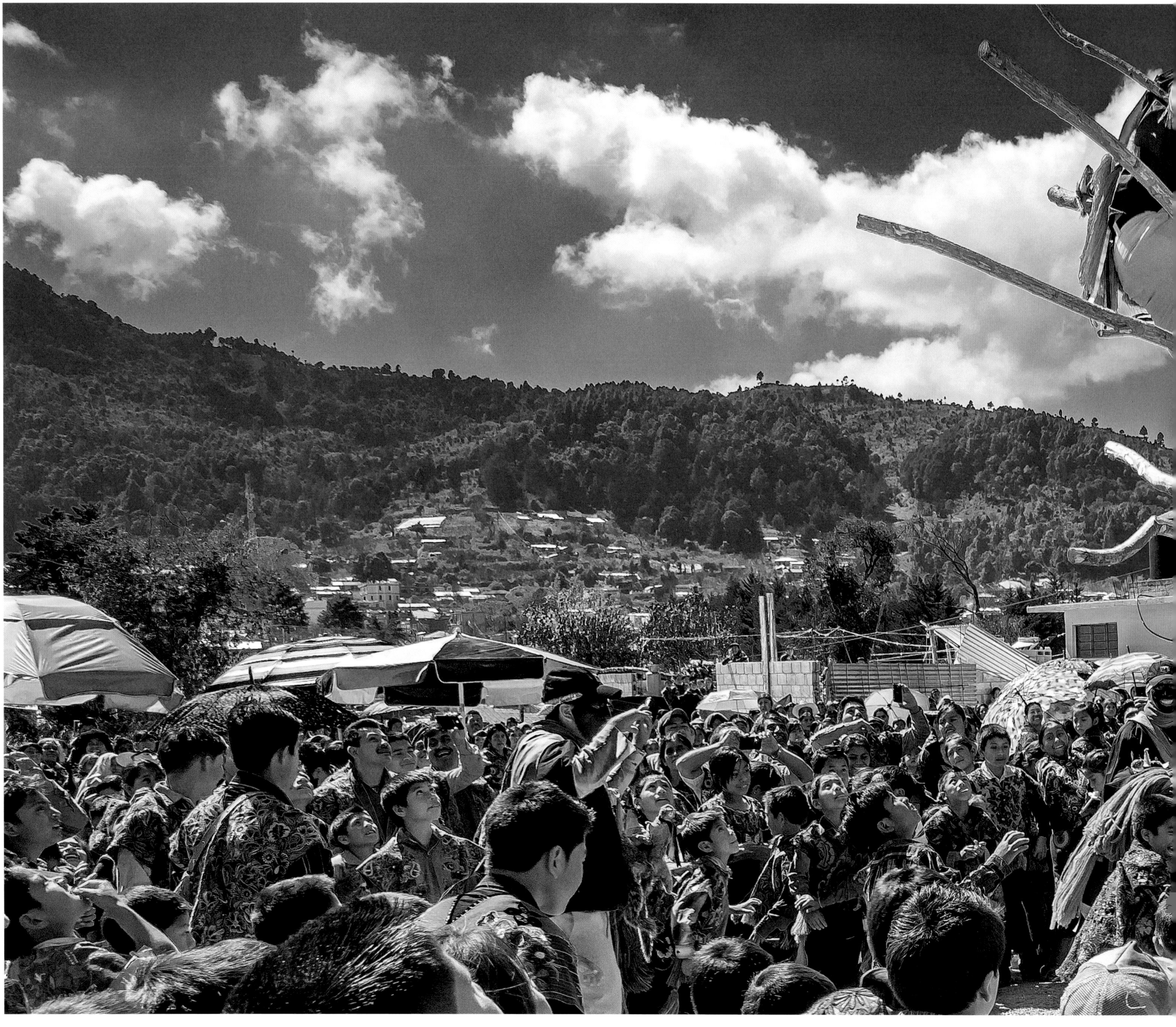

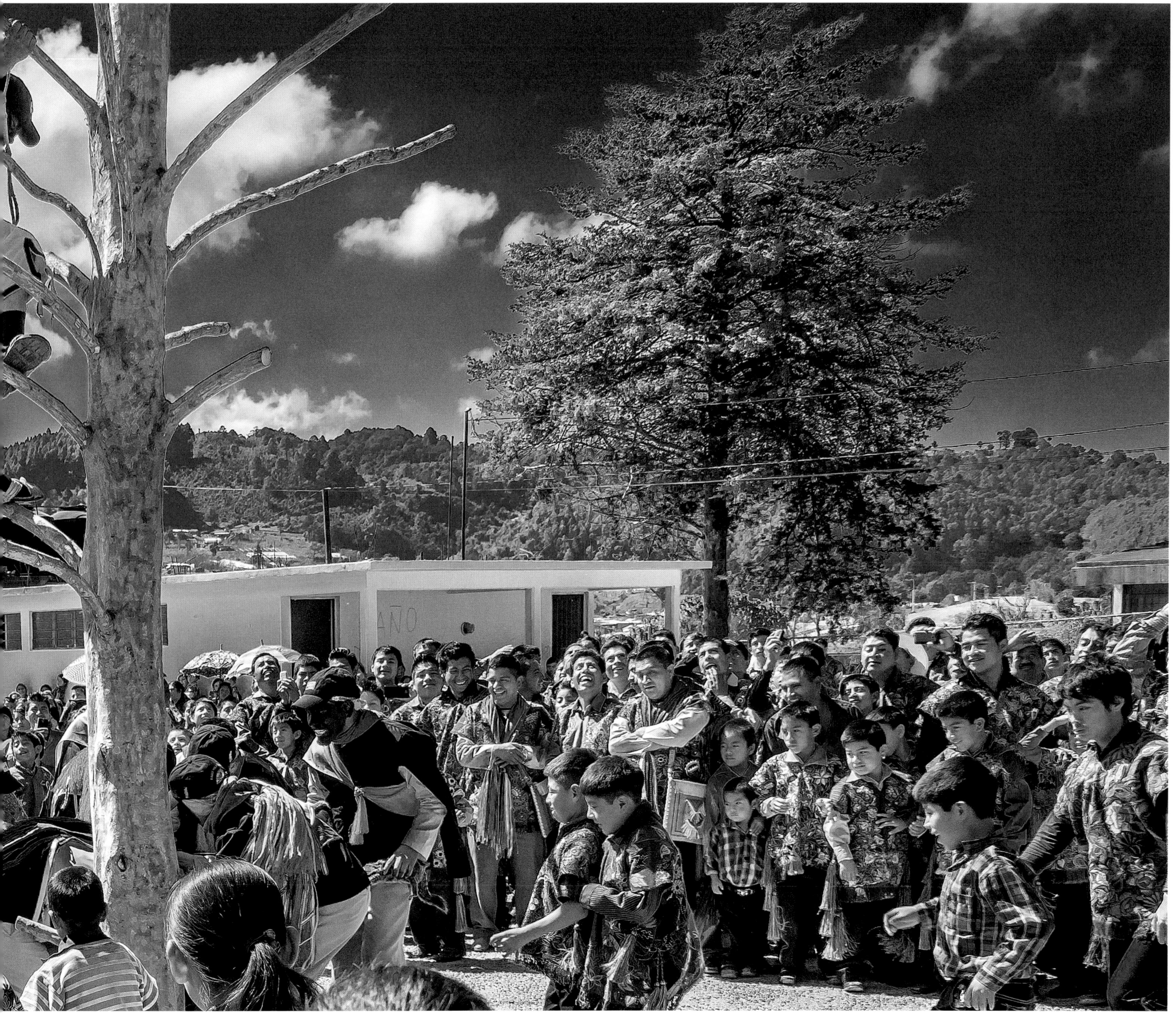

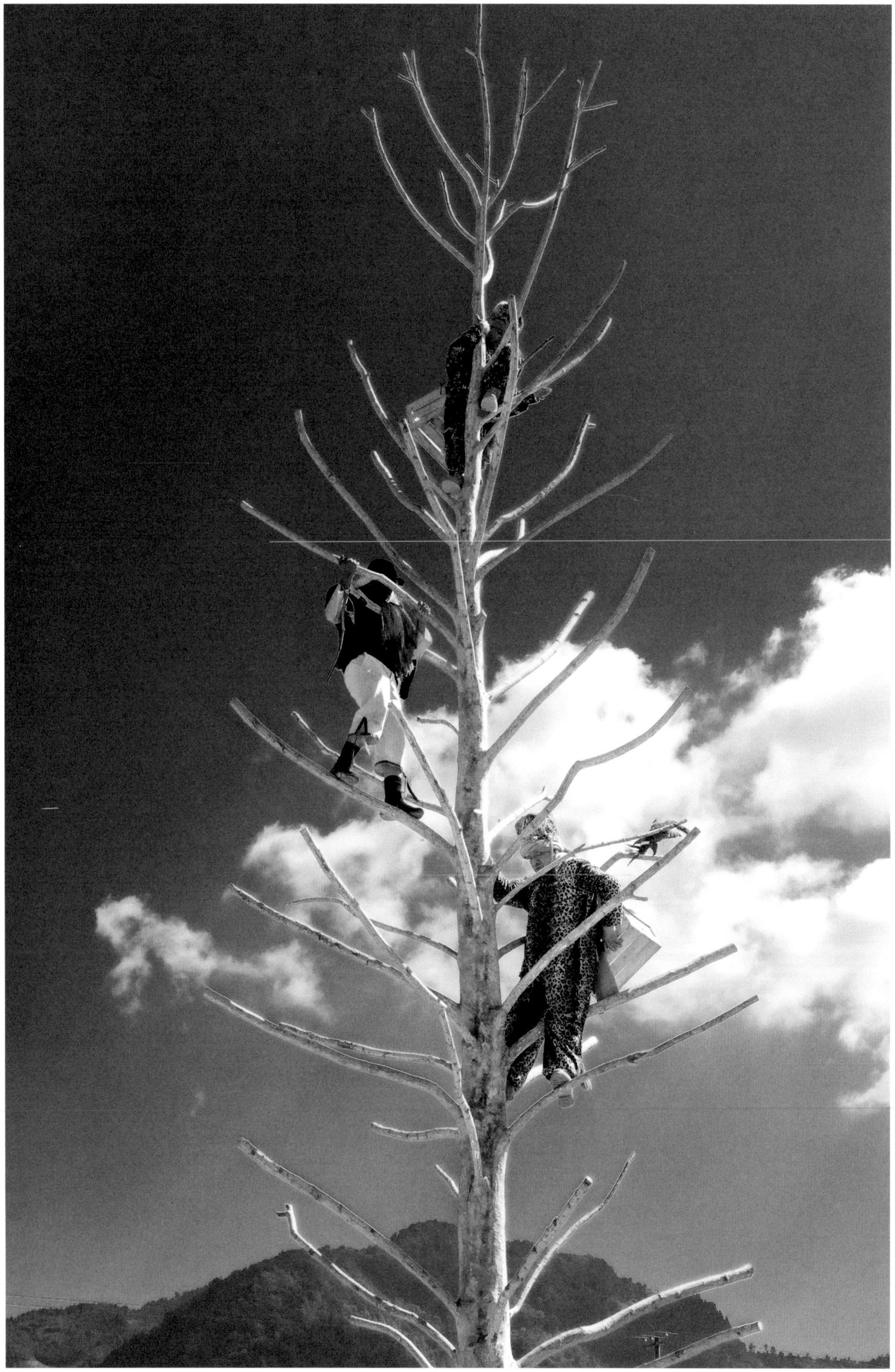

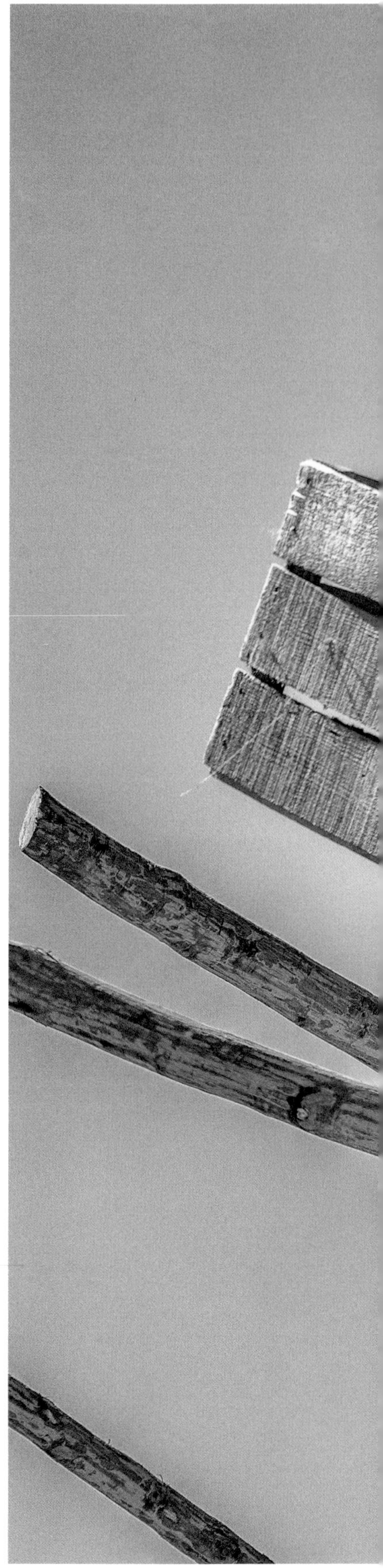

JAGUARS DESCENDING, 2015

opposite: A JAGUAR CHARACTER WITH HIS BOX OF SQUIRRELS, 2015

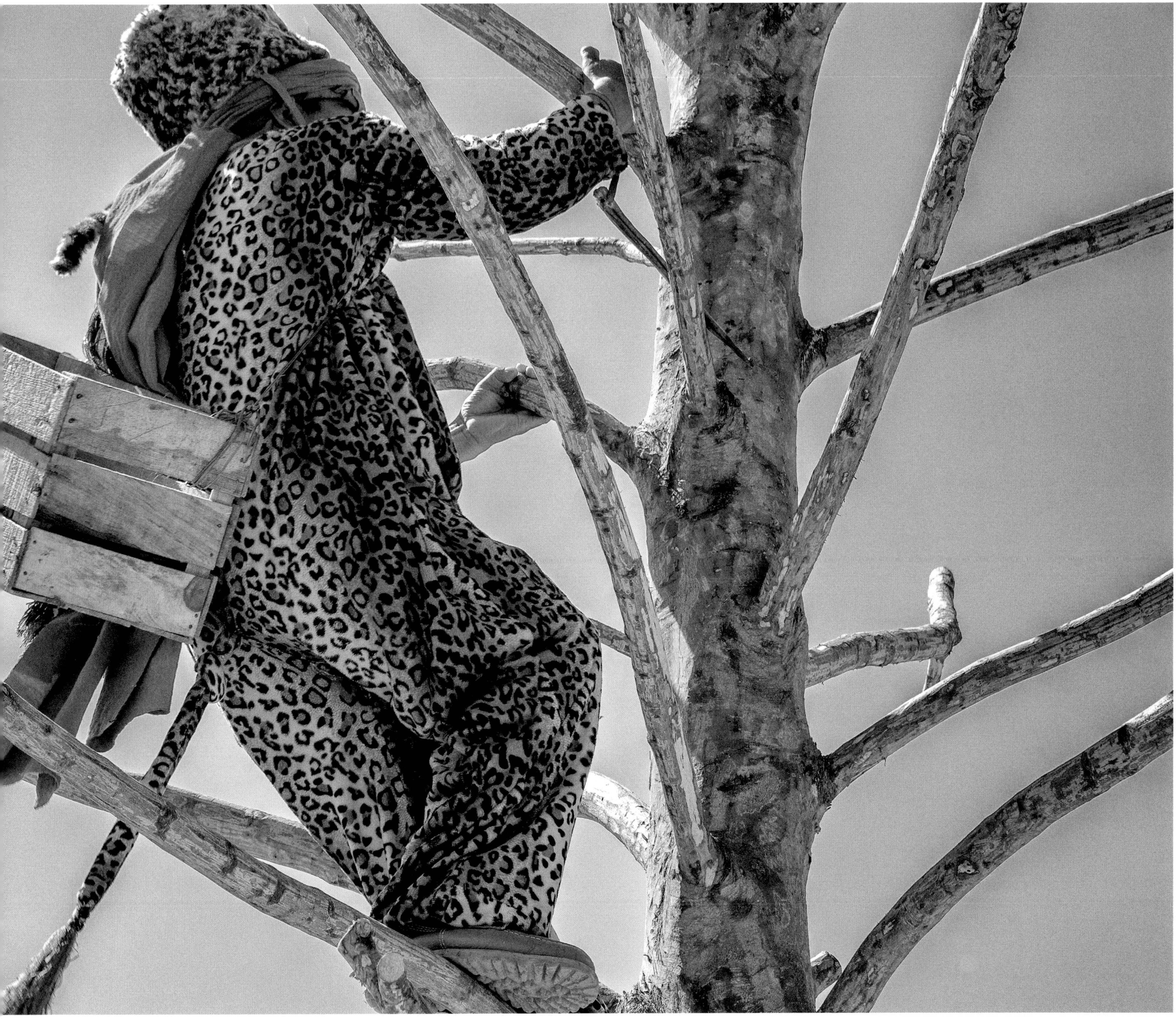

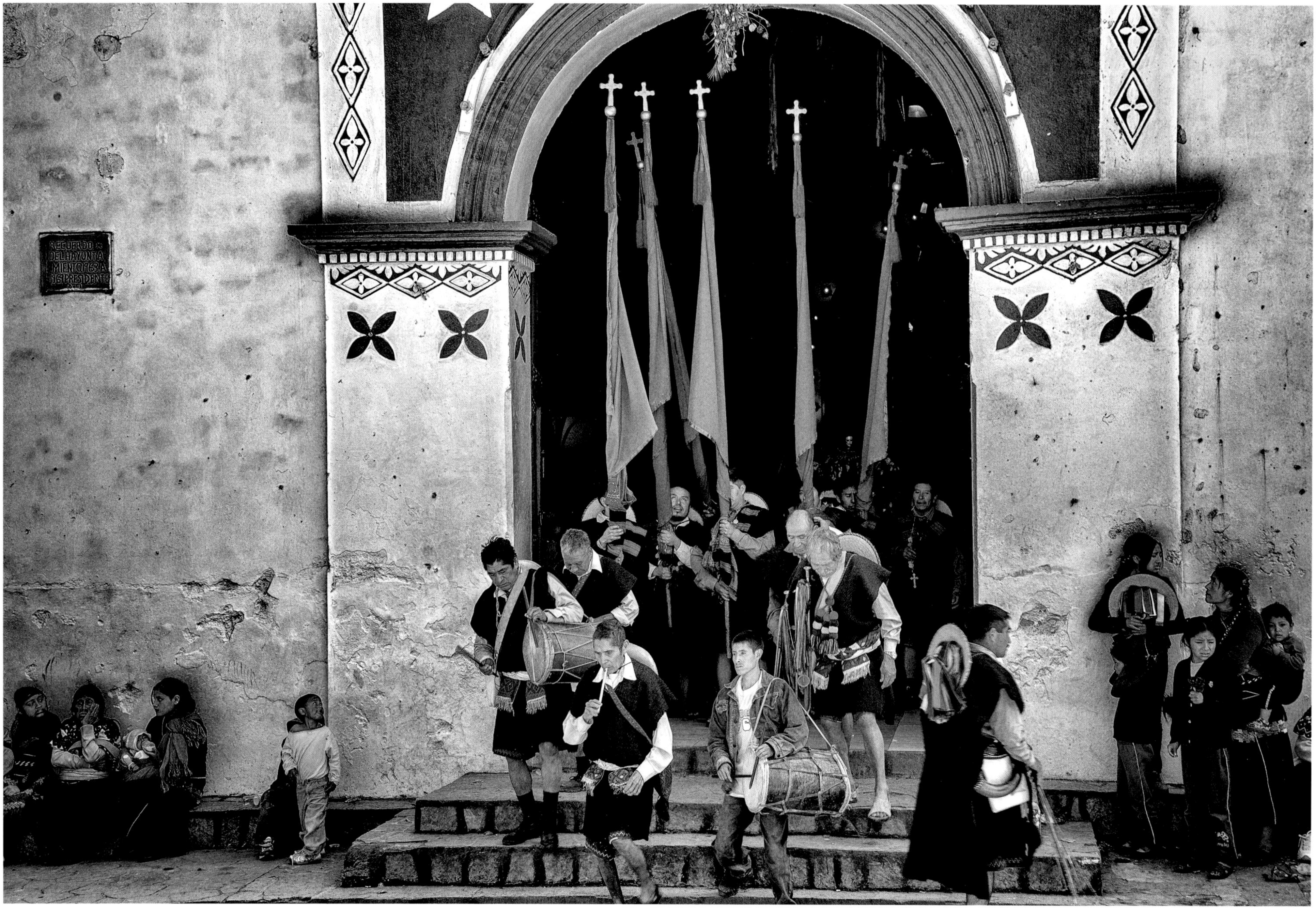
RECUERDO
DEL H AYUNTA
MIENTO 1963 A
1967 PRESIDENTE

Feast of San Ildefonso

January 23
Tenejapa, Chiapas, Mexico

The history of Tenejapa can be traced to pre-Hispanic times when a group of descendants of the early Maya settled in Chiapas. After the Spanish colonization of Chiapas in the mid-sixteenth century, Dominican priests made active attempts to bring Catholicism to this region. Tenejapa was one of the towns in which the Dominicans established a parish church, the church of San Ildefonso, which serves more than one hundred small villages in the area, as well as the inhabitants of the town of Tenejapa.

The Feast of San Ildefonso honors the patron saint of Tenejapa on January 23, the day of his death in 667. Born in 607 in Toledo, Spain, Ildefonso began his religious journey as a deacon and ended it as Bishop of Toledo. A favorite of the Catholic missionaries, he espoused good deeds throughout his life, which served to inspire the missionary communities. Perhaps even more important, he was known to have experienced two significant visions. The first was a vision of the martyr Saint Leocadia rising from her tomb to thank Ildefonso for his devotion to the Mother of God. The second was a vision of the Blessed Virgin herself, who also thanked then-Bishop Ildefonso for his devotion and presented him with a special vestment to be worn during Marian ceremonies.

In Tenejapa, the procession of the Feast of San Ildefonso begins in the church, after the town's mayordomos wash the clothing of the wooden saints that remain in the church during the year. No Catholic priests participate as pine boughs are spread on the floor of the church, and rituals commence: prayers, the burning of incense before the altar, and preparation of the saints for the procession. The procession leaves the church with statues of the Blessed Virgin and San Ildefonso on palanquins carried by the villagers, alongside musicians and men holding banners aloft. Hundreds of Tenejapans join in a solemn march that slowly encircles the town and returns to the church, where the saints are retired until the next feast day.

opposite: THE PROCESSION OF SAN ILDEFONSO LEAVING THE CHURCH, 2015

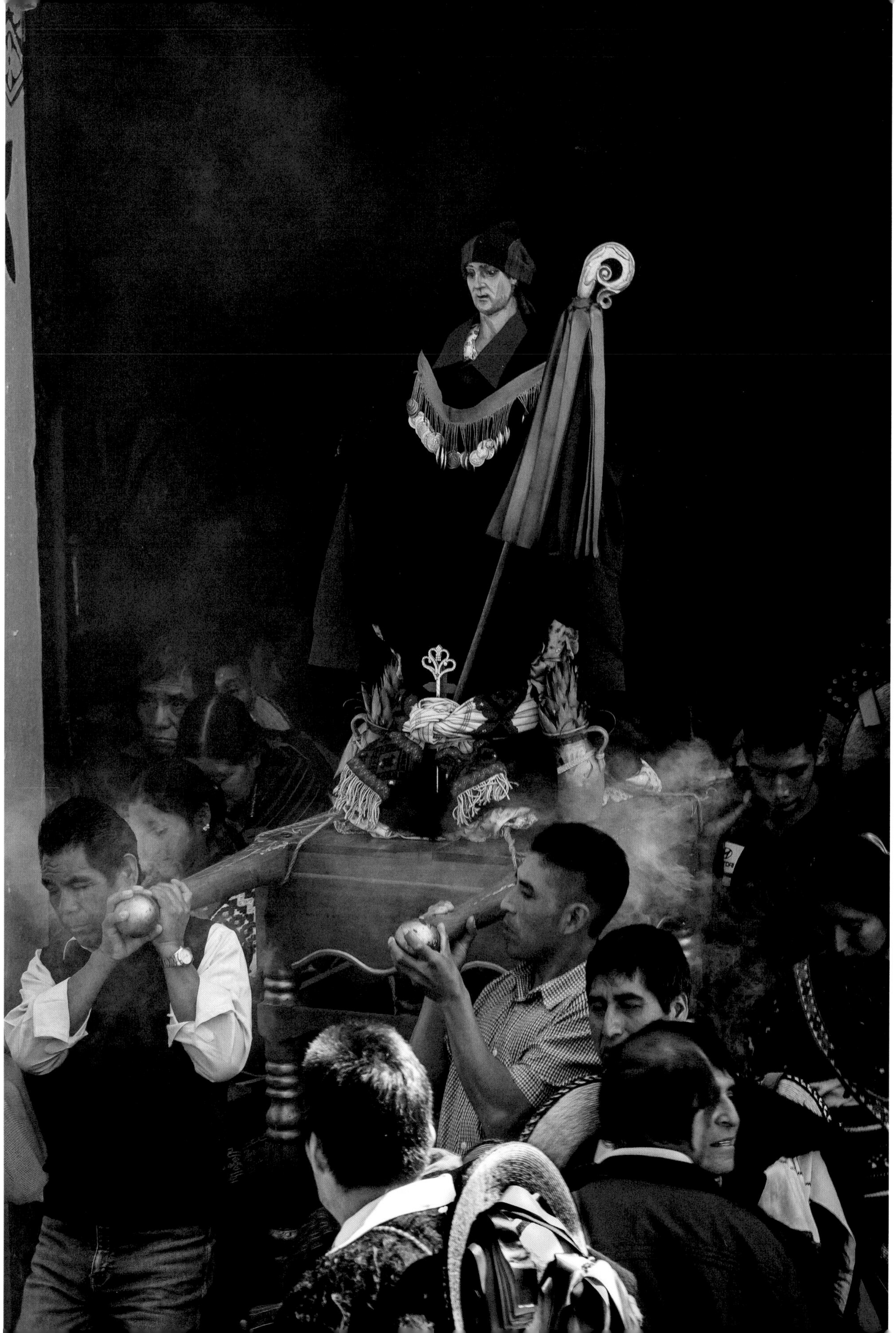

SAN ILDEFONSO, THE PATRON SAINT OF TENEJAPA, 2015
opposite: MEMBERS OF THE PROCESSION, 2015

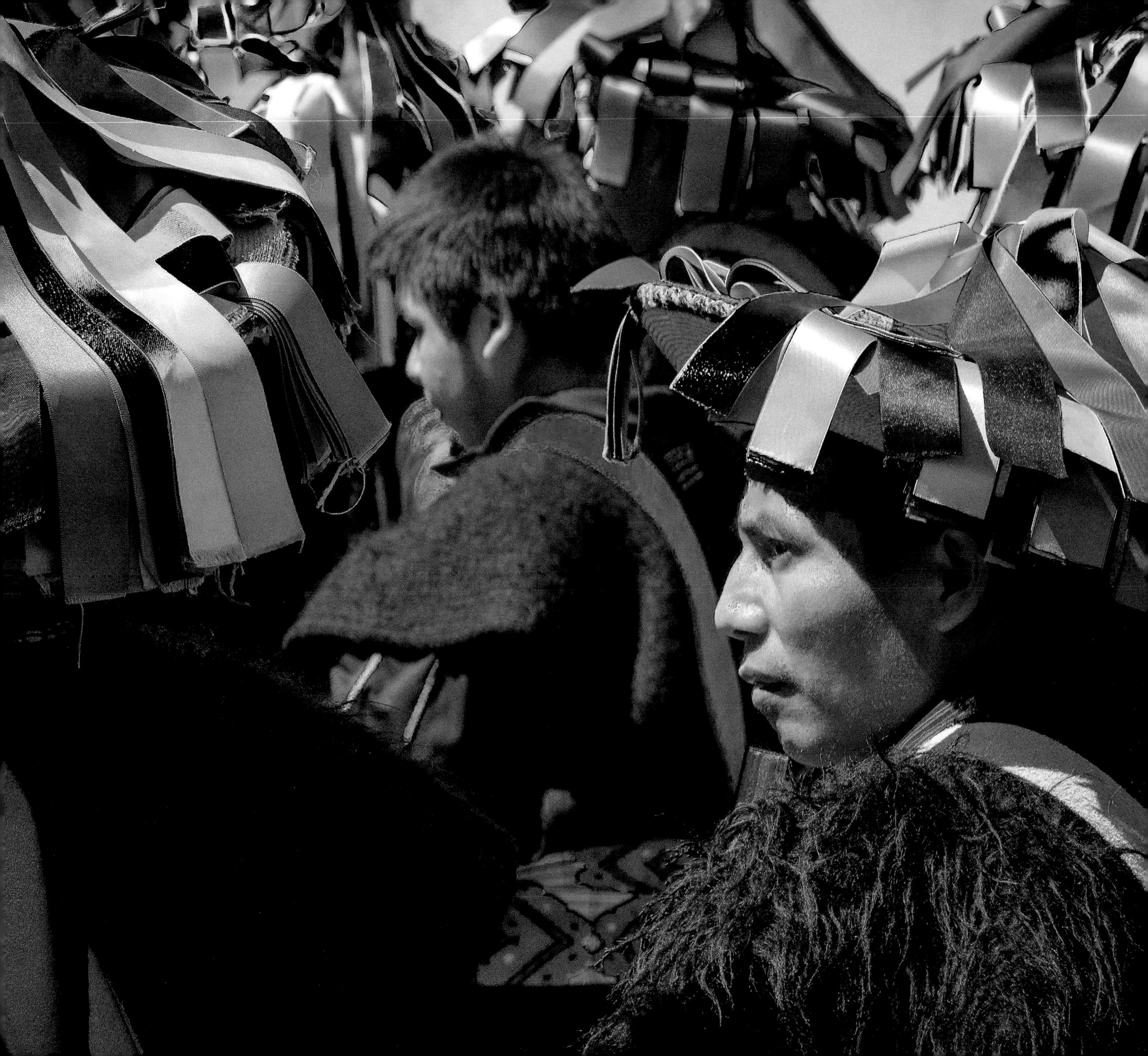

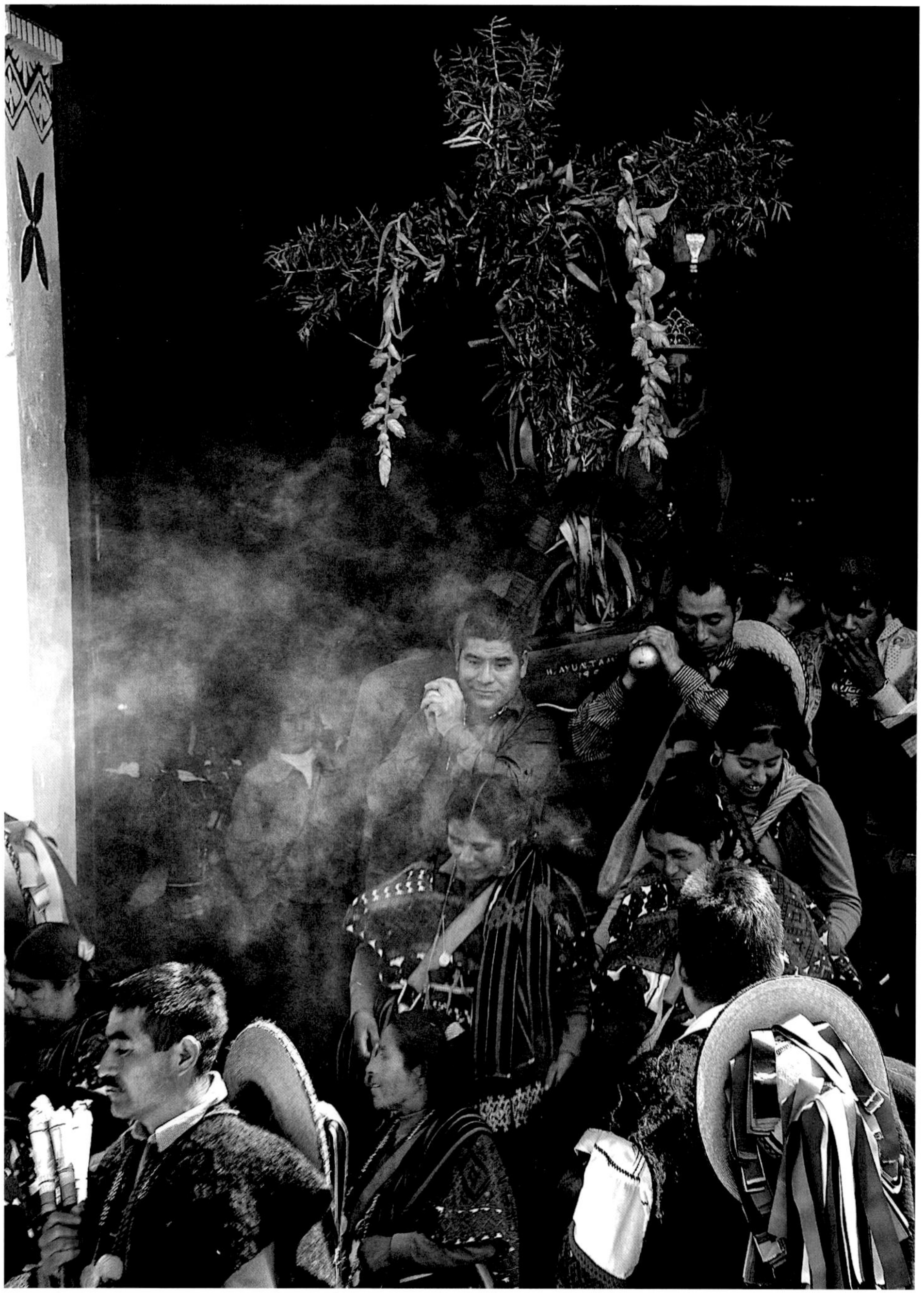

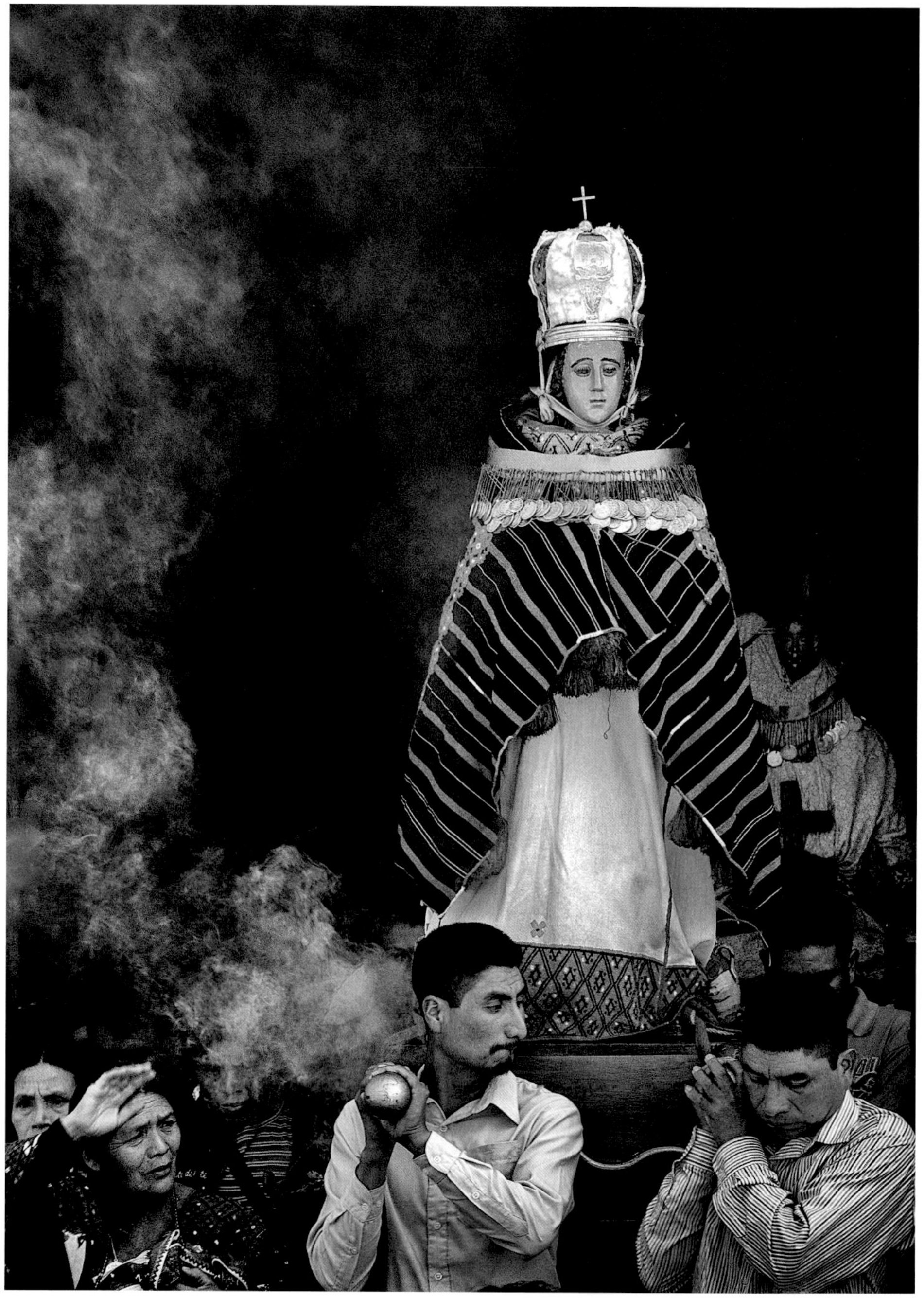

A HANDWOVEN CRUCIFIX CARRIED IN THE PROCESSION, 2015

center: THE SAINTS LEAVING THE CHURCH, 2015

opposite: THE SAINTS CARRIED ON WOODEN PALANQUINS, 2015

following spread: THE PEOPLE OF TENEJAPA JOINING THE PROCESSION THROUGH THE TOWN, 2015

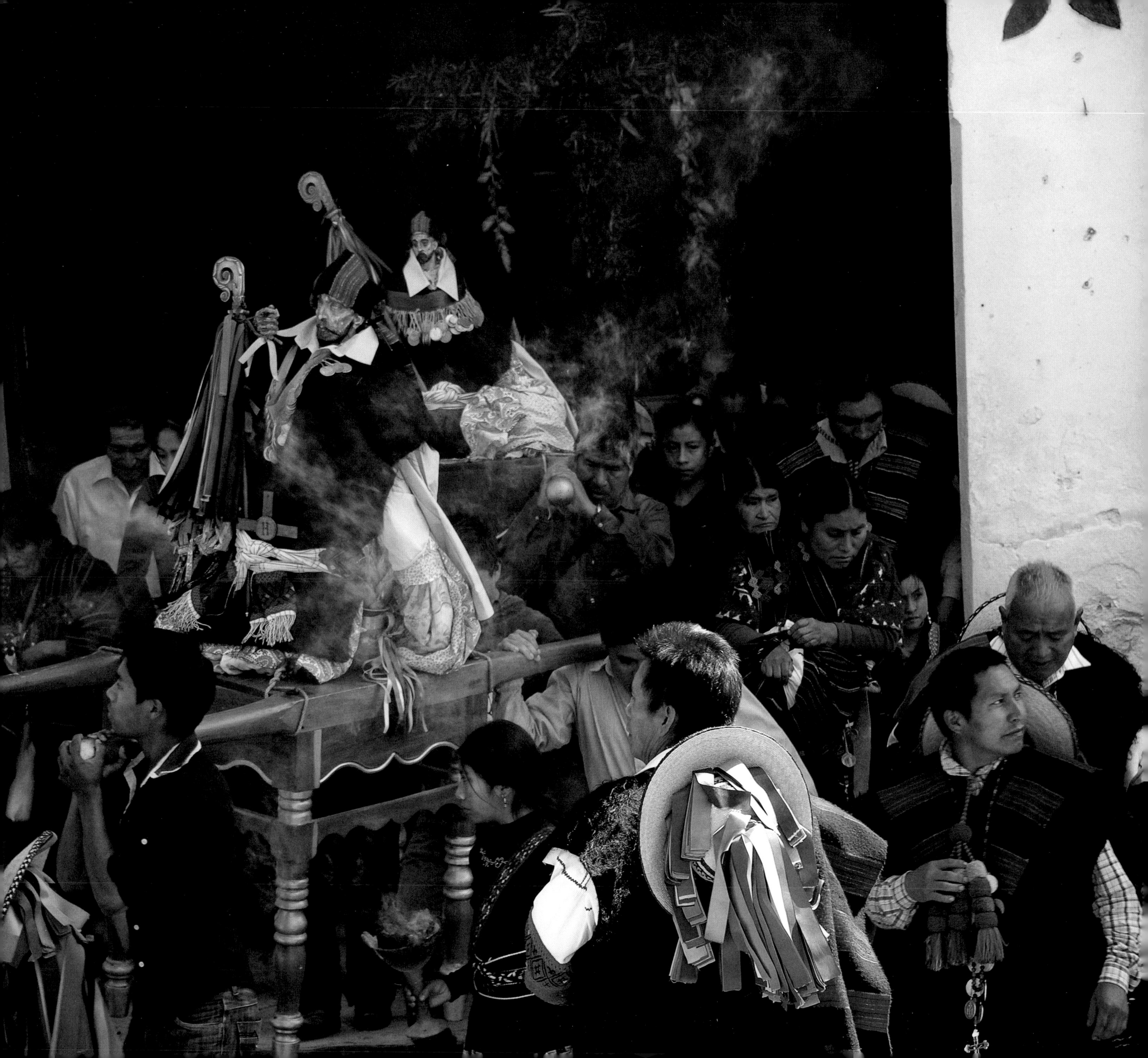

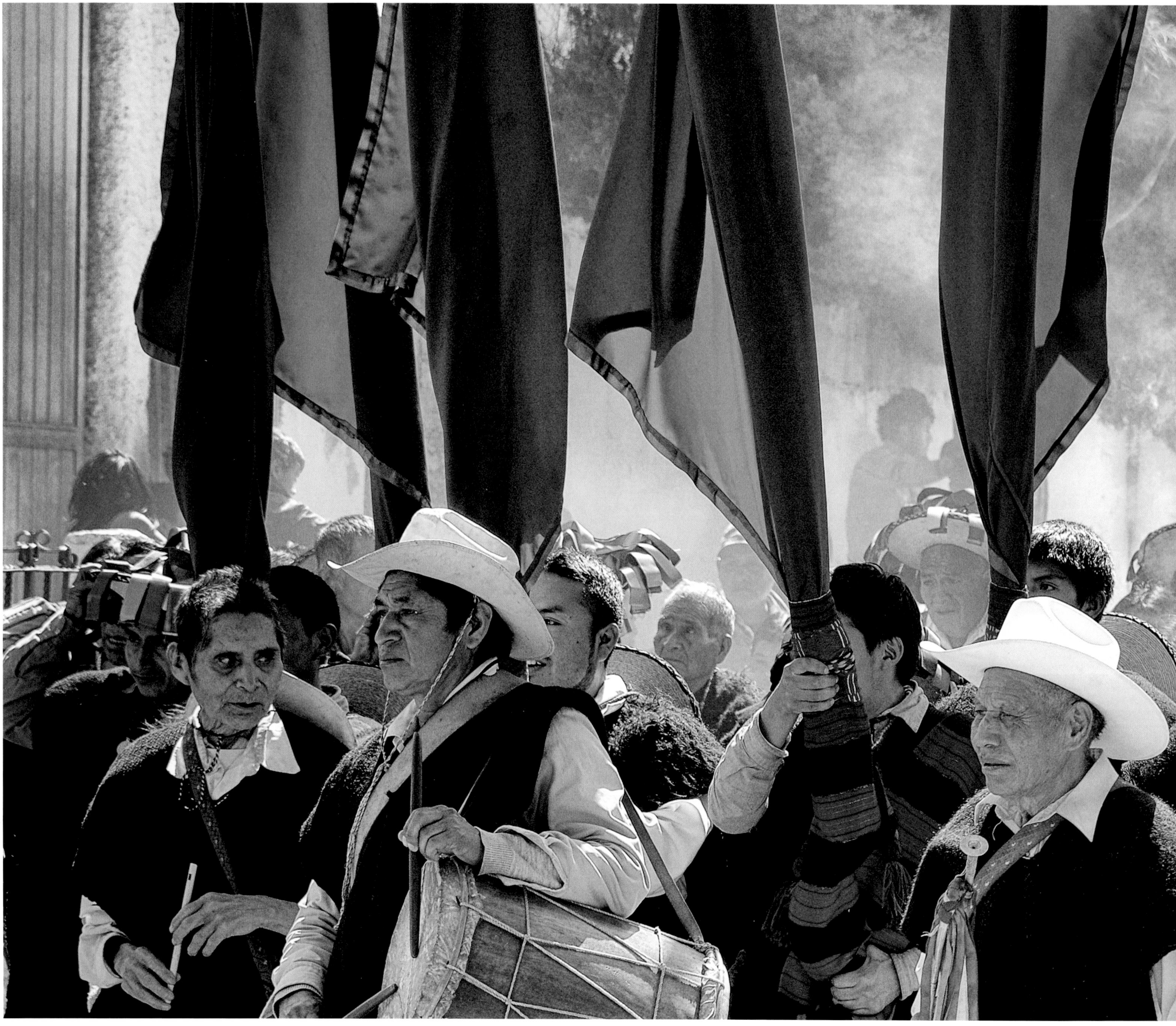

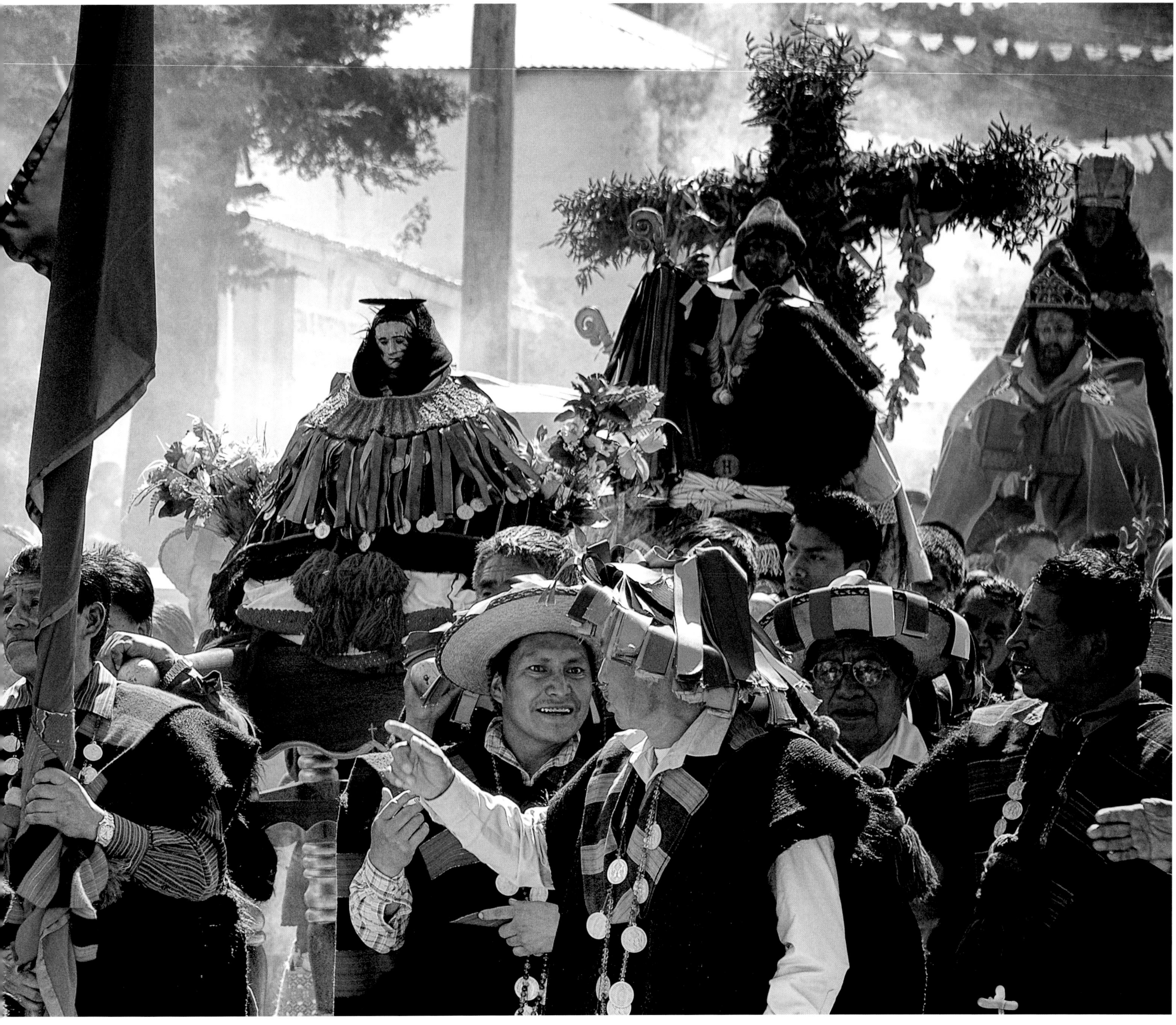

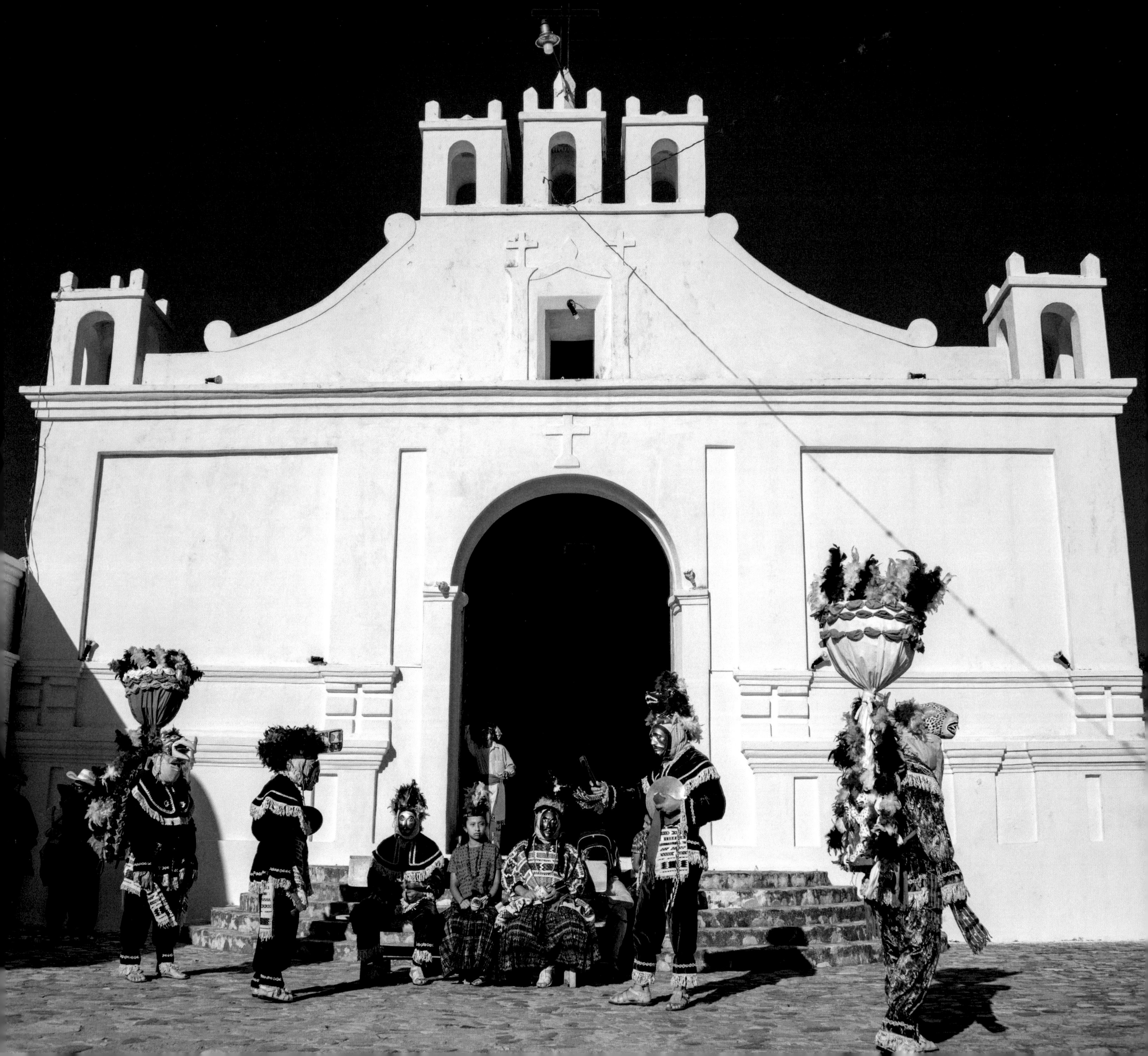

Rabinal Achí and Feast of San Pablo

January 25
Rabinal, Baja Verapaz, Guatemala

The Rabinal Achí is one of the very few remaining Maya song-and-dance dramas dating to the the pre-Hispanic period. Written in the Maya K'iche' language, it portrays a story of political rivalry between two neighboring kingdoms and the ultimate triumph of the people of Rabinal. Like many other ritual performances throughout Mesoamerica, it has deep-rooted meanings related to cultural identity and ways of understanding the world. In 2005 it was proclaimed a Masterpiece of Oral and Intangible Heritage of Humanity by UNESCO.

Performances of the Achí are enacted every year on January 25 in the small town of Rabinal, located in the highlands of Guatemala. In conjunction with the Achí are celebrations for the Feast of San Pablo, on the same day, and the Feast of San Sebastián, on January 20. San Pablo is the patron saint of Rabinal—perhaps to placate the Spanish conquerors, Rabinal leaders designated his feast day as the day for the Achí performance. In this way, the community was able to retain its pre-Hispanic roots while demonstrating acceptance of the religious precepts of the colonizers.

The whole town has a festive air during this period, but the feast-day celebrations, which are conducted by the *cofradía* (local brotherhood associated with church parishes and dedicated to its patron saint) are especially intense, featuring music, masked dances, and large quantities of food and drink for the crowds. Huge, hand-carried floats decorated with flowers and feathers and containing images of saints are carried through the streets to the cathedral.

Performances of the Rabinal Achí take place at locations throughout the town. The four-act narrative is long and takes hours to complete. There is a large cast of characters bedecked in ornate costumes, headdresses, and beautifully carved masks, but only a few of them speak. The primary characters are two warriors: the Rabinal Achí (Man of Achí) and Cawek, the K'iche' Achí (Man of K'iche'). Other important characters include the king, or leader, of Rabinal; his wife; his servant; his maiden daughter; numerous eagles and jaguars representing warriors; and other dancers.

The drama details the good deeds—as well as the crimes—committed by the noble but renegade warrior Cawek. As a result, he is tried, and it is ultimately decided that he should be killed. He dreams about his native land but submits to execution, bringing justice back to Rabinal. Music from wooden slit drums, cymbals, and trumpets typically accompanies the performance, resulting in a dreamlike state that helps transport those in the audience back to the world of their ancestors.

opposite: THE ACHÍ PERFORMANCE IN FRONT OF THE CHURCH OF EL CALVARIO, 2020

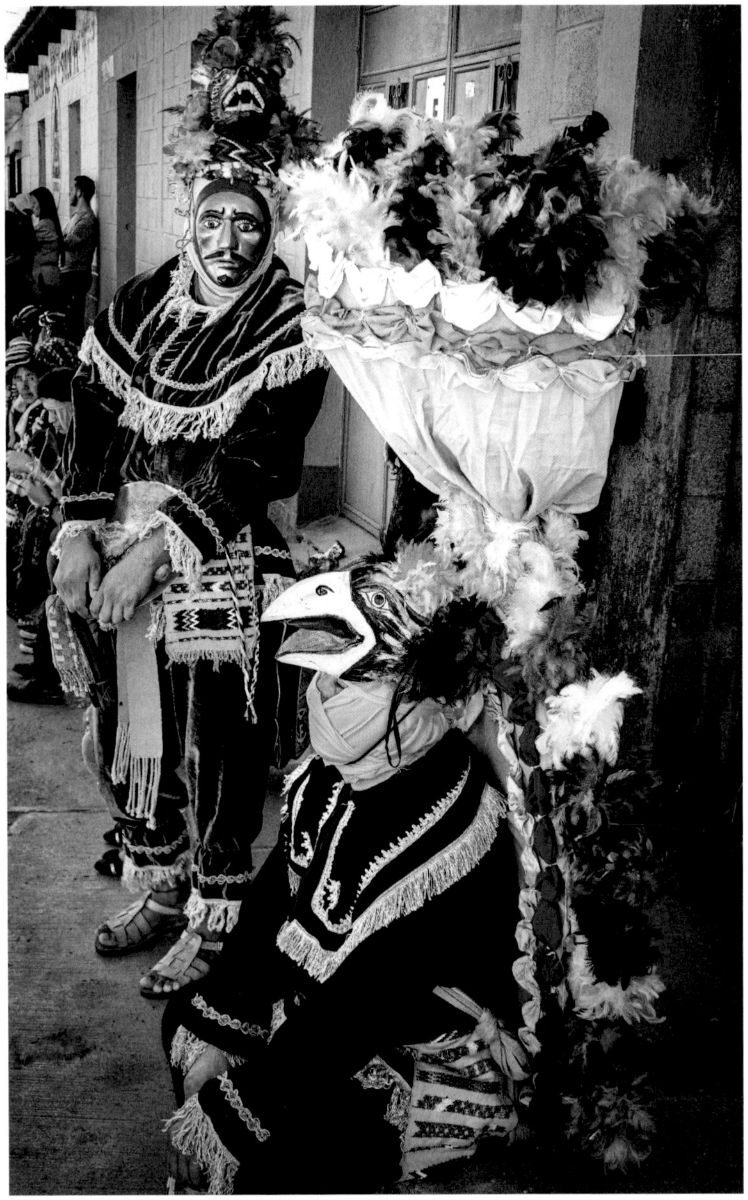

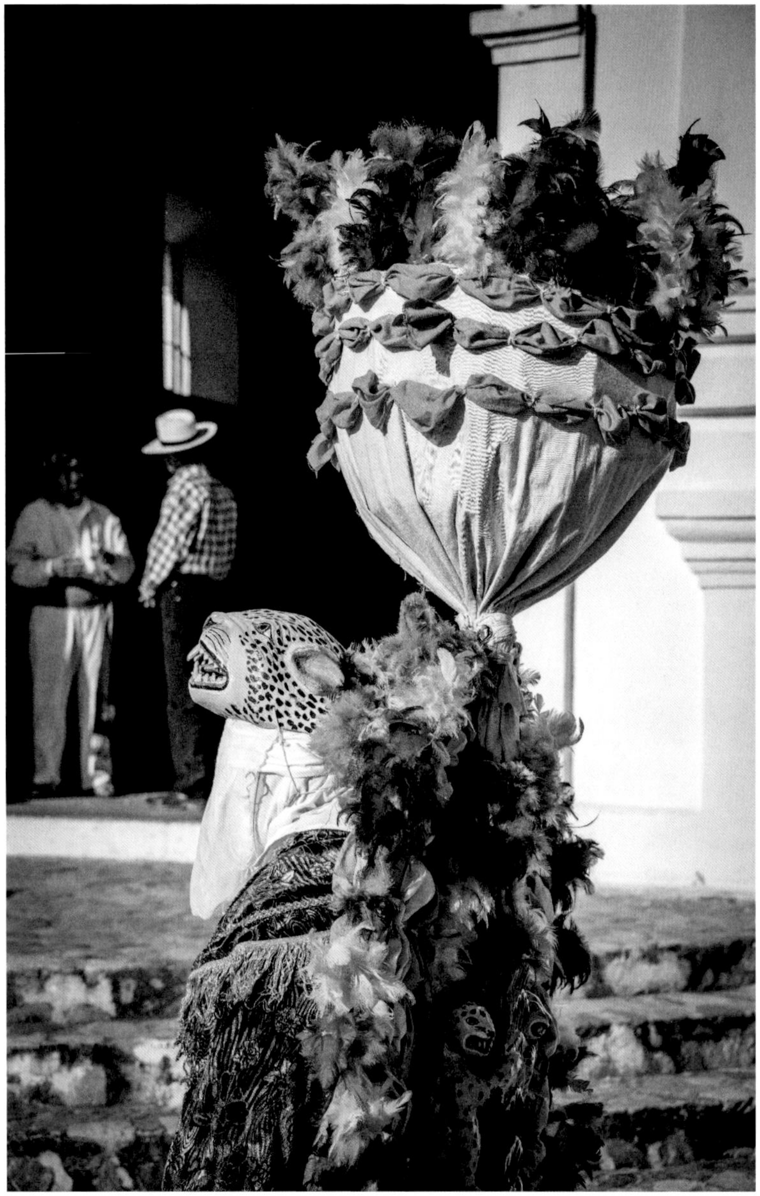

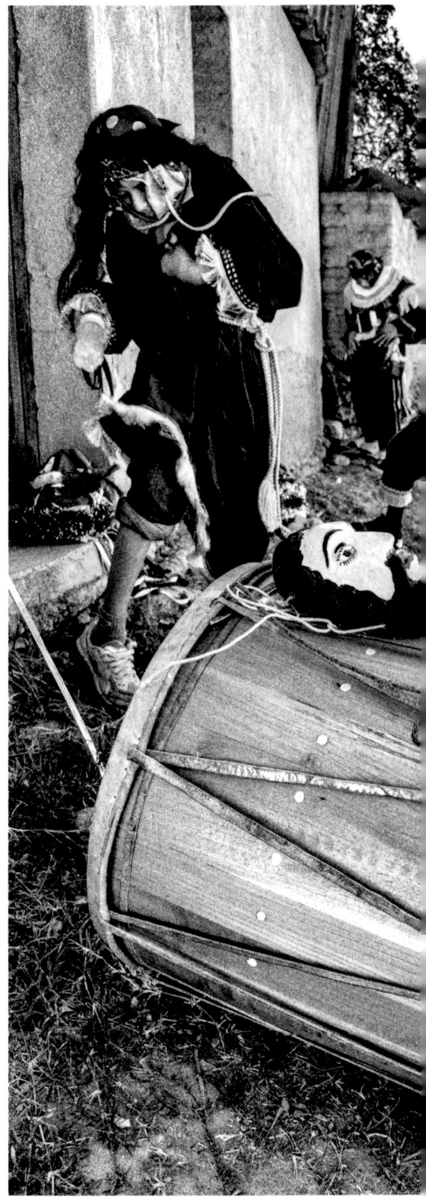

THE RABINAL ACHÍ AND AN EAGLE WARRIOR IN THE ACHÍ, 2020
center: A JAGUAR WARRIOR CHARACTER IN THE ACHÍ SONG-AND-DANCE DRAMA, 2020
right: THE START OF AN ACHÍ PERFORMANCE, 2020

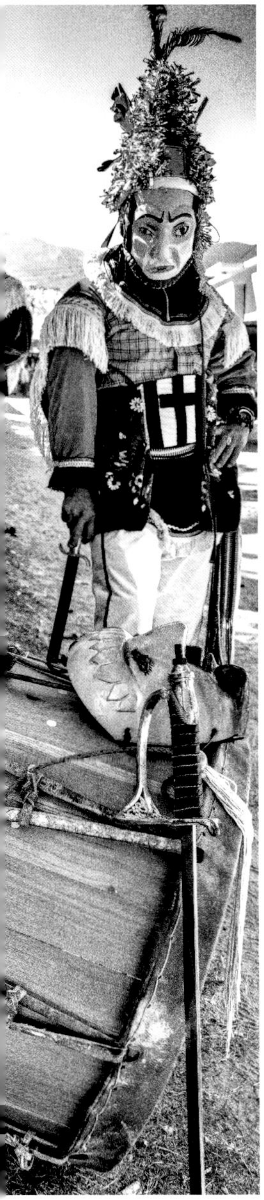

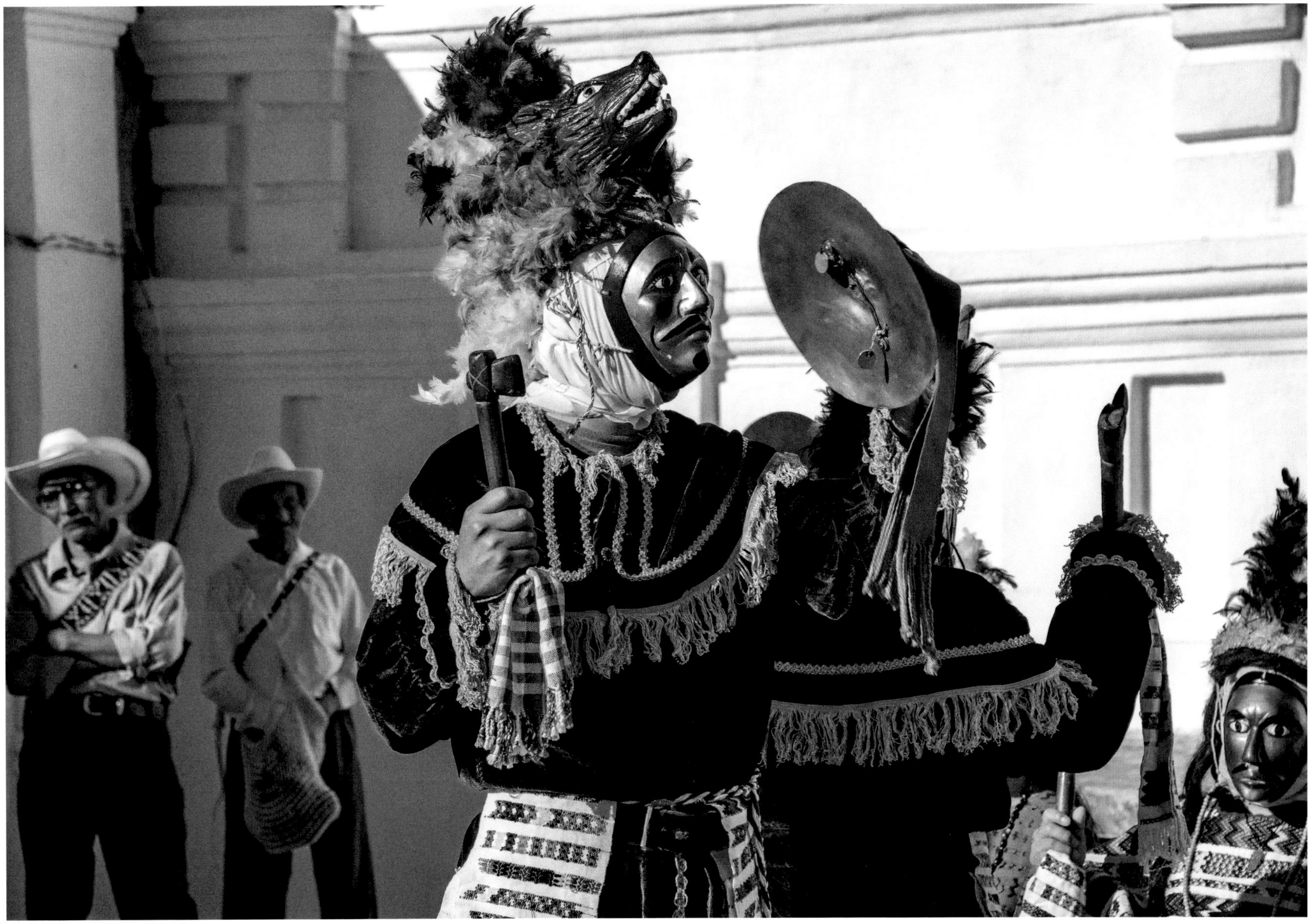

THE ACHI PERFORMANCE, 2020

following spread: MEMBERS OF THE PARISH GATHERING IN FRONT OF THE CHURCH OF EL CALVARIO, 2020

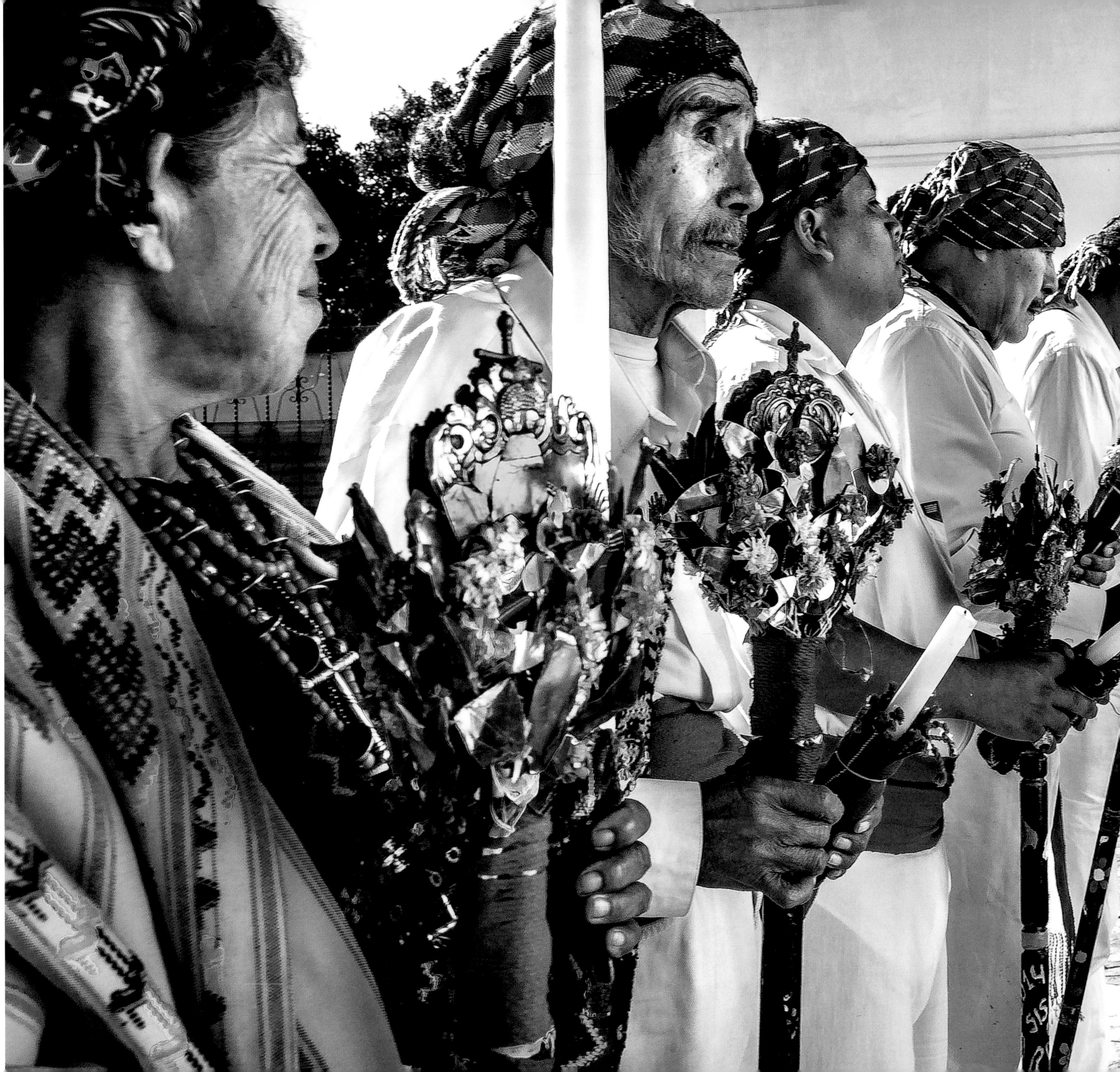

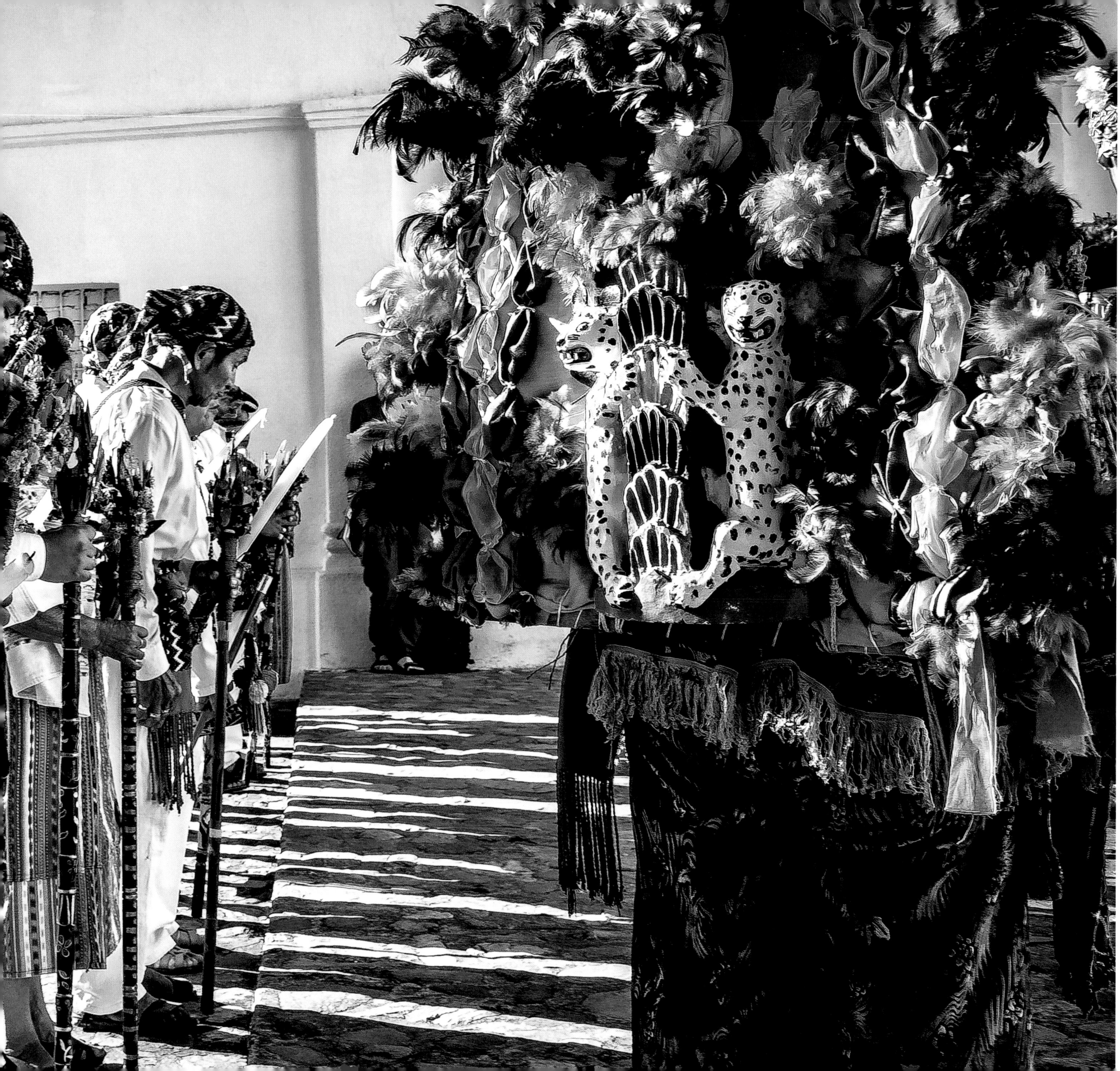

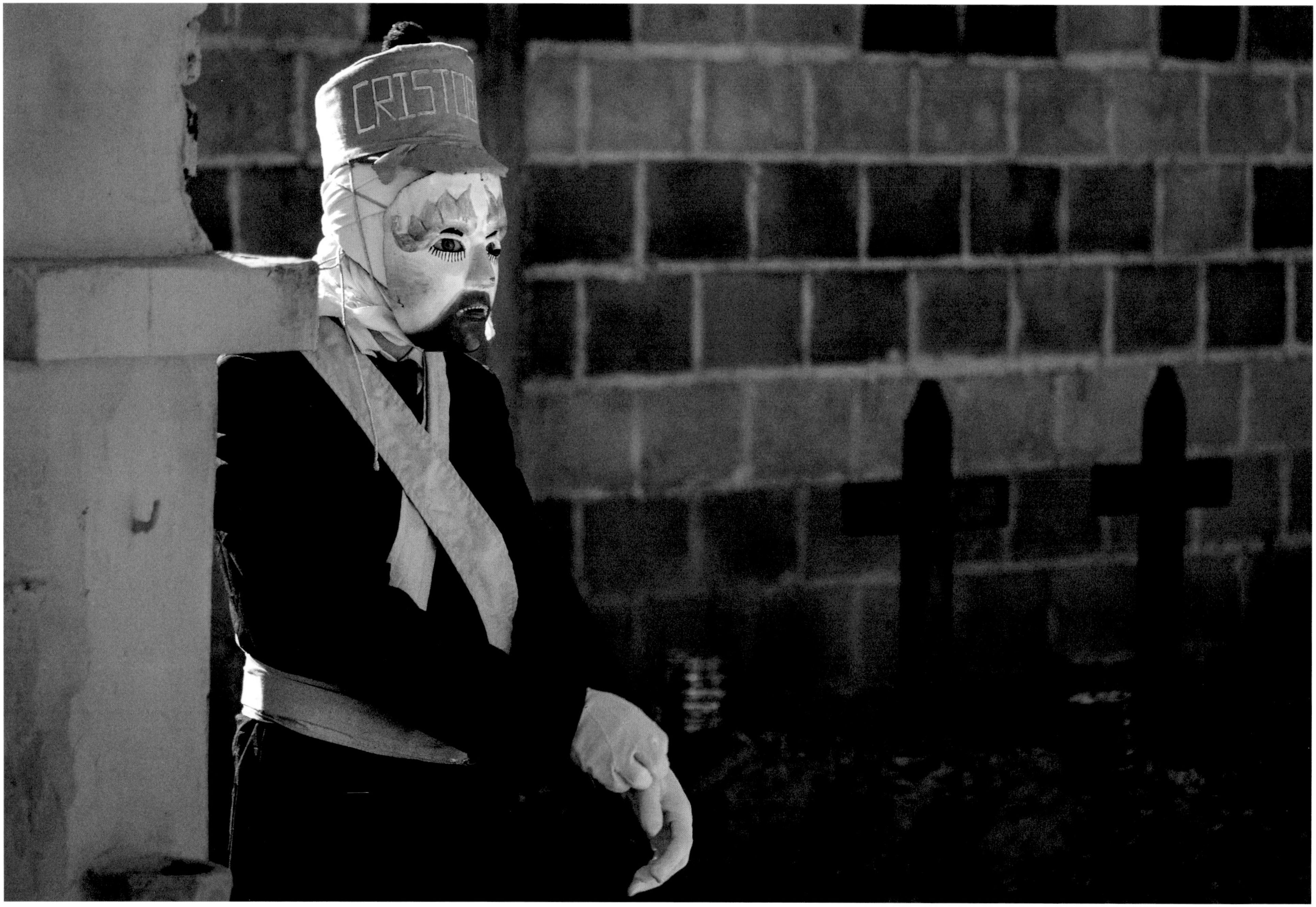

AN ACTOR WAITING TO PERFORM, 2020

opposite: MASKED SAILORS AWAITING THE PROCESSION OF SAN PABLO, 2020

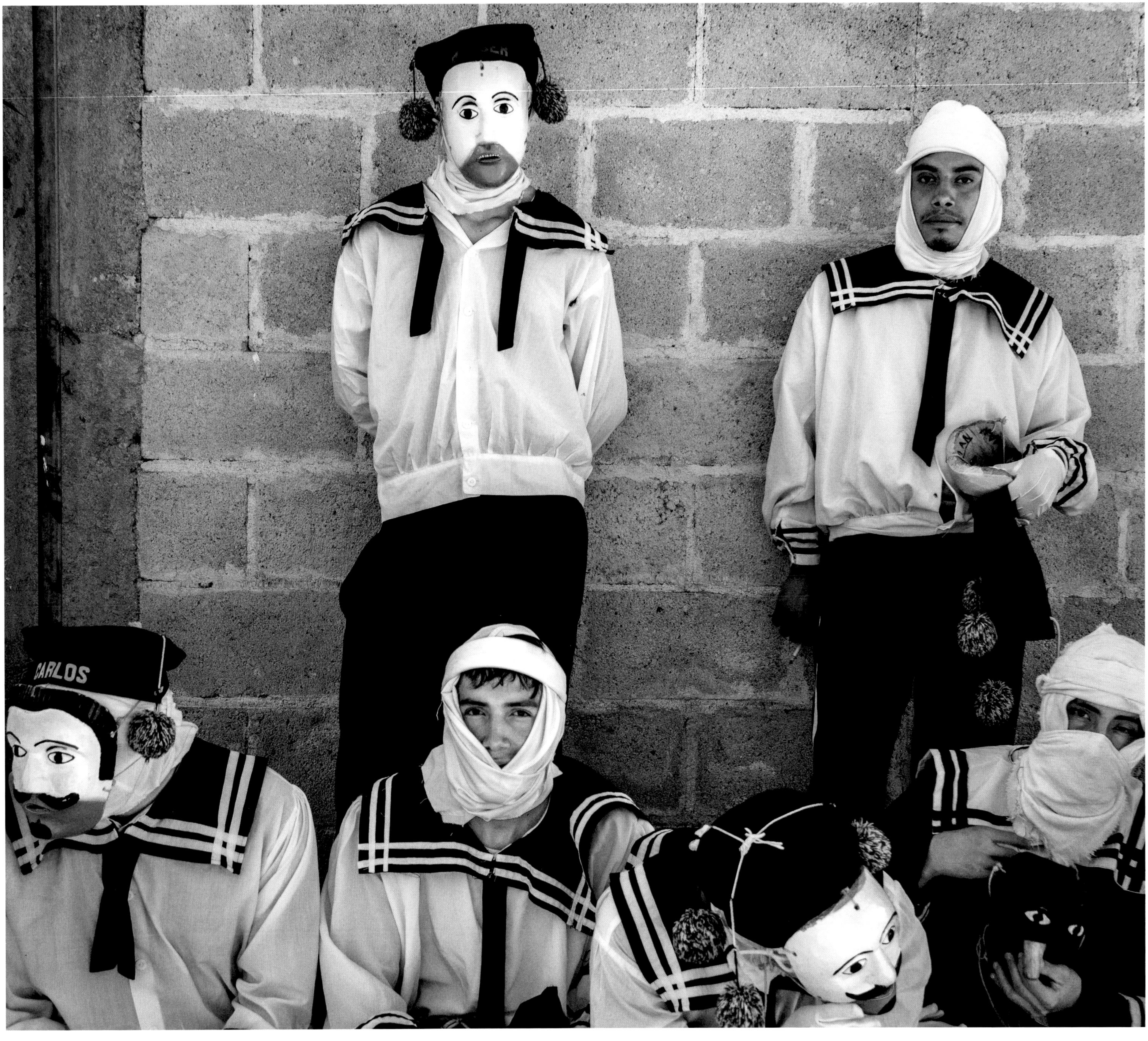
CARLOS

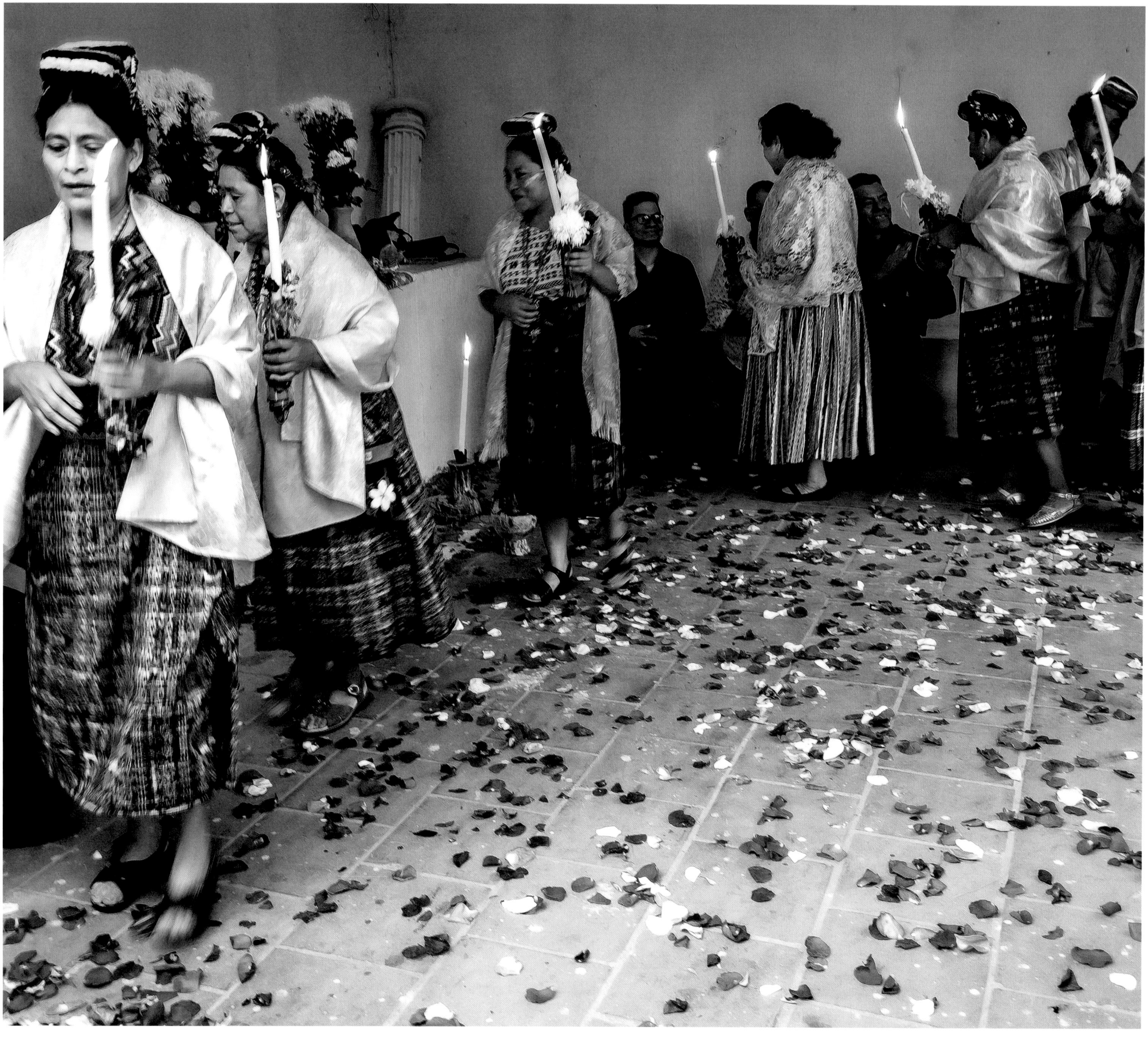

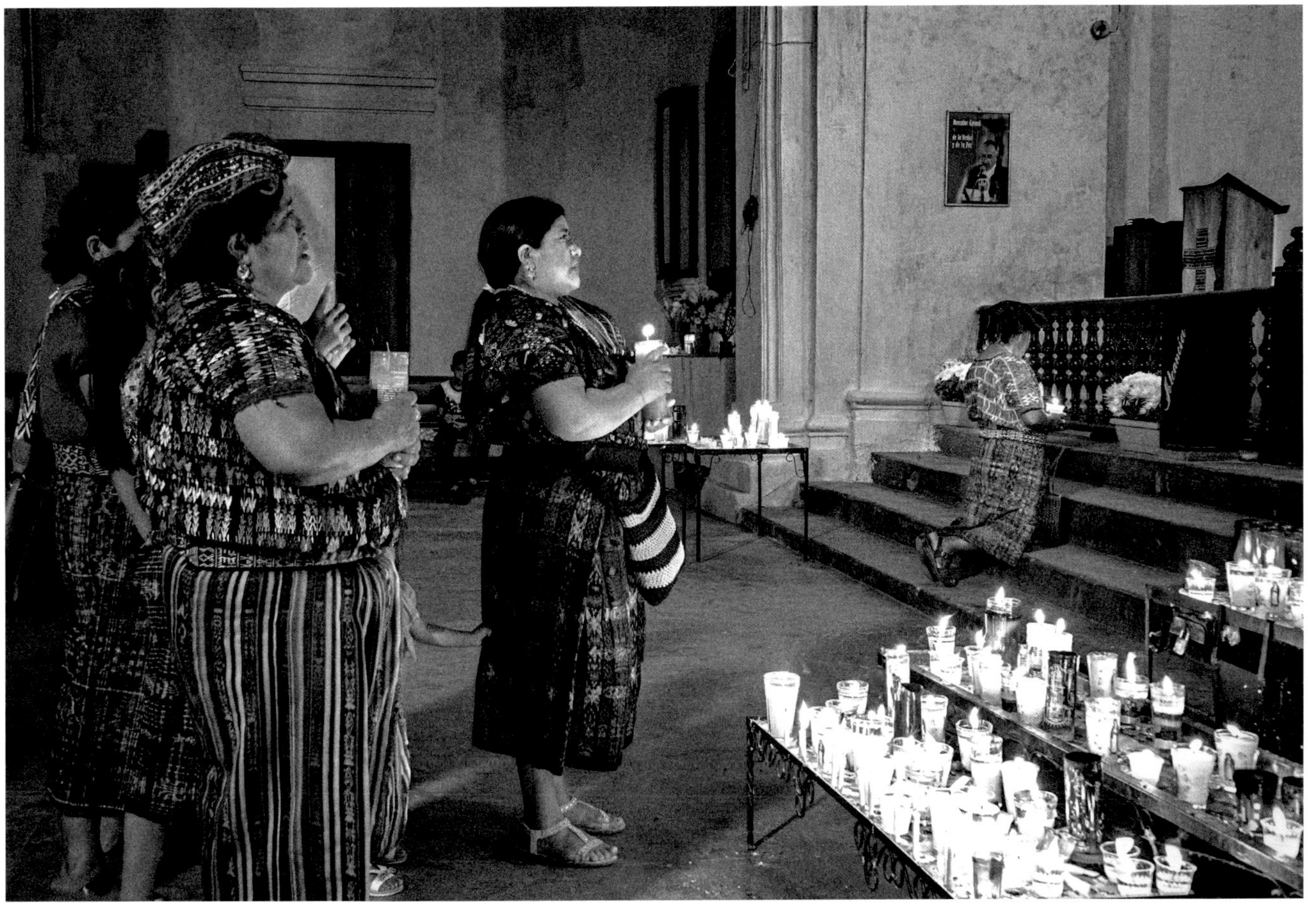

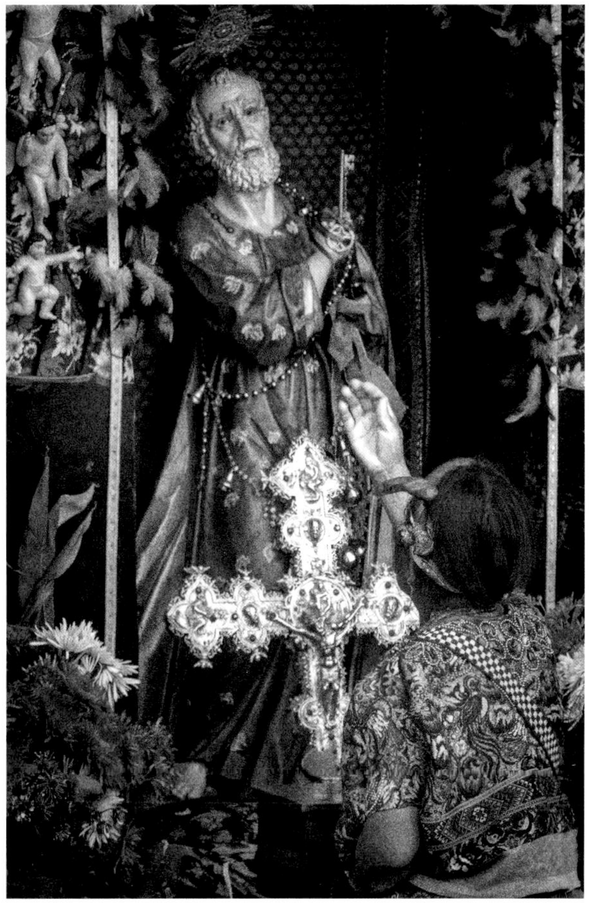

opposite: PAYING HOMAGE TO THE TOWN'S MAYORDOMOS, 2020

PRAYERS IN THE CATHEDRAL DURING THE FEAST OF SAN PABLO, 2020

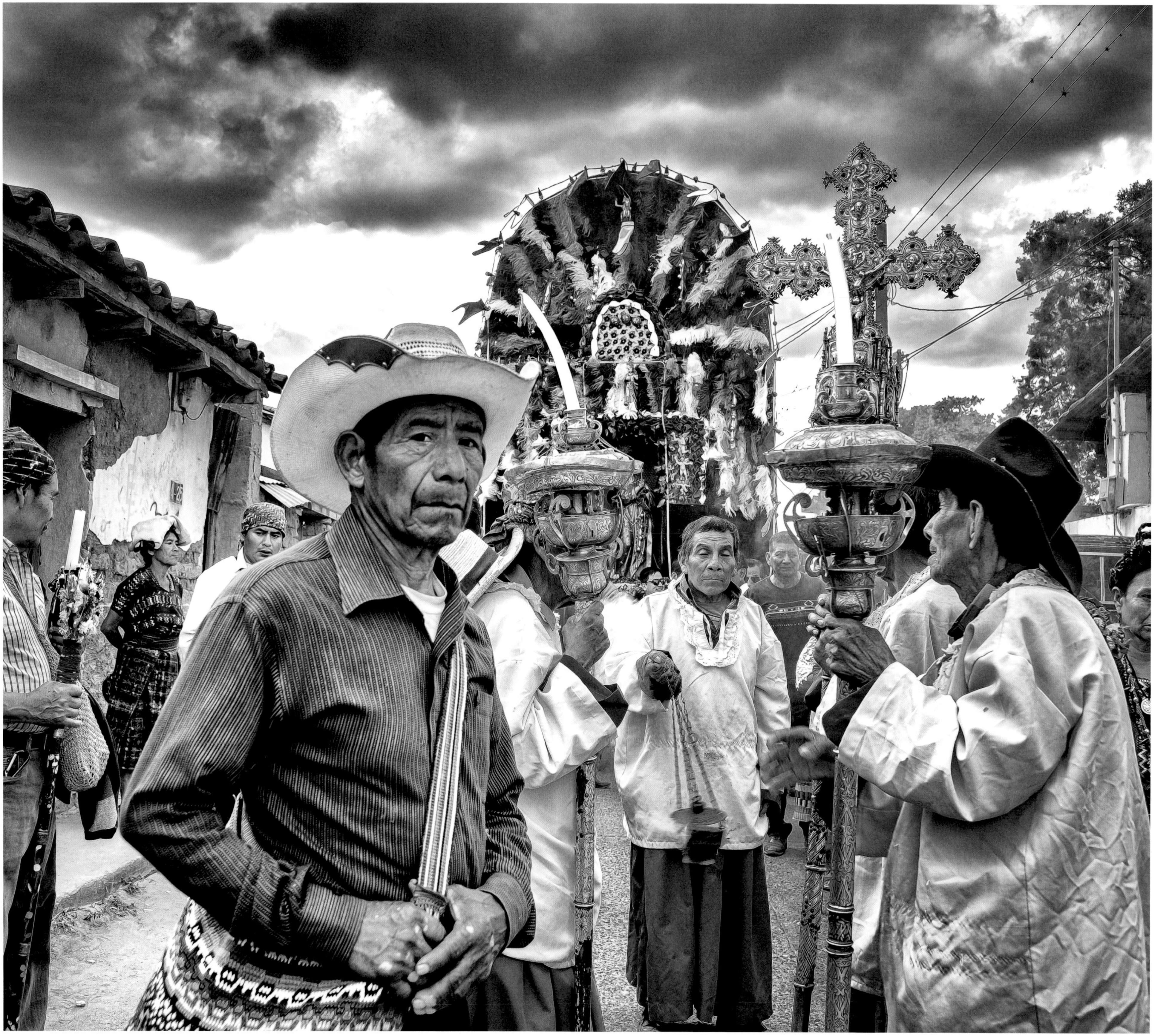

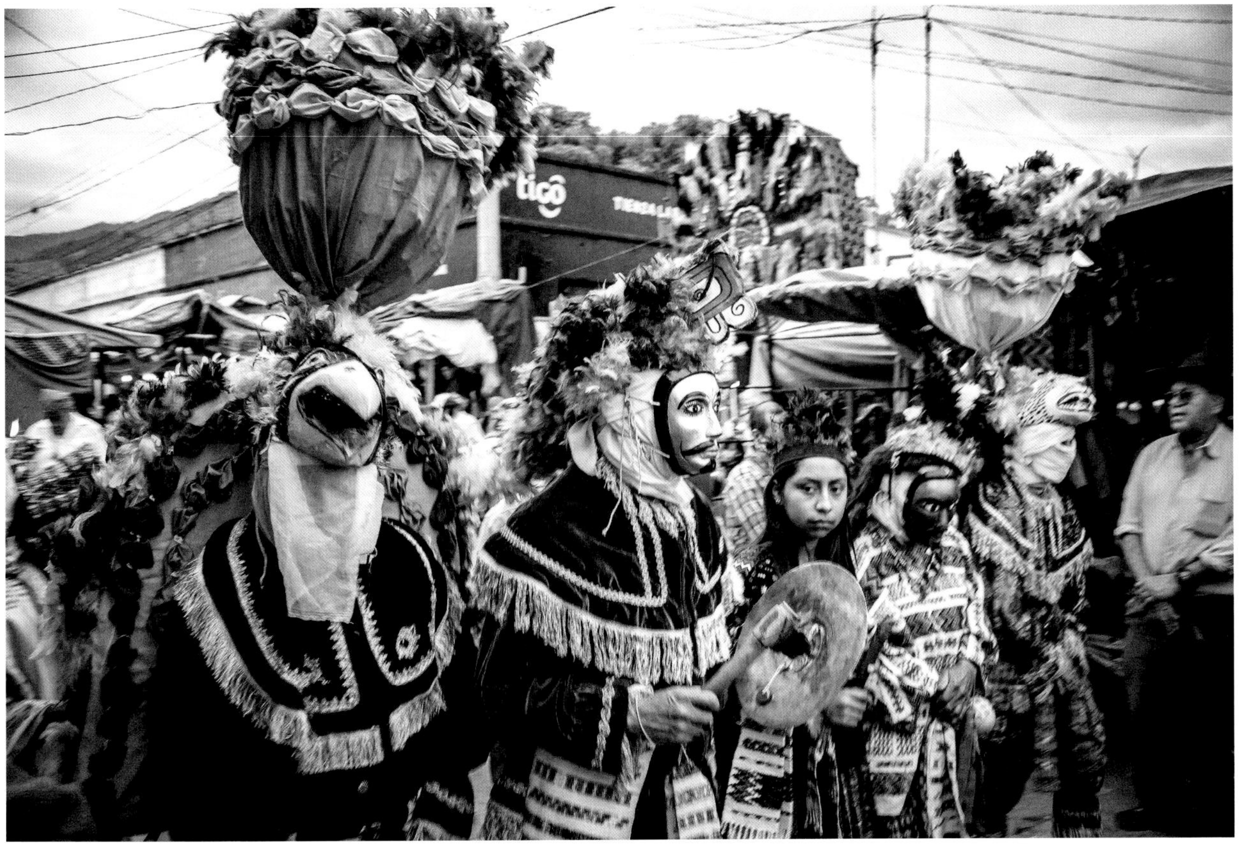

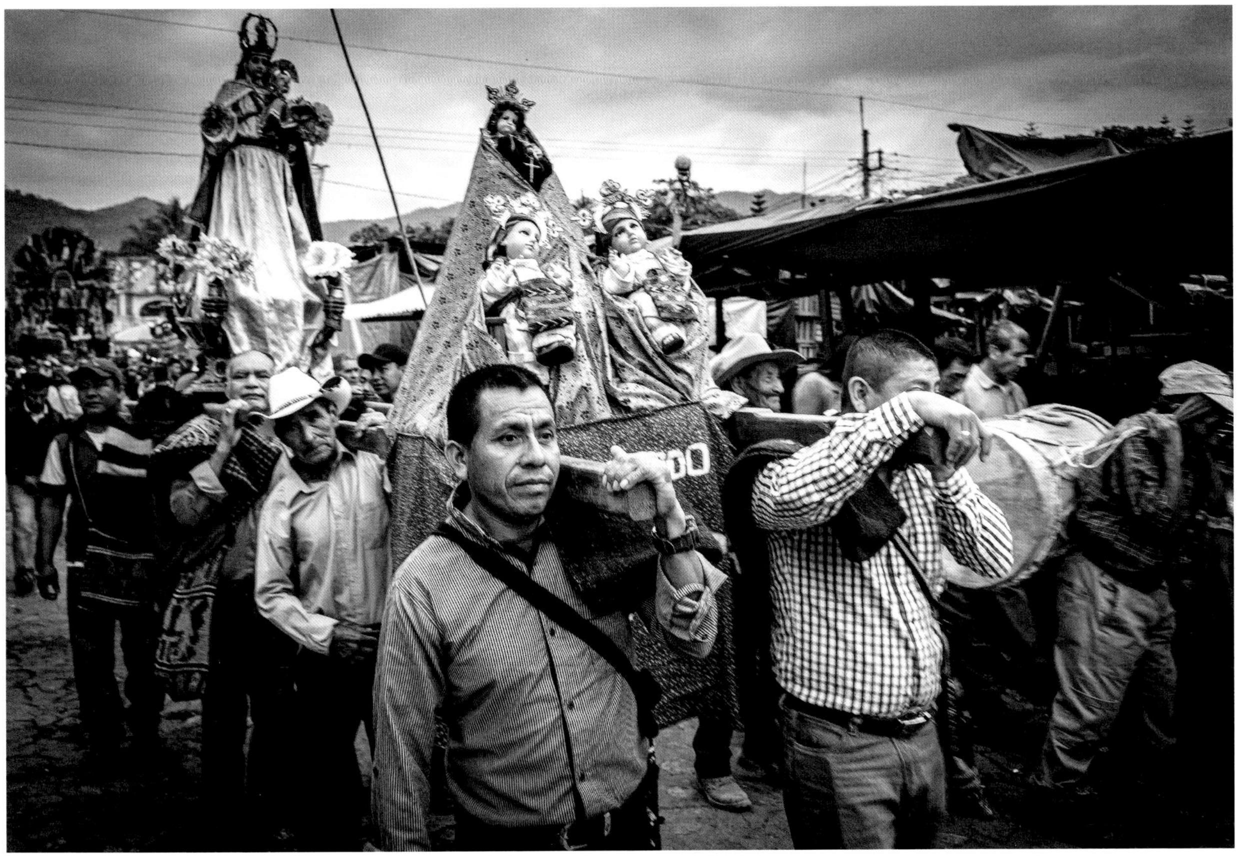

opposite: THE PROCESSION OF SAN PABLO, 2020

above: EAGLE AND JAGUAR CHARACTERS
REPRESENTING WARRIORS FLANKING THEIR PRINCE, 2020
below: THE PROCESSION OF SAN PABLO, 2020

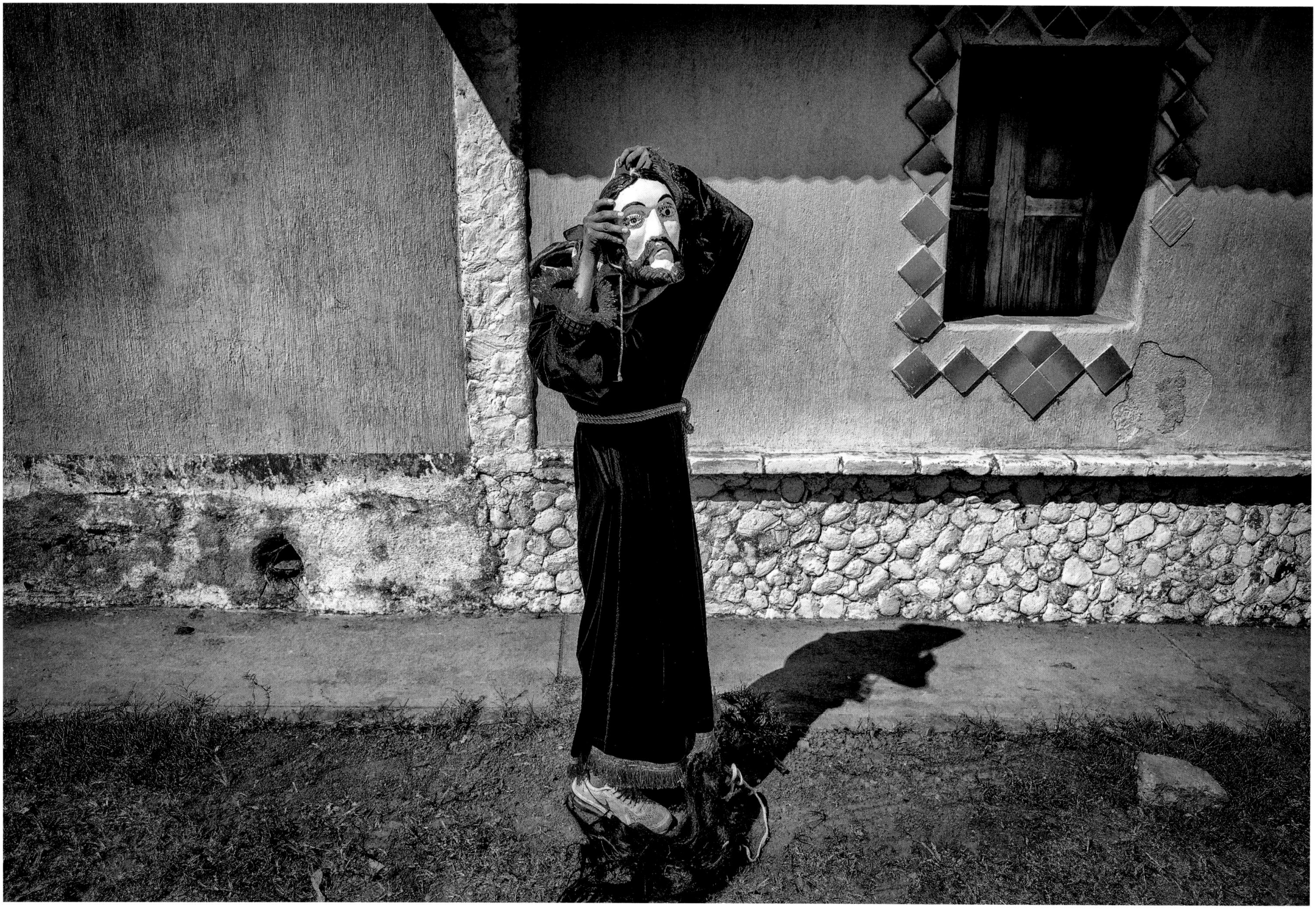

PREPARING FOR THE PROCESSION OF SAN PABLO, 2020

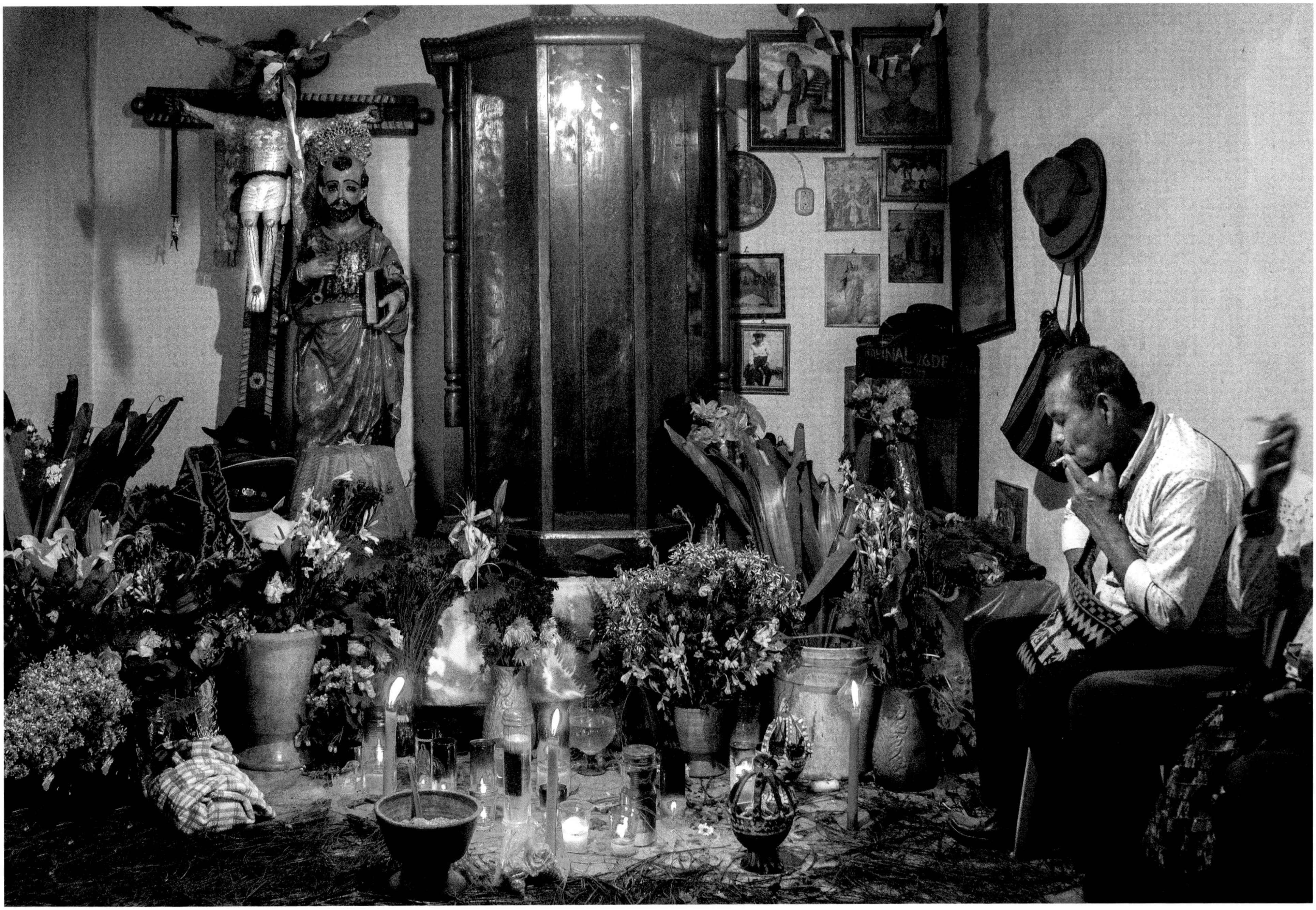

INSIDE THE SAN PABLO BROTHERHOOD ROOM FOR THE SAINTS, 2020

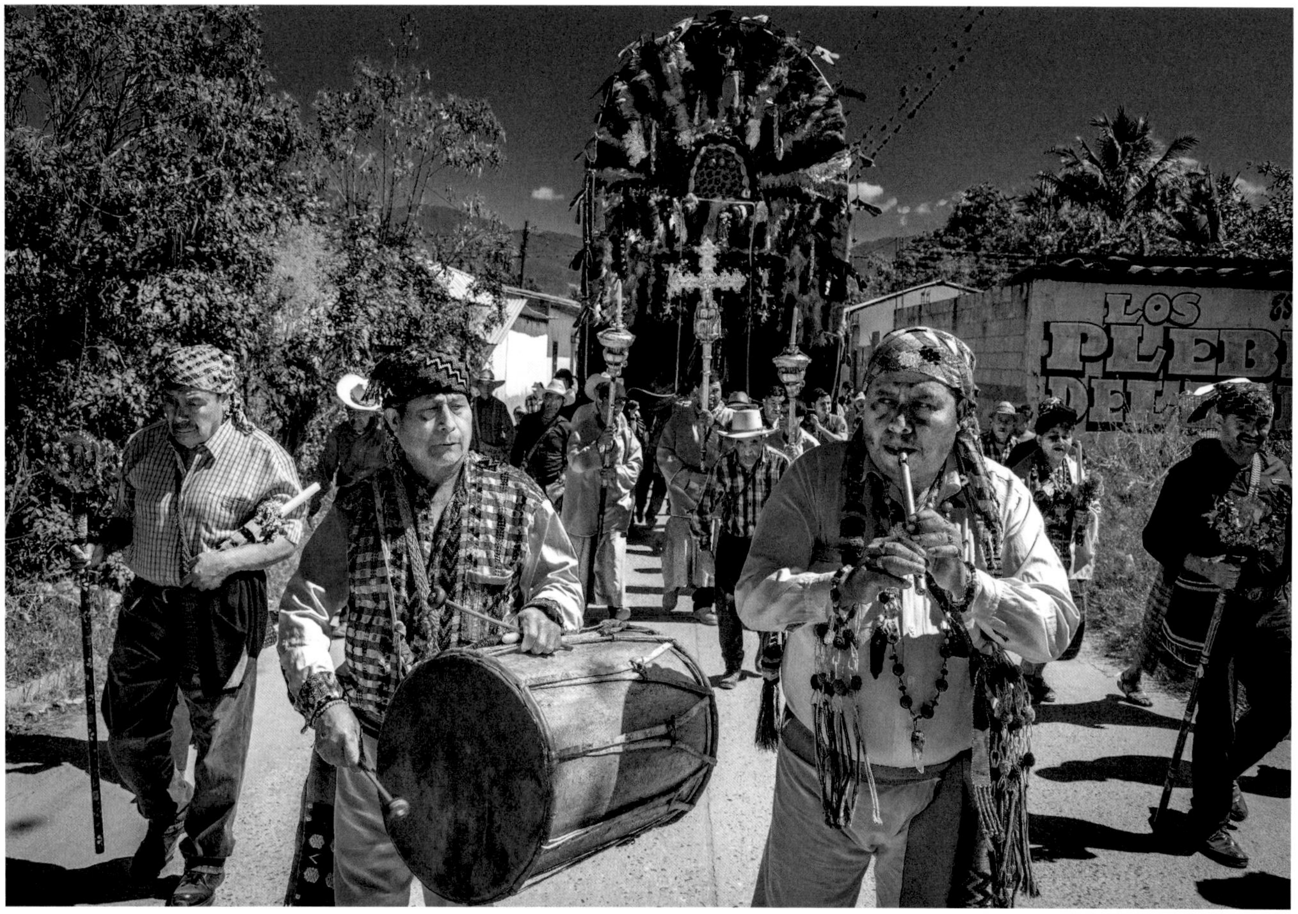

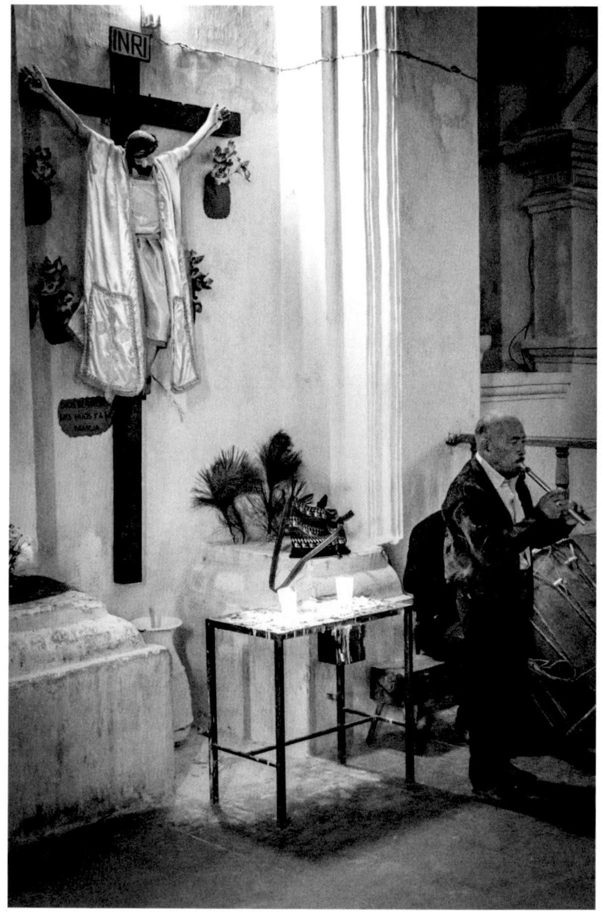

MUSICIANS LEADING THE PROCESSION OF SAN PABLO, 2020
center: A FLUTE PLAYER PREPARING FOR SAN PABLO'S ENTRY INTO THE CATHEDRAL, 2020

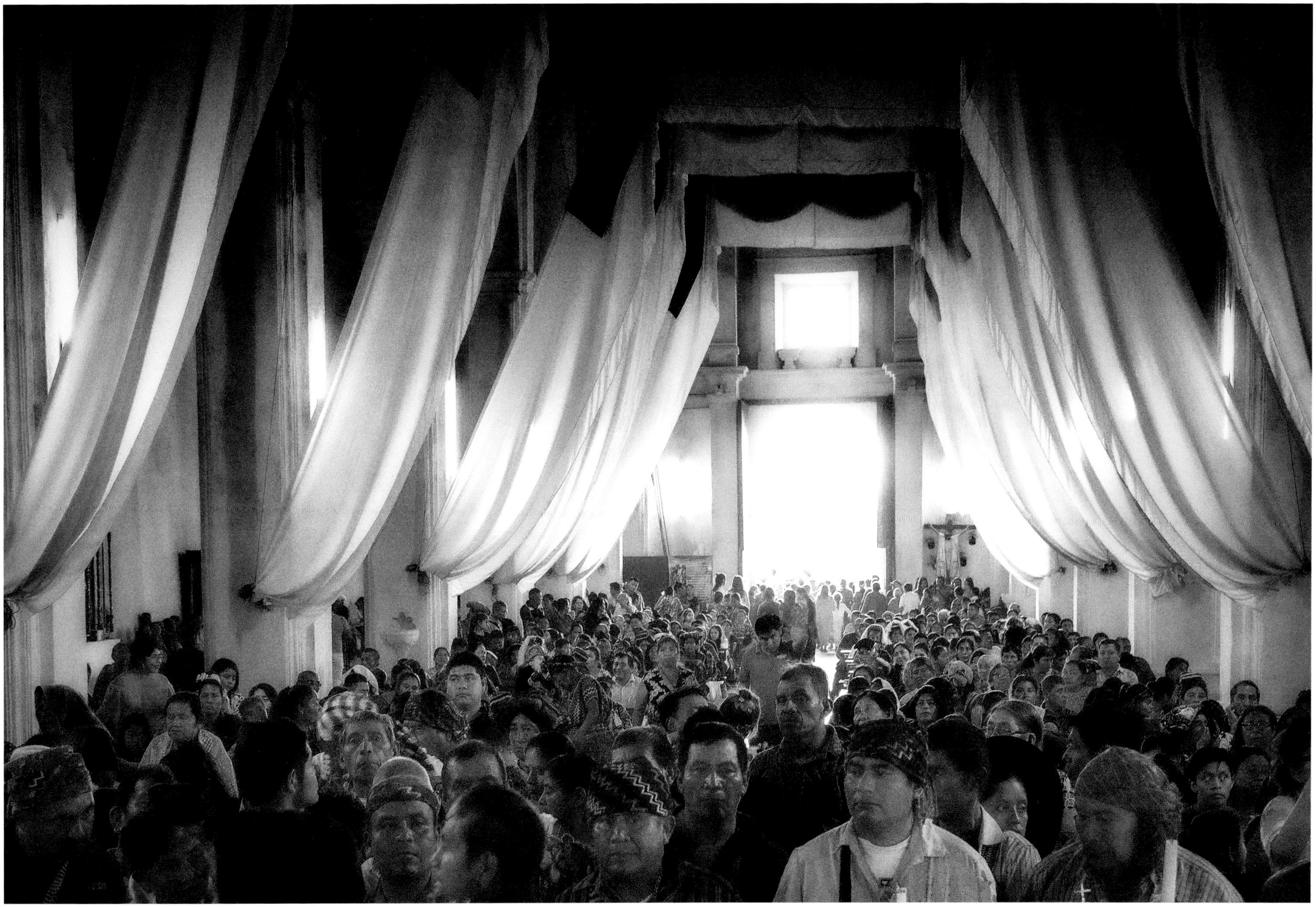

THE BLESSING OF SAN PABLO INSIDE THE
CATHEDRAL IN RABINAL, 2020

SAN MIGUEL, WEIGHING SOULS ON JUDGMENT DAY, LEAVING THE CATHEDRAL, 2020

opposite: SAN PABLO CARRIED IN PROCESSION THROUGH THE STREETS OF RABINAL, 2020

following spread, left and right: FLOATS ENTERING THE PORTALS OF THE CATHEDRAL IN RABINAL, 2020

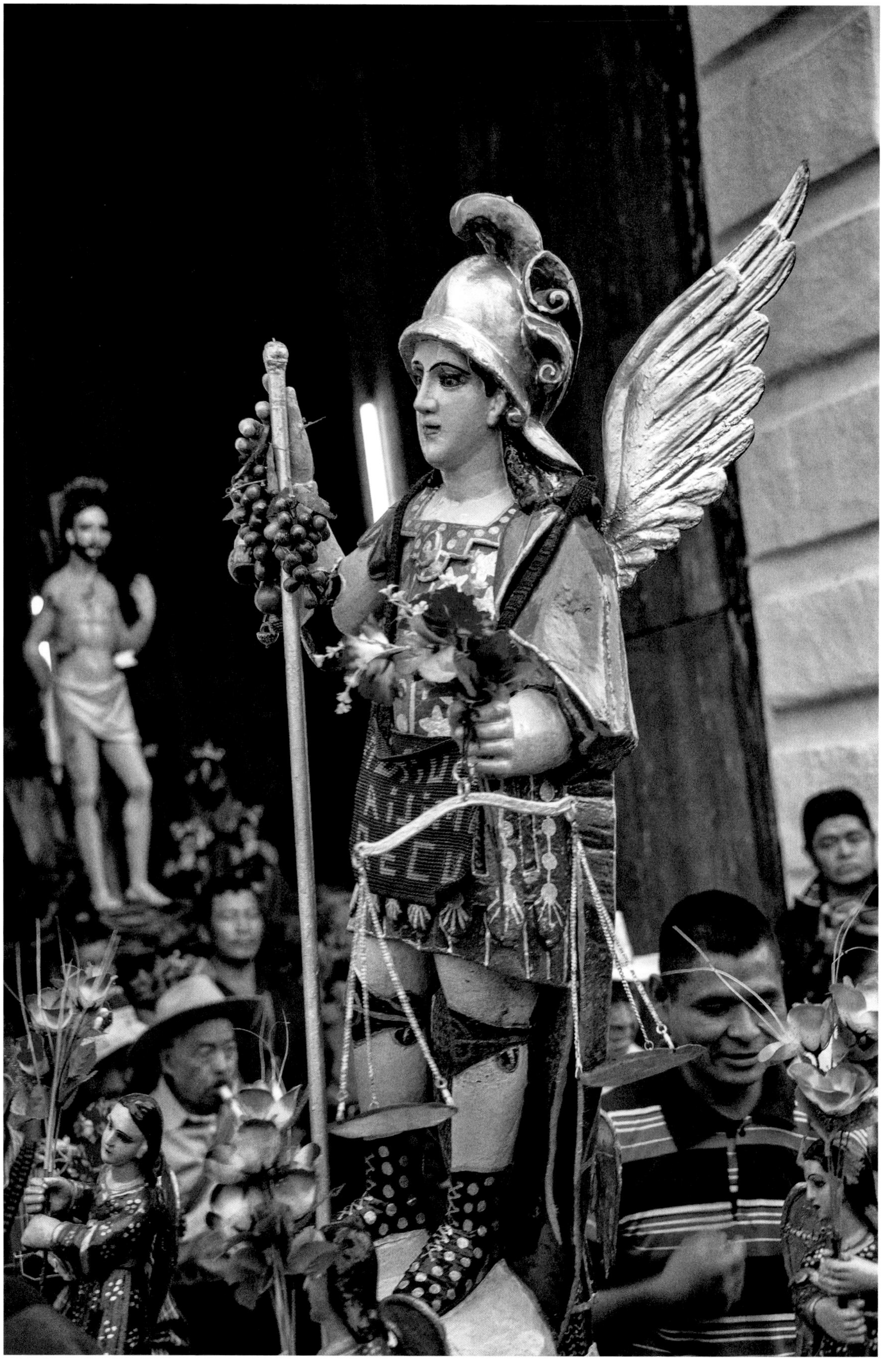

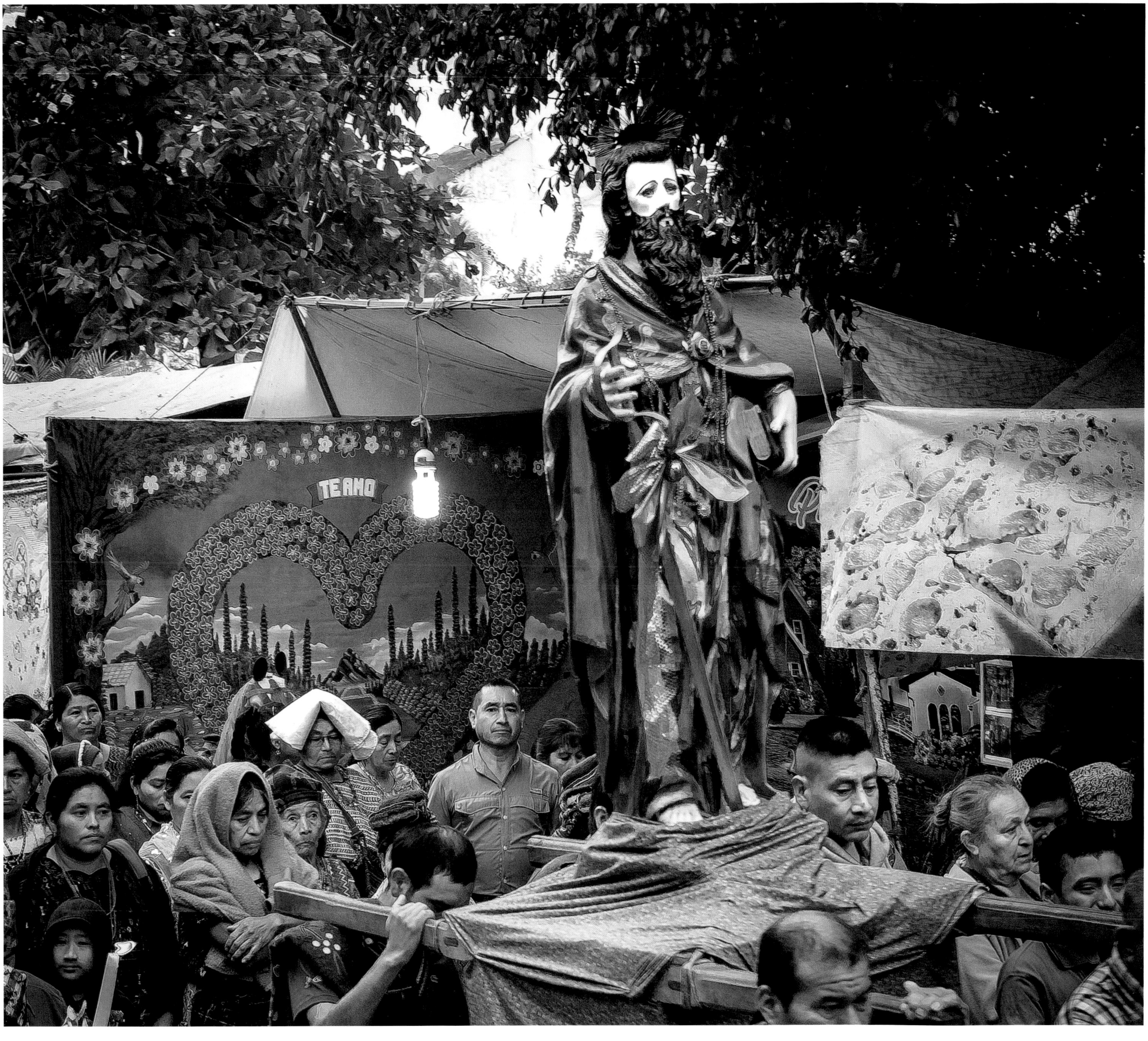
TE AMO

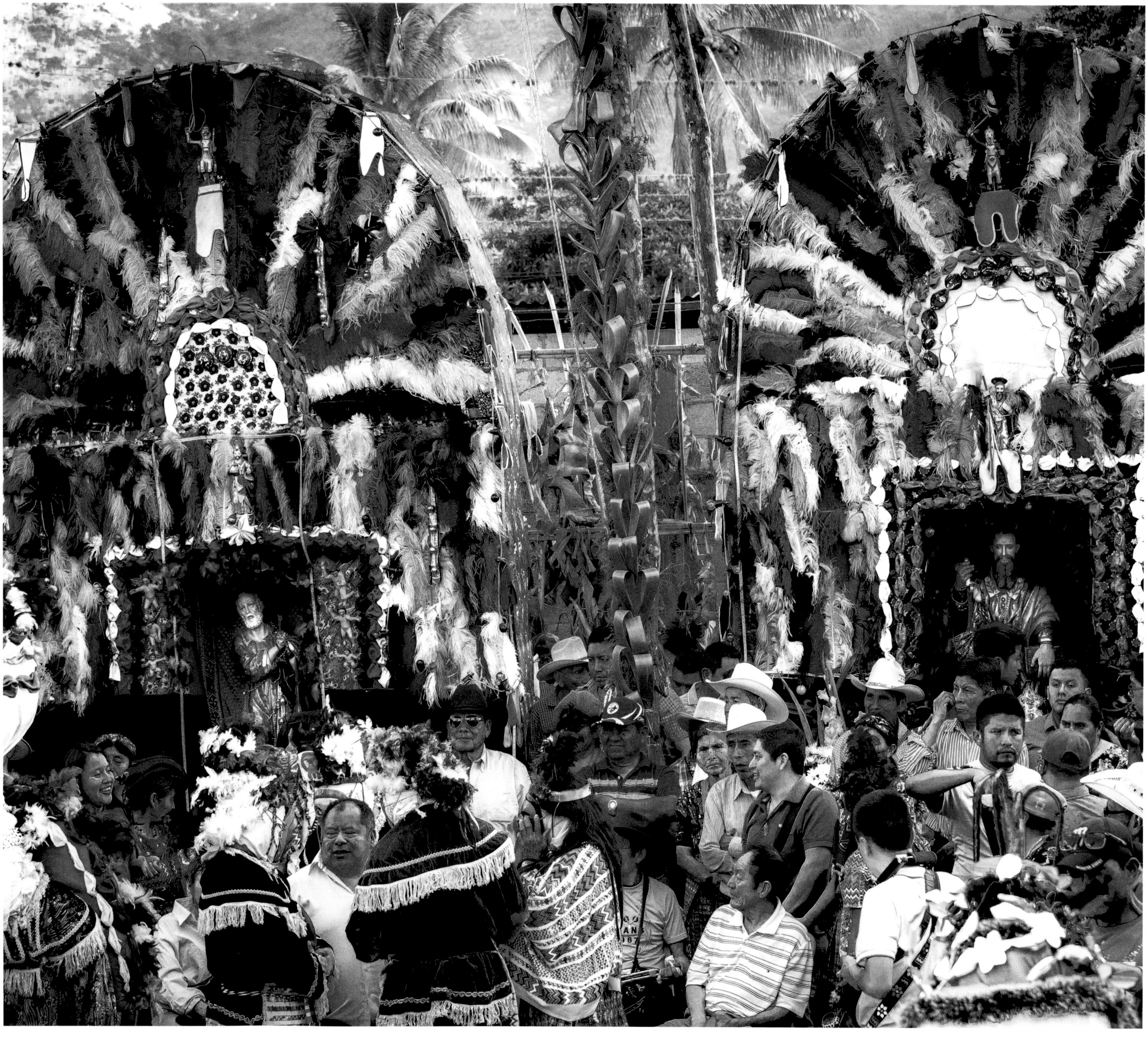

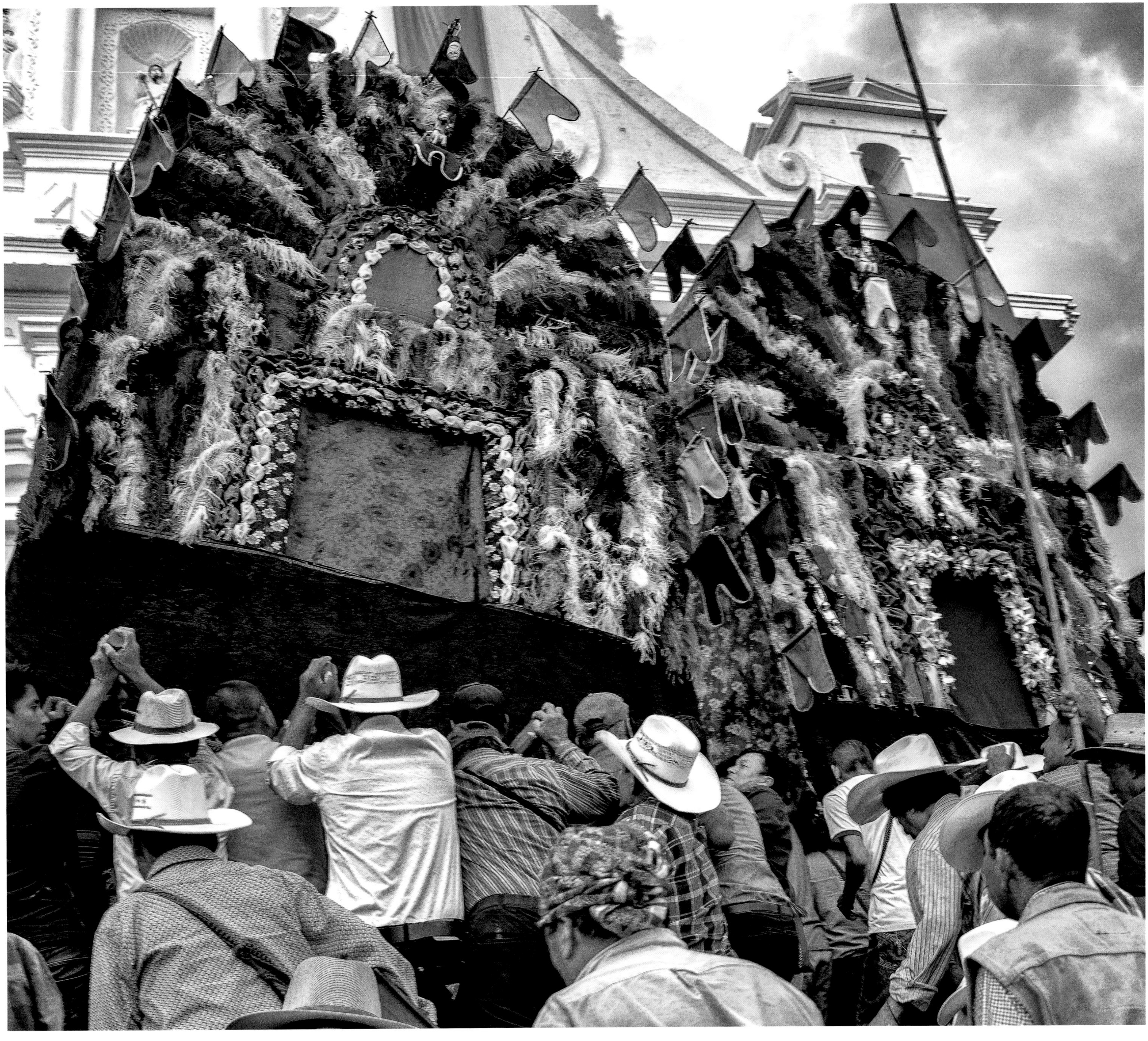

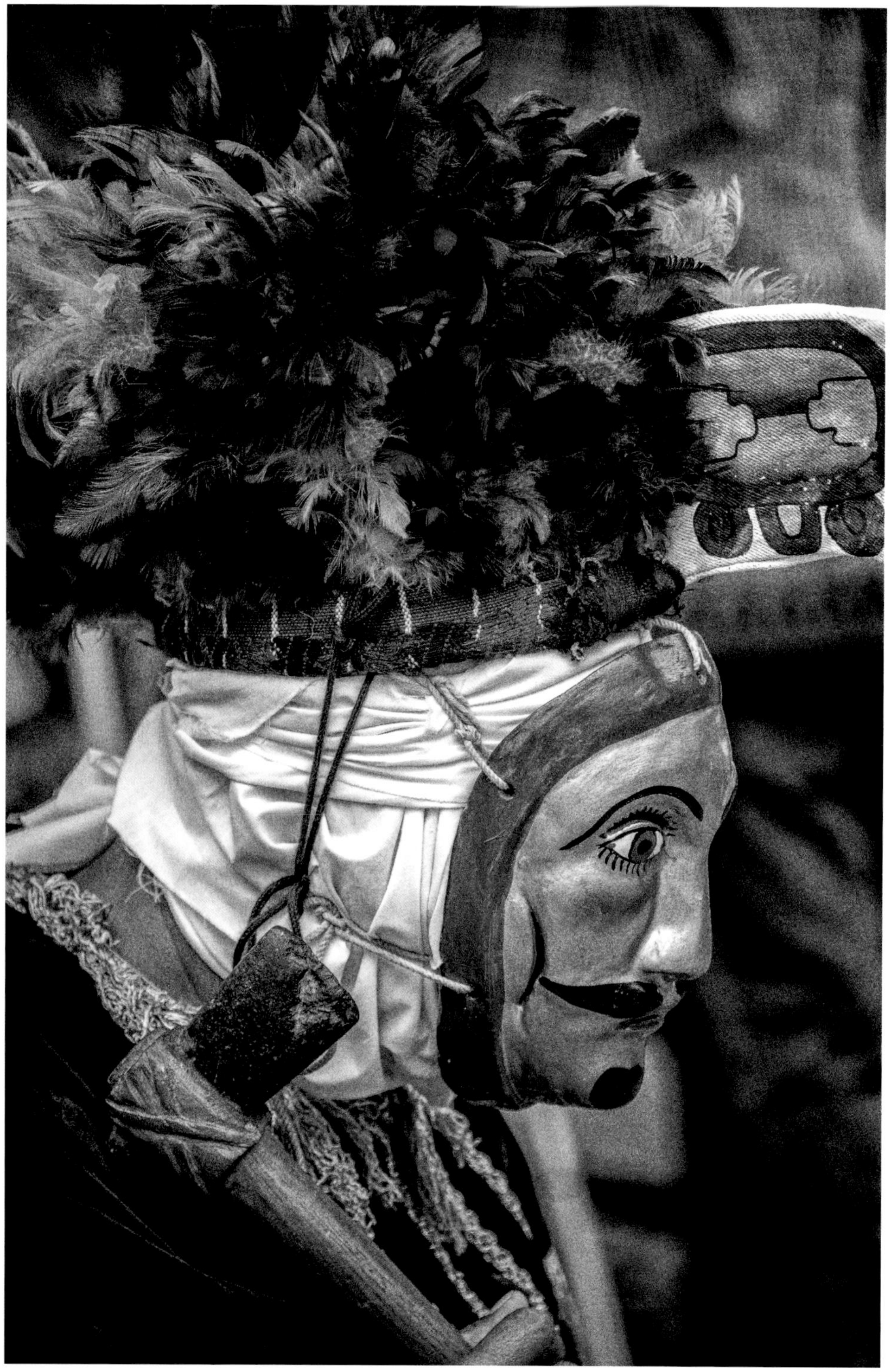

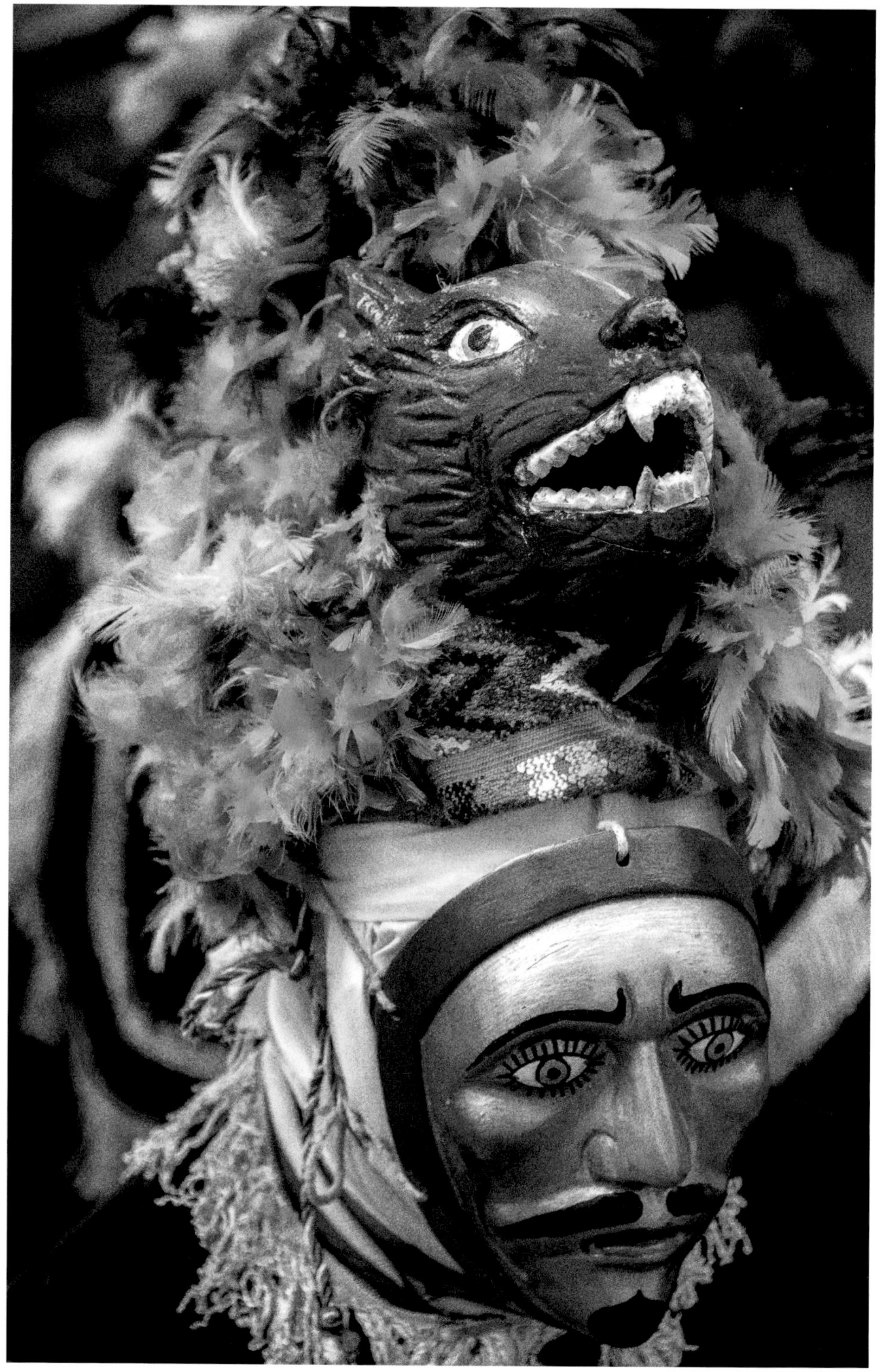

CAWEK, A PRIMARY ACTOR IN THE ACHÍ, 2020
center: RABINAL ACHÍ, THE TRIUMPHANT WARRIOR, 2020; opposite: BALAM, A JAGUAR WARRIOR IN THE ACHÍ, 2020

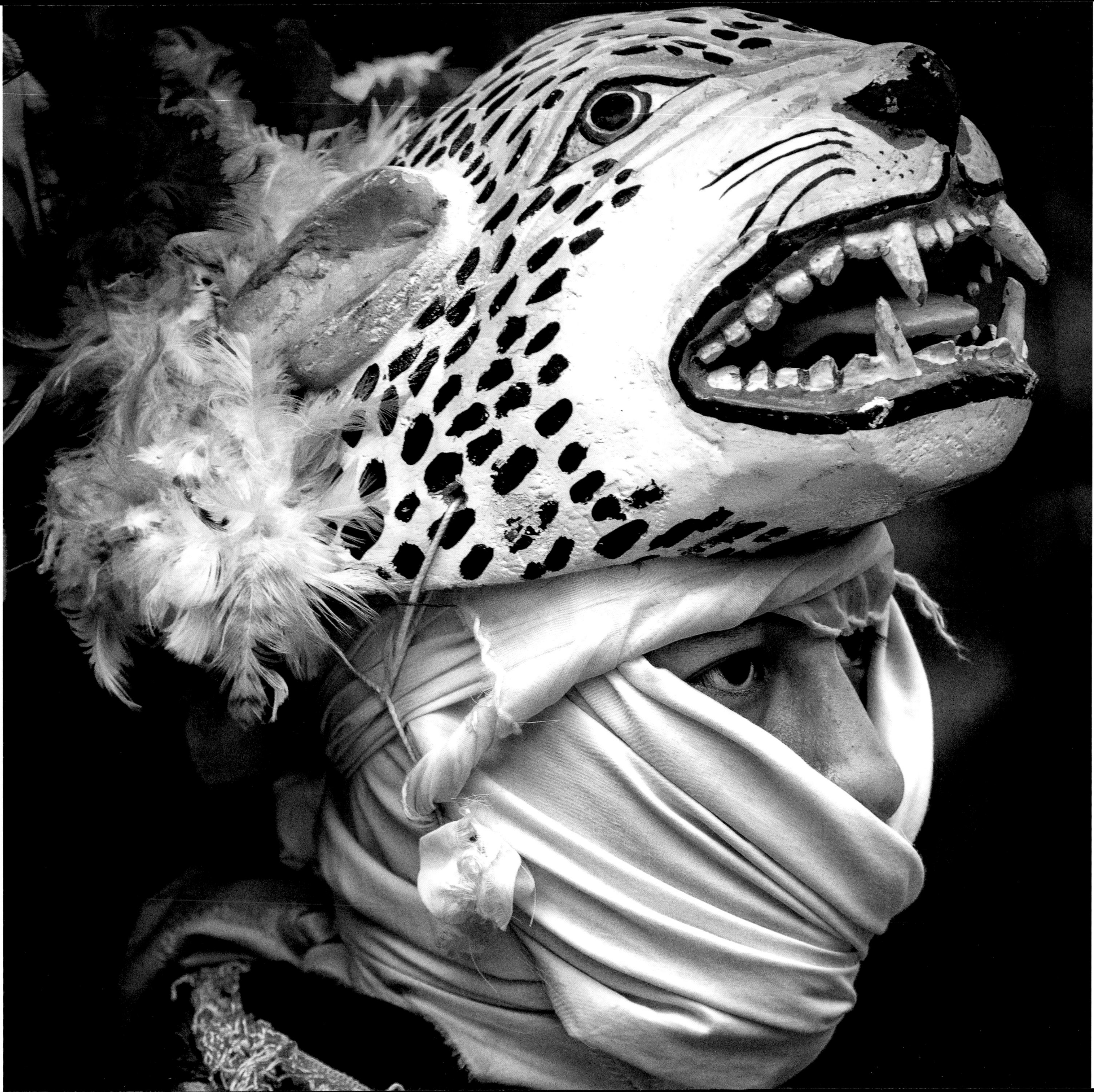

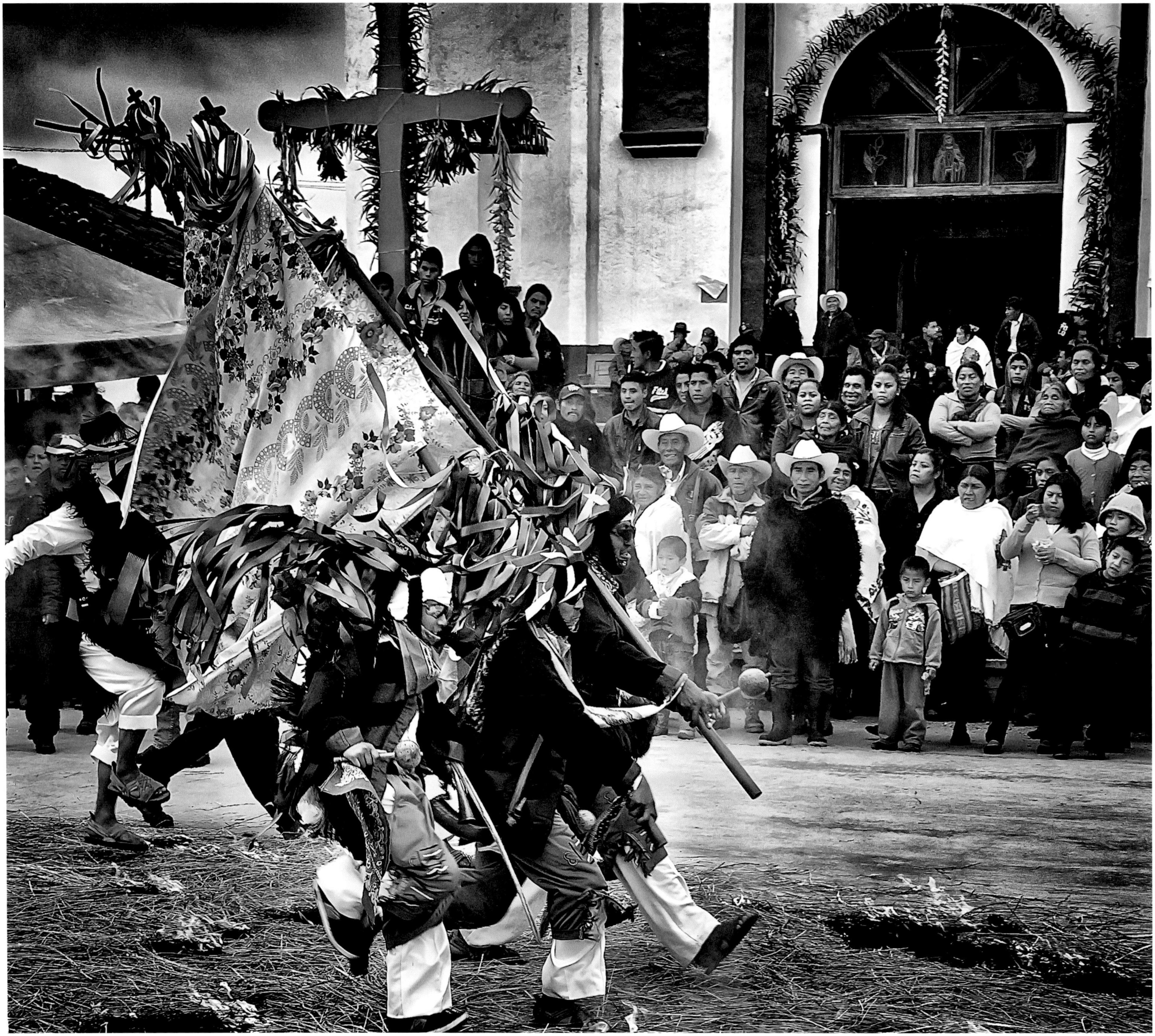

Carnival, Huixtán

January/February
Huixtán, Chiapas, Mexico

Huixtán is a small town in Chiapas with a population of approximately 1,700 people who speak both Tsotsil and Spanish. The Carnival of Huixtán is celebrated on each of the four Sundays prior to Ash Wednesday before Easter. During this period, people from surrounding communities gather in Huixtán for a celebration that serves to reinforce their identity and traditions. The religious aspects of Carnival combine indigenous Maya and Catholic beliefs that include Maya prayers for rain and bountiful harvests, as well as Catholic prayers for a holy and pious forty days of Lent. Distinctive and characteristic of this tradition are the interactive games the dancers play with the spectators through jokes and humor.

On the first day of Carnival, participants gather in the morning in the home of an elder to begin the ritual of dressing. After the ritual dressing, an elder mixes lime with water, places this paste in the form of a cross on the foreheads of men and boys, and adds the mixture to their arms, transforming them into Tanchaketik (Men with Whitewashed Bodies). Some also wear scarves adorned with the image of Our Lady of Guadalupe on their bare backs, as well as straw hats with ribbons. Each bears an instrument or item of ritual paraphernalia that is used during the ceremony, including guitars, harmonicas, and horns, as well as stuffed armadillos, skunks, squirrels, and other animals to be used as props as the men imitate their movements and prod spectators, to the amusement of all.

Two other characters play a major role in Carnival: the Potses, who wear masks representing the sun, and the K'ameel, who represent women with faces covered by a red scarf or a scarf bearing the image of Our Lady of Guadalupe. There is also a Huixteca man and a woman wearing traditional clothing and masks. These dancers represent the Grandfather (or Old Bearded Man) and the Grandmother (Old Woman), both of whom are responsible for giving life. They dance to the rhythm of huge drums in order to purify the soul, remove evil spirits, and ask God for forgiveness for the damage caused to Mother Earth.

Performers enter the church and dance and blow their horns and other instruments before praying to the Christian God and Maya gods to ask for their intercession for a productive year. They then leave the church and lead a boisterous parade through the town, ending in the main plaza where the Tanchaketik continue their wild dancing for hours and chase a bull that represents the Devil and that is led by a lasso-carrying corporal who symbolically sacrifices it in front of the church. The ceremonies end with a dramatic Firewalk in front of the church.

opposite: CARNIVAL PERFORMERS RUNNING THROUGH BURNING THATCH, 2016

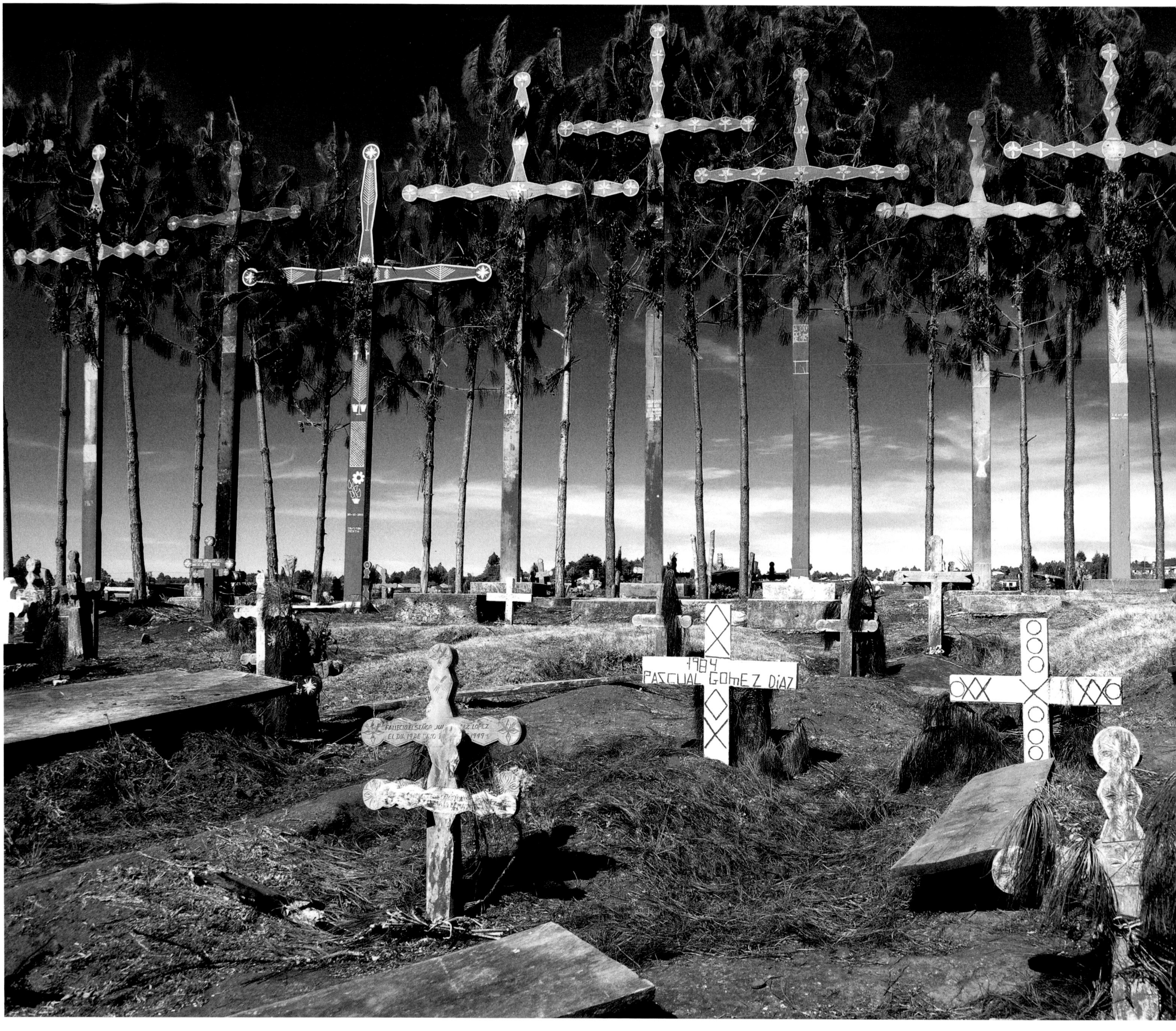
1984
PASCUAL GOMEZ DIAZ

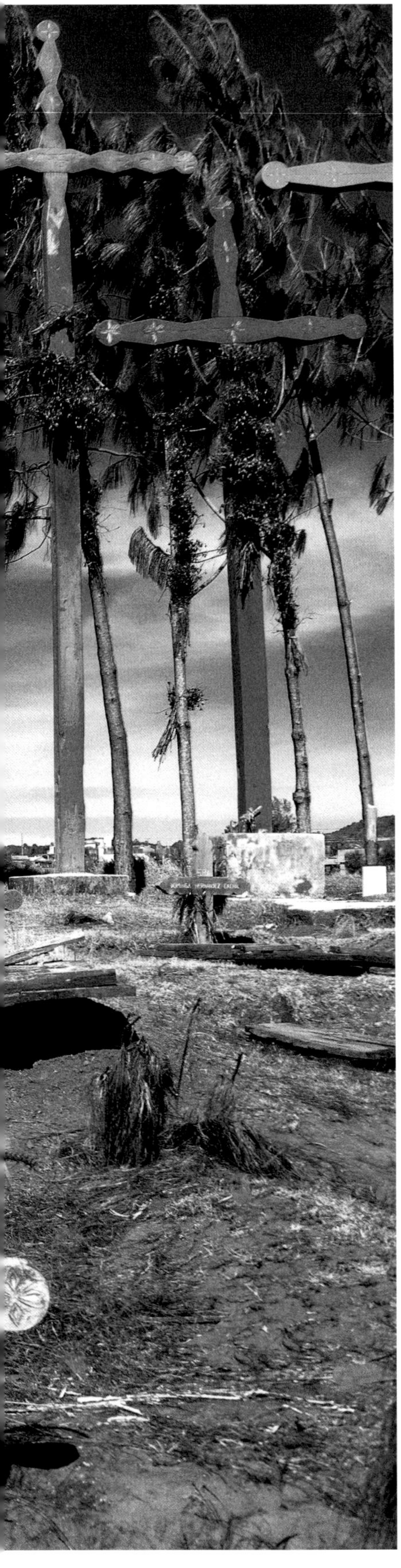

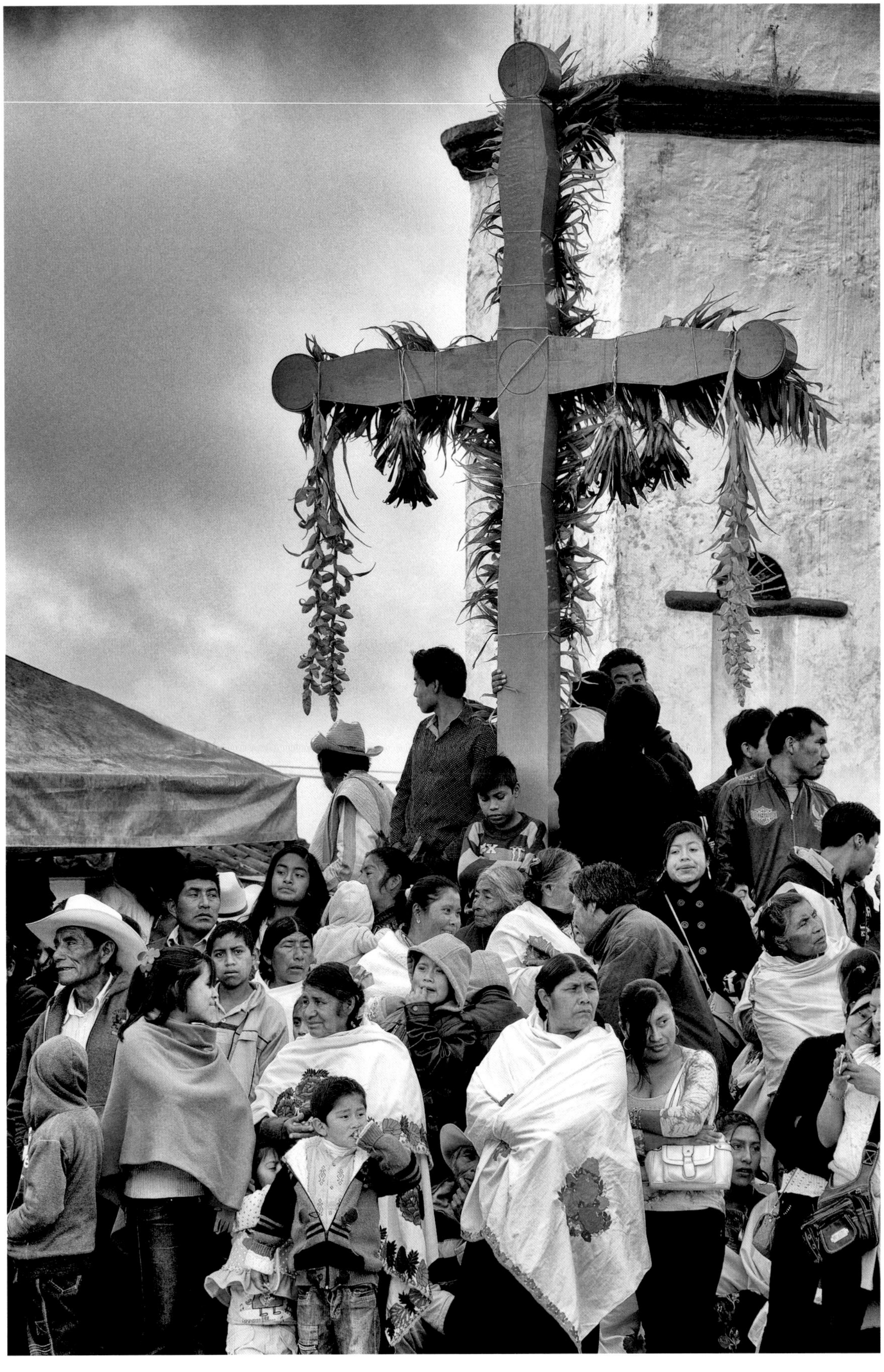

opposite: CEMETERY IN THE CHIAPAS HIGHLANDS OUTSIDE HUIXTÁN, 2016

PEOPLE GATHERING TO VIEW CARNIVAL CEREMONIES, 2016

following spread: MAYORDOMOS OVERSEEING THE CARNIVAL CELEBRATIONS, 2016

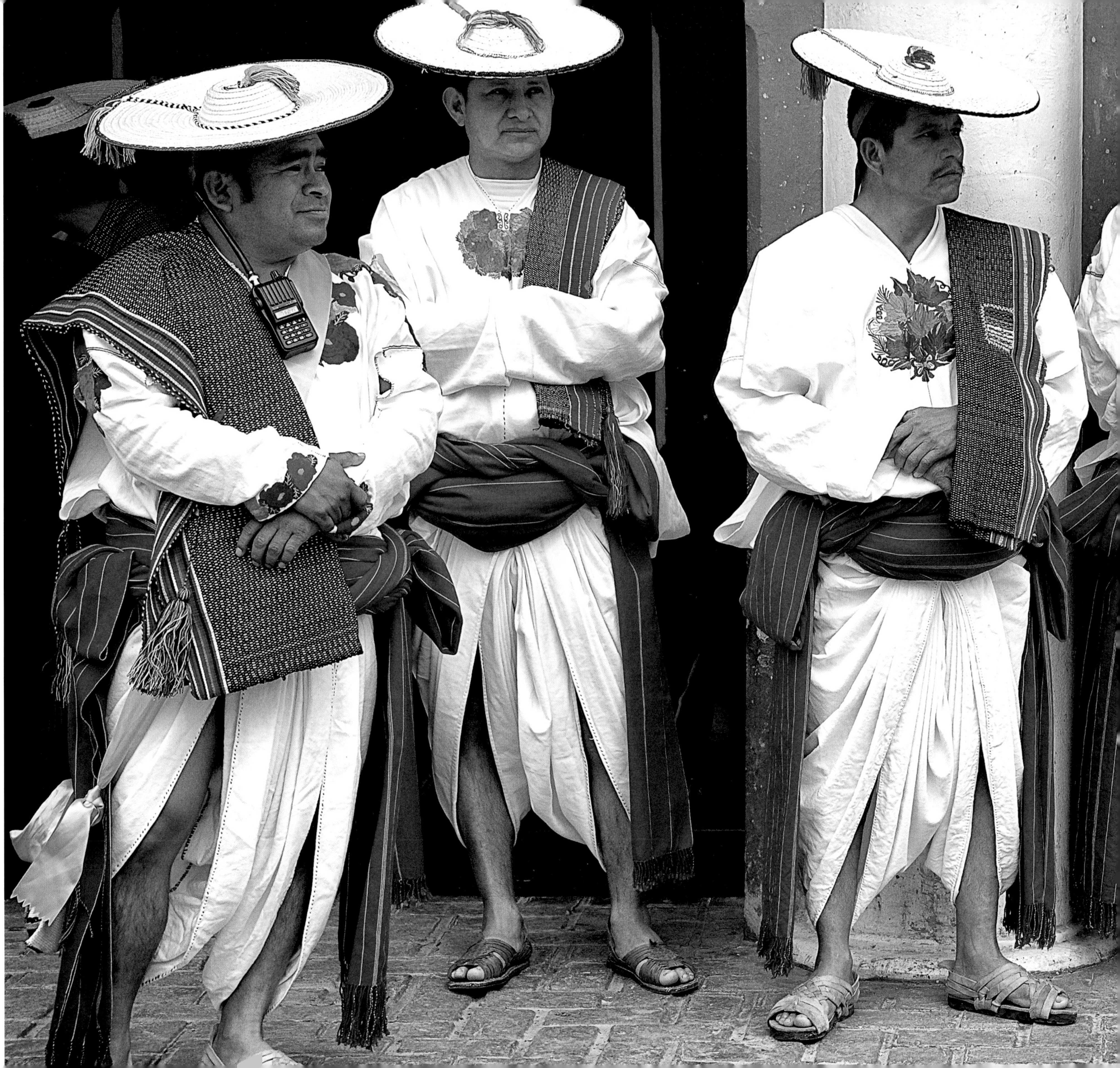

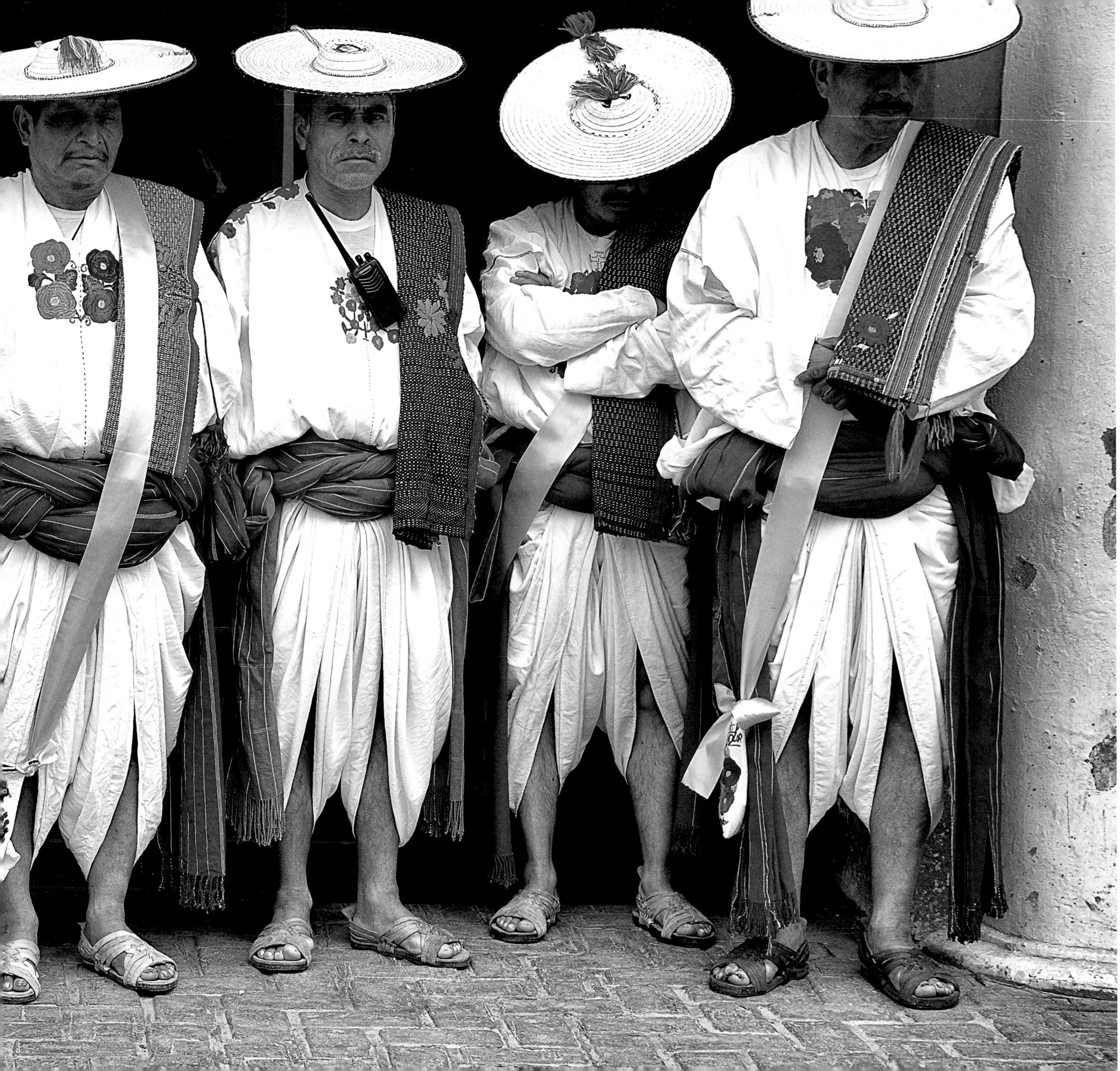

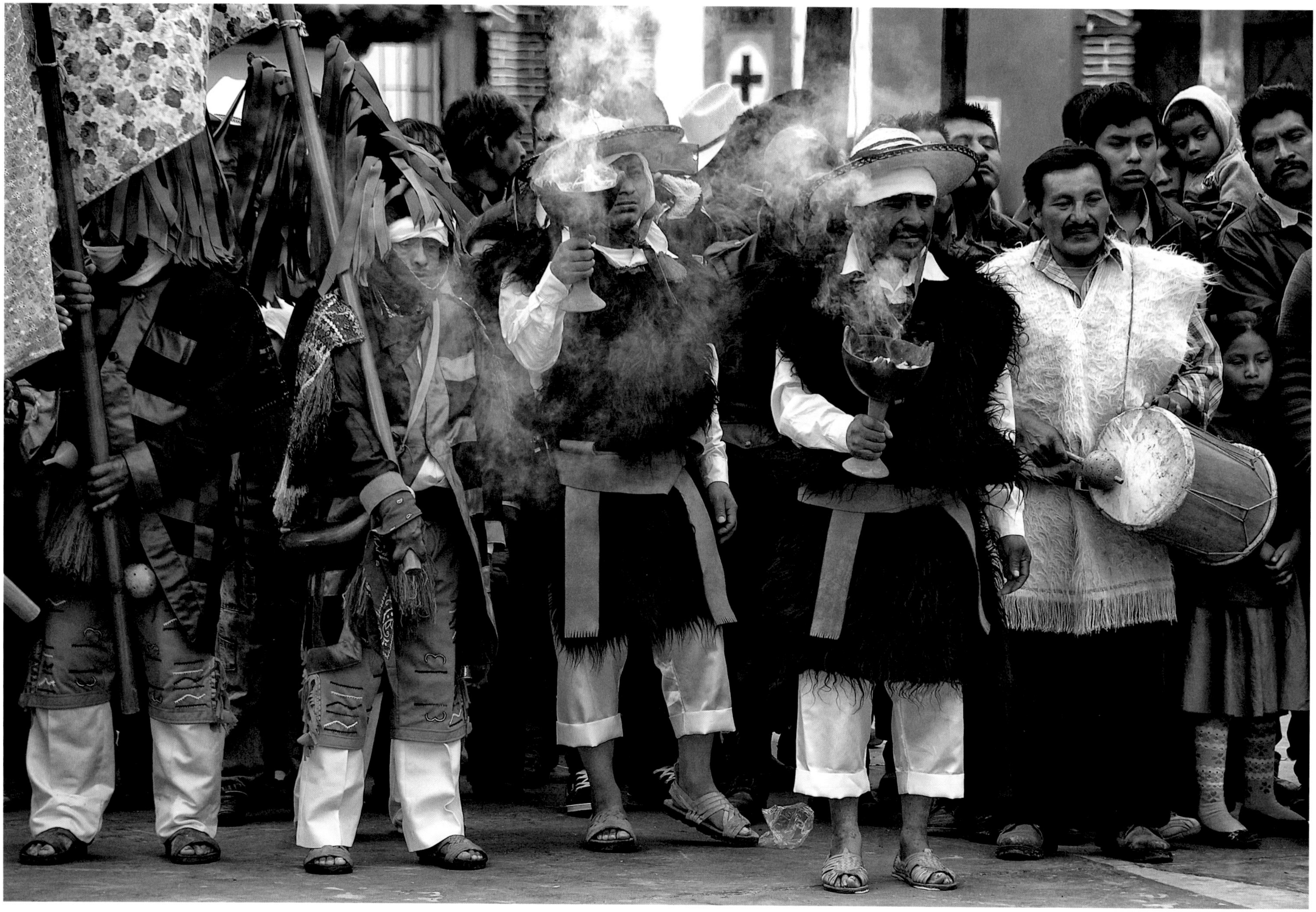

SMOKE FROM BURNING COPAL PERMEATING THE CELEBRATIONS, 2016

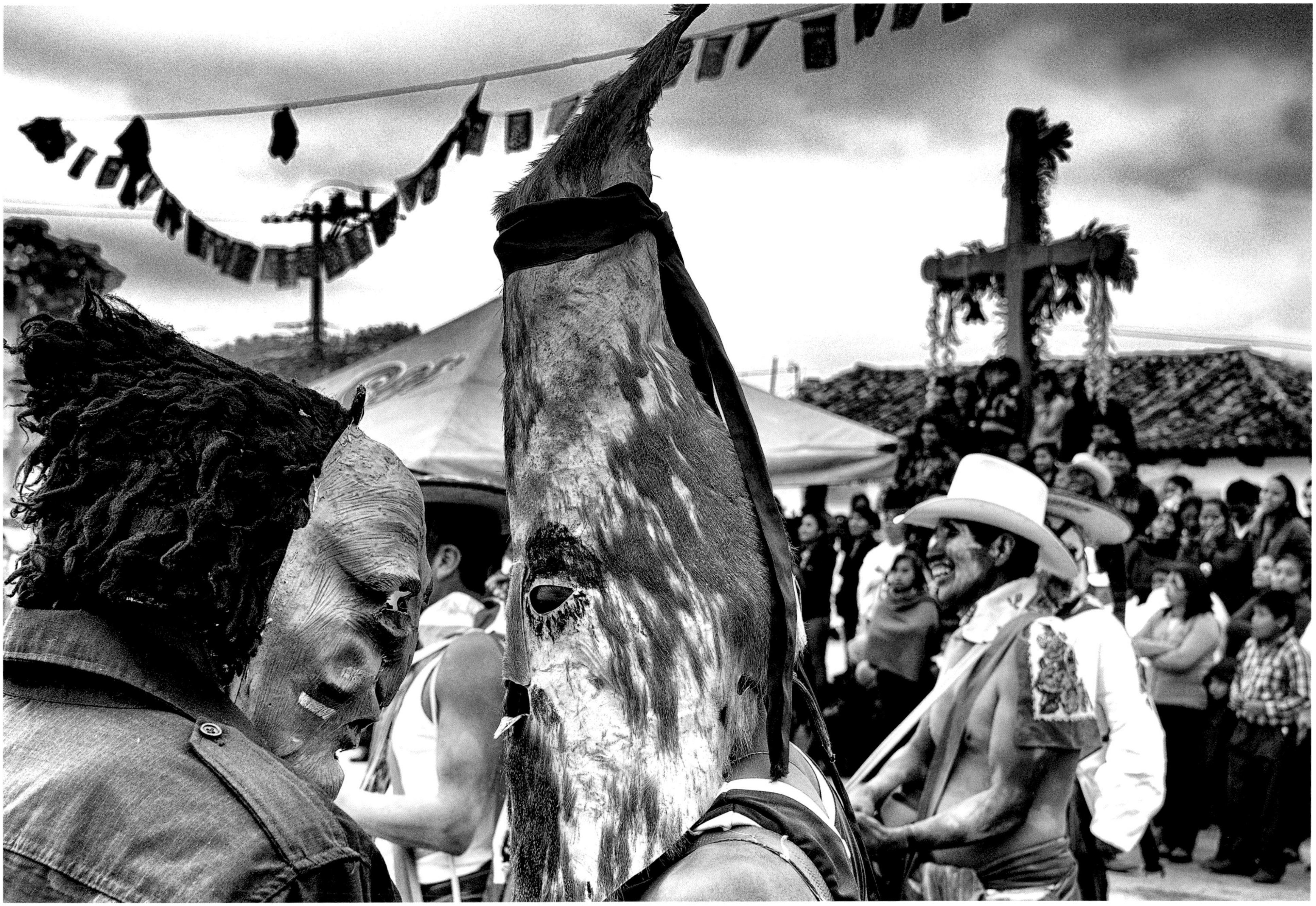

DANCERS WITH PAINTED FACES AND ANIMAL MASKS, 2016

following spread, left: A DANCER WITH HIS STUFFED ARMADILLO, 2016
center: MUSICIANS IN TRADITIONAL PANTS AND SASHES, 2016
right: DANCER IN DEER MASK, 2016

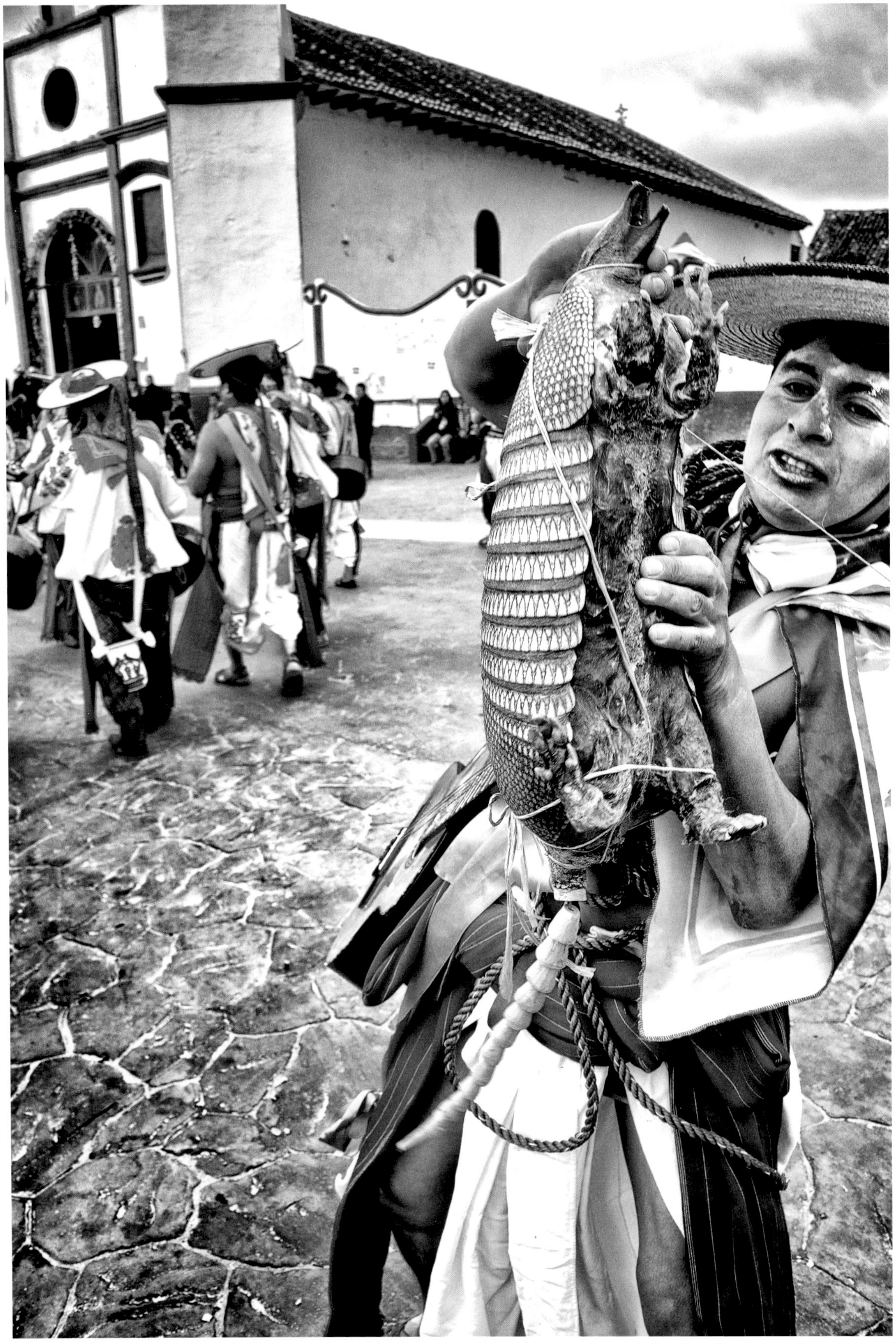

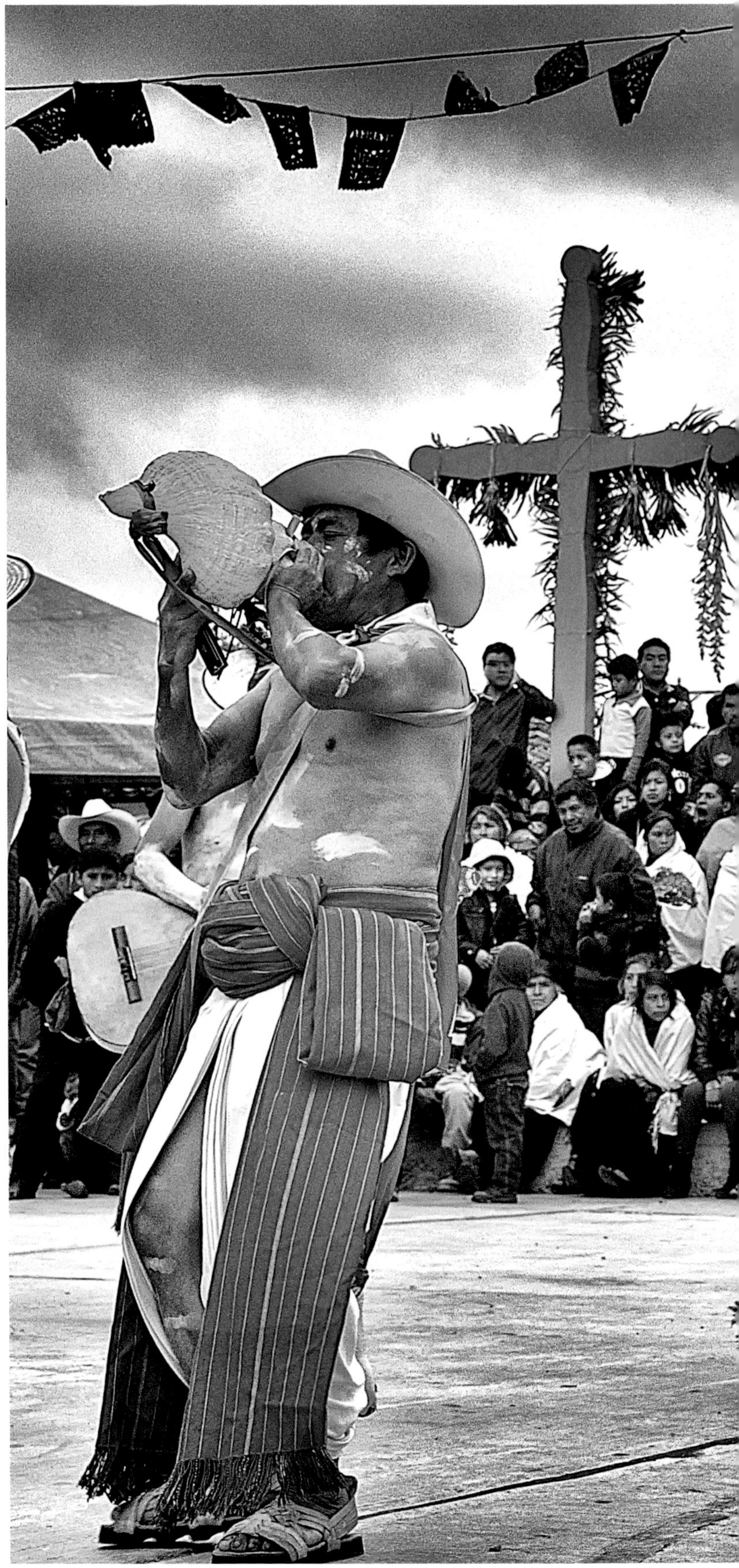

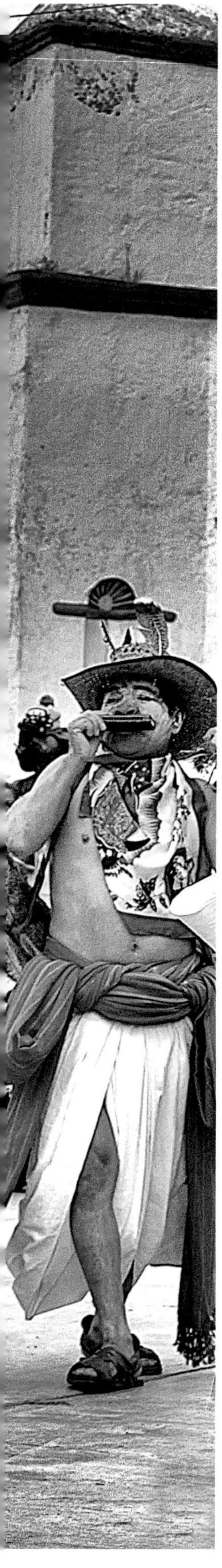

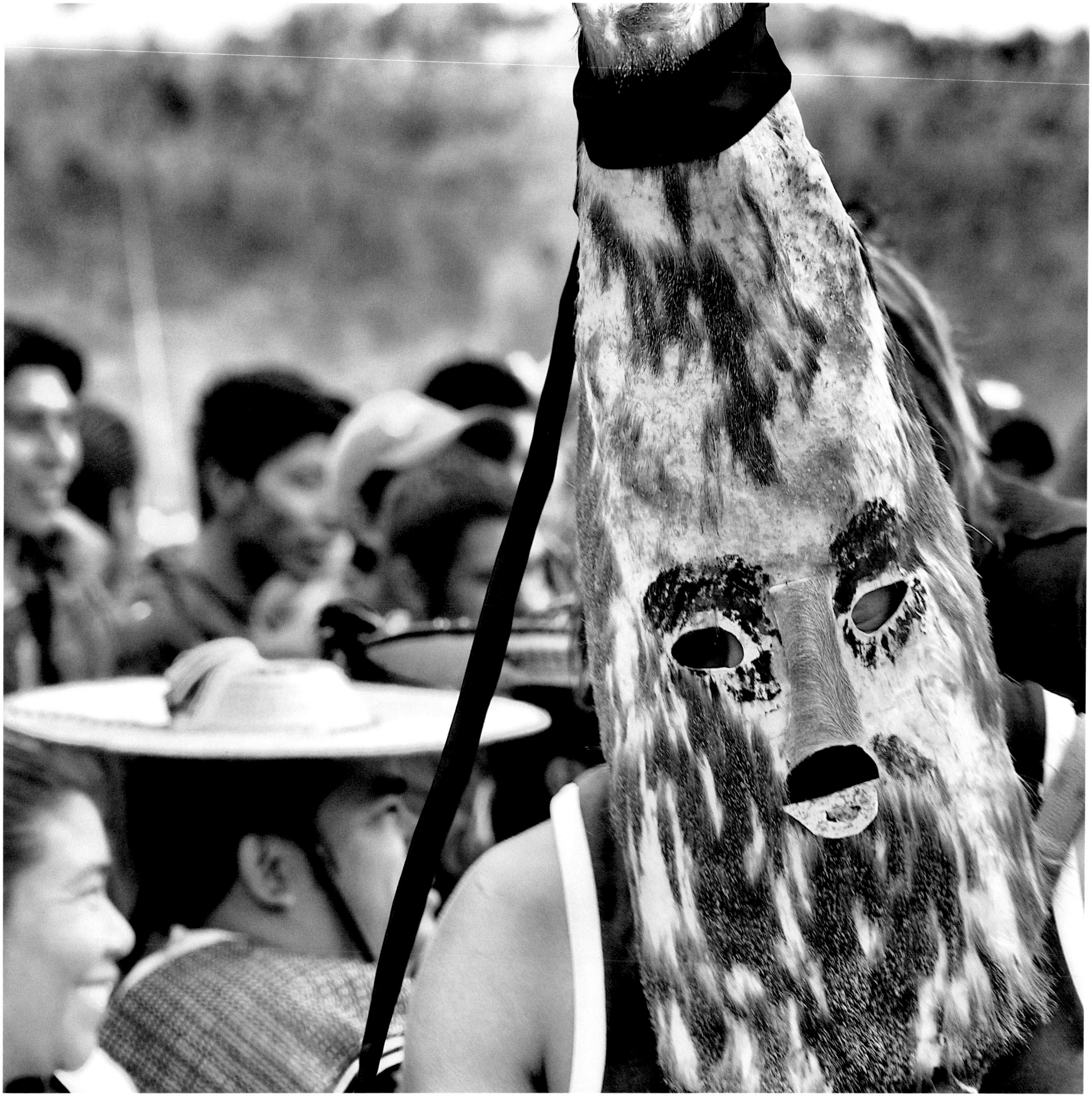

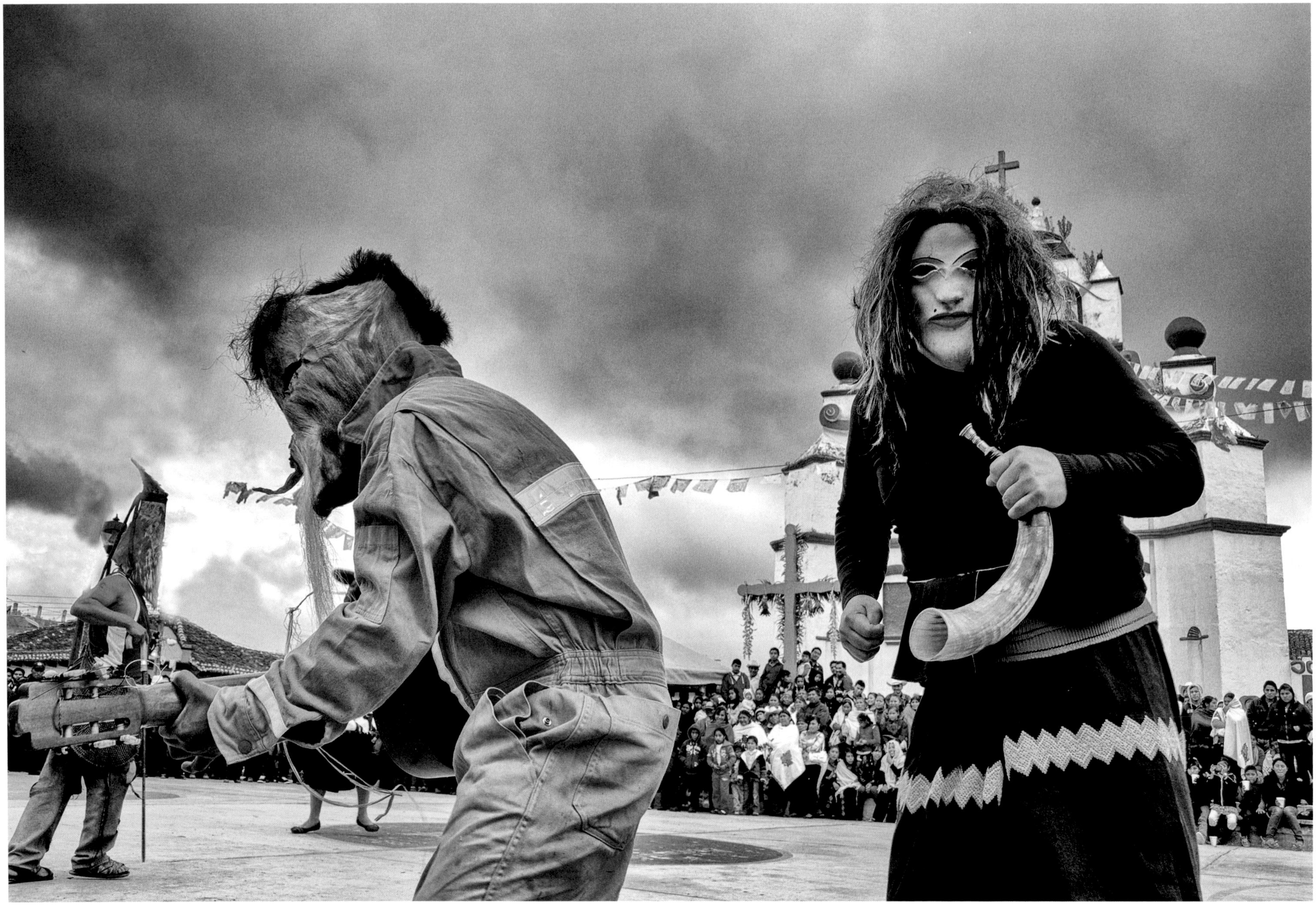

THE OLD MAN AND OLD WOMAN, IMPORTANT CARNIVAL CHARACTERS, 2016

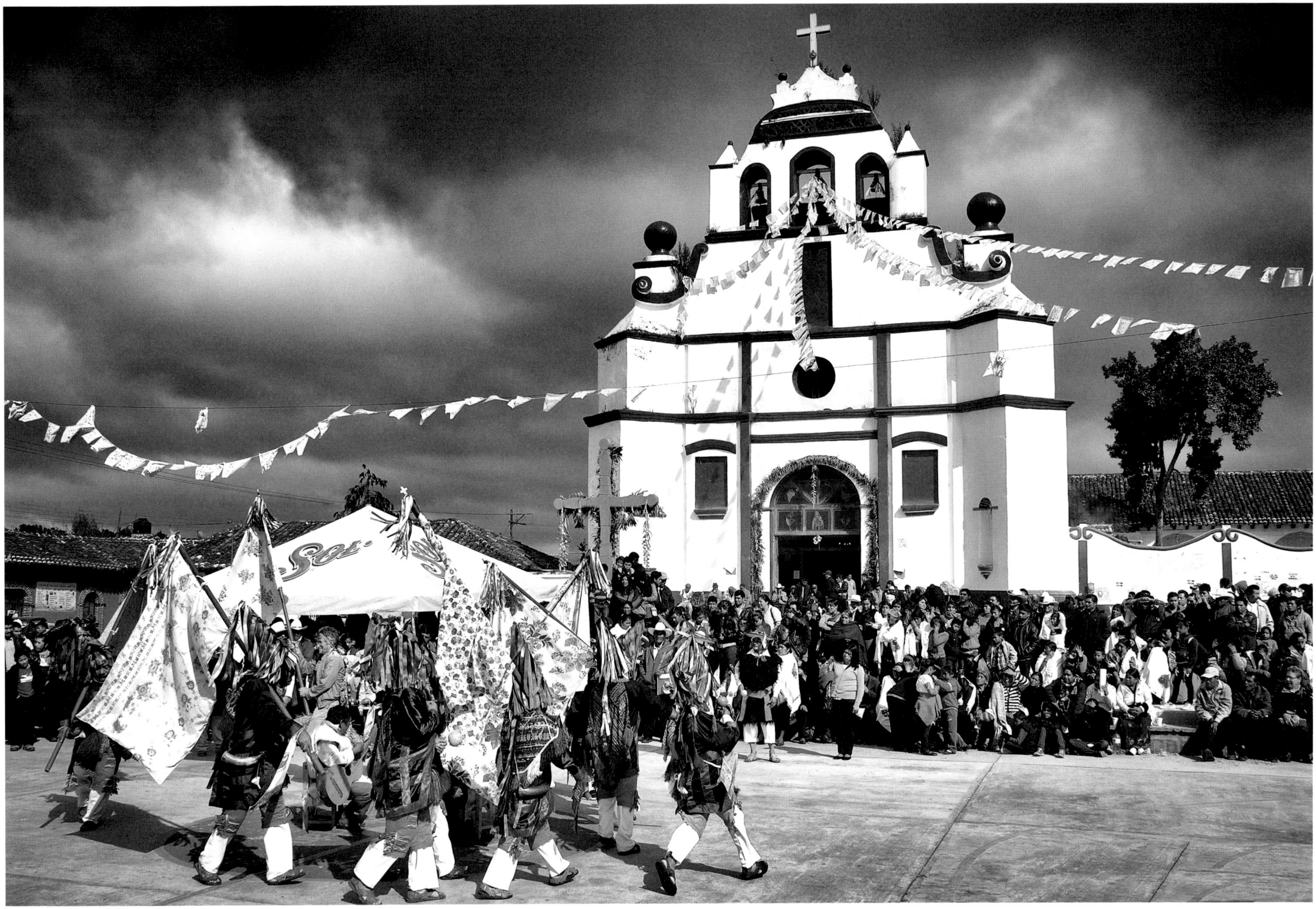

PERFORMERS ASSEMBLING IN THE PLAZA IN FRONT OF THE CHURCH, 2016

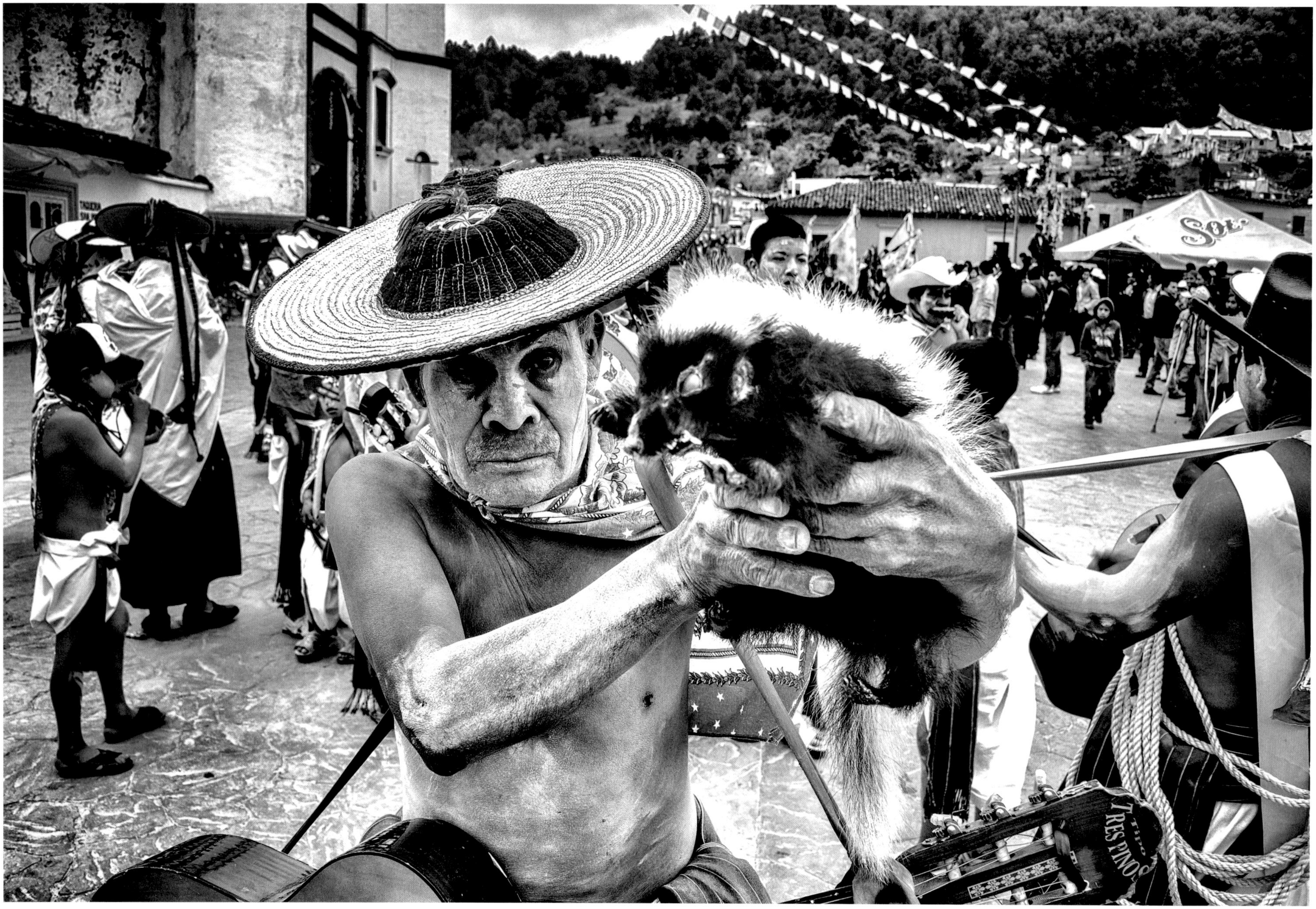

MUSICIAN WITH STUFFED SKUNK, 2016

opposite: THE CARNIVAL PROCESSION ENCIRCLING THE MAIN PLAZA, 2016

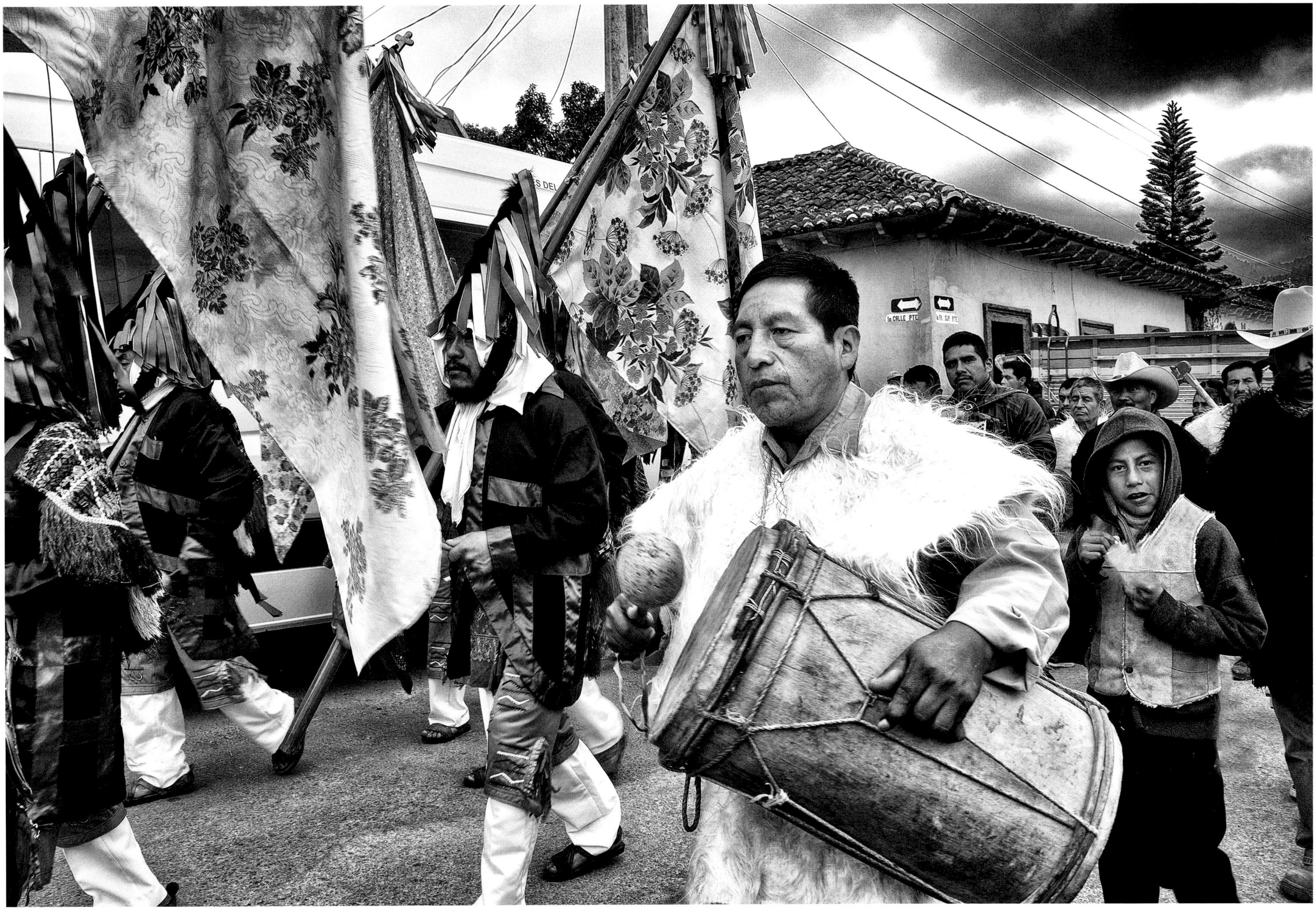

following spread, left: DANCER WITH DEER MASK, 2016
right: YOUNG BOY PAINTED WITH WHITE LIME PASTE, 2016

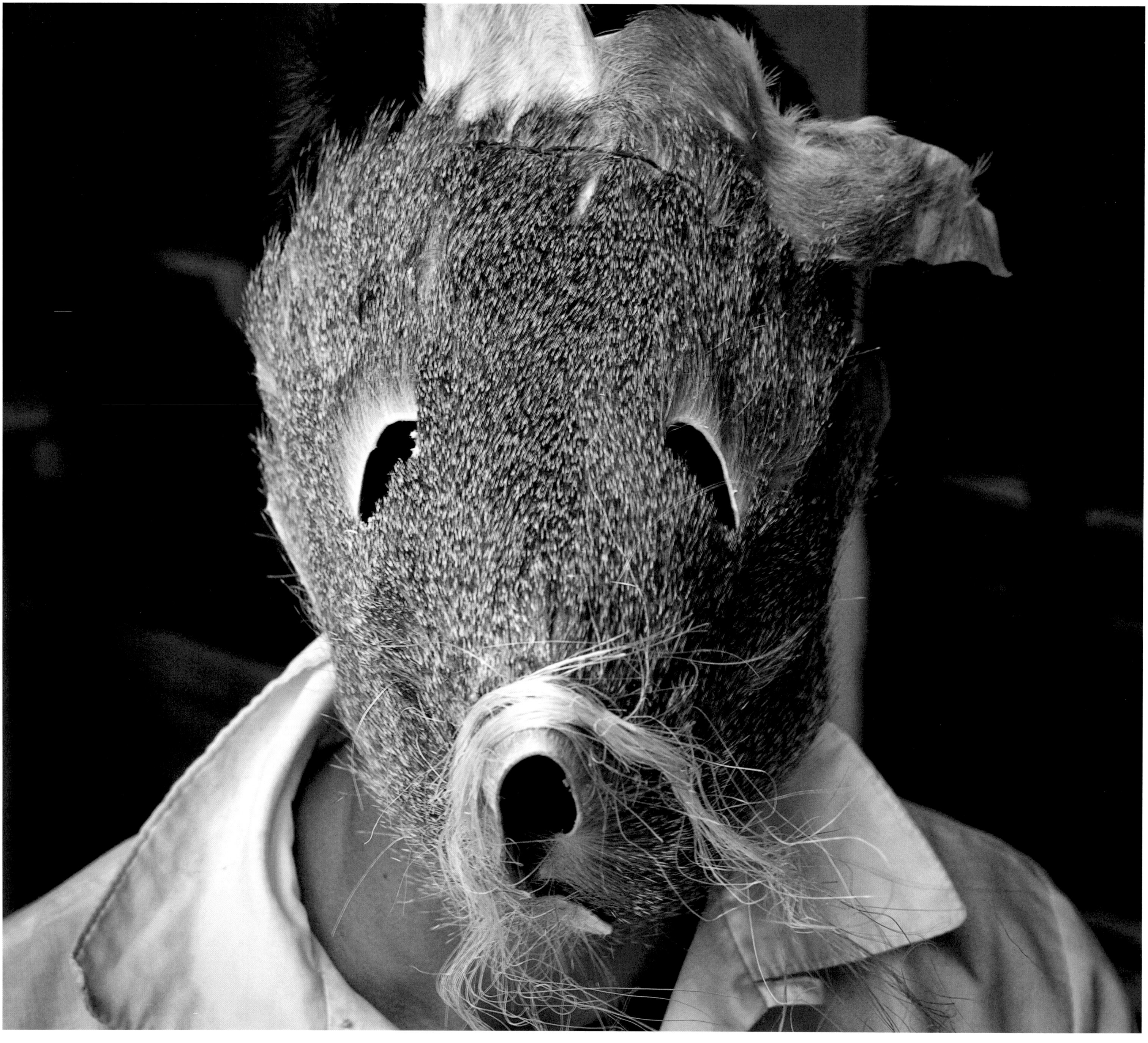

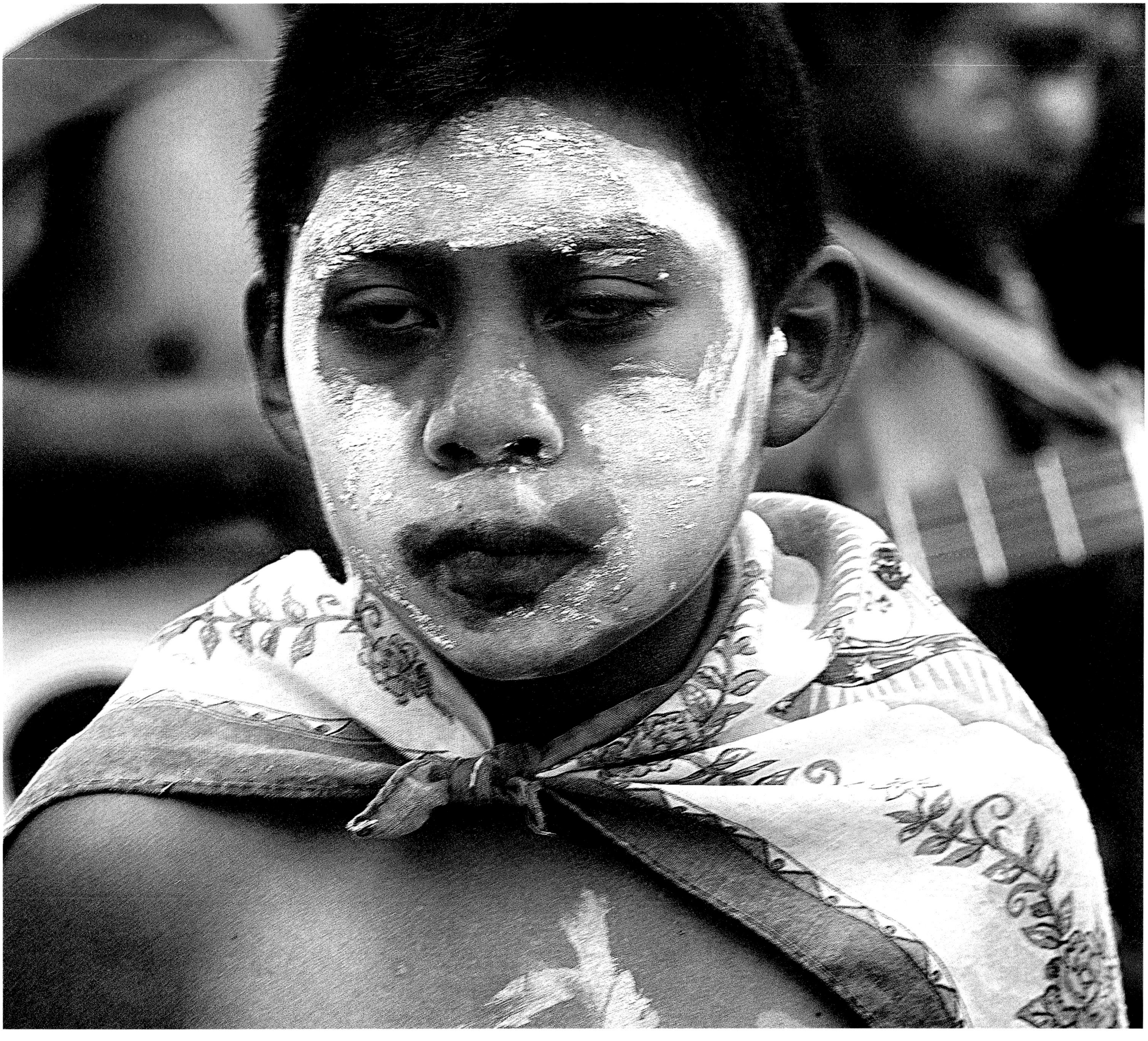

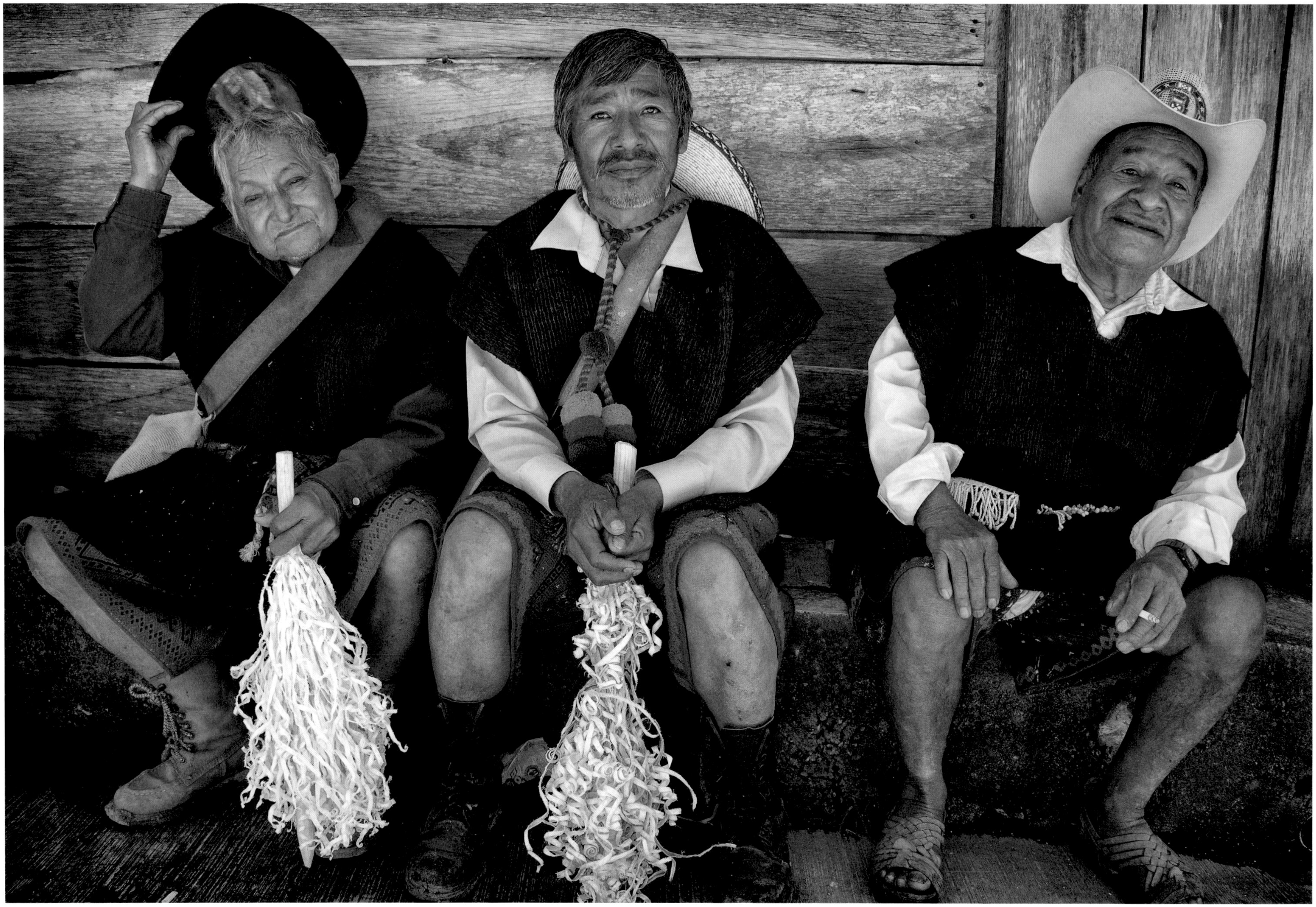

Carnival, Tenejapa

January/February
Tenejapa, Chiapas, Mexico

The Carnival of Tenejapa begins in the *pocolum* (center of town), the first place where the ancestors settled according to local legends. Mayordomos oversee these activities, drinking a sacred distilled elixir called *posh*, which they share with others involved in managing the festivities. The area is filled with men and boys wearing traditional dark tunics, scarves, and straw hats covered in ribbons. They run in circles, carrying red flags, musical instruments, and drums. Men in masks depicting devils, animals, and grotesque human faces run through the crowds, poking and prying onlookers.

Led by a group of mayordomos, the Tenejapans then proceed to the main plaza in front of the Church of San Ildefonso. Flag-bearers encircle the plaza while men march to the beat of the drums. People in the crowd pursue El Torito, a bull represented by a man encased in a wooden frame covered by straw mats and topped by a set of bull horns. The bull runs through the plaza and through nearby streets. He is chased and followed by flag-bearing men and young boys, shouting that they must rid Tenejapa of the evil demons.

Animals that appear in these dances are generally those that were religiously significant to pre-Hispanic Indigenous people; after the Spanish conquest, dancers added other animals, such as the bull, which represents evil. Several different men wear the bull costume during these festivities, and at its conclusion, the costume is dismembered and its pieces handed over to the Tenejapans as blessings for their homes. On the last day of Carnival, a real bull is sacrificed, and its meat is provided to the community. The demons disappear from Tenejapa for another year.

opposite: WAITING FOR FESTIVITIES TO BEGIN, 2016

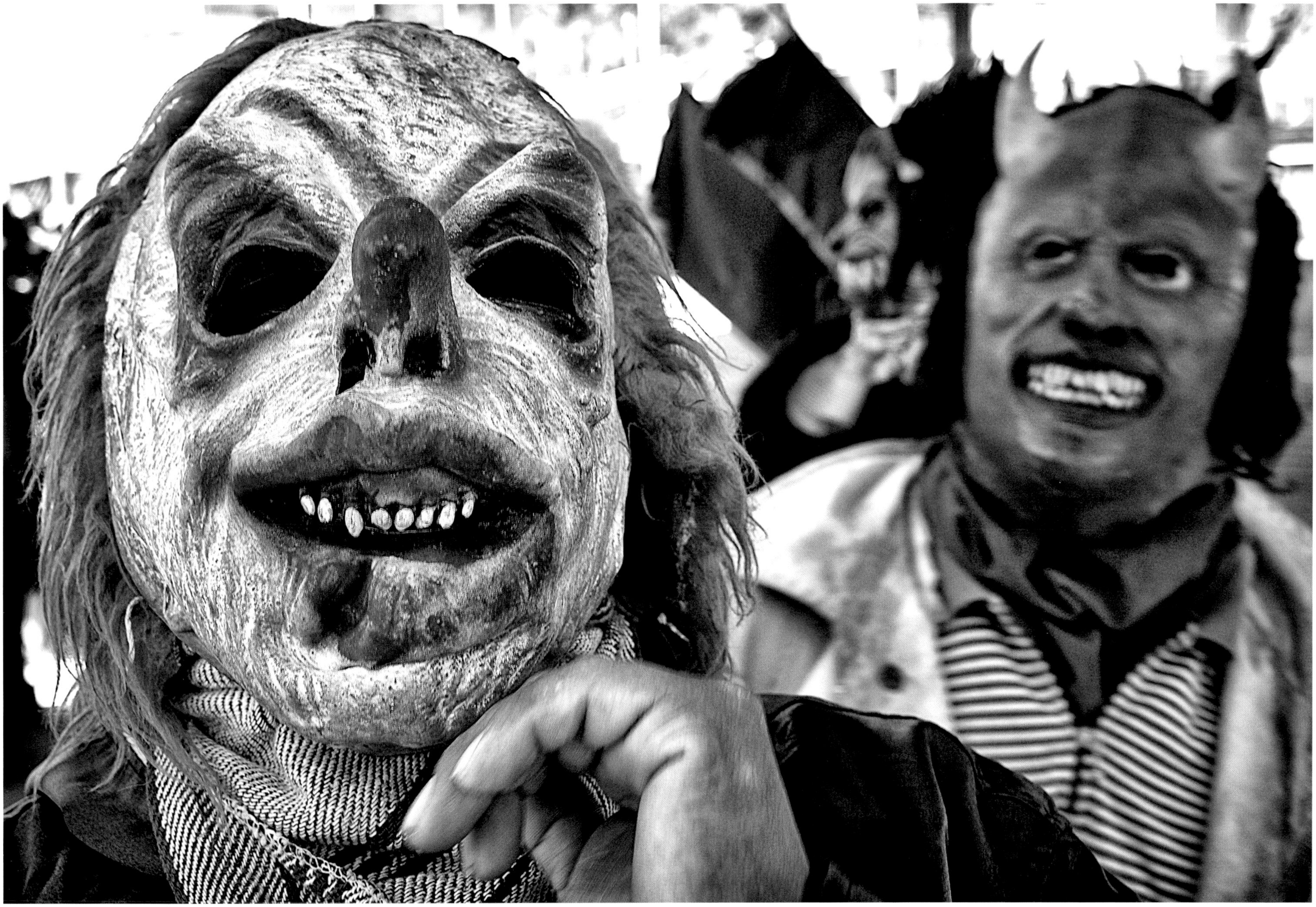

MASKED DANCERS, 2016

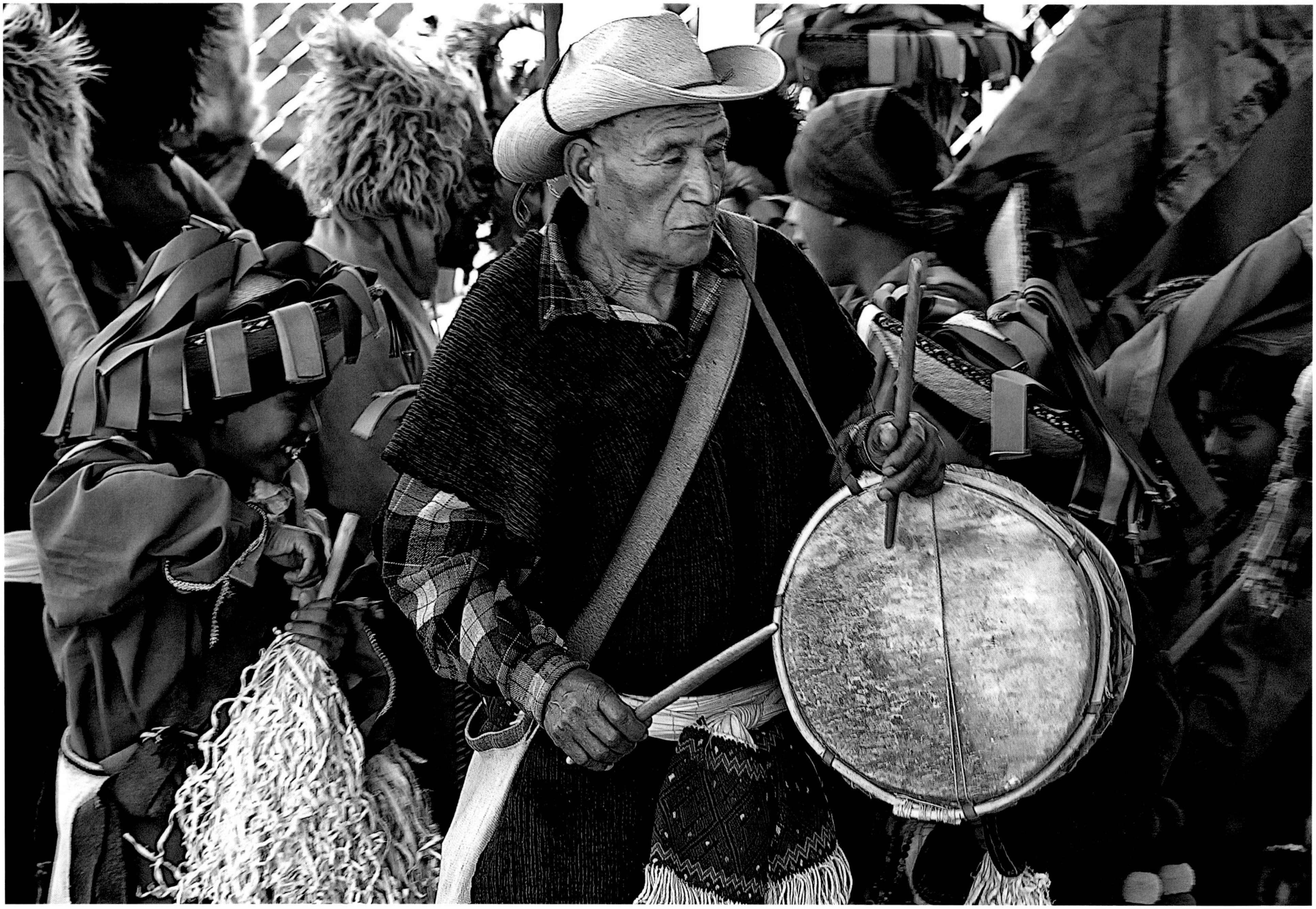

A DRUMMER PLAYING THE BEAT FOR THE PROCESSION, 2016

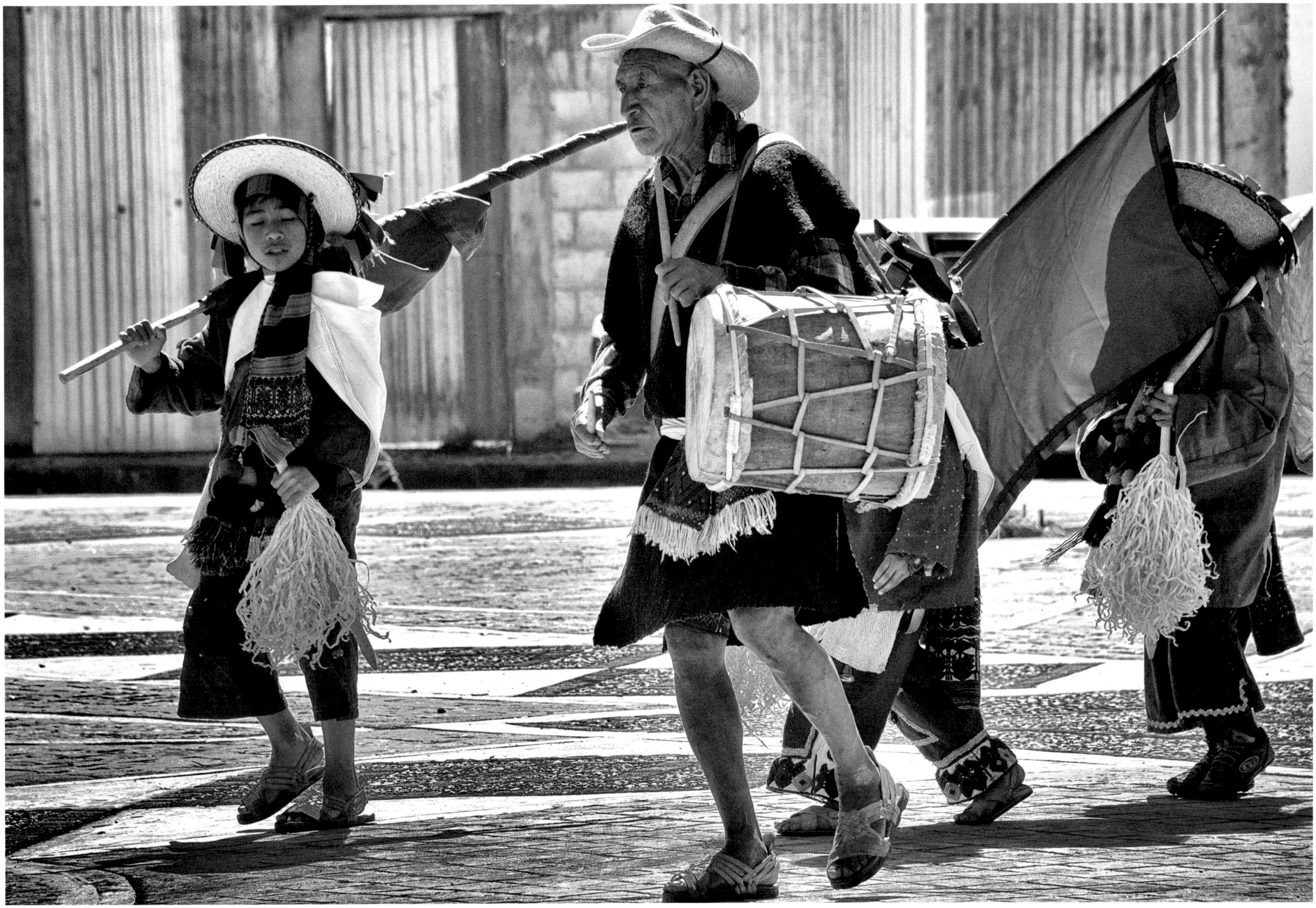

DRUMMER CIRCLING AROUND THE CHURCH, 2016

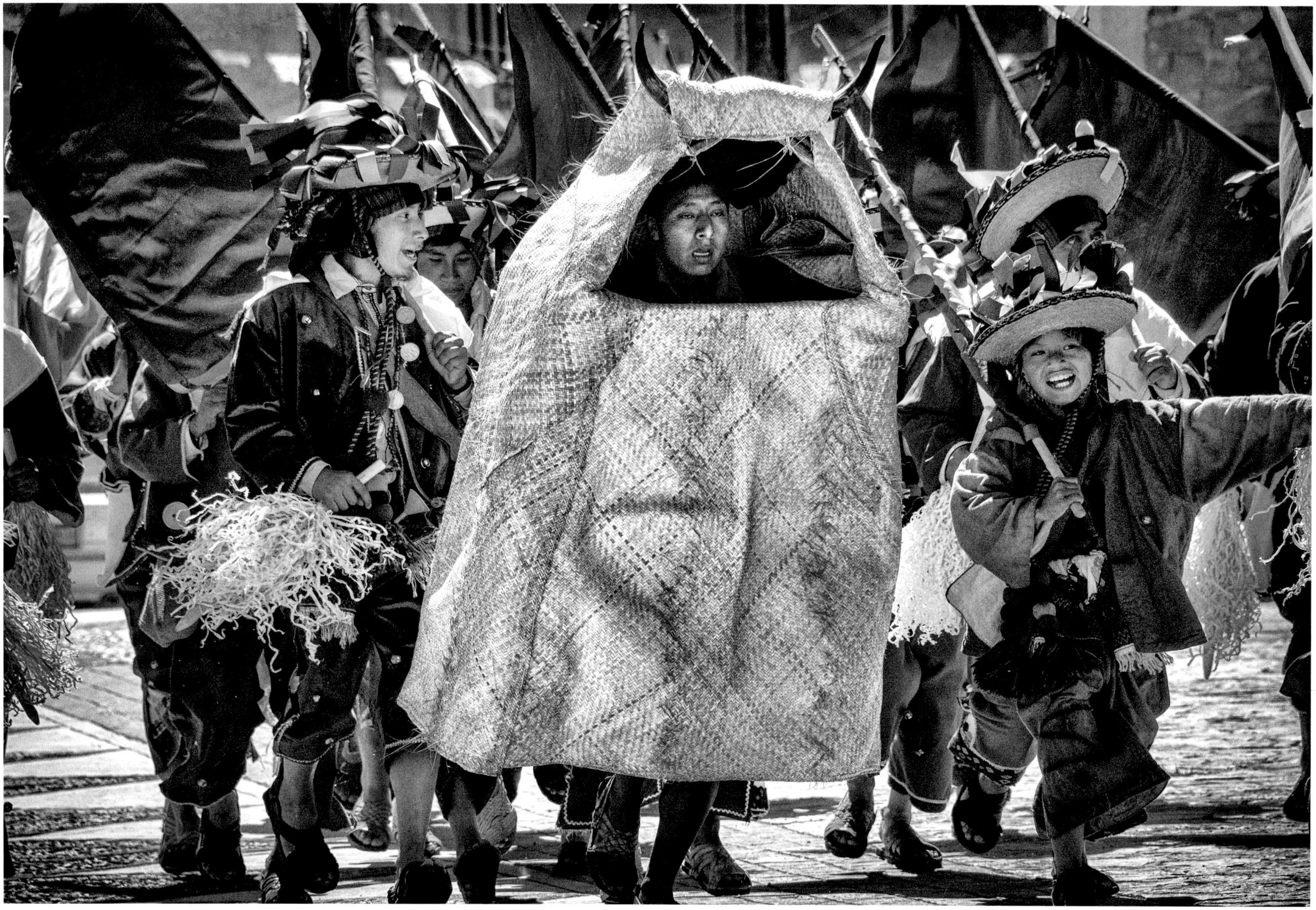

THE BULL CHARACTER LEADING THE CARNIVAL PROCESSION, 2016

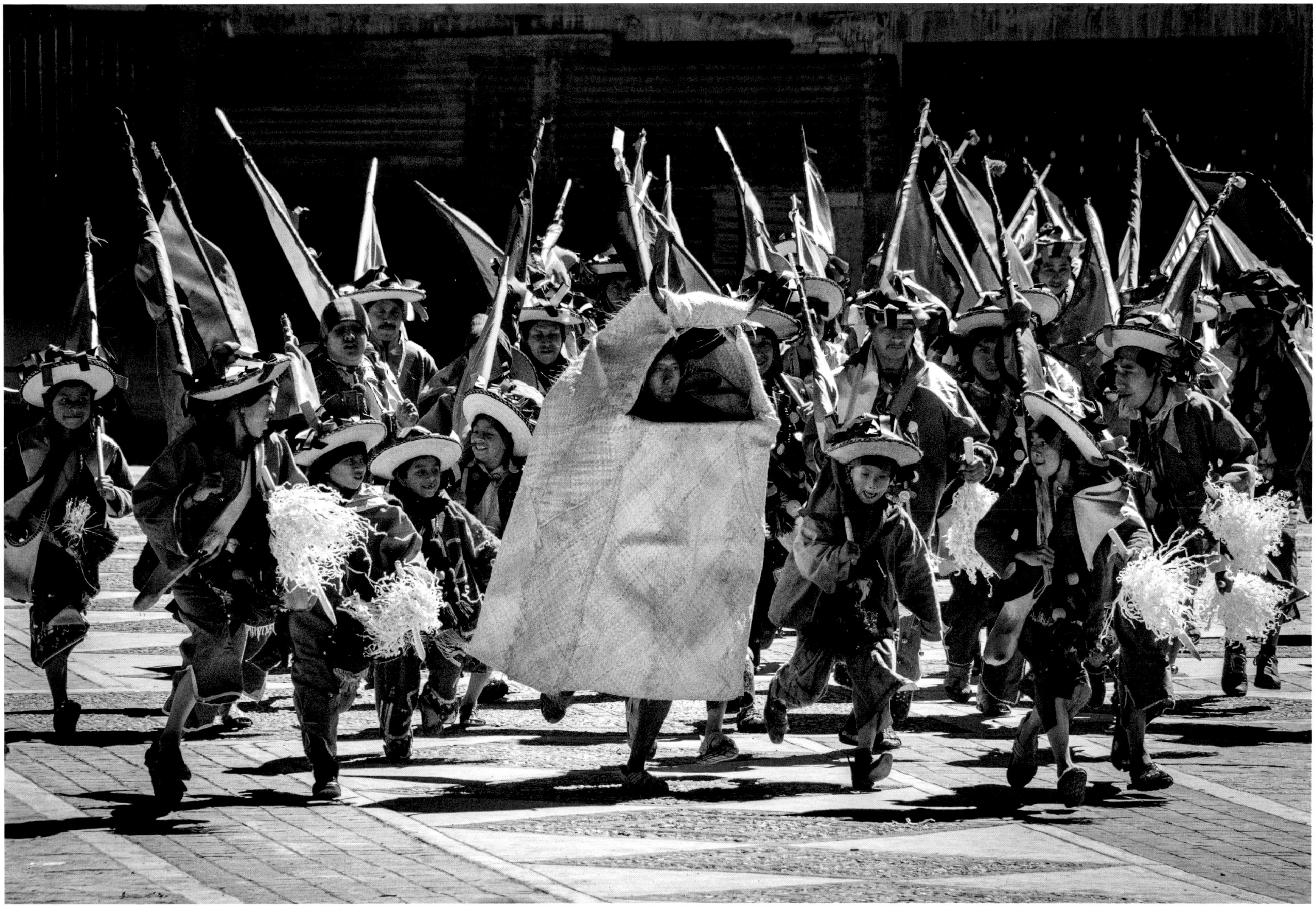

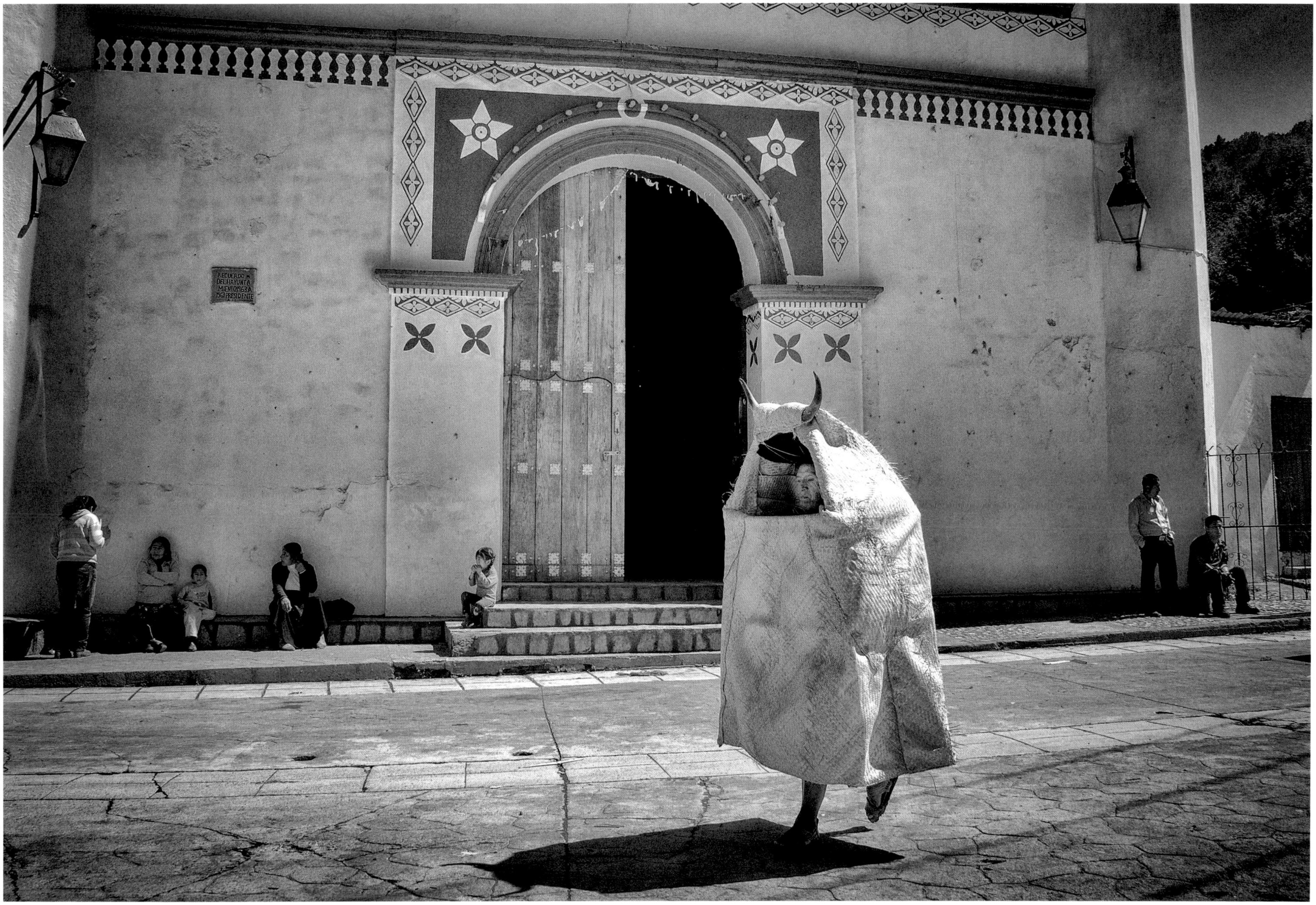

BULL BEING PURSUED THROUGH THE STREETS, 2016

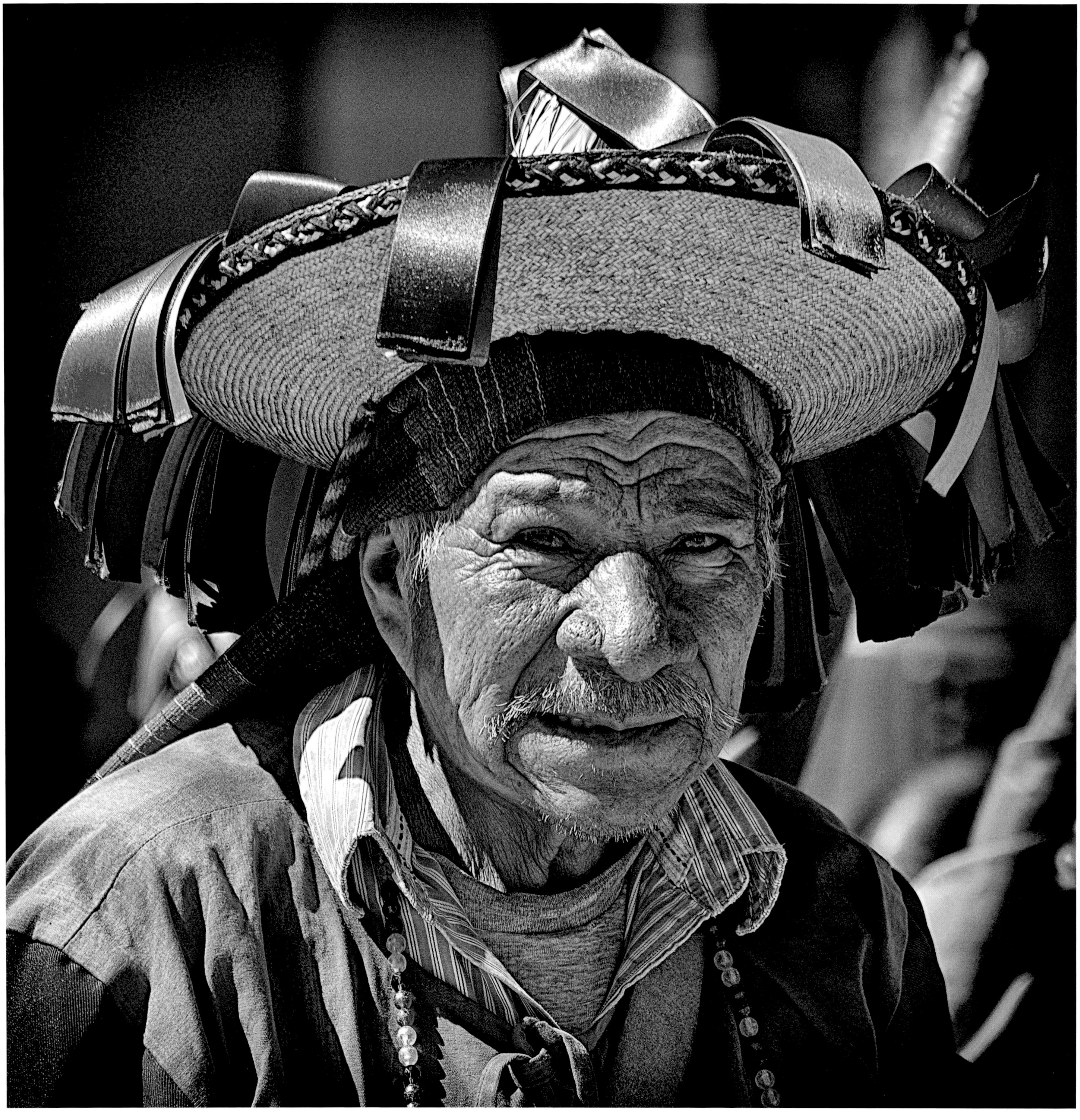

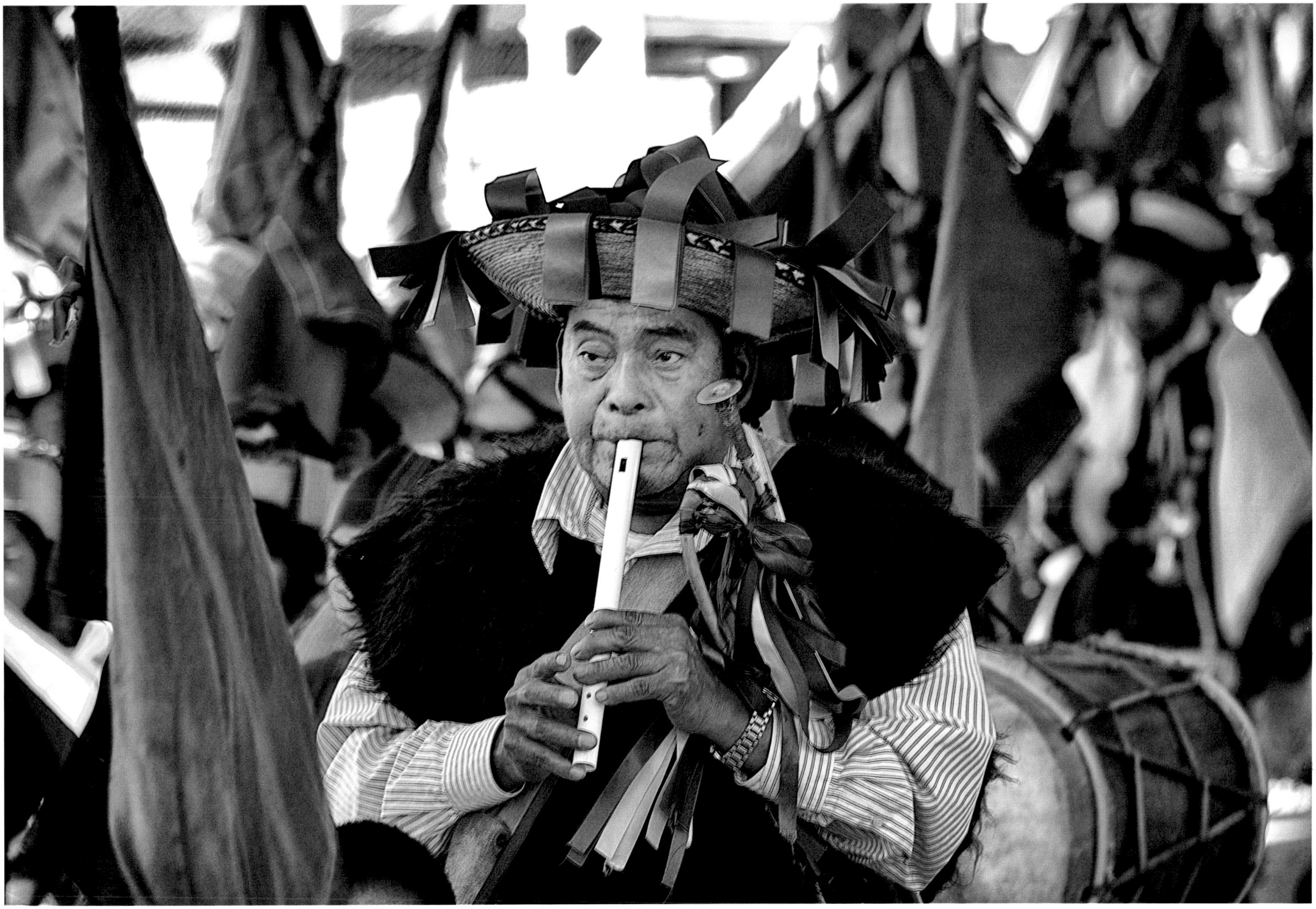

opposite: MAN IN TRADITIONAL STRAW HAT WITH RIBBONS, 2016

MAN WITH FLUTE, 2016

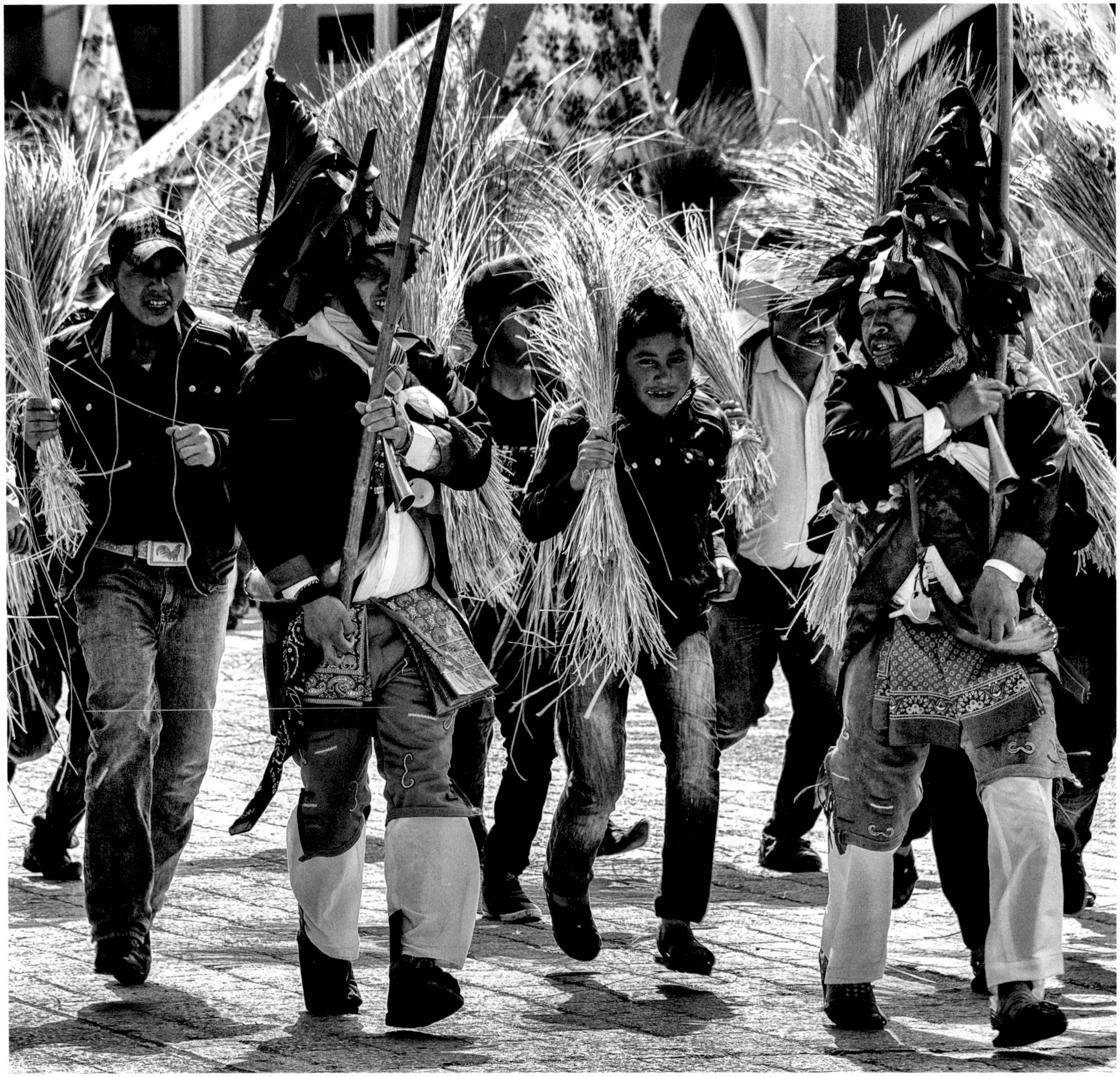

Boys carrying dried grass for the Firewalk during the Festival of Games, 2015

The Chamula Festival of Games: A Complex Self-Portrait

GARY H. GOSSEN

Author's note: This essay is excerpted from *Symbol and Meaning Beyond the Closed Community: Essays in Mesoamerican Ideas*, which I edited, and which was published in 1986 by the Institute for Mesoamerican Studies at the State University of New York at Albany.

A NUMBER OF MAGNIFICENT PHOTOGRAPHS INCLUDED in this book focus on a spectacular festival that is celebrated each year in February by the Maya community of San Juan Chamula, which is located in the central highlands of the state of Chiapas, Mexico. This annual ritual, known in Tsotsil, the local Maya language, as *k'in tahimoltik* (the Festival of Games), coincides with Carnival time, the four days preceding Ash Wednesday in the Christian liturgical calendar. However, as this essay reveals, the Festival of Games, as crafted and staged by the Chamulas over the past four hundred years, has little to do with the Passion of Christ but is rather a tribute to Our Lord in Heaven, the sun deity who the Chamulas believe created and presides over the universe as their preeminent divine being.

Chamula's self-portrait, as revealed in the Festival of Games, is more than a folk spectacle put on by an isolated community. It is, in fact, an eloquent dialogue by a municipality with the external and internal forces that impinge upon its fate. The Chamulas emerge from this self-appraisal as a highly self-conscious, historically conscious, and class-conscious people.

San Juan Chamula is one of about twenty Indian municipios (the Mexican political division below the state level) in the highlands of Chiapas in which Tsotsil[1] is spoken by a majority of inhabitants, who are corn farmers, traders, artisans, and day laborers. During my fieldwork in the community from 1966 to 1990, I had the opportunity to participate in the Festival of Games as a minor assistant, and was able to observe firsthand their elaborate preparations as well as the festival itself. The Chamulas numbered more than 100,000 at that time and lived then and now not only in their home municipio but also in more than one hundred colonies scattered all over the state of Chiapas.[2]

San Juan Chamula is acknowledged by many to be both the real and symbolic center of Indian cultural presence in the Chiapas Highlands, a situation that has been a conscious creation of the Chamulas themselves. The town is one of only a handful of Native communities in the Chiapas Highlands that do not permit non-Indian Mexicans or foreigners to own land—or even spend the night in their boundaries without the permission of municipal authorities. In the recent past, the community was infamous among other Indian groups and Mexicans alike for being ruthless to foreigners and Mexicans who wandered within its boundaries without the permission of authorities. Even today, photography of rituals in San Juan Chamula is limited and is not permitted inside the church.

Location in Time and Space

Chamulas describe the Festival of Games affectionately as the best (*mas lek̦*) of all the events in their annual ritual cycle. Of the more than twenty major public ritual events that occur annually in the town's ceremonial center, it is the best attended. Hundreds of men come home from the coffee plantations throughout the region, and thousands of families travel on foot and by truck for the lost days of *lok̦o pebrero* (Crazy February), which is the Tsotsil pronunciation of the Spanish *loco febrero*.

Crazy February refers to the well-known Carnival season preceding Lent in the Christian calendar. However, like so much of the thematic content of the event, there are Christian and traditional Maya references for most symbols. The festival also coincides with the ancient Maya month of *čay k̦'in*, which in Tsotsil means "lost festival," "lost days," or "lost heat." It came around the time of the winter solstice in the ancient Maya solar calendar and was the five-day odd month in this system (eighteen months of twenty days plus a five-day special month equals 365 days). This calendar persists in Chamula and remains in use as an agricultural almanac; however, the five-day month is adjusted by officials to coincide with the traditional pre-Lenten Christian calendar of four days (Saturday through Shrove Tuesday) plus Ash Wednesday. Whatever its Christian and ancient Maya history, the festival now falls during a time of agricultural dormancy—the cold, dry season—a betwixt and between time when no one is planting, tending, or harvesting corn.

The anomalous time in the annual cycle complements other peculiar traits of the festival. It is five days in duration, while all other festivals in the annual cycle are three days long. It is also the most expensive festival in terms of ritual sponsors' expenses, and it comprises the major annual effort of the highest-ranking religious officials. However, it is peculiar in that it takes place entirely outside the church and involves no cults to the saints.

A key to all of these anomalous themes is the name of the event itself, k'in tahimoltik, which refers to a time of intense ritual play and games, a reenactment of the awful childhood of humankind before the establishment of day and night—a time when there were no rules (cosmic, supernatural, or human), a time before the sun had risen into the sky to differentiate day from night and to bring forth the first heat that destroyed its mythical adversaries. There is a well-known Chamula mythical referent that provides the details of the death of the Sun/Christ deity at the hand of the forces of evil. Briefly paraphrased, the story is as follows:

> The Sun/Christ is born to the Moon/Virgin Mary as her second son. He is slain and nailed to a tree, but comes back to life. On this, the first day of the primeval myth era, he goes to the edge of the Earth, marked by the western horizon, known in Tsotsil as the place of waning heat. On the second day he descends into the southwestern quadrant of the universe, which is the Underworld. On the third day he moves past the nadir of the universe, still in the

> Underworld, and into the southeastern quadrant of the universe. On the fourth day, he rises from the eastern horizon, emerging from the Underworld into the northeastern quadrant of the universe. This marks the great cosmogonic moment, the first rising of the Sun/Christ into the new universe. Upon reaching the zenith of the sky at the end of the fourth day of creation, the Sun/Christ gives to the universe for the first time sufficient heat and light to kill his adversaries. On the fifth day order is established in the universe as the Sun/Christ moves into the northwest quadrant, descending to the western horizon to mark the end of humanity's first real day. With this, the categories of time, space, and cosmic order are established in the beginning of the First Creation. This creation is subsequently destroyed and restored three more times by the Sun/Christ as punishment for human ineptitude. The last of these is the present, Fourth Creation.[3]

It is precisely the five primeval days of the First Creation that are recapitulated ritually in the five-day Festival of Games: four days of chaos and anticipation, culminating in a Firewalk over burning thatch and grass (symbolizing the first ascent of the Sun/Christ to the zenith) at noon of the fourth day, followed by the first day of Lent, known in Tsotsil as Fish-Eating Wednesday.

The Sequence of Events

The scale of the Festival of Games is monumental, and the grand total of individuals with official roles to play each year comes to more than 2,000. The festival requires the participation of two hereditary positions that are passed from father to son—the Lord of the Drum, of which there is one for each of the three barrios, and the Crier, who serves as the master of ceremonies. There is but one Crier for the whole community, and he is also the sacristan of the Chamula church.

There are also a large number of rotating positions. These public-service jobs are requested many years in advance, with waiting lists kept in the town hall in a locked safe. All of these positions exist in triplicate, for each of Chamula's three political divisions or barrios: San Juan, San Pedro, and San Sebastián. Each of the rotating positions must be occupied for two consecutive years, first as an incoming official and then as an outgoing official. There is a veritable army of supporting personnel required for each of the official positions, for all have complex service responsibilities involving preparation and distribution of ritual meals and elaborate exchanges of ritual goods.

The principal sponsors and leading ritual figures are the Pasyonetik (Passions), named for the Christian Passion, which is one of the historical overlays represented in this pre-Lenten festival. There are two Passions for each of Chamula's three barrios. They are striking figures to behold, wearing a costume that looks rather like a loose, two-piece suit of red pajamas with knee-length legs and headgear consisting of a long piece of white cotton that is wound as a great turban, with loose ties hanging in the back. It is useful to consider the Passions as symbols of the festival itself, for they embody the two opposing aspects of good and evil, as do many of the dual-aspect deities of Mesoamerican antiquity. Each of the six Passions has an associated second-ranking personage called Ničim (Flower). Like the Passions, the Flowers contribute heavily to the annual maintenance of the cult of the Sun/Christ. In an explicit sense, the Passions and Flowers are a team, responsible for the different parts of the Sun/Christ's body. The Passions also have lower-ranking officers, known as Commissaries and Ordinaries, plus a large number of servants to help fulfill the vast network of ritual obligations. Groups of musicians associated with all the major ritual officers play and sing for endless hours during the five-day festival. Their role is of critical importance, for the words of their songs, formulated in traditional couplets, offer a running narrative of what is happening at each stage.

Roaming through the festival, joking and threatening bystanders, are hundreds of men and boys dressed as nineteenth-century French soldiers, complete with red-and-black frock coats, short trousers, and conical monkey-skin hats. These Mašetik (Monkeys) represent the evil monkeys of primeval antiquity, who, with the demons and the Jews, killed the Sun/Christ. Like other ritual personnel at the festival, they have a dual aspect and are also the policemen of the festival, the keepers of the public order.

Preparations for the festival begin in earnest on the Feast of San Sebastián, which takes place on January 20 and is a major festival in its own right. On this occasion, all Festival of Games personnel appear in full costume at around noon to request permission to stage the festival. All participants, surrounded by their entourages of Monkeys and other servants, get on their knees at the southwestern corner of the walled atrium compound of the church and beg the Presidente Municipal for permission to stage the festival. The Crier reads for the first of many times the Carta Española (Spanish Letter), a kind of charter myth that is delivered in mock seriousness at many times during the festival. This incitation to war, destruction, and immortality is read in brutal, almost mocking Spanish.

In the weeks leading up to the five-day festival there are many ritual activities that take place. After a wood-gathering expedition that begins at night, the time of pre-cultural chaos, drunkenness, and cold, there is a feast at the ritual official's home in the ceremonial center. The theme of this meal is primitive food and primitive behavior. The menu consists of beans and tortillas and cow tripe soup. The soup significant because it is greasy, which is specifically repugnant to Chamula food aesthetics. Significantly, the Monkeys celebrate and praise the virtues of greasy food—Mexican food—in Spanish. They perform with mockery and laughter and offer the audience drinks of rum from their cow-horn flasks. Beginning with this event, interior hearth fires are extinguished, and all ritual meals of the festival are prepared in crude shelters outside the ritual official's home. This recapitulates the themes of negation of heat and light, which are central to the destructive theme of the first phases of the festival. Ordinary domestic and public life is suspended, and there is the total segregation of males and females in all activities.

Three major events take place during this period. First, all Passions and Flowers must present formal ritual petitions to the Lords of the Drum to appear with their drums at appropriate times during the festival. Second, the outgoing Passions must arrange for the bulls that will be ritually sacrificed to provide meat for the ritual meals of the festival. Third, flower-gatherers are dispatched for each of the twenty-four major ritual positions. These crews of four to twelve men go by foot, truck, or bus to tropical or subtropical areas to gather necessary plants and flowers for the adornment of altars, porticos, and shrines. They also collect pine needles to cover the floors of their patrons' homes with the required carpet of green.

Bull-Pulling Monday is the day that sacrificial bulls are taken to the ceremonial center. Each party departs in the early morning darkness, amid fireworks and laughter, for the site in a distant hamlet where their bull is held. The bull is then lassoed, and lines of men and boys grab the ropes amid great hoopla as the party departs for the five- to six-hour trip to the ceremonial center.

Several hours before dawn on Bull-Killing Tuesday, each of the Passions pray over their sacrificial bull, stating pointedly that the bull is not only the Sun/Christ, but a substitute

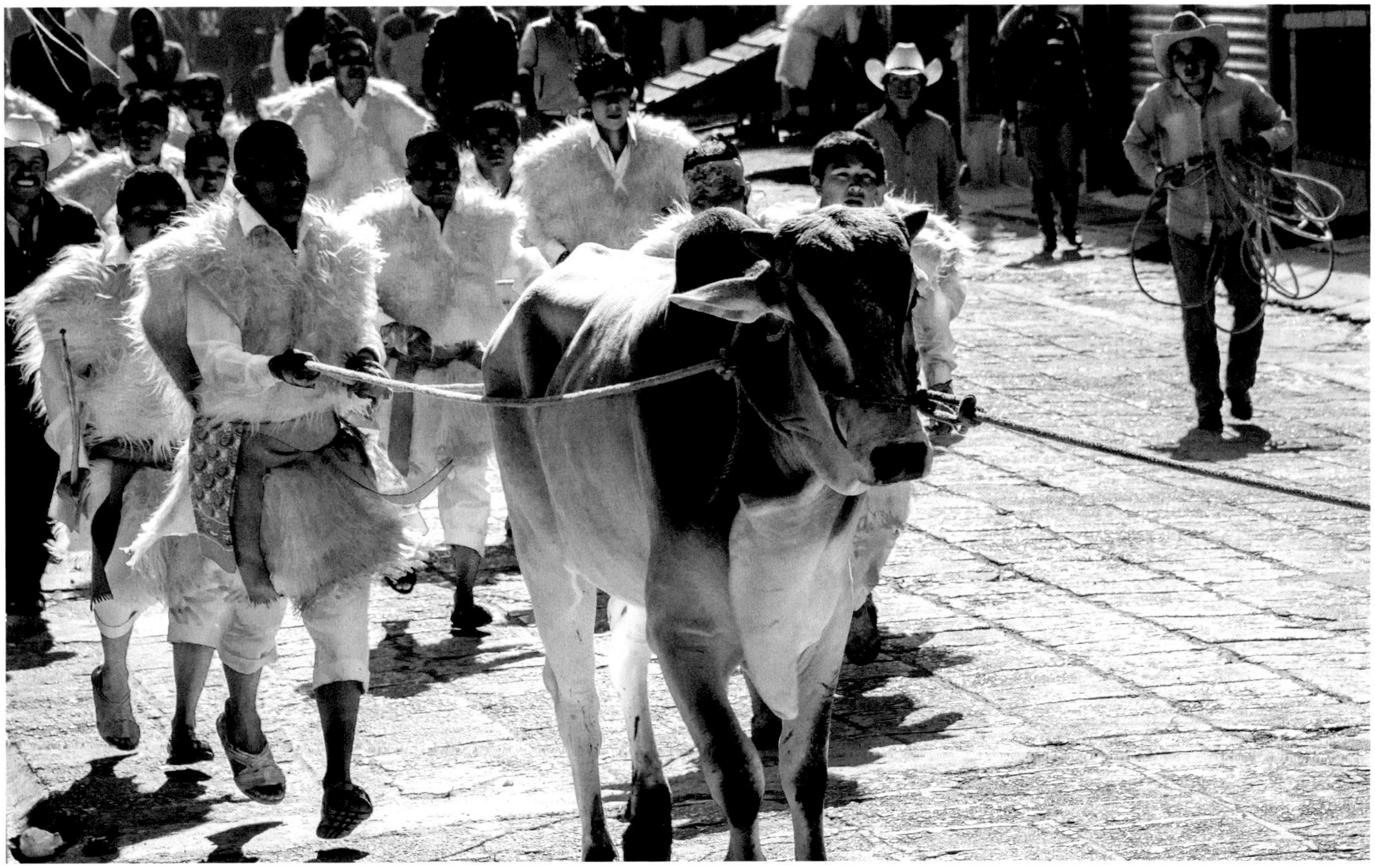

A team of men and boys pulling a bull toward its sacrifice, 2015

for everyone. As the sun appears, skyrockets are launched and hand cannons are fired as a signal to the butchers at the three sacrificial sites. Knives are thrust into the jugular vein of the bulls' exposed throats, and as the blood rushes out, it is caught in buckets and taken to the outdoor kitchen to be prepared as blood soup, which is served in gourd bowls at noon.

On Shopping Wednesday the Passions' entourage departs at sunup for a collective ritual shopping expedition to the town of San Cristóbal de las Casas, where Mexican sweet buns, coffee, sugar, citrus fruit, and other non-Indian goods are purchased, and hundreds of kilos of corn are brought for custom grinding into flour for use in the vast amounts of sweet gruel that will be prepared on Gruel-Cooking Friday. On the next day, Sweeping Thursday, ritual cleaning crews sweep the major thoroughfares and paths in the ceremonial center and make sure that proper decorations of ritual plants and pine-needle carpets are in place.

Gruel-Cooking Friday is a day of massive food preparation. Tens of thousands of bean tamales are prepared, wrapped in calla lily leaves, and steamed for hours. In addition, hundreds of gallons of sweet gruel are slowly cooked in great clay pots. The gruel is a snack food served to guests, but it also symbolizes the radiance of the Sun/Christ deity and the life force itself, since it is made of corn, said originally to have been given to humankind by the Sun/Christ, regarded as the supreme creator of all life. After emerging from the intense gruel-making ritual, the outgoing Passion in each barrio and his wife go in ritual procession to present freshly made gruel and what is known as a baby tamale to the incoming Passion of the same barrio. This baby tamale, which is actually a baby-sized bean tamale wrapped in calla lily leaves, is a symbol of the mythological sins of the ancestors, who practiced the custom of eating their own children as toddlers and were destroyed by the Sun/Christ at the end of the First Creation for this crime.

On Saturday, the first day of the Festival of Games, the focal activity is the Dance of the Warriors, which takes place around the sacred kettledrums on a dance ground located in front of each Passion's patio shrine. Hundreds of men from the community are captured in rank order and recruited to the Passions' army to be initiated through the dance. Over four days this dance is performed almost incessantly, and virtually every man who has ever in his lifetime performed a civil or religious job is reincorporated into the corporate community through this ritual.

Sunday, the second day of the Festival of Games, is a replay of the first day except that fatigue and excitement make the events even wilder. There is a huge influx of outside vendors, for Sunday is the regular market day, and this attracts not only a larger crowd but also a more diverse crowd, including tourists. It is as though Chamula is indeed being invaded by cultural "others," in a sense fulfilling the war proclamation of the Spanish Letter. Roaming around among the ritual personnel is a costumed character known as the Spanish Lady, or in Tsotsil as the Stinking Woman. The character is played by a male accused of sexual infractions who wears a tattered white Mexican wedding dress. The Stinking Woman's presence is a constant reminder of the strict Chamula moral code.

Monday, the third day of the Festival of Games, is also known as Water-Drinking Monday, because there are no banquets and the only ritual item formally given to all is rum. Events reach a fever pitch on Tuesday, the fourth day of the Festival of Games. It begins with torch and lamplight processions at around midnight to the Mount Calvary hilltop shrines associated with the three barrios. The ritual visits to the shrines represent explicitly the defeat of the Chamulas at the hand of generic invaders. Shortly before dawn, at a signal from activated skyrockets and hand cannons, masses of people representing the three barrios descend from the mountains, running and shouting, for the final assault on Chamula. They converge in the walled atrium of the church to witness the symbolic nailing of boards across its main entrance. The three mobs move to the sacred waterholes, a location that seems to symbolize the taking of the Chamula hinterlands from their rightful owners.

After a noontime feast, a mock battle between Mexico and Guatemala takes place. The two armies group on facing hillsides and, at the signal of a trumpet, charge each other, throwing hard pellets of horse manure as ammunition. Meanwhile, a team gathers thatch and dried grass and carries it to the ceremonial center, where it is spread into a path across the plaza from the church to a cross shrine at the opposite end. The thatch is ignited, and even before the flames die down, the key officials from the three barrios run back and forth over the flames and coals. This dramatization of the cosmogonic moment—the first ascent of the Sun/Christ into the heavens, purging evil and vanquishing the evil forces of the cosmos—never fails to achieve a stunning dramatic effect. With this event, the ambiguity of the Passions cease, and the Chamulas are on the Sun/Christ's side. With the fireworks over, the tension and stress of the four previous days dissolve into a kind of secular carnival.

Wednesday, the fifth day of the Festival of Games, is known as Fish-Eating Wednesday, an obvious thematic link with Ash Wednesday in the Christian calendar. It is an anticlimax from the previous days, and the major activities are rest, prayers of penance by the Passions, and household visits. In the evening, flagpoles with banners which represent the Sun/Christ are dissembled, wrapped in white cotton and placed in storage boxes.

Motivations for the Festival of Games

Why do the people of San Juan Chamula invest such time, such social energy, and (relatively speaking) such vast sums of money and resources in staging an event whose script is set and whose outcome is fixed? Why does it matter so much? No single answer suffices, but the most compelling answer to this comes from the Chamulas themselves. They respond quite simply: "It is the custom. If we don't do it and do it properly, we will die." What exactly are they getting at?

I believe that they are appraising, in a complex idiom, who they are as a successful, if besieged, minority in modern Mexico. The anthropologist Victor Turner,[4] in one of his many brilliant forays into the meaning of ritual action, said that ritual expresses "quintessential custom . . . the refined extract . . . of many long-standing customary ways of behaving, thinking, and feeling." Elaborating the idea in another way, he said that ritual is "the periodic restatement of the terms in which men of a particular culture must interact if there is to be any kind of coherent social life . . . it creates, or re-creates, the categories through which men perceive reality—the axioms underlying the structure of society and the laws of the natural and moral orders."[5]

The Festival of Games achieves such a self-appraisal by ritually destroying and reconstructing the moral fabric of the community. Chamula stages and wins a moral, military, and ethnic battle that is not unlike its everyday battle with disruptive forces from within and from without. The slow motion of ritual action at the beginning of the festival is focused on peripheral social space comprising the forests and lowland cattle ranches, both of which are associated with evil beings and with the Mexican mestizo world. The disruptive forces invade the ceremonial center itself as preparations for the festival proceed. At an accelerating pace, the familiar daily scenes—the hearth, sleep, work, leisure, having sex—fall by the wayside, as Chamula returns to primeval mode, its childhood. The fires go out inside homes, and life goes primitive. There is no work, sleep, or sex—only running and the feverish activity of warfare and destruction.

The temporary ritual victory of the sinful past of human experience is achieved as the triumphant "bad" armies invade Chamula. They descend from the mountaintop shrines on Tuesday morning to symbolically vanquish all of Chamula by ritually boarding up of the church door. Finally, the Sun/Christ prevails and defeats the soldiers and Monkeys, as the whole ritual entourage purges its negative mode by running the Firewalk (the Path of God), as though they themselves were the Sun/Christ embarking upon his first ascent into the heavens. Thus, Chamula reconstitutes itself through the Festival of Games, taking the whole community on an immense journey through space and time. Recreating on the ritual stage what they have experienced as a people within the greater social universe of Mexico and the world at large is a powerful reminder of why they believe as they have for centuries that it is crucial to keep the center of the moral universe, San Juan Chamula itself, free from foreign intervention and moral corruption.

The Festival of Games relives the dialectic of the story of creation of the past and present conflict between rule-governed and non-rule-governed forces. It is a folk commentary in the mode of macroanalysis, a reenactment and appraisal of centuries of ethnic conflict that the Chamulas have seen and survived as a people. It shows clearly that they are aware of where they have stood in these centuries of conflict as tribute-paying victims, not beneficiaries of the larger world's interventions in their affairs. The festival sheds some light not only on why Chamulas have assumed a defensive posture toward the world at large, but also on how they have coped with the threat of intervention. They do so by keeping a fanatically centralized political and religious organization that systematically purges unwanted foreign presence and militantly discourages intra-community factionalism. This political style of Chamula is expressed in the obligatory ritual reincorporation of past and present officials in to the central moral community through the Dance of the Warriors. As though this gesture were not sufficient, undesirable behavior and devious motives are finally purged through the Firewalk.

The Festival of Games is also an economic commentary. It clearly acknowledges economic dependence on the larger Mexican community, but also reveals that Chamula wants Mexico's goods and services on its own terms, in the service of the Sun/Christ in Chamula, not in the service of becoming Mexican. Through the rituals performed, the festival provides a poignant commentary on the traditional agricultural cycle, an appeal to the Sun/Christ for another warm growing season, and to the Earth Lords at the water hole to supply rain, in order to make the sacred food-producing drums and the Passions' banquet everyday possibilities, not just symbolic tokens. Even the burning grasses of the Firewalk and the horse manure pellets of the mock battle are key elements in Chamula traditional agriculture. Each spring, corn stubble, dry grass, and weeds are burned in the fields. The resulting ash together with any available sheep or horse manure is dug into the impoverished soils of Chamula to encourage another annual crop of corn.

The festival is also a commentary on human psychology that recognizes in all of us the capacity to hold ambivalent, sometimes contradictory opinions about the same individual situation or external reality. Just as the Passions are at once the representations of the Sun/Christ and of ethnic forces that would destroy Chamula, so each Chamula is an amalgam of good and evil. The ambivalence in the Passion, with his coterie of Monkeys on the one hand and his holy coffer containing the symbols of the head of the Sun/Christ on the other is perhaps in all Chamulas, and may be in all of us. Indeed, all of the communities whose festivals are represented in this book are much more than the colorful and exciting spectacles that they create for themselves and for visitors. All of these festivals are complex ritual dramas that tell us much about the communities that stage them. Mined for implicit meaning, they provide an opportunity to glimpse, from a local perspective, how they view their lives and times and their place in the world.

NOTES

1. "Tsotsil" is the most commonly used spelling of the word today, but older sources may use "Tzotzil."

2. The ethnographic data and commentary in this essay are based on the author's fieldwork in Chamula for a total of four years over the period 1966 to 1990. The isolated small village of San Juan Chamula is no more. Between 1990 and 2020 it has been transformed into what looks like a small Mexican town of perhaps 2,000 people. It remains, even in its transformed state, a highly self-conscious identity as an Indian community.

3. Variants of this narrative differ on many details, especially whether the ascent of the Sun/Christ to the zenith of the sky occurs on the third or fourth primeval day.

4. Victor Turner, *The Drums of Affliction: A Study of the Religious Processes Among the Ndemdu of Zambia* (Oxford: Clarendon Press and the International African Institute, 1968), 23.

5. Ibid., 6–7.

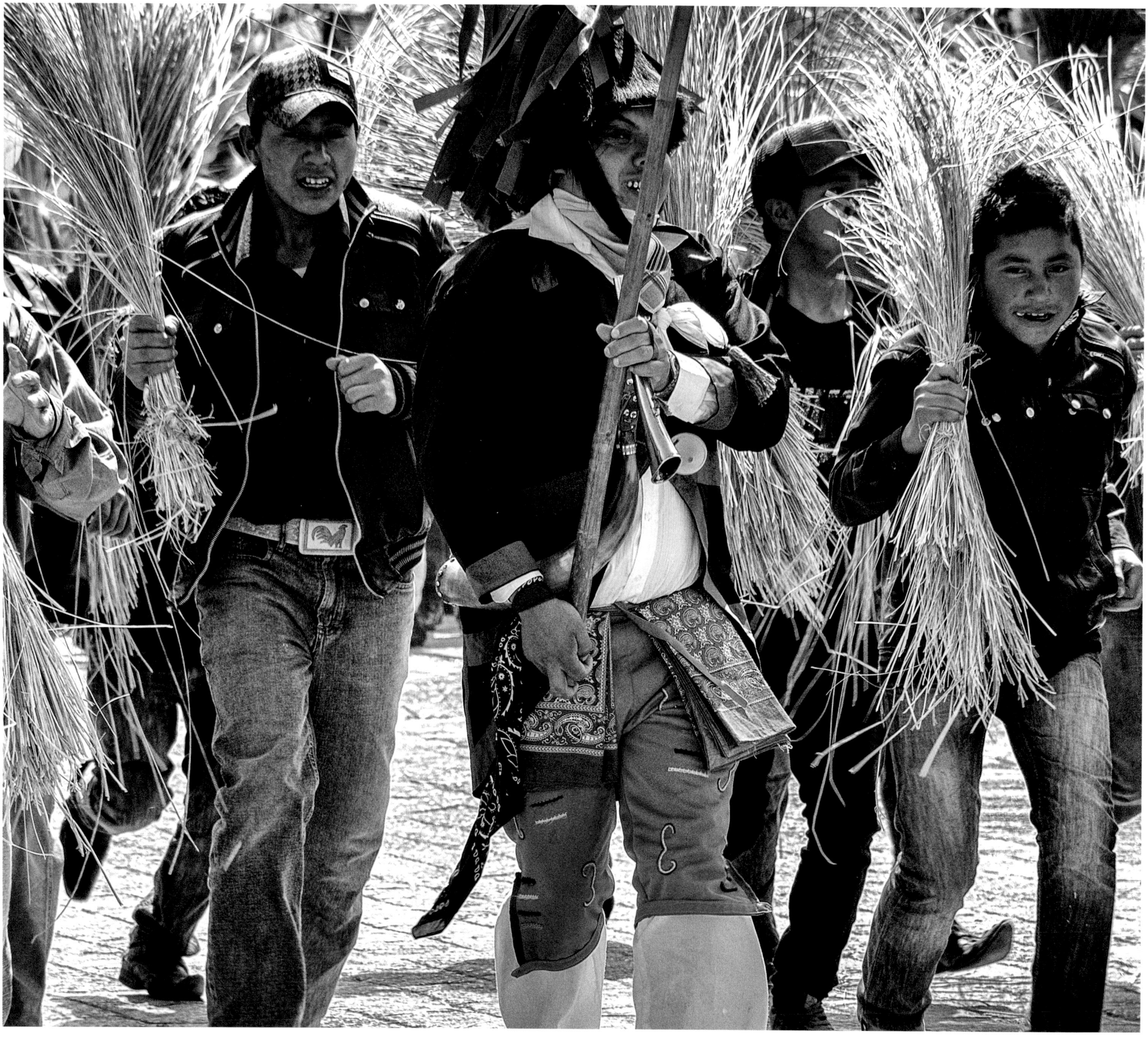

Festival of Games

January/February
San Juan Chamula, Chiapas, Mexico

The Festival of Games in San Juan Chamula takes place over a five-day period coinciding with Carnival, the days leading up to Lent in the Christian calendar. This spectacle, which involves thousands of participants and onlookers, is the most expensive and labor-intensive of all the events celebrated in the community throughout the year. The festival tells the story of the five primeval days of the First Creation: four days of chaos that culminate in a Firewalk over burning grass on the fourth day, symbolizing the ascent of the Sun/Christ, followed by the first day of Lent.

Preparations for the festival begin on the Feast of San Sebastián on January 20. In the subsequent weeks leading up to the festival, there are many ritual activities such as gathering wood at night (considered to be the time of pre-cultural chaos), preparing meals with symbolic importance, and gathering flowers and pine needles in the countryside. On Monday and Tuesday before the festival, bulls are lassoed and taken to the ceremonial center of the town for sacrifice. On Friday, hundreds of gallons of sweet gruel and thousands of bean tamales are prepared and distributed.

The Dance of the Warriors takes place on Saturday, the first day of the Festival of Games. Hundreds of men participate in this performance, which continues throughout the next four days. On Sunday, the activities intensify with the arrival of more outside visitors and vendors for the weekly market. Events reach a crescendo on Tuesday, a day that begins with torch and lamplight processions to hilltop shrines After hearing skyrockets and hand cannons just after dawn, masses of people descend from the hills into the town, running and shouting as they recreate a symbolic invasion. At noon, a mock battle between Mexico and Guatemala takes place. Afterward groups of boys and men collect dried grass and carry it into the town center, where it is spread into a path and ignited. Key officials run back and forth over the flames and coals in a dramatization of the first ascent of the Sun/Christ into the heavens, which vanquishes the evil forces of the universe. The final day, Wednesday, is quieter by comparison and is devoted to rest, prayers, and household visits.

opposite: BOYS CARRYING THATCH TO THE CEREMONIAL CENTER, 2013

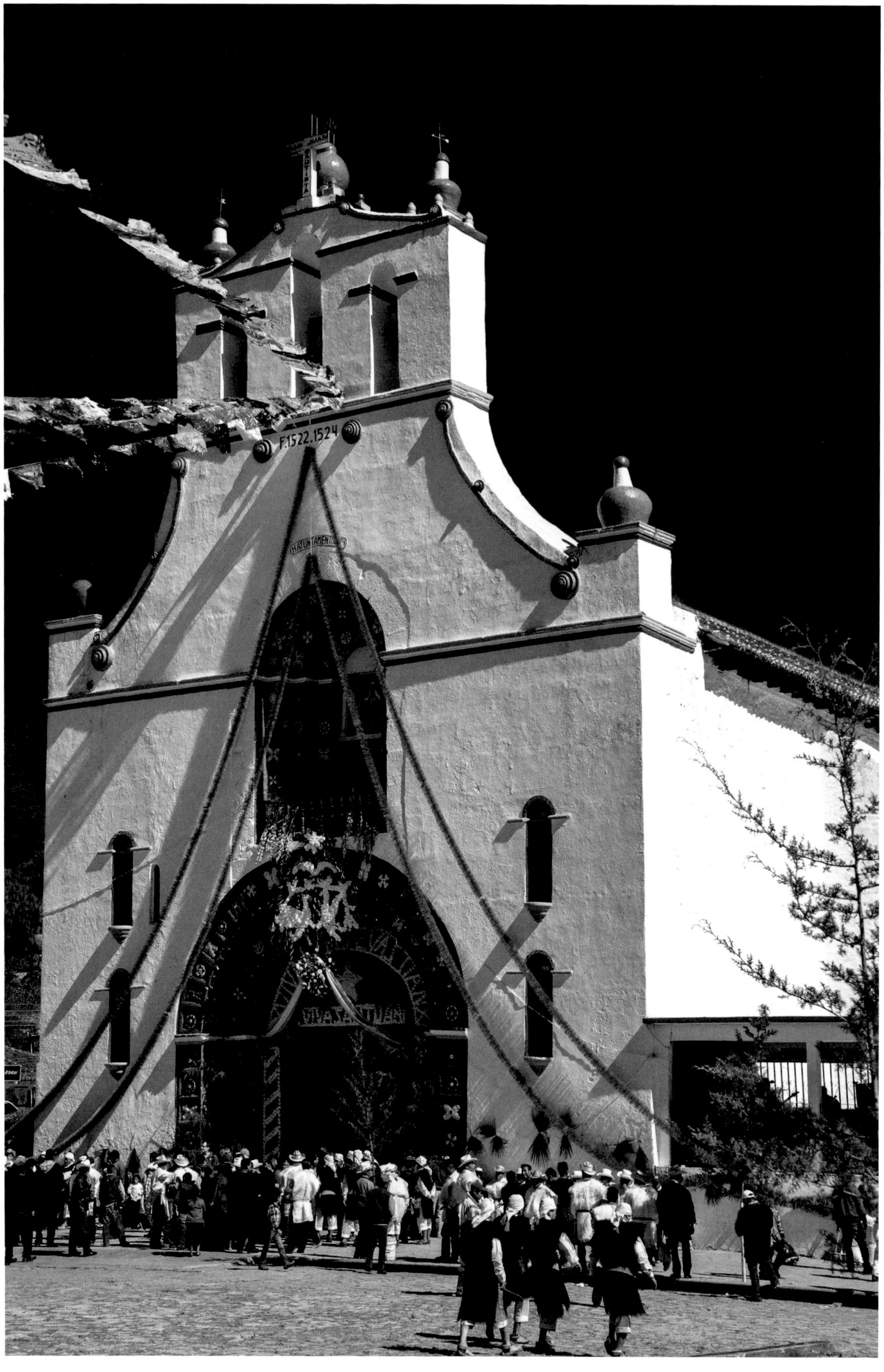

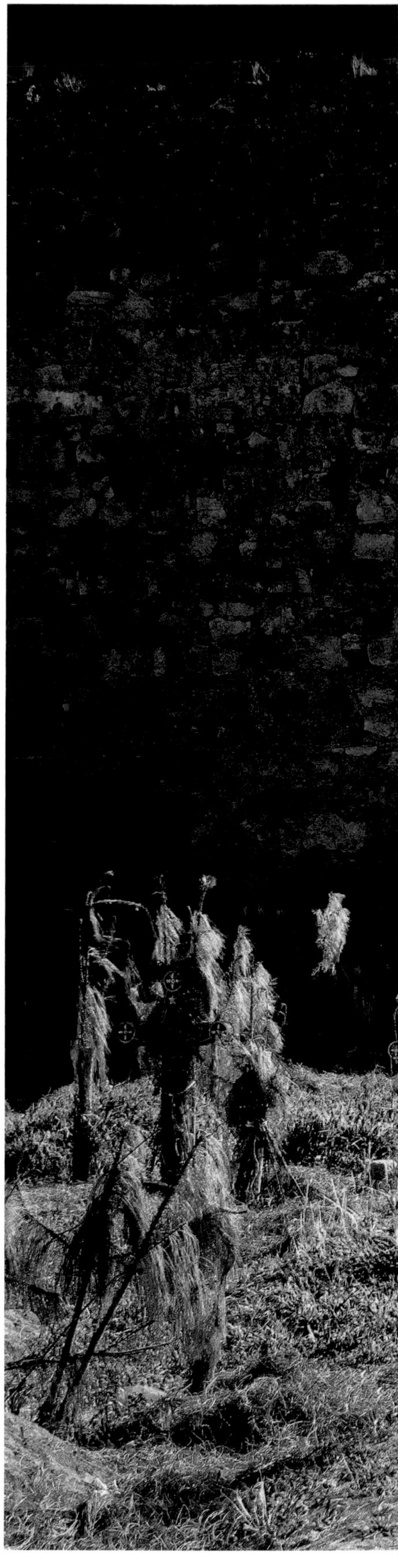

THE CHURCH OF
SAN JUAN BAUTISTA, 2015

opposite: THE CEMETERY OF
SAN JUAN CHAMULA, 2015

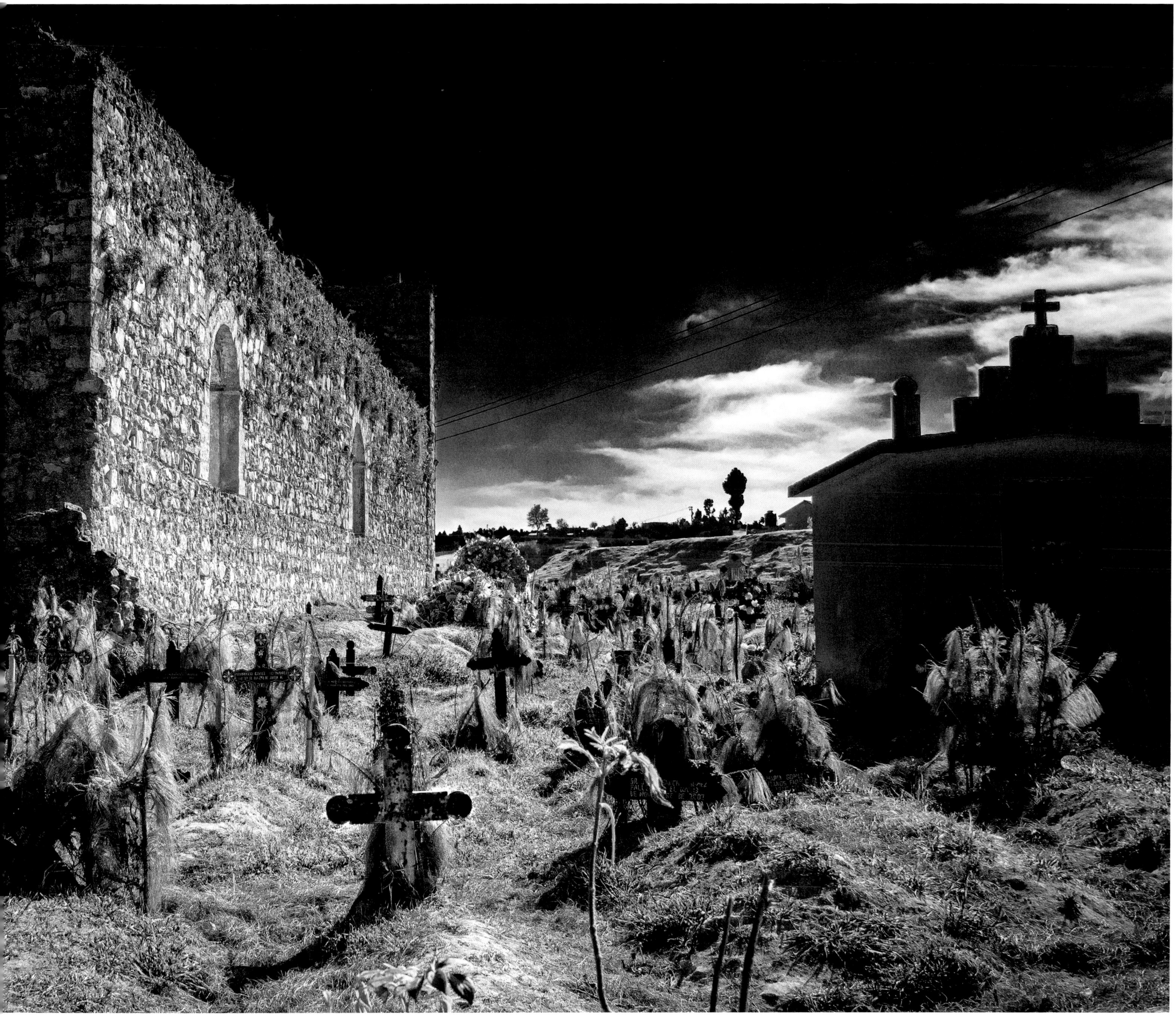

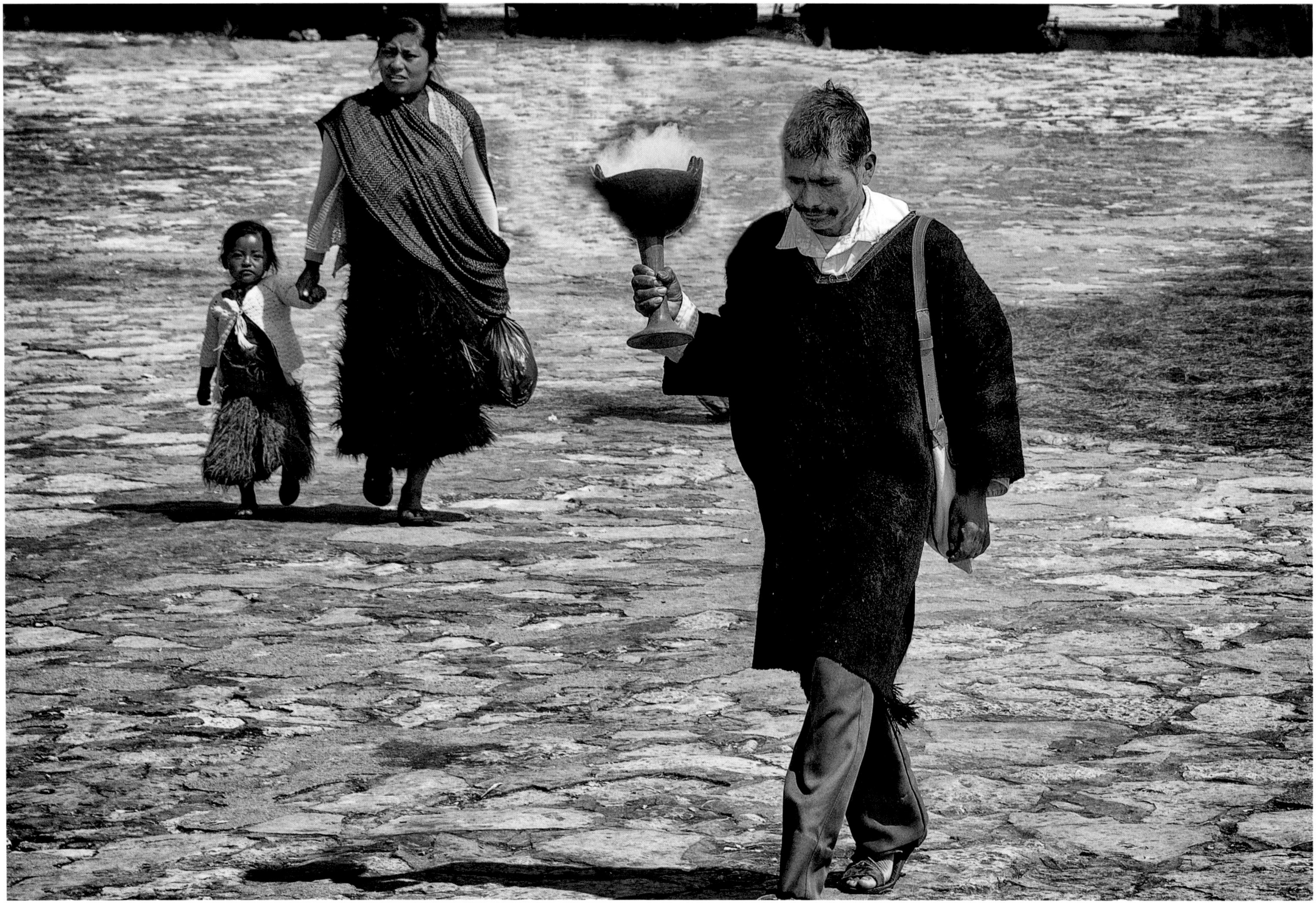

PREPARATIONS FOR THE FESTIVAL OF GAMES, 2015

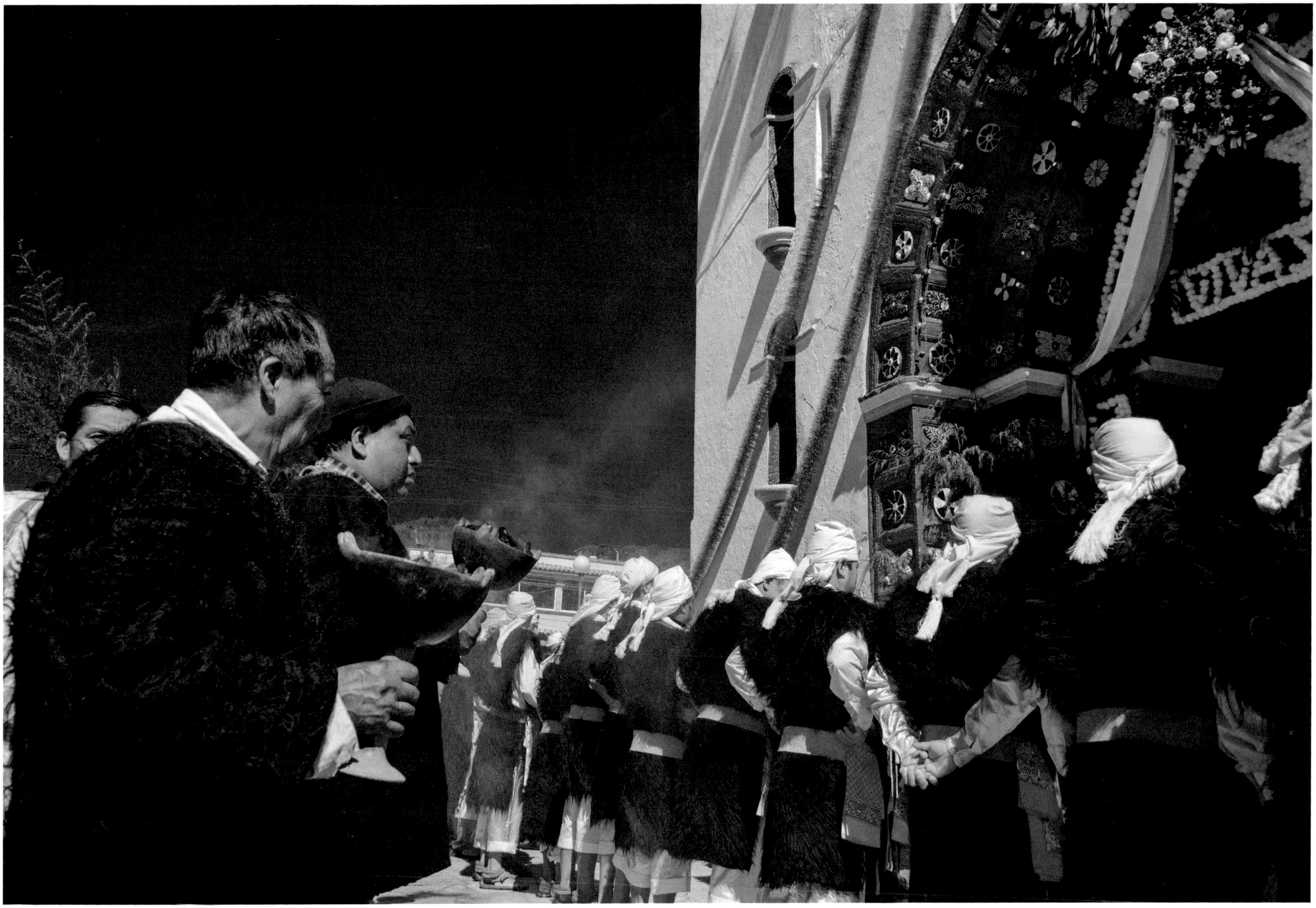

MEN FROM THE COFRADÍA OF SAN JUAN CHAMULA
PRAYING BEFORE ENTERING THE CHURCH, 2015

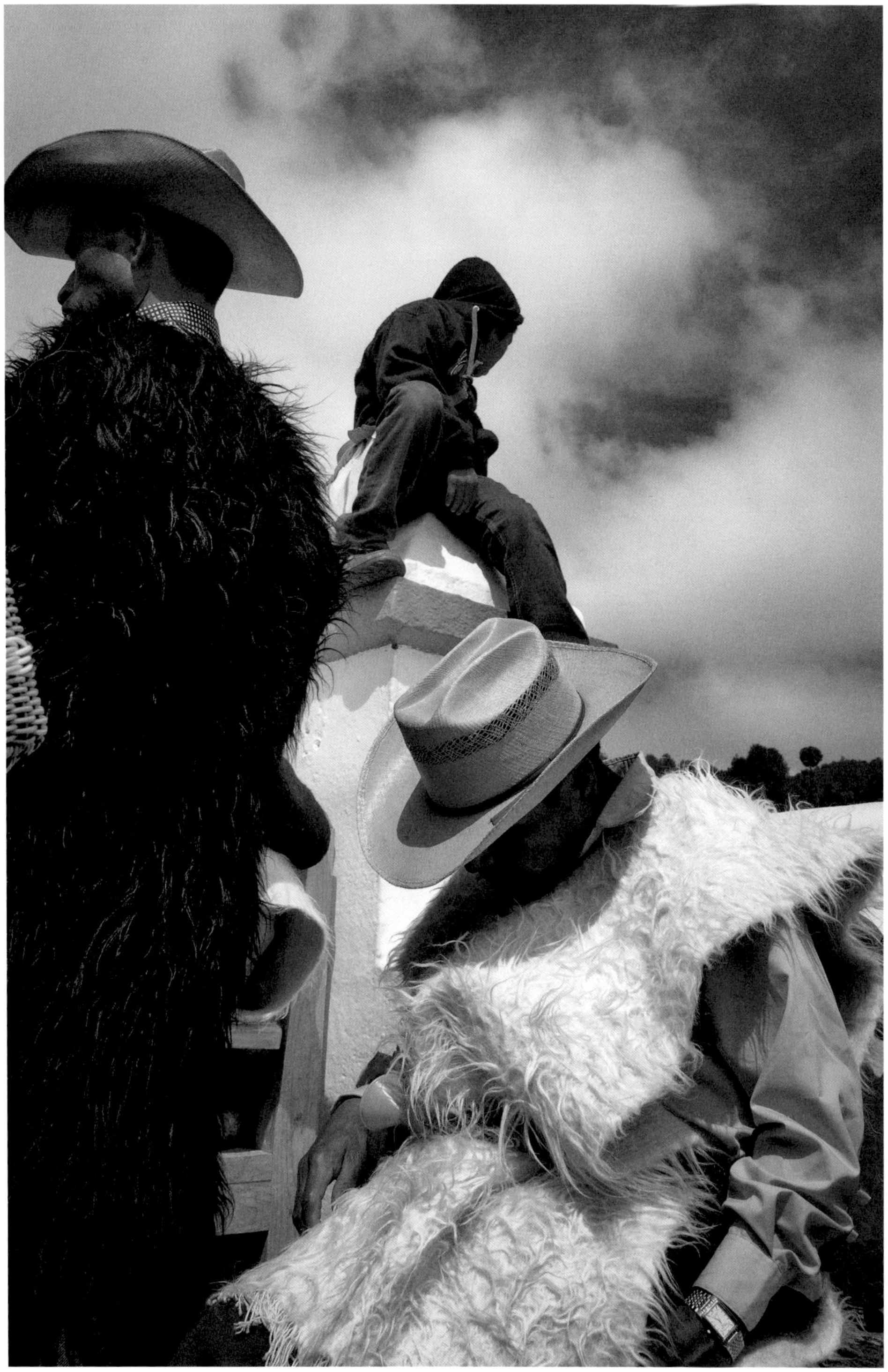

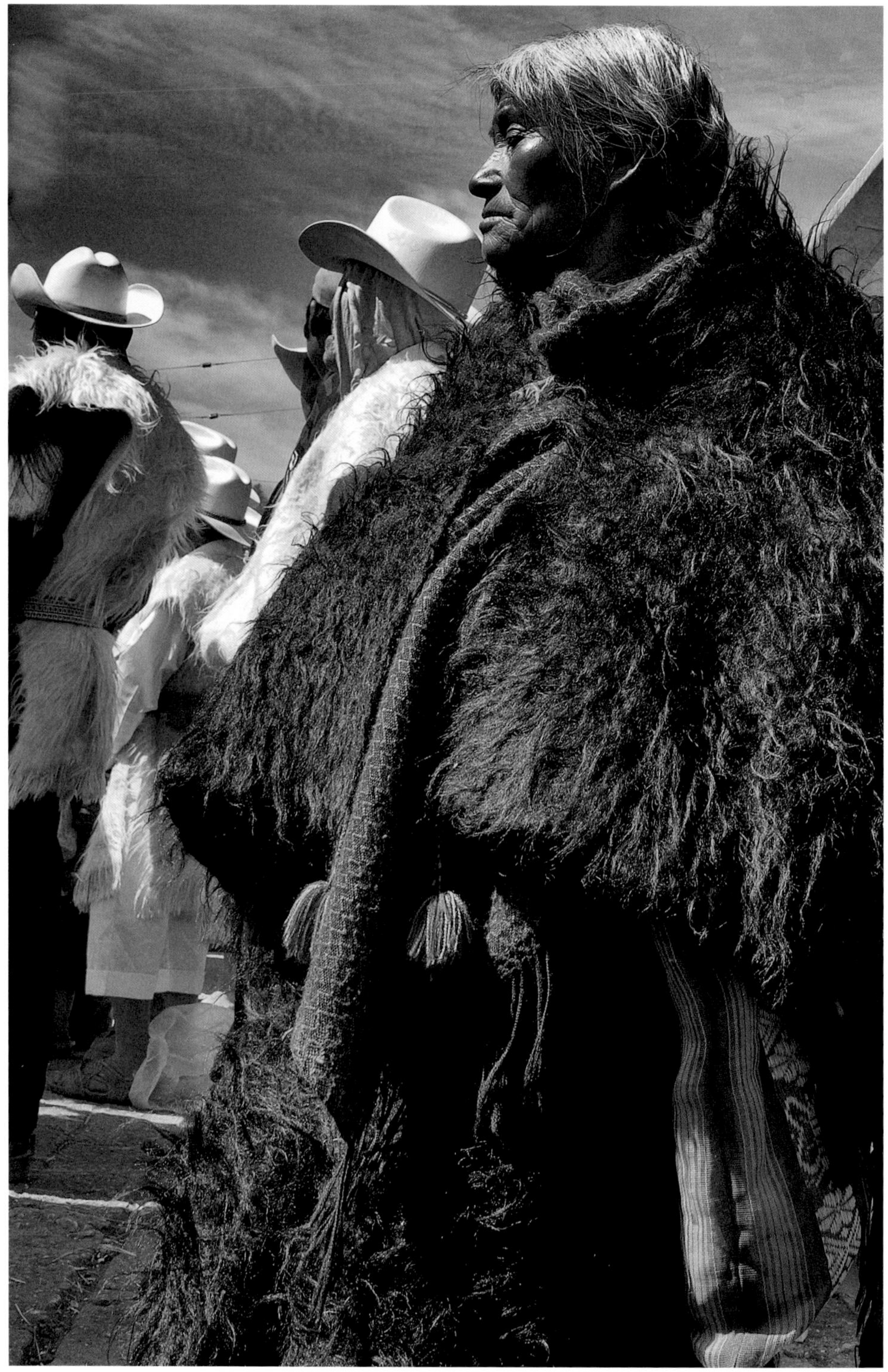

TSOTSIL MAYA PEOPLE OF SAN JUAN CHAMULA, 2013

opposite: A MAYA MAN, 2013

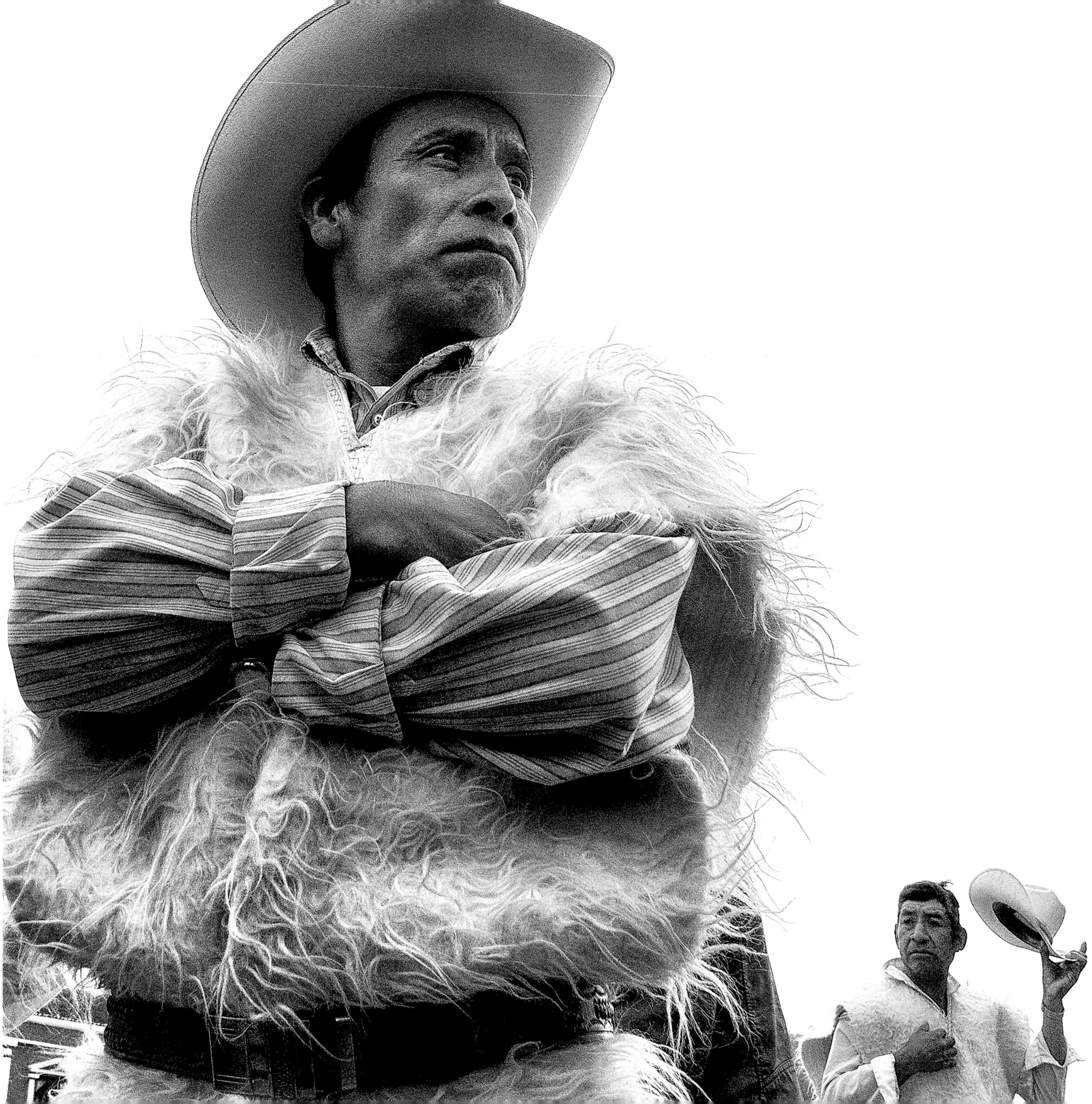

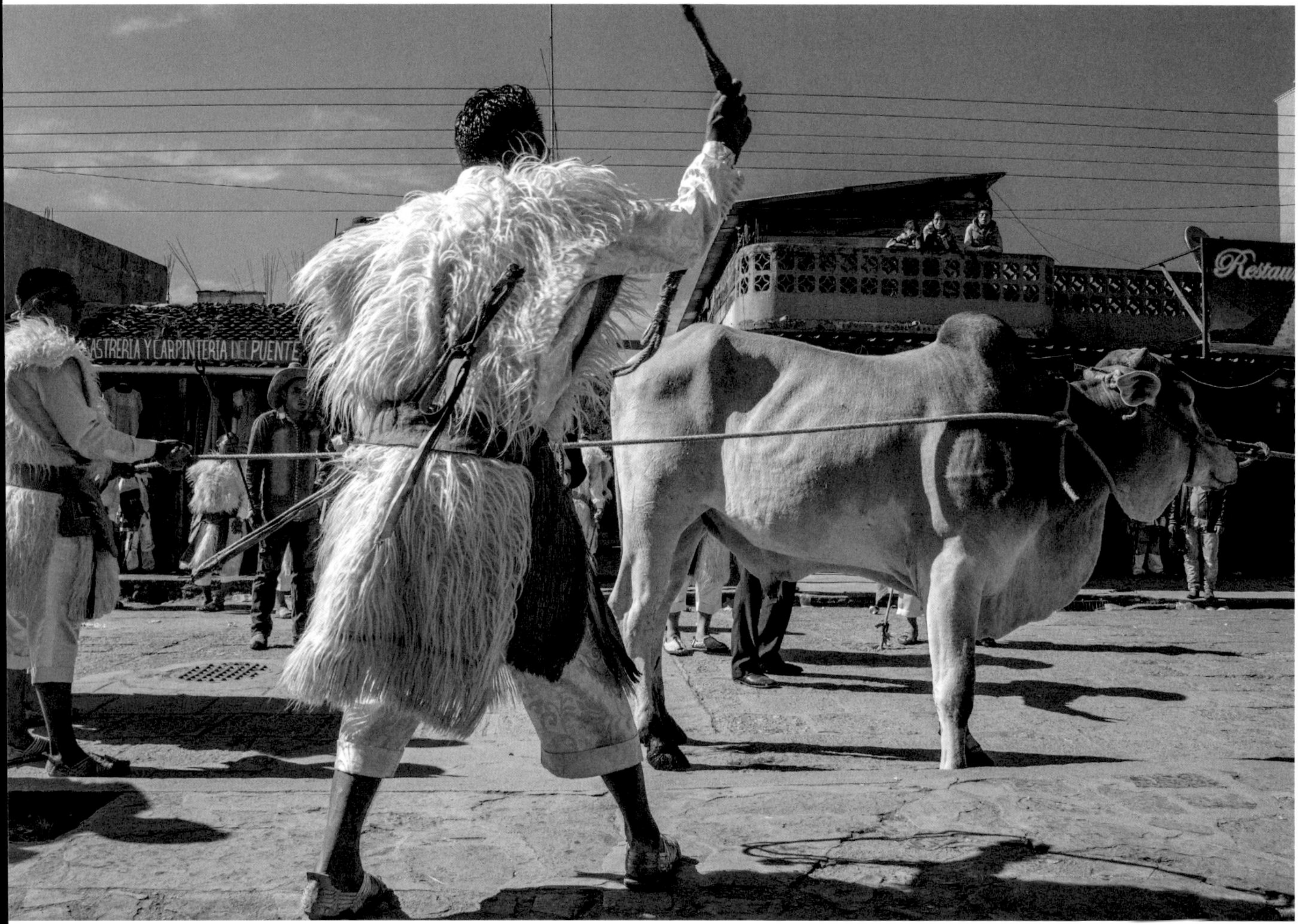

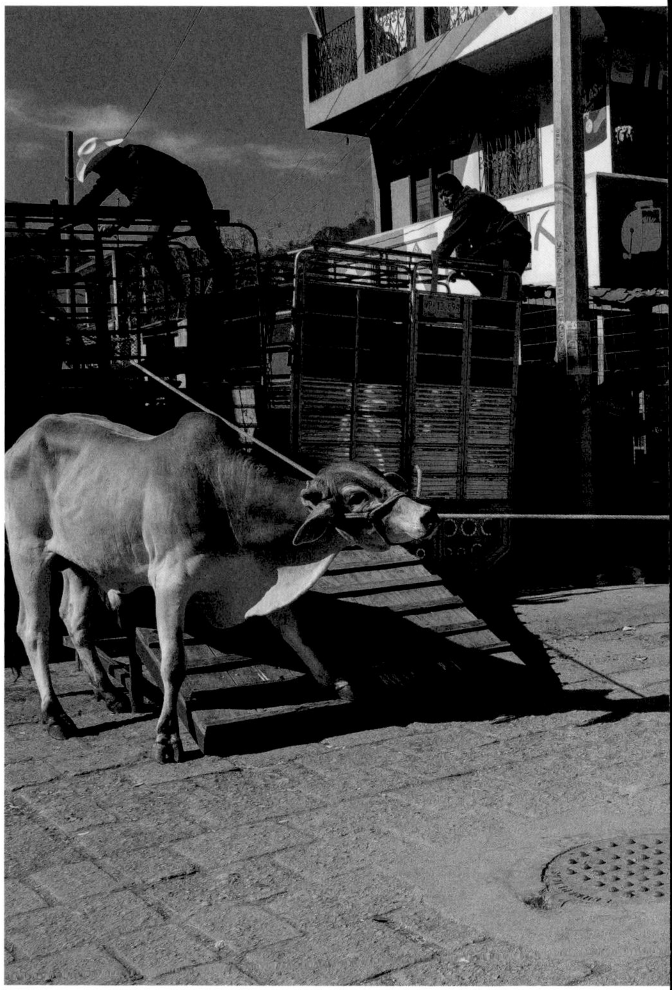

BULL-PULLING MONDAY, 2013

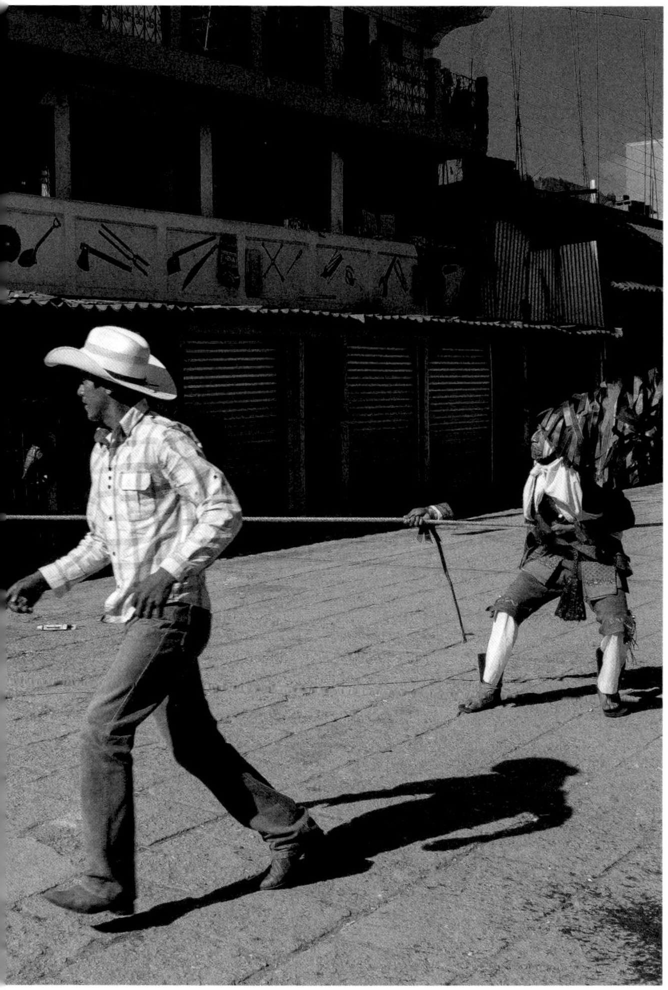

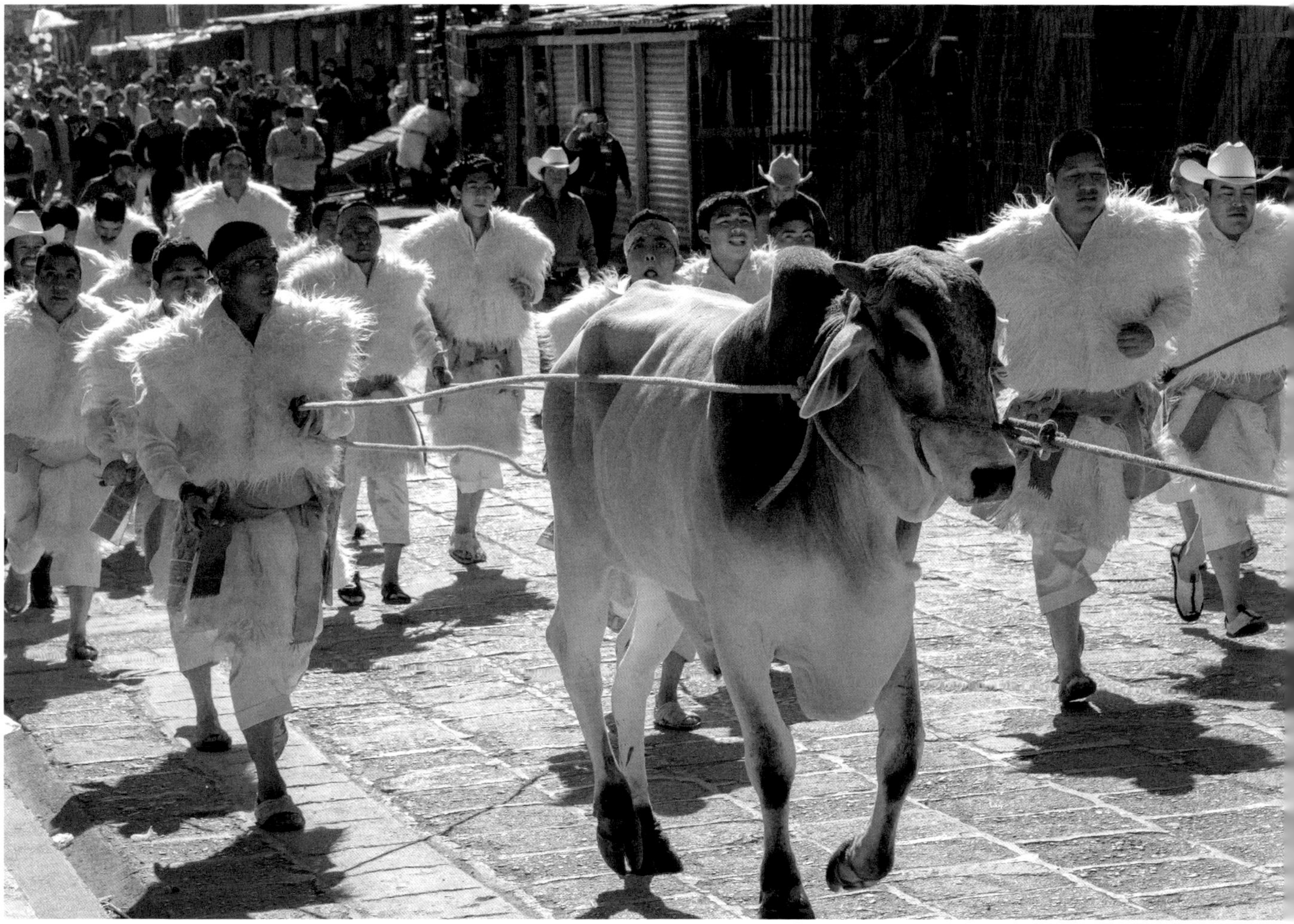

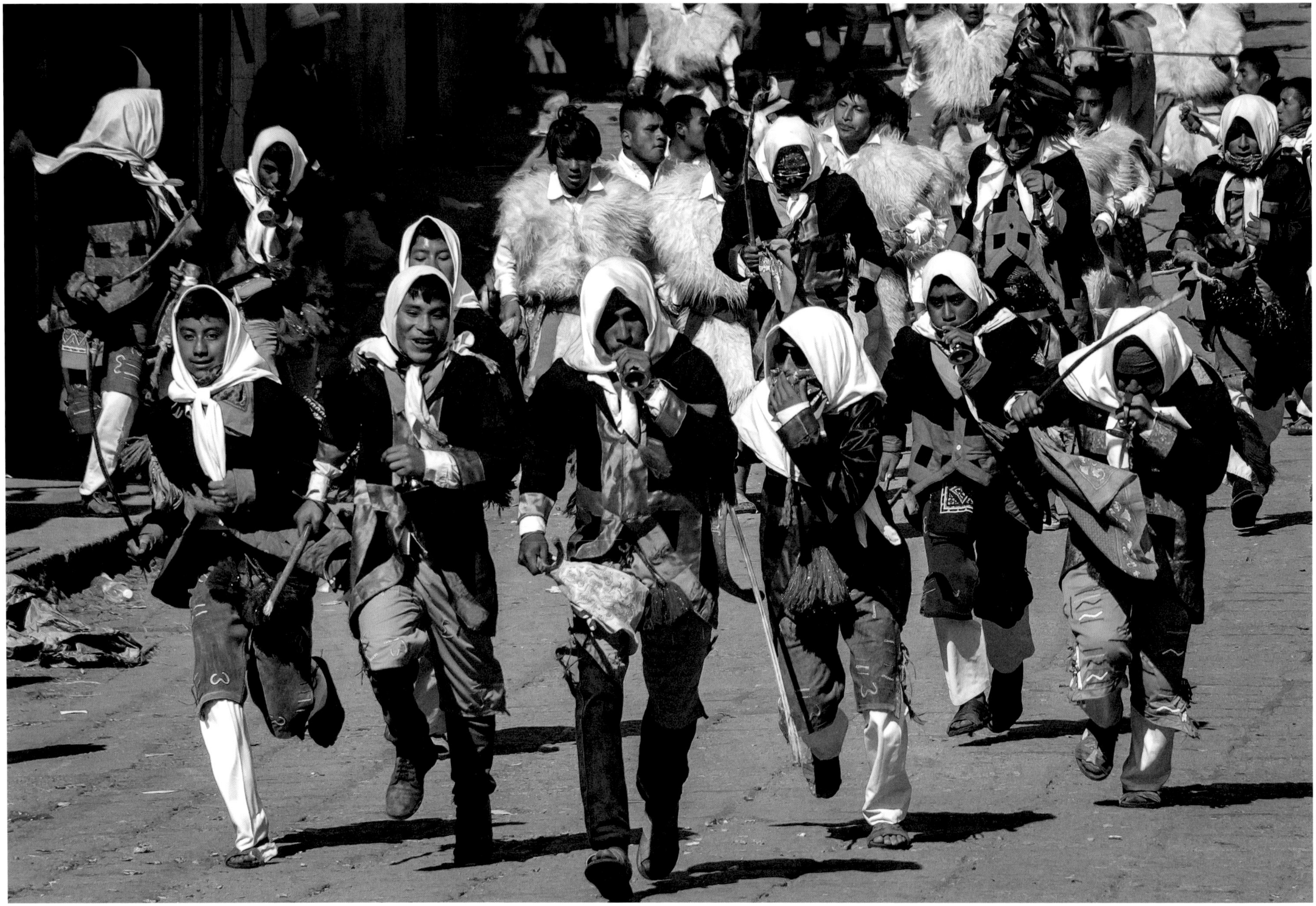

THE FESTIVAL OF GAMES, 2013

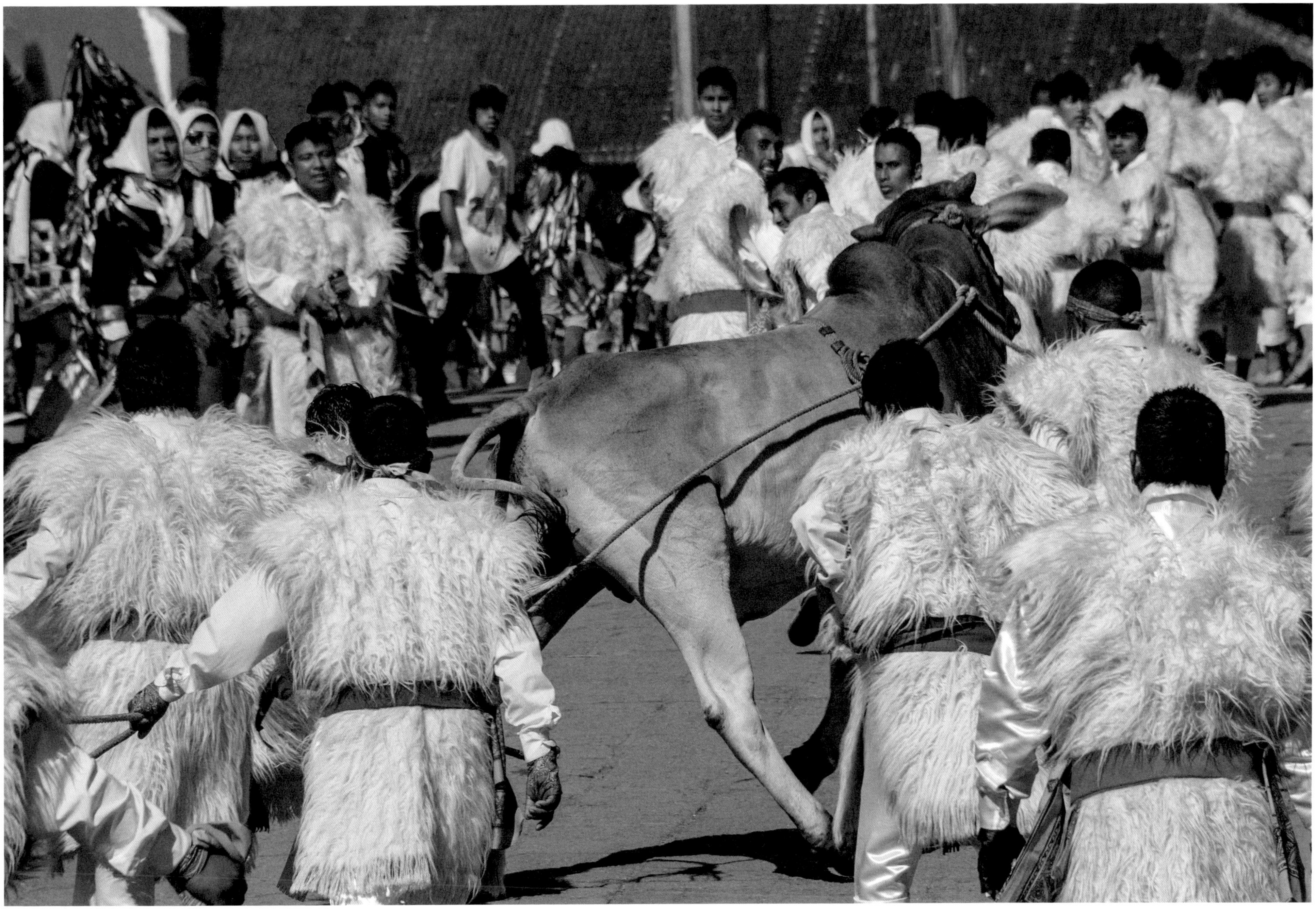

PREPARING FOR THE KILLING OF THE BULL, 2013

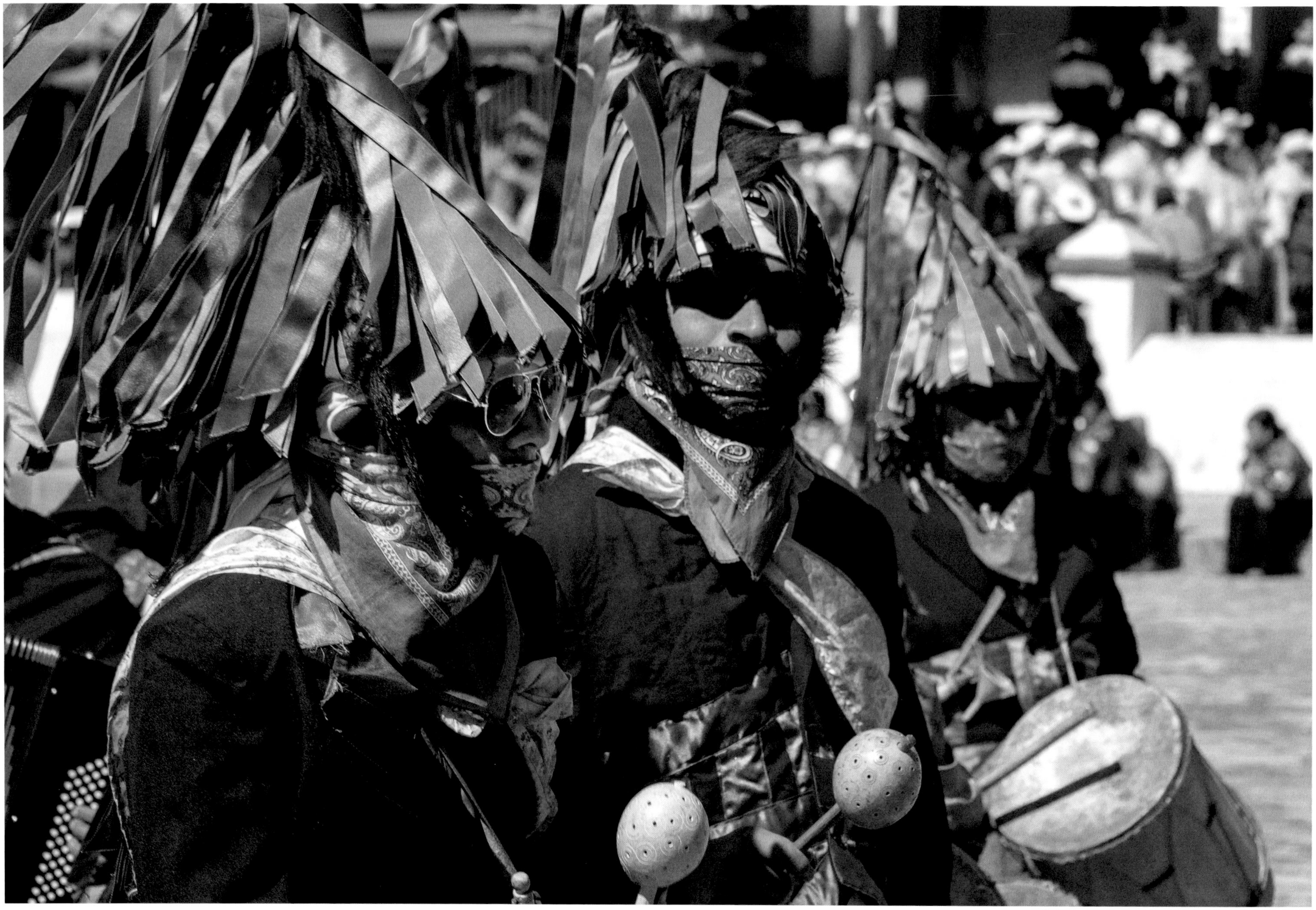

MUSICIANS AT THE FESTIVAL OF GAMES, 2013

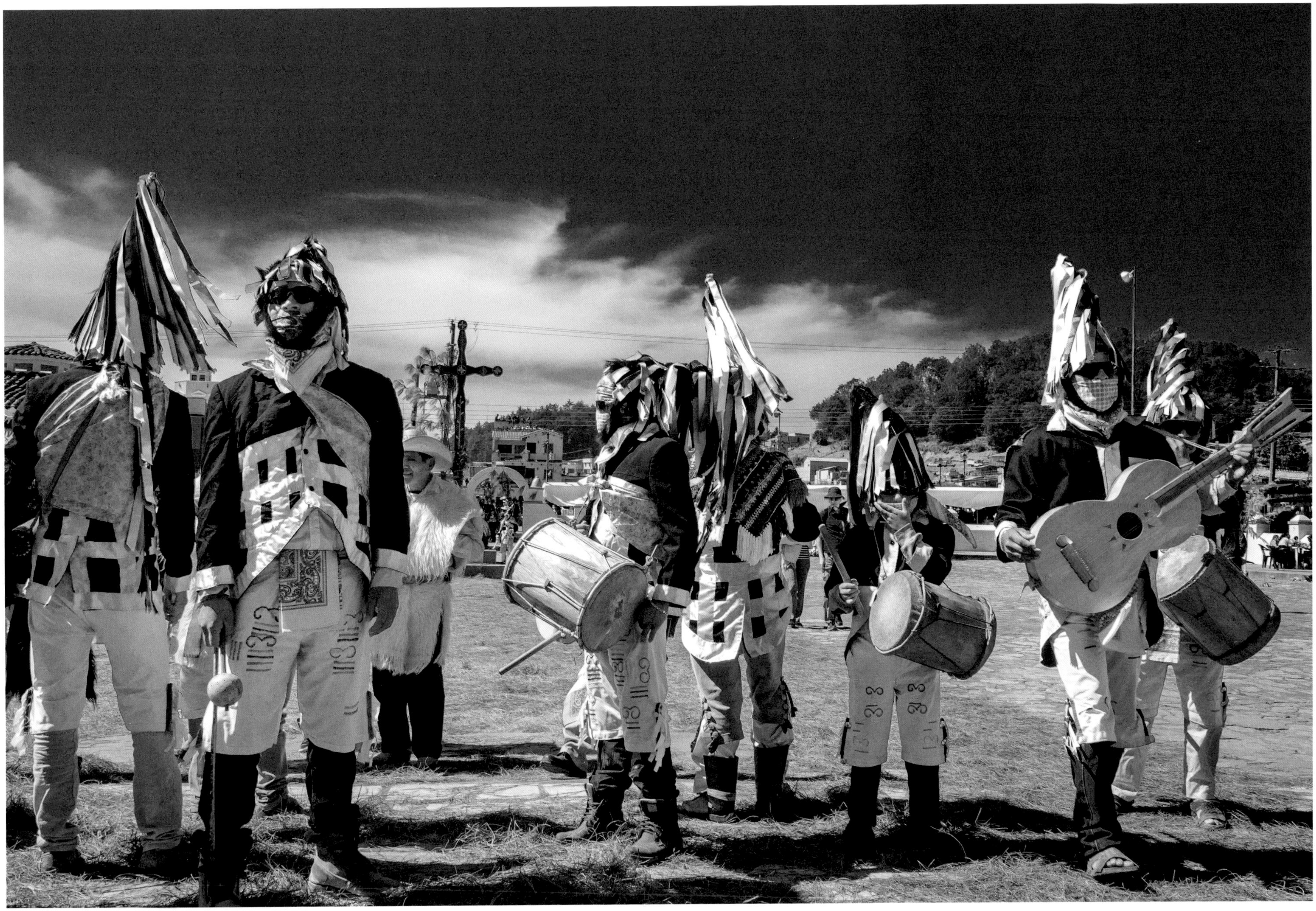

SIX MUSICIANS OFFERING A RUNNING NARRATIVE, 2013

Spring

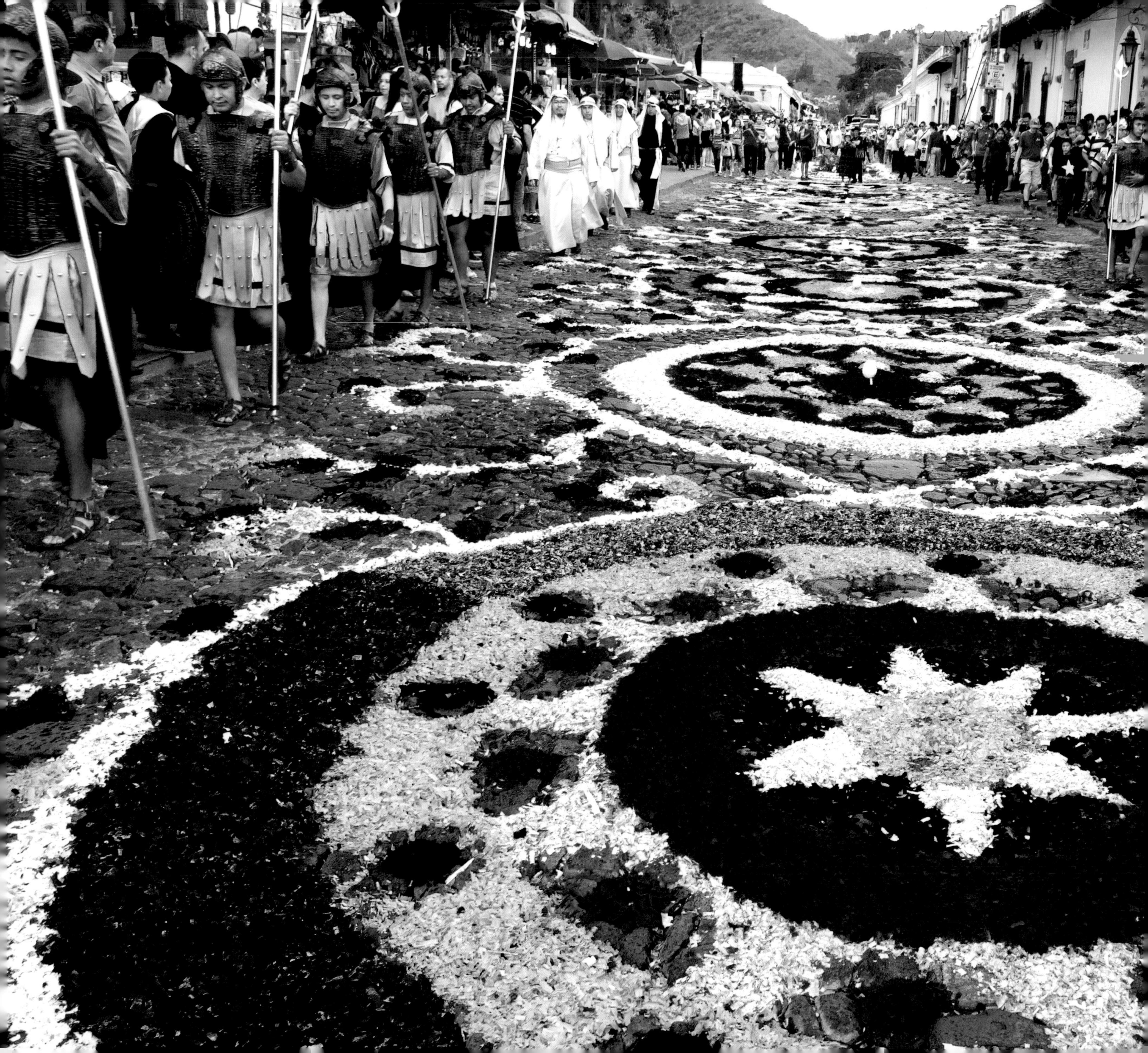

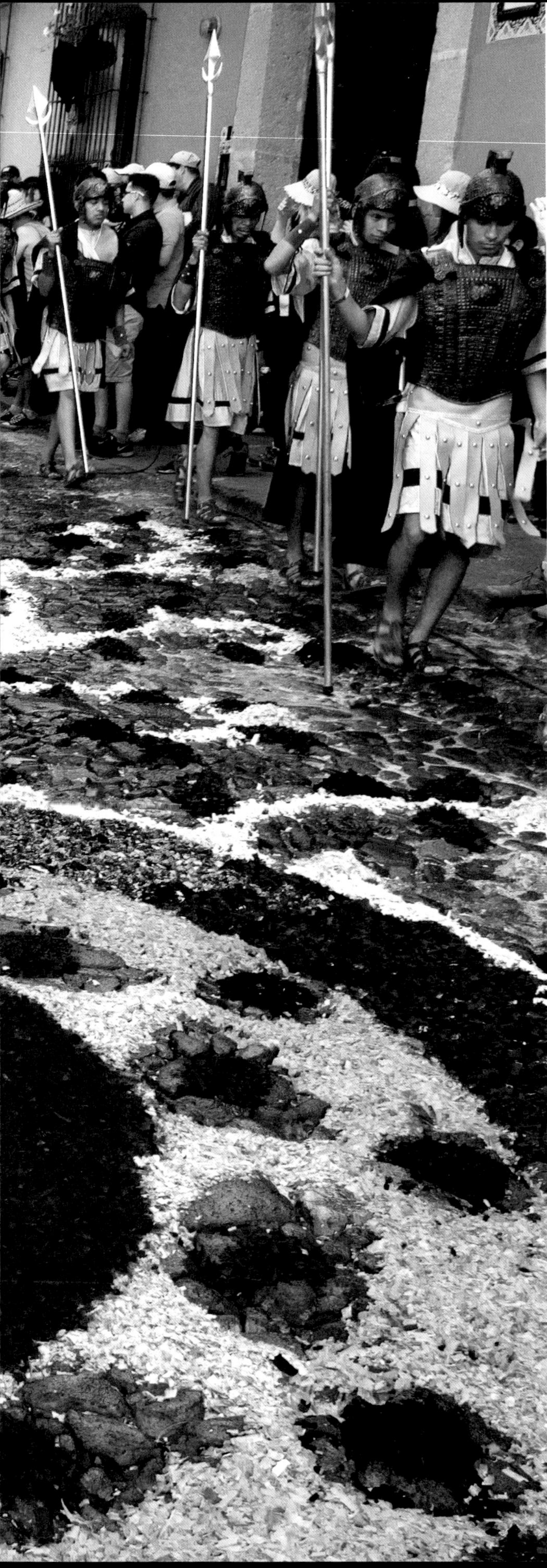

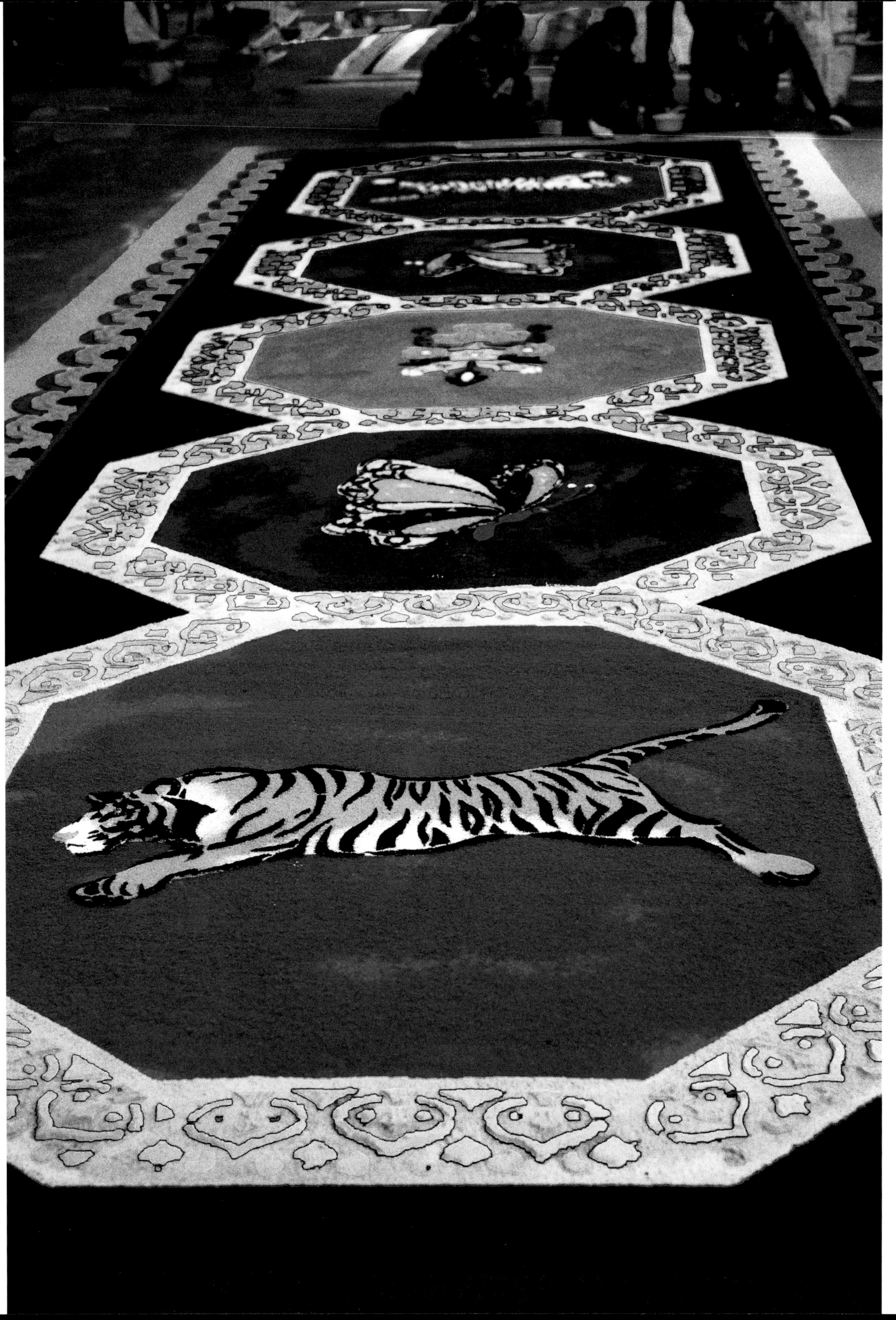

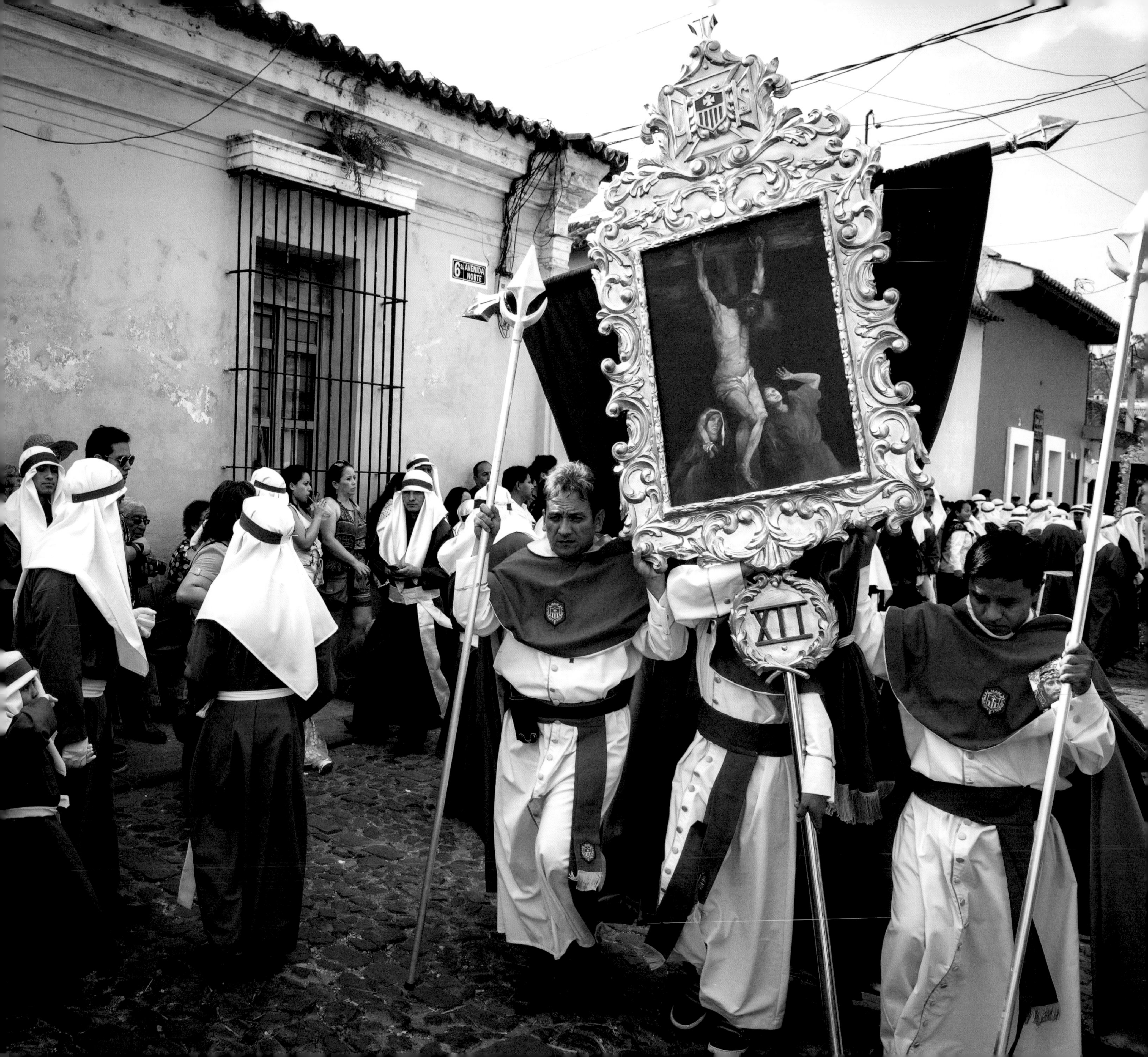
6a. AVENIDA NORTE
XIII

Semana Santa

March/April
Antigua, Sacatepéquez, Guatemala

Semana Santa, or Holy Week, is a major week-long ceremony celebrated throughout Guatemala and Mexico during the week before Easter. In Antigua, Guatemala, thousands of people participate in religious activities, processions, and the creation of colorful *alfombras*—rectangular carpets made of flowers, pine needles, sawdust, and other natural materials placed on the streets of the city. Although they are a fleeting sacred art form destined to be destroyed by the processions that walk over them, they are carefully designed and assembled by groups of family and friends on the section of the street in front of their homes or businesses.

The Spanish brought Holy Week to Guatemala in the early 1500s. While these celebrations are undertaken within a Catholic framework, the Maya incorporated Indigenous religious beliefs and symbols into the Catholic rituals. This syncretism can be seen in a variety of examples during Semana Santa in Antigua. The alfombras on streets and inside churches often display pre-Hispanic Maya iconography. The jaguar, considered the ruler of the Underworld in Maya mythology, symbolizes darkness. The butterfly is a symbol of the god Hanab Ku, who represents the consciousness of all living things and signifies life after death. The palanquins that carry the wooden statues of saints can be up to seventy feet long and require fifty to one hundred bearers who carry the weight on their arms and shoulders. The palanquins bear statues of Jesus, the Virgin Mary, Our Lady of Sorrows, and other wooden images of saints that date to the sixteenth and seventeenth centuries.

Holy Week ceremonies begin on Palm Sunday, which commemorates the entrance of Jesus into Jerusalem. Holy Thursday commemorates the Last Supper, the final night Jesus spent with his apostles before his crucifixion and death. In the churches of Antigua, priests wash the feet of twelve common people, stand-ins for the twelve apostles whose feet Jesus washed at the Last Supper.

On Good Friday, processions from La Merced Church begin in a more somber mood. Throughout Antigua black decorations replace the previously bright, colorful ones. The palanquin bearers now wear black robes to mourn Christ's crucifixion, and many palanquins depict scenes of Jesus carrying his cross. On Holy Saturday, more processions with palanquins, these carried by women, portray the mourning of Mary, the mother of Jesus. Late on Saturday evening, Antigua's faithful begin celebrating the resurrection of Jesus Christ. Easter Sunday itself is quiet, but an atmosphere of joy pervades the town.

previous spread, left: AN ENTIRE STREET COVERED WITH ALFOMBRAS MADE OF FLOWERS, SAWDUST, AND OTHER MATERIALS, 2017
right: JAGUARS AND BUTTERFLY MOTIFS ON AN OUTDOOR ALFOMBRA, 2017

opposite: HOLY WEEK PROCESSION ON HOLY WEDNESDAY, 2017

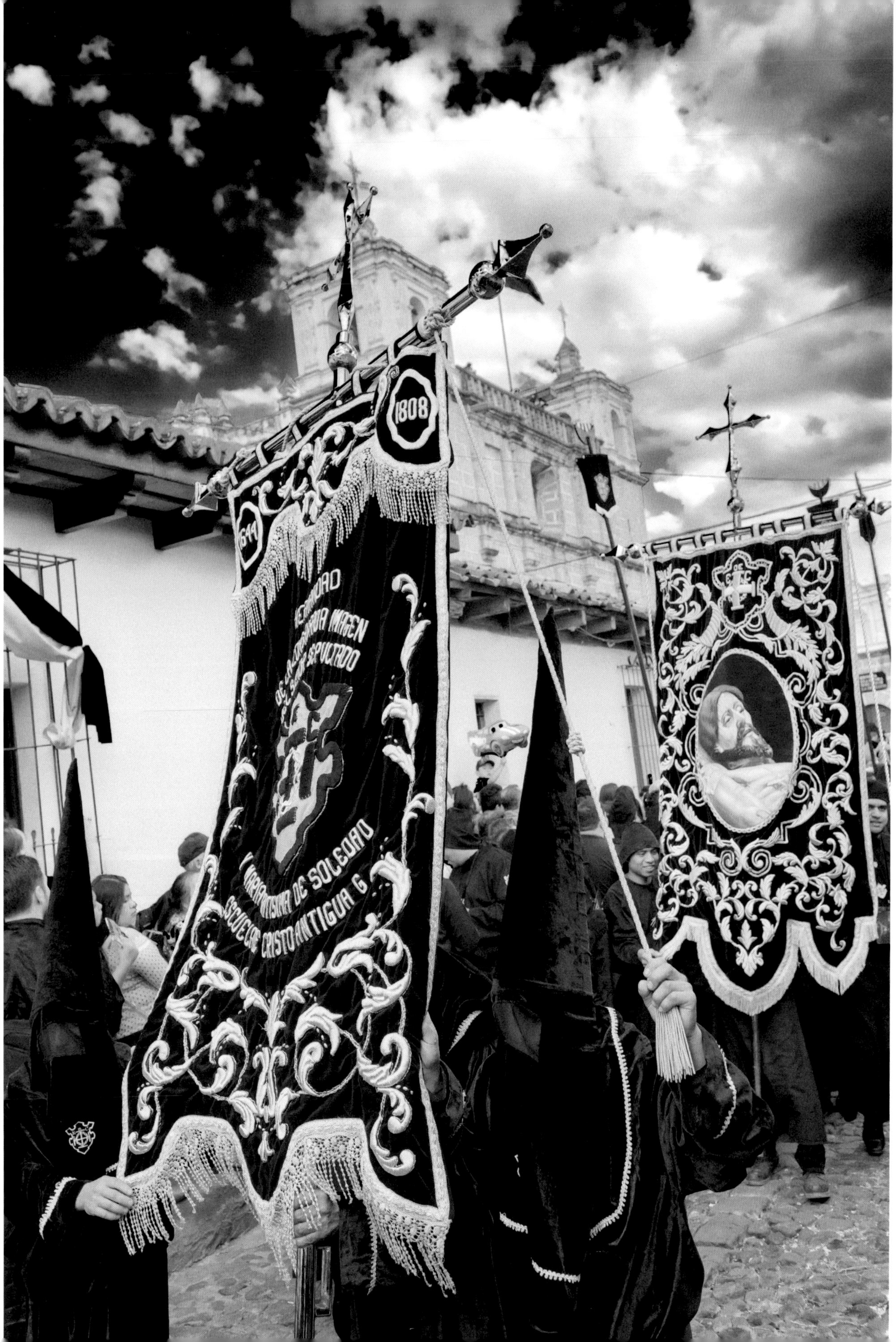

HOLY WEEK PROCESSION ON
HOLY WEDNESDAY, 2017

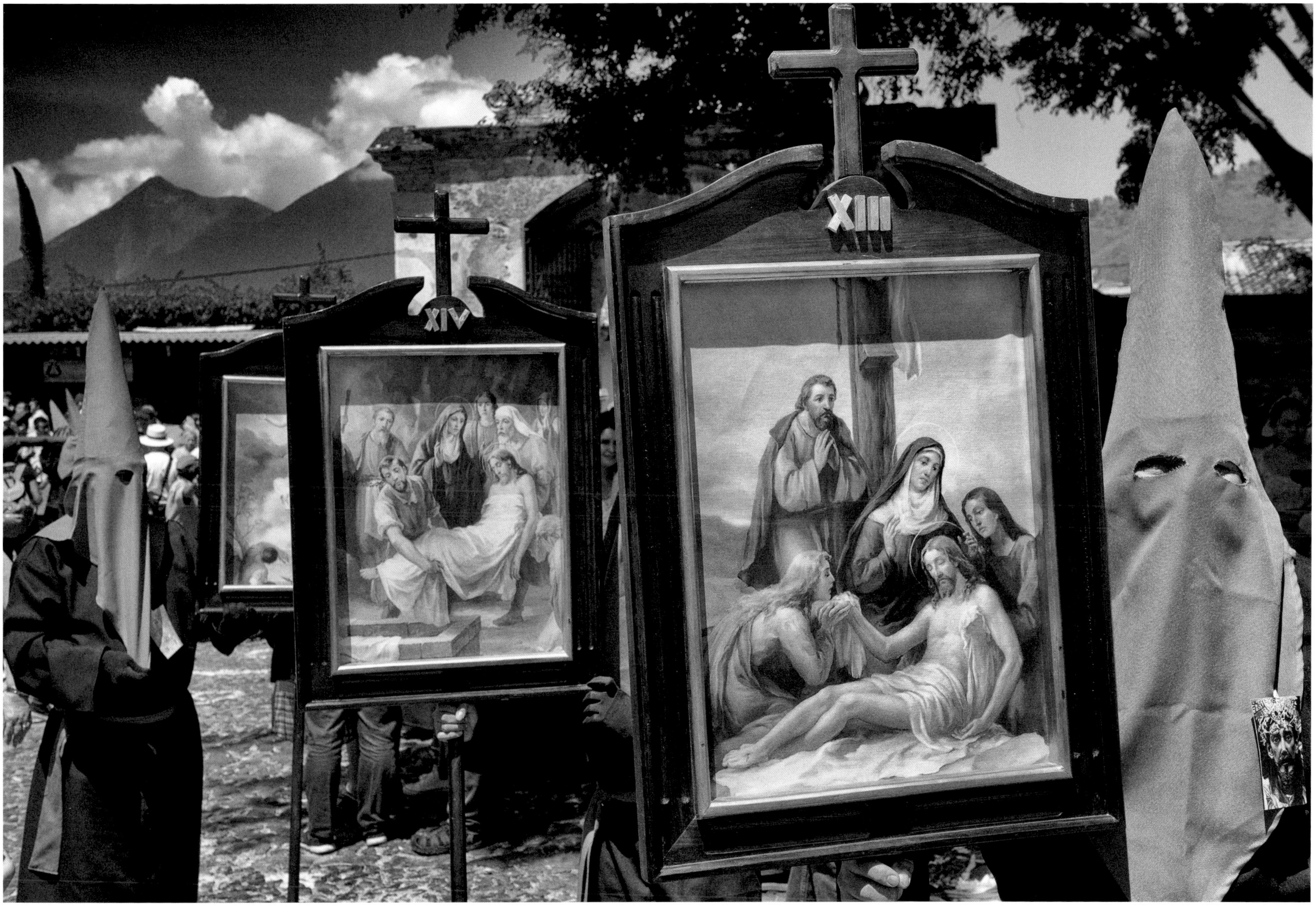

AT THE CHURCH OF SAN FRANCISCO EL GRANDE, 2017

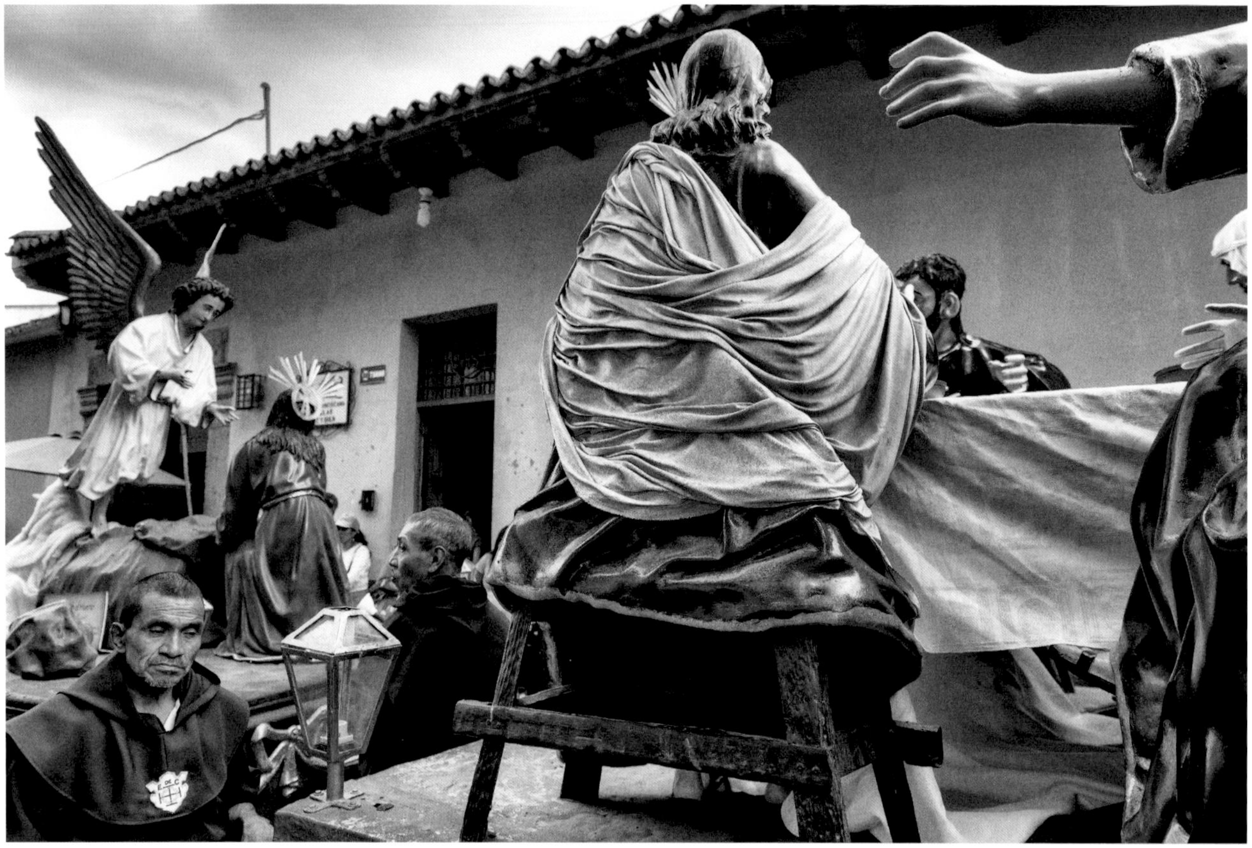

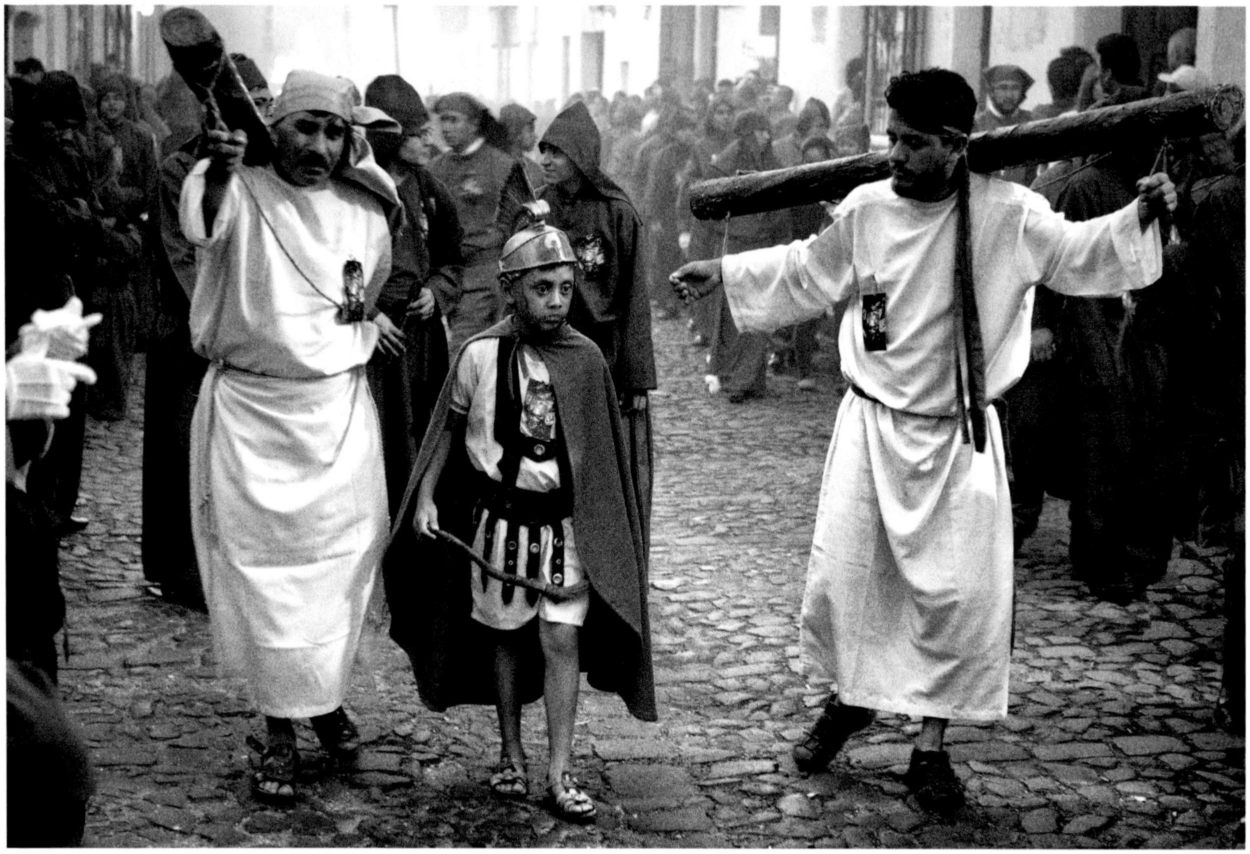

above: PREPARING A PALANQUIN FOR THE HOLY THURSDAY PROCESSION, 2017
below: PORTRAYAL OF THE SORROWFUL WAY TO CHRIST'S CRUCIFIXION ON GOOD FRIDAY, 2017

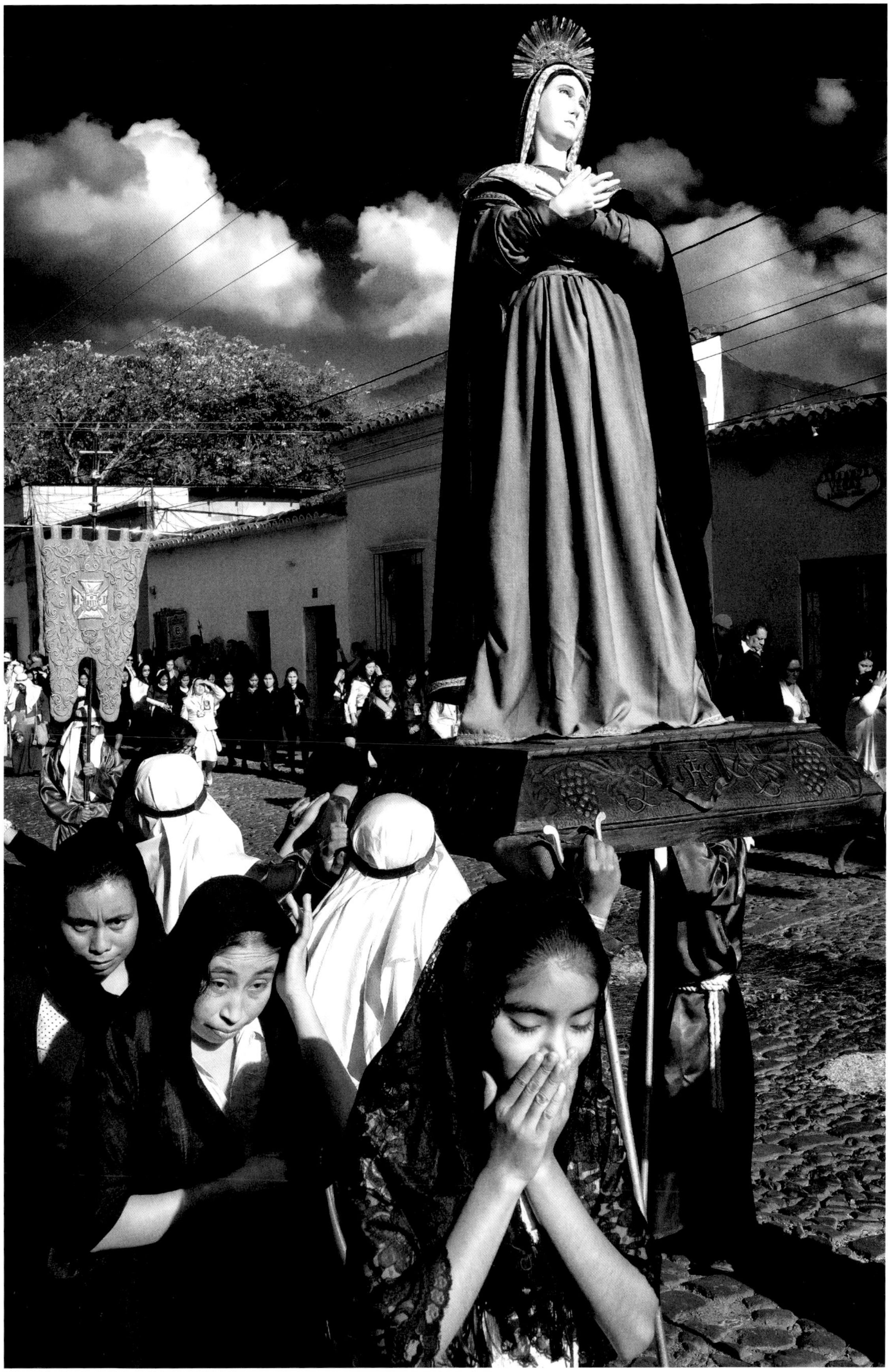

GOOD FRIDAY PROCESSION
OF WOMEN, 2017

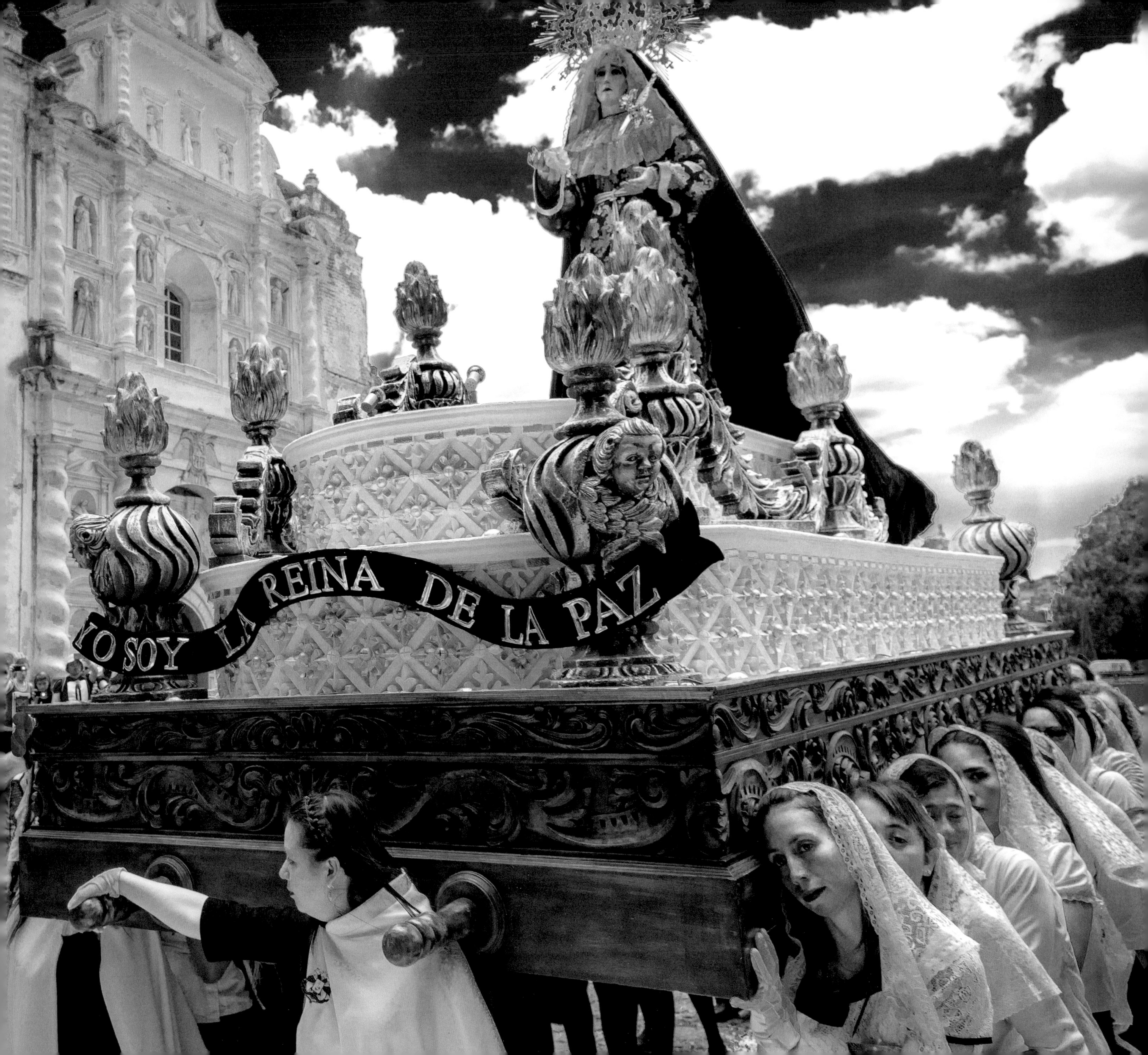
YO SOY LA REINA DE LA PAZ

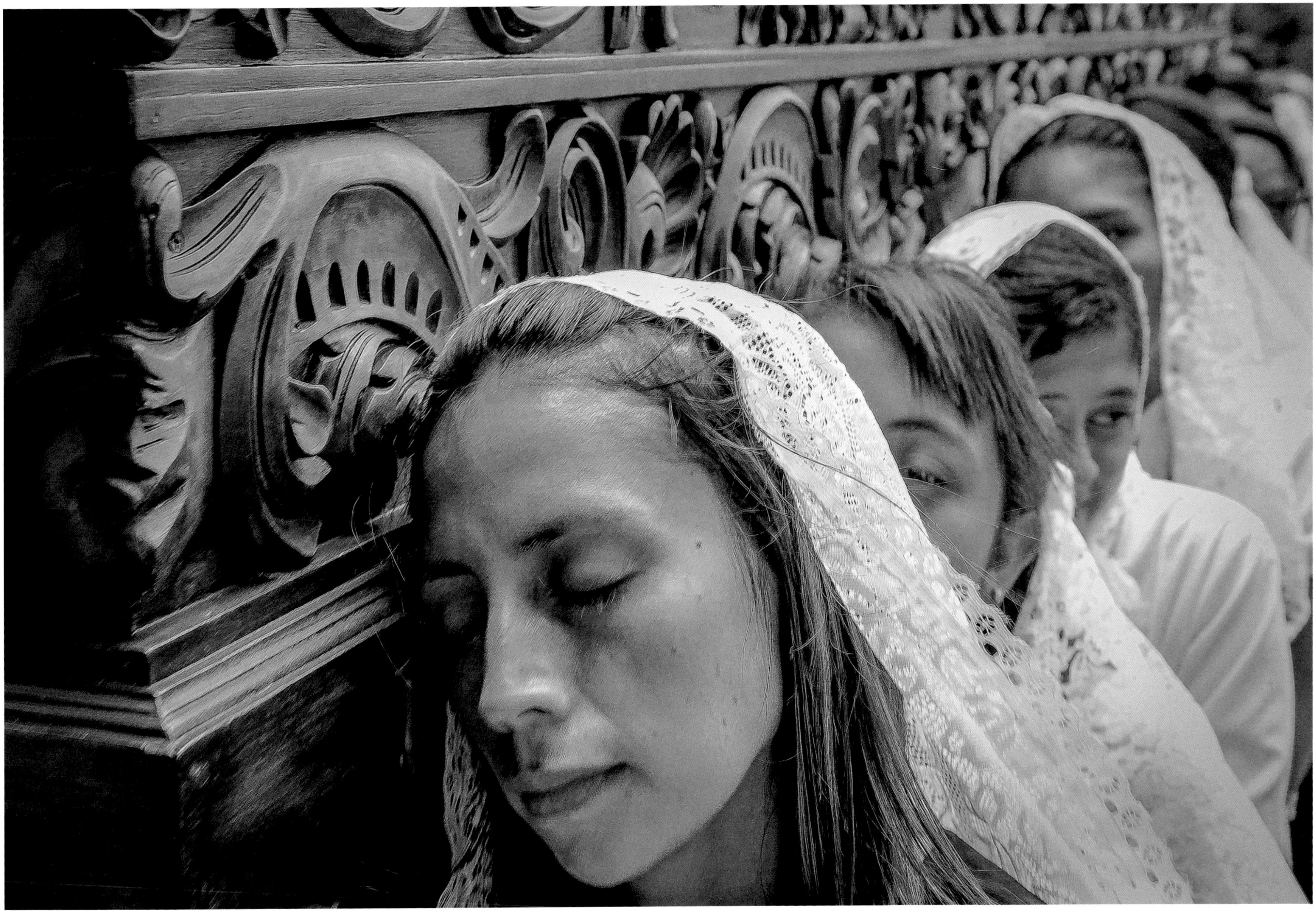

opposite: PROCESSION WITH OUR LADY QUEEN OF PEACE, 2017

PALANQUIN BEARERS FOR OUR LADY QUEEN OF PEACE, 2017

opposite and following spread: INCENSE AND SMOKE AT THE HOLY WEEK PROCESSION, 2017

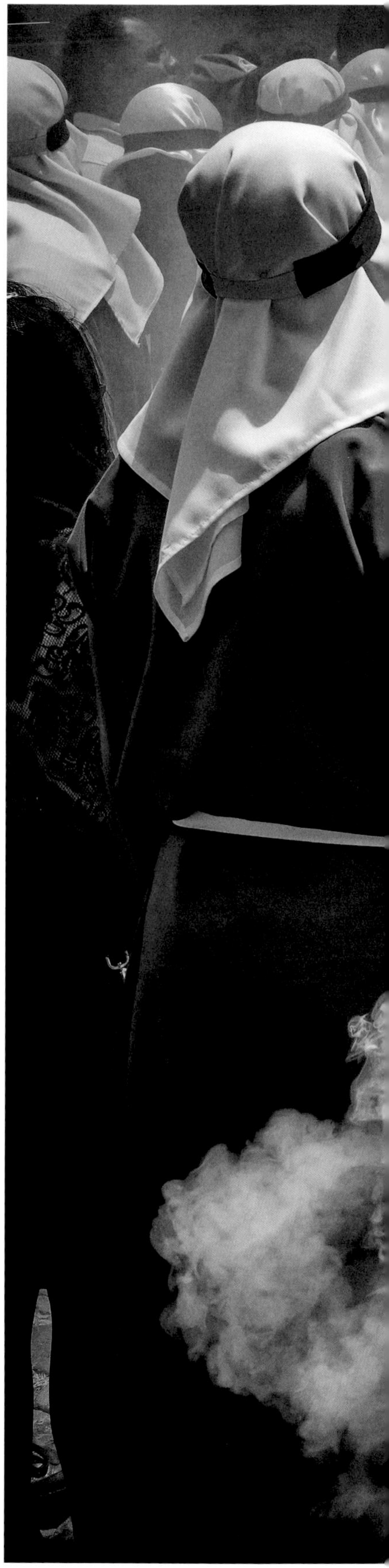

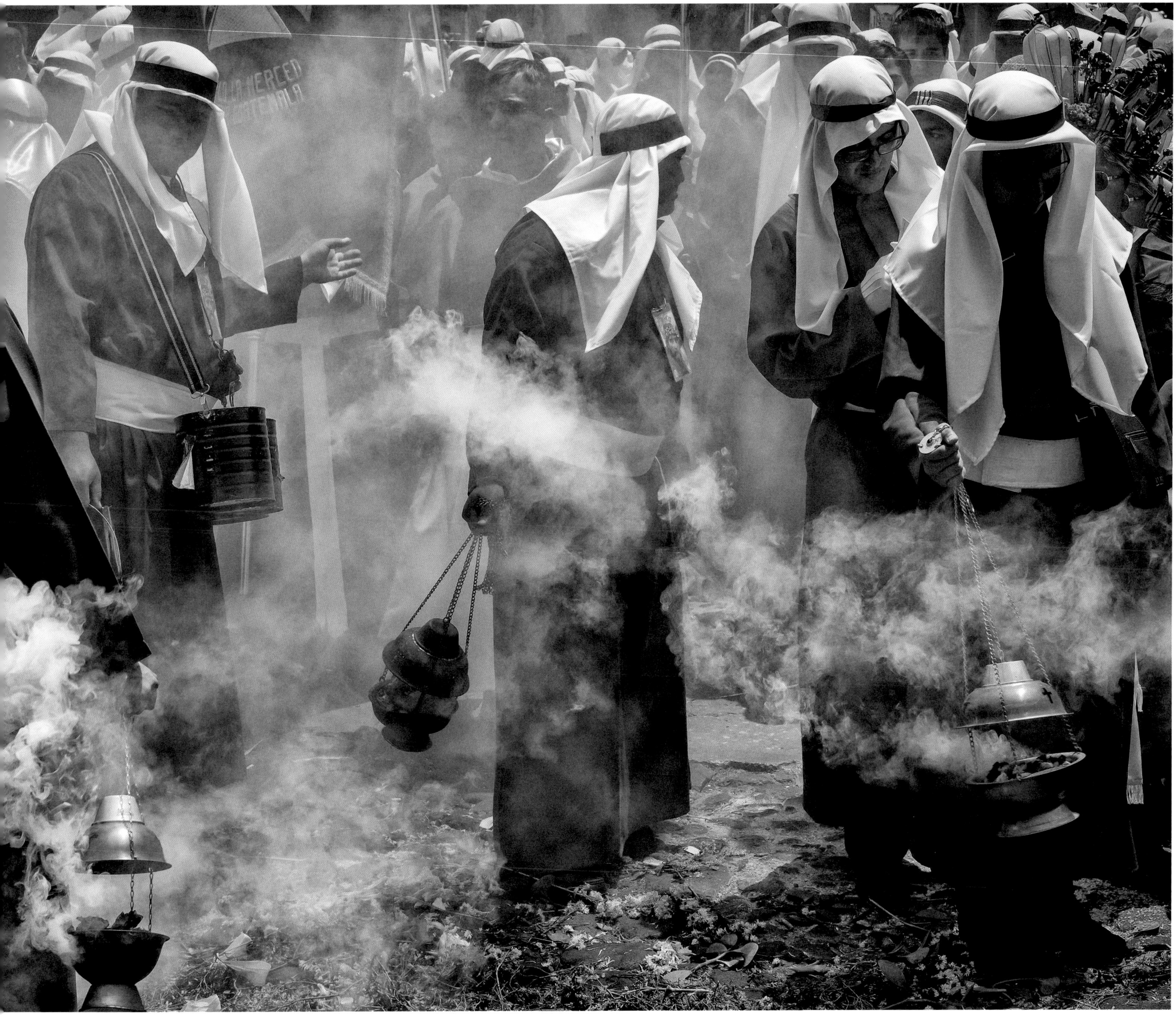
MERCED

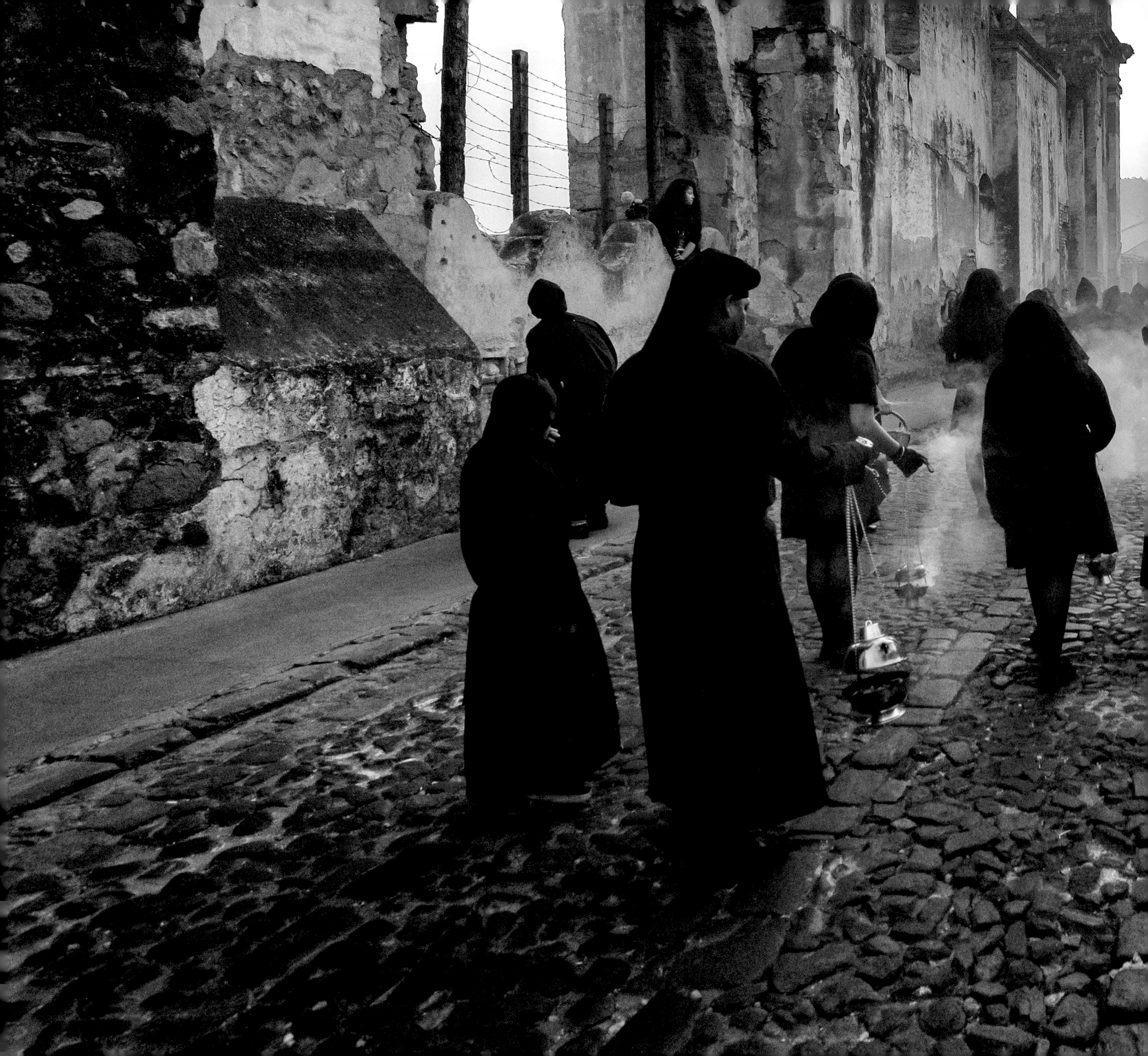

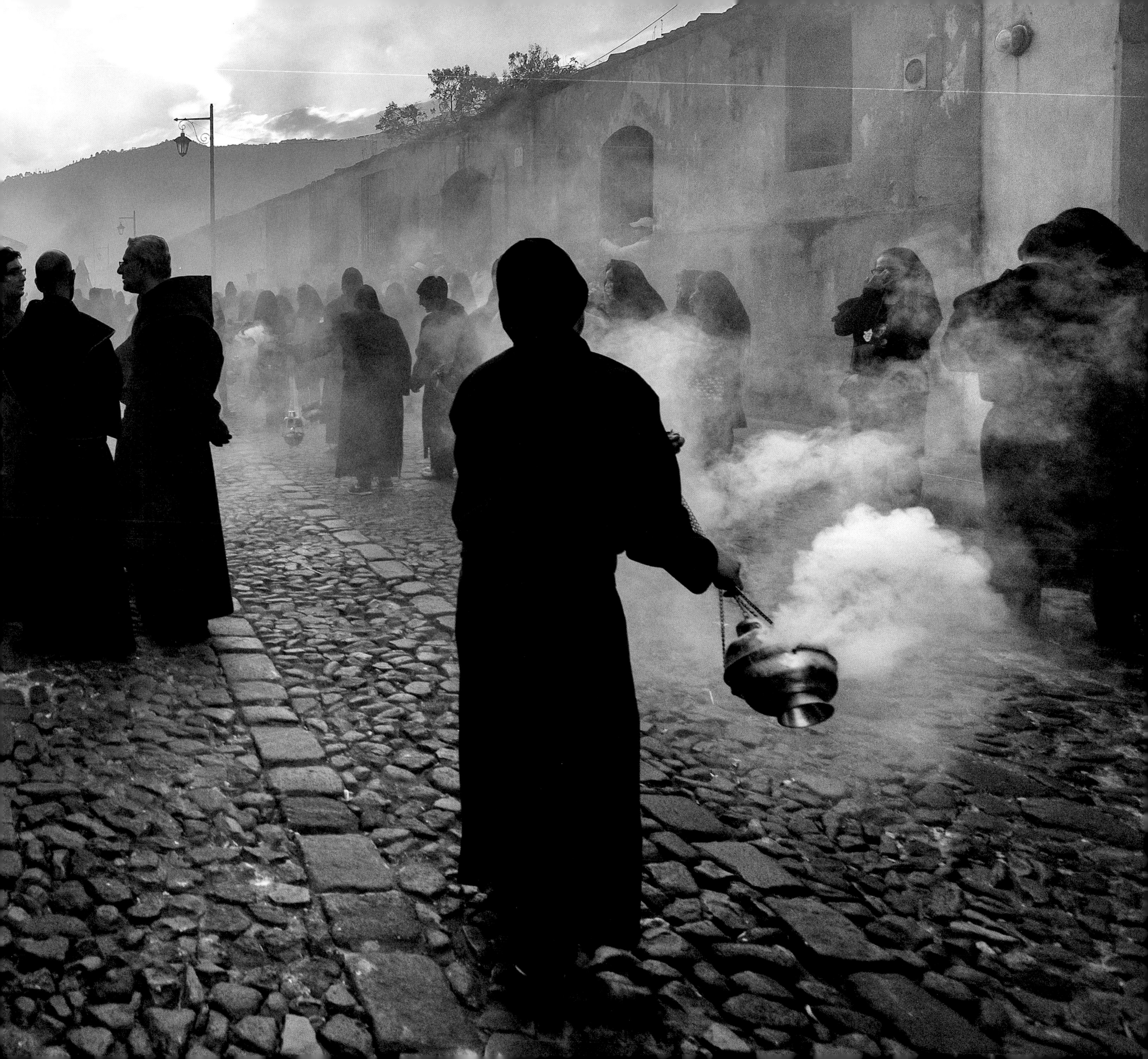

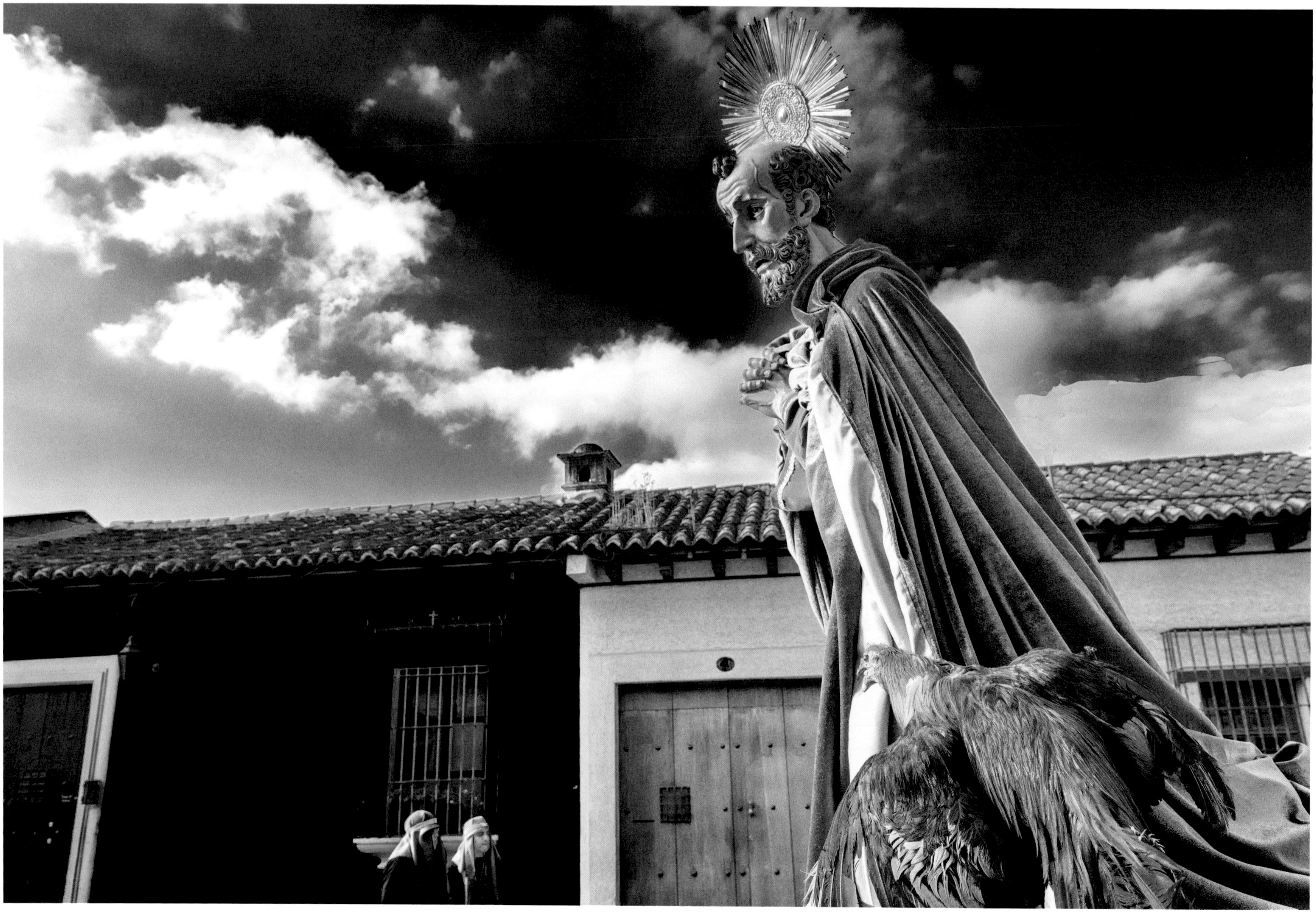

SAN PEDRO AND ROOSTER, 2017

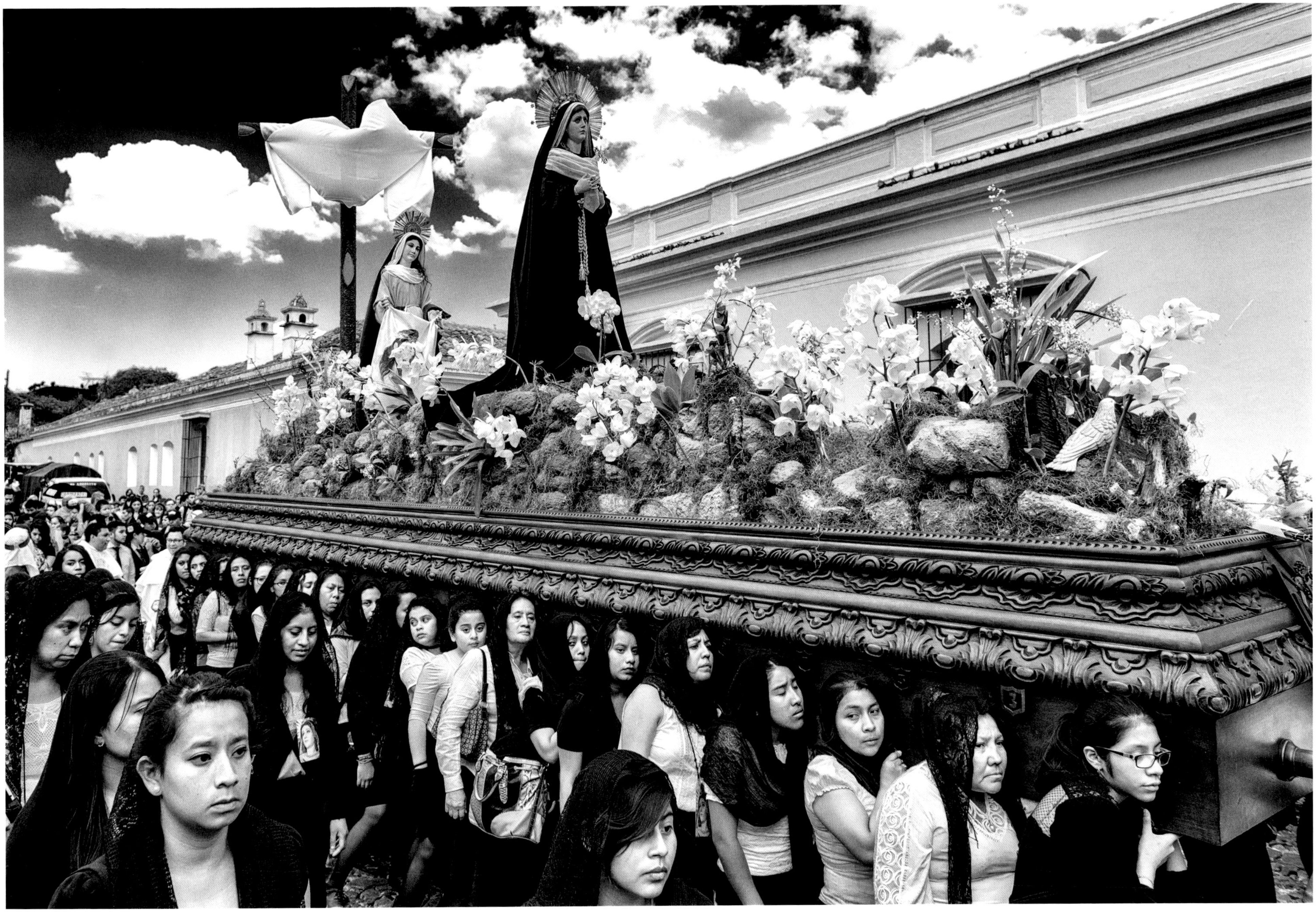

GOOD FRIDAY PROCESSION OF WOMEN, 2017

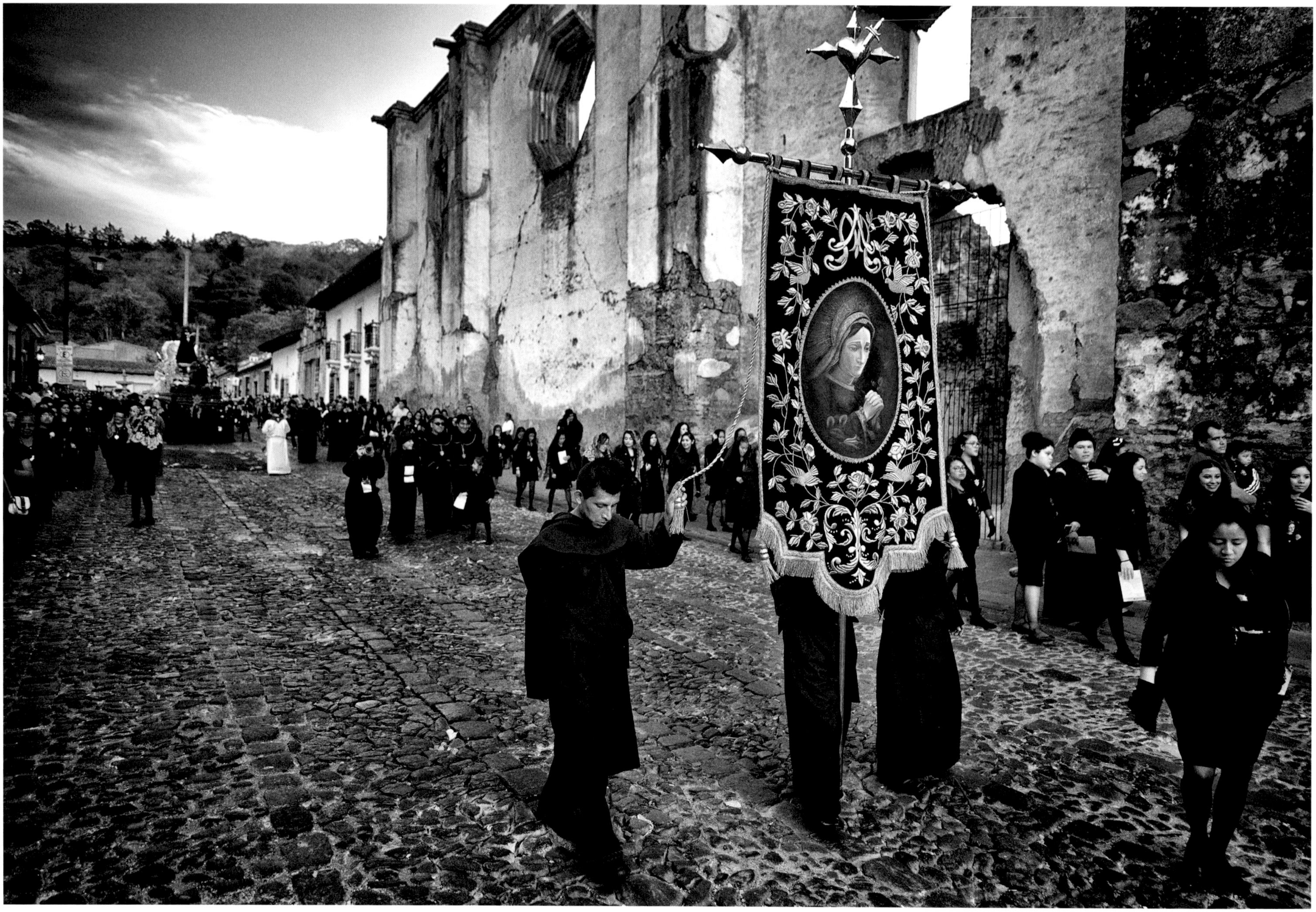

ADORATION OF THE BLESSED VIRGIN, 2017

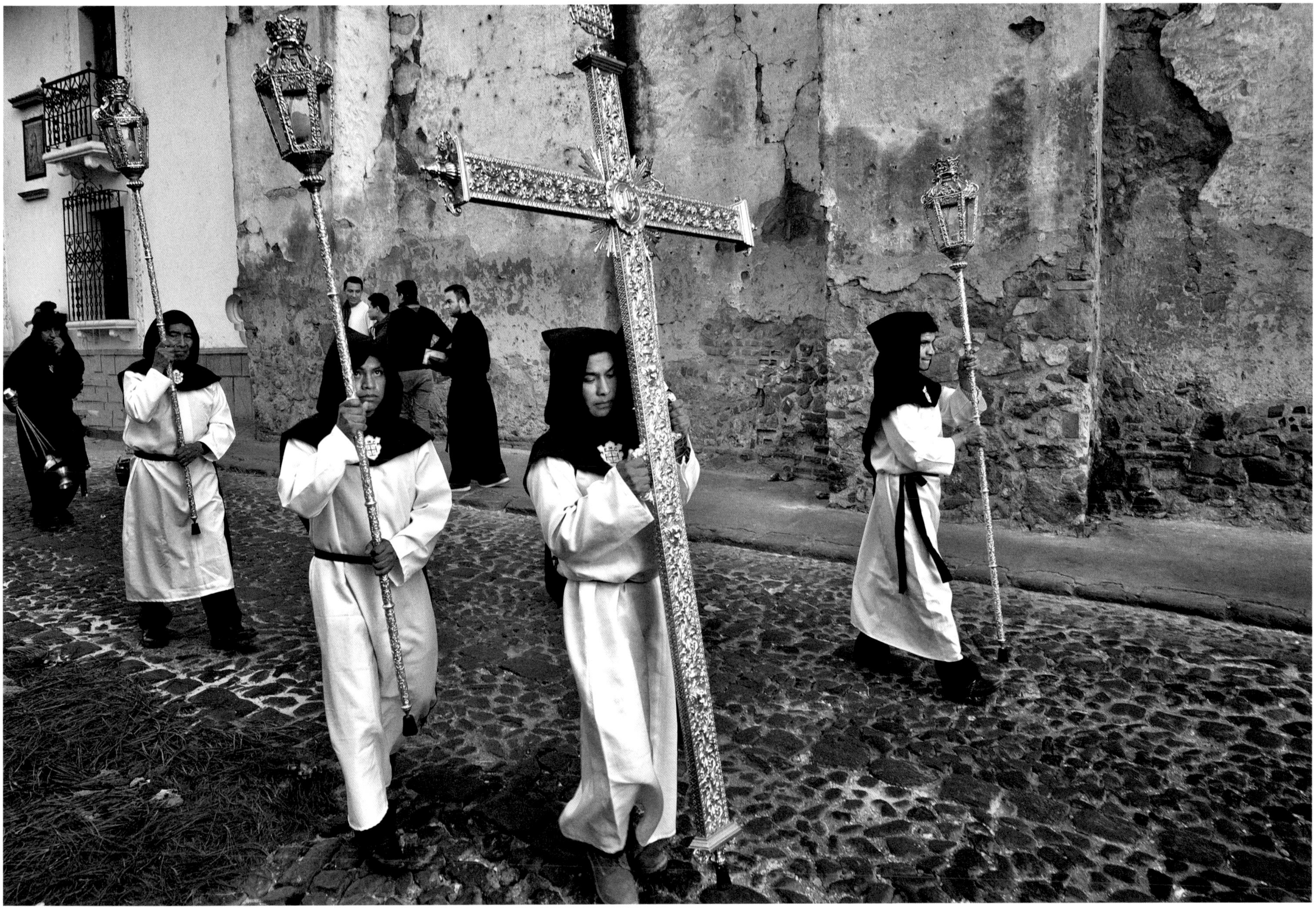

HOLY SATURDAY, 2017

following spread: HOLY SATURDAY PROCESSION, 2017

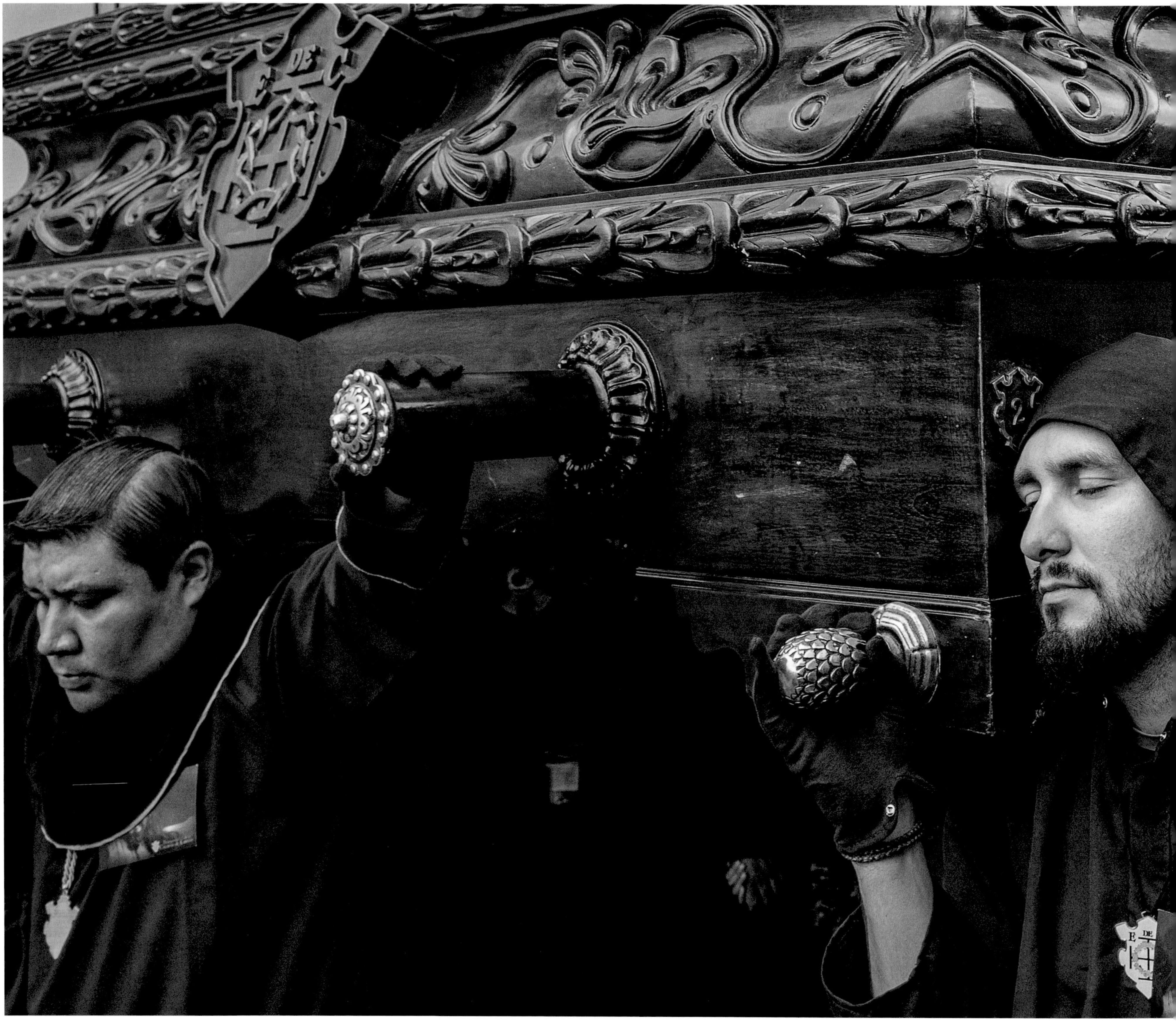

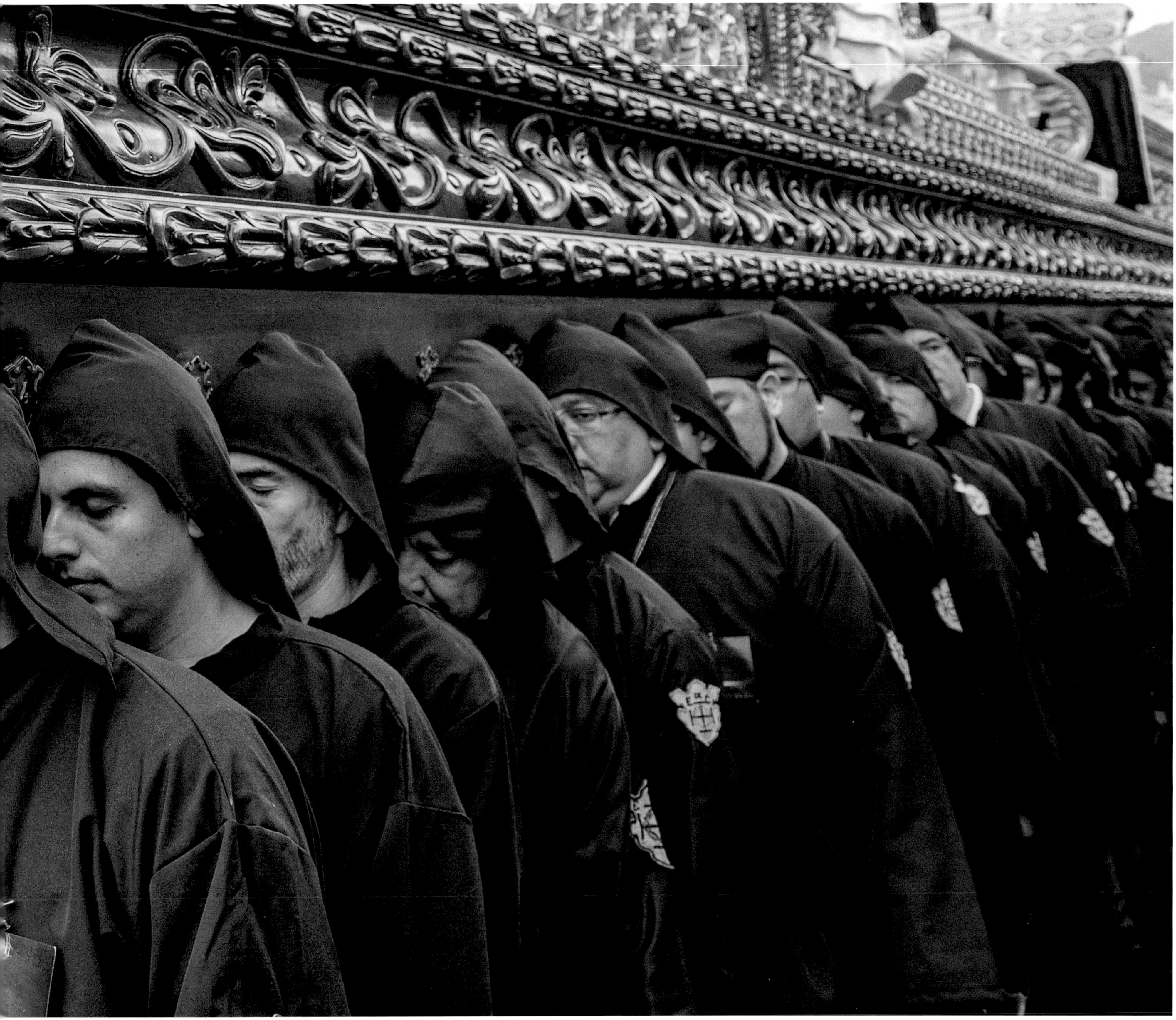

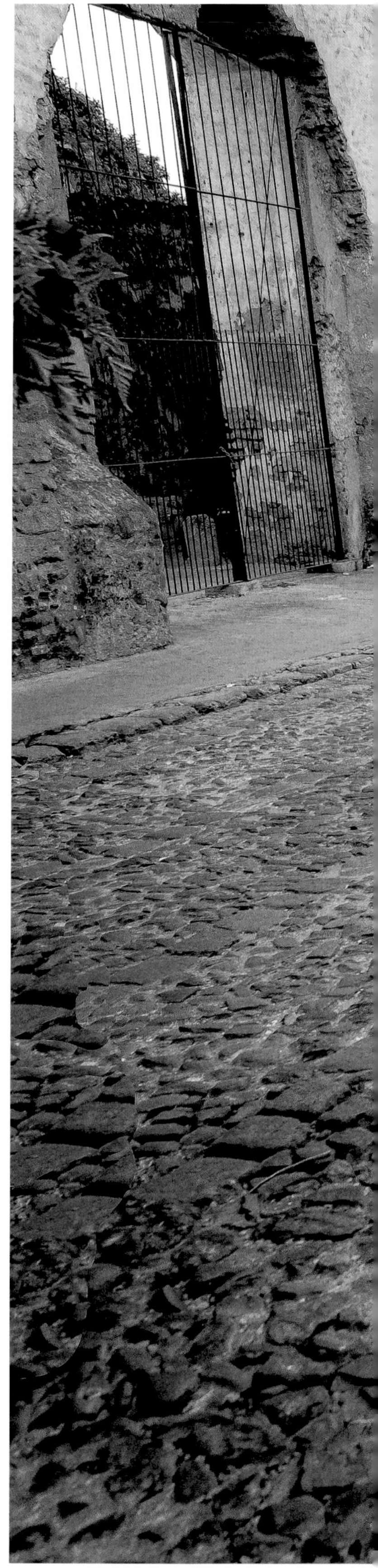

MEN OF THE COFRADÍA ASSEMBLING ON HOLY SATURDAY, 2017

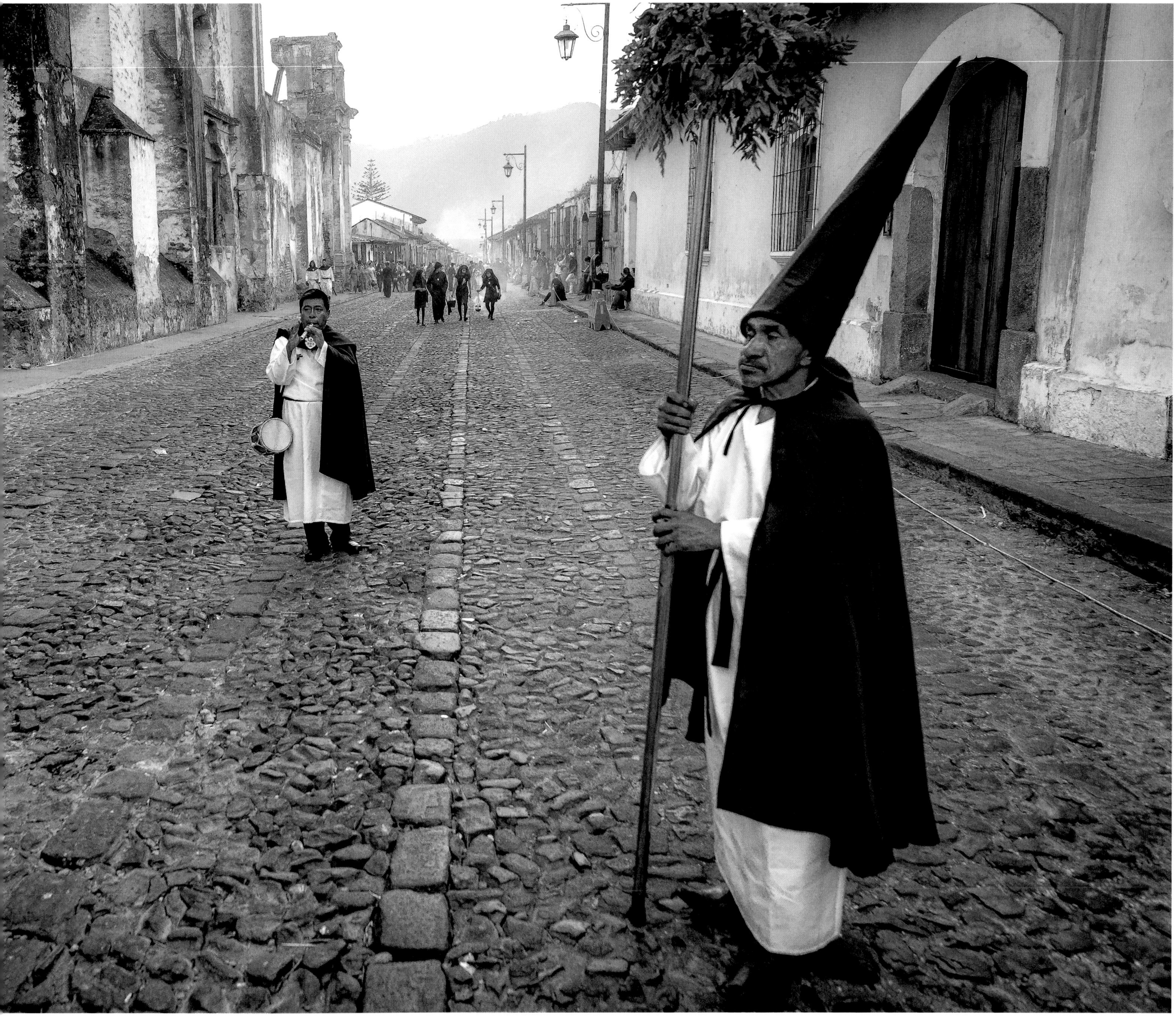

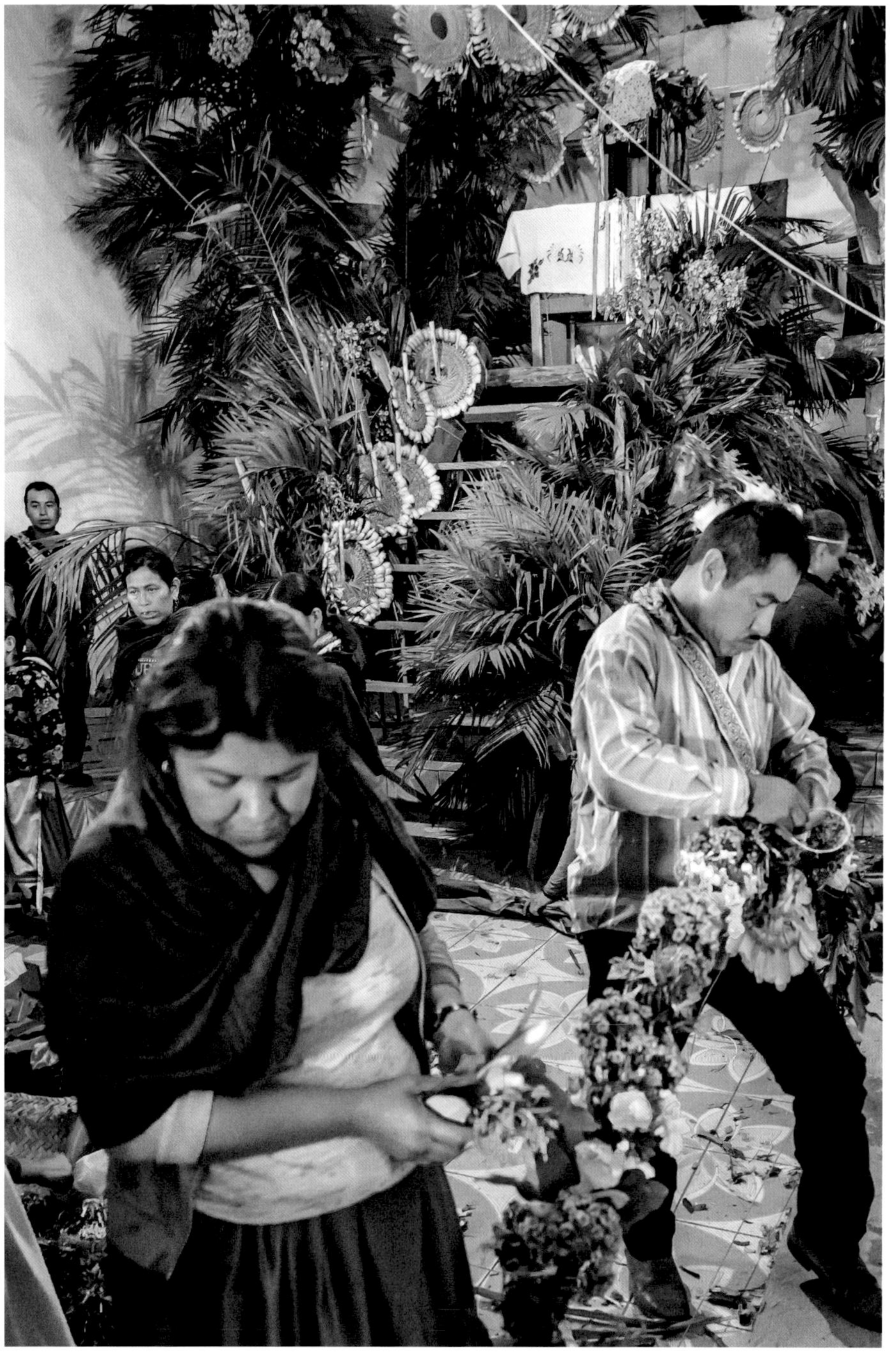

Garlands of fresh flowers assembled inside the church, 2019

The Holy Week of Puáaxku jitsé in Santa Teresa

FRINE CASTILLO BADILLO AND PHILIP E. COYLE

The spectacular and mysterious festivals of the Indigenous peoples of Mexico and Guatemala have drawn observers for centuries, as they also attract participants themselves, who come in from their homes, outlying hamlets, and even distant cities to celebrate and reconnect. Masked dancers appear out of the mountain mists. The sound of their jingling costumes echoes off courtyard walls. Clacking wooden rattles add earthy undertones. Fireworks explode over enticing food stands. Wooden images of saints appear and disappear, one minute hidden alone in the darkest recesses of the church, the next paraded together into the full light of day. Anthropologists or documentary photographers may also be there, trying to capture an angle, a moment of insight.

But the fiesta keeps moving, circling, adding groups from side streets or shifting its center of gravity from one part of town to the next. The music and drinks thicken with the night. A giant copper cauldron of *atole* (a corn-based beverage) may be stirred by torchlight, while masked dancers hover on the edges of darkness. Every festival is different, but all depend on the spirit and willingness of the local people who make the festivals their own, and use them to move forward from year to year and from one generation to the next.

Among the Náayeri people—also commonly called the Cora people—a mind-bending and visually stunning Easter-time festival has drawn the interest of photographers, journalists, anthropologists, tourists, and many other observers for generations. Interest in the festival by outsiders and by the Náayeri people themselves shows no sign of waning. Despite all this attention, however, the significance of it for the Náayeri people has too often been diluted by imposed agendas and points of view, often having more to do with popular cultural trends than with the festival as it is lived. The haunting and evocative photographs presented here give us an opportunity to move beyond the edge of the plaza—where most observers gather—and to glimpse its heart.

The celebration is referred to by the Náayeri people of Santa Teresa as Puáaxku jitsé (which means “at Easter”). The term is an old loan from the Spanish word for Easter (Pascua), but refers to all the culminating Náayeri ceremonies of the period corresponding with Holy Week. The event is known regionally, nationally, and even internationally as La Judea Cora. This name refers to the Judíos, or Jews, who are principle characters of the festival, which is often considered a kind of Passion Play like those performed worldwide during Catholic Holy Week. They are also referred to as the Borrados (the Erased) or the Tiznados (the Ash-Covered) in Spanish. In the Náayeri language they are called the Xumuávika (the Blackened) for the dramatic black body paint that seems to transform them from humans into otherworldly creatures.

Although ceremonies of the Puáaxku jitsé are related to what might be considered the death and resurrection of Christ, as understood locally, this is only part of the story. They are also linked to all aspects of ritual and social life in the town and very much require the participation of Náayeri women, who often have been omitted in descriptions, giving a false impression that the ceremonies are oriented entirely to the boys and men who are its most obvious participants as the black-and-white-painted Xumuávika. Indeed, the significance of these ceremonies goes far beyond the analytical categories typically used by anthropologists and others to describe them—and even undermines European colonialist assumptions about reality more generally.

The assumed distinction between nature and culture, for example, and all the corresponding oppositional categories related to it (e.g., body/mind, ritual/belief, earth/heaven) are not helpful for understanding Náayeri ceremonialism, which is not considered by Náayeri people to be any more or less supernatural than their day-to-day existence as people in the world. The Puáaxku jitsé festival of the Náayeri, then, should be understood on its own terms and not as an example of a Mexican folk Catholic Holy Week. A brief summary of Náayeri history and ethnographic writing on the Puáaxku jitsé provides some context for what we hope will be an understanding of its meaning and significance that more closely approximates explanations provided by Náayeri people themselves.

The homeland of the Náayeri people is located in what is now the Mexican state of Nayarit, which is named for the Náayeri people. Most of the inhabitants speak their own ancient Náayeri language, which belongs to the Uto-Nahua linguistic family and has eight dialects. It is closely related to the Uto-Nahua language of the better-known Wixárika (Huichol) people, famed for their peyote pilgrimages. The dialect of the Náayeri language spoken in Santa Teresa is called *kwéimarusa'ana*, which is also the name of the people from the town.

The Náayeri region is unique in the history of Mexico for its late conquest at the hands of Spanish colonial forces and their Indigenous allies in 1722, nearly two hundred years after the fall of the Aztec capital of Tenochtitlán. The narratives of this late conquest were written by participating Spanish captains, soldiers, and missionaries, and they all have a triumphalist tone. One example is the work of Joséph Antonio de Ortega, a Jesuit priest who spent time in Nayarit from 1727 to 1754. He wrote of the "general history of the conquest" as a completed fact.[1] Nonetheless, after the conquest was supposedly complete, missionaries, soldiers, Spanish authorities, and (later) Mexican officials all found it very difficult to maintain an active presence in the area, which is characterized by very rough terrain. Indigenous uprisings and rebellions continued, even as many Náayeri people were also eager to relate to the colonial world, "which, despite the reports of missionaries and civil authorities—that spoke of the ruggedness of the sierra—was well-known to regional Spanish or mestizo Vecinos, who were able enter and establish contact with its inhabitants without apparent conflict."[2]

Despite Spanish historical discourses that portrayed the Indigenous groups of the region as isolated, static, and unchanging, the Náayeri people incorporated many Spanish cultural elements into their ongoing way of life. It should also be pointed out that even though the missions lasted only a relatively short time—because the Jesuits were expelled from New Spain in 1767—the entry of Spanish Catholic evangelizing missions, starting in 1722, did bring about important changes, including the veneration of Catholic-derived saints in ceremonies like the Puáaxku jitsé. As the Mexican scholar Raquel Eréndira Güereca Durán points out, "conversion to Christianity and incorporation into the colonial world can be resisted even as Hispanic technological elements, food, and ideas are accepted with ease and enthusiasm, without implying the loss of cultural identity, but rather its reformulation and re-articulation."[3]

Given the ethnocentric blindness of Spanish chroniclers, little is learned from Spanish colonial sources about Náayeri rituals and belief systems prior to Spanish attempts at Catholic missionization in the area. Rosa H. Yañez, a Mexican academic and scholar in the use of Indigenous language during evangelization, mentions reports that say that the Náayeri,"had the sun as the most important deity or *tecuat*, to whom they offered arrows with beads and feathers."[4] Ortega describes the existence of Indigenous ceremonies and sacred places and glorifies in their destruction at the hands of Spanish soldiers, but even the close descriptions that he might have provided were at that time considered a kind of diabolical threat to Catholicism. What is certain, however, is that the Náayeri people actively and enthusiastically participated in the ancient Mesoamerican worldview and religion.

Even though their dispersed mountain settlements lacked the large cities and monumental architecture common to the lowlands, they were never isolated from contact with larger Mesoamericans civilizations like the Teuchitlán tradition, the Aztatlán complex, and the Chalchihuites culture. The eradication of such ancient belief systems by the Spanish was not easily accomplished, if—as we argue here—it was accomplished at all. For example, baptism with holy oil or water was considered by the Spanish to be proof that the group in question was under control. But it also seems likely that a leader may have offered his children for baptism, as was the case with the Náayeri king once the surrender of his group was negotiated, because this sacrament removed the parents as a probable cause of diseases, and not because of an actual religious conversion to Catholicism.[5] In other words, the ancient religion of the Indigenous people of the region was maintained through the Catholic-seeming cult of the saints, and it continued to function for Náayeri people not as an acceptance of Catholic belief, but rather as protection against adversity and illness, as it presumably had for centuries—if not millennia—before.

Currently in Santa Teresa, Náayeri practice of their ceremonies during the Puáaxku jitsé focuses on a church built by the Franciscans during the nineteenth century, which houses their saints from the previous Jesuit era: Saint Anthony, Saint Joseph, the Virgin of Dolores, Saint Teresa, the Virgin of Guadalupe, and Saint Michael the Archangel. Another important building is the courthouse across the plaza from that church, where part of the celebrations of Puáaxku jitsé take place. The ruins of a never-completed Jesuit-era colonial church are also located on the town's plaza. After the Jesuits were expelled from what was then New Spain, in 1767, the elaborately carved altar and entrance arch were left exposed to the elements. Local Náayeri emphasize that it was their own fasting and prayers that drove out those colonial-era missionaries, leaving them relatively free to continue their ancestral religion. A bronze bell from the time still hangs in the unfinished bell tower, and it is decorated with flowers in what is now a reference to the pre-Lenten Pachitas festival that leads toward the Puáaxku jitsé each year.

A number of Náayeri people have abandoned their difficult and time-consuming ancestral religion—also referred to as *costumbre* because of the many customs, or ceremonial practices, required for its successful completion—for versions of evangelical Christianity promoted by outside missionaries. These evangelical Protestant missionaries from the United States began visiting the town in small airplanes after the construction of an airstrip by the Mexican government in the 1970s. Mestizos in the town, some of whom married local Náayeri women, are predominantly Catholic and attend mass in a small chapel that was added to the visiting Catholic priest's parsonage in a corner of the plaza, leaving the larger Franciscan-era church for Náayeri costumbre-oriented ceremonialism.

The Náayeri ceremonialism of which the Puáaxku jitsé is a part is connected to the two dramatically distinct seasons of the year: the dry season, which extends from November to April, and the wet season, which begins in May and continues until October. The Puáaxku jitsé can be seen as a culmination of the dry season, which also includes the cycles of ritual office transfers (cargos) that occur over the previous months. The yearly ceremonial calendar also includes a series of maize-oriented ritual dances, commonly called *mitotes* in Spanish, that are held during the wet growing season in family compounds and in a larger dance patio on the slopes of the town's principle mountain, called Tayaxuri in the Náayeri language (Our Grandfather). The sets of ceremonies for transferring cargo offices constitute two smaller cycles within the larger, yearlong cycle of ceremonies that take place in Santa Teresa's ceremonial plaza. The first of these cycles begins its rotation during the Festival of the Birth of Our Mother, on September 8, and concludes during the Festival of Santa Teresa, on October 15, when lower-level incoming officeholders formally accept their offices during an elaborate ceremony called *la entrega de los bancos* (passing on the seats of office). The higher church-based offices, as well as all of the courthouse-based offices, are transferred during the subsequent cycle that begins immediately following the Festival of Santa Teresa. During the Day of the Dead (November 1–2) and the Festival of Guadalupe (December 12), the courthouse- and higher church-based officers are publicly presented at their own installments.

Recent ethnographic approaches provide deeper insights for understanding the Puáaxku jitsé specifically and Náayeri ceremonialism more generally. They build on the rediscovered work of Konrad Teodor Preuss, which is also connected to the recent ontological turn in global scholarship that is finally able to comprehend Indigenous understandings of a much more complex being-world than envisioned by previous generations of anthropologists. From the point of view of this ontological approach, it is not only people who are recognized as subjects with agency in the world. Ritual objects, costumes, and beings (like flowers) also have their own perspectives with the capacity to bring health or harm. Preuss documented such Náayeri understanding of an ontologically complex being-world, but because of the loss of his main manuscripts and the difficulty of comprehending the significance of his ethnographic data at the time, it was slow to be fully appreciated.

Preuss' fieldwork among the Náayeri people at the beginning of the twentieth century was sponsored by eminent Mesoamericanist Eduard Seler, who was seeking ongoing remnants of Mesoamerican religion among the j54

peoples of Mexico.[6] Preuss recorded ritual songs and myths, and witnessed many Náayeri ceremonies, including the Puáaxku jitsé, which he not inaccurately described as a kind of cosmic battle between day and night, such as was also described by Seler for the Aztecs. The blackened Xumuávika men and boys were "white stars of the dark night that allow themselves to fall to earth as spring-time spirits of renewal, fertilizing the earth through their sexual acts and so making the plants and animals grow."[7] Afterward, these "demonic stars"[8] are defeated by the resurgent sun, much as played out on the grander stage that was the Aztec capital of Tenochtitlán. Mexican anthropologist Jesús Jáuregui, who republished Preuss' work along with Johannes Neurath, also wrote about such ancient Mesoamerican connections, comparing the Náayeri worldview to that of the Aztecs and describing the Puáaxku jitsé as a violent spring-equinox "astral drama" between the sun and the moon.[9] Johannes Neurath similarly describes the Puáaxku jitsé of the Náayeri town of Mesa del Nayar as such a "cosmic battle" between day and night, as well as other dualistic forces of the universe.[10]

Importantly, Preuss also recognized a fundamental underlying Mesoamerican metaphysical logic that motivated Náayeri people to continue ceremonies like the Puáaxku jitsé, and that, we argue, continues to motivate them today. As Preuss put it, Náayeri people feel that there are "natural forces" that are condensed into "clouds and animals, and particularly into deceased elders and 'the ancient ones' and that, as a result, these beings have a certain 'magical power.'"[11] Even a young boy casually playing a reed flute as he fishes in the river in anticipation of becoming a Xumuávika during the Puáaxku jitsé—a moment that seems like nothing more than "playful fun"—is in fact carrying out "an important religious ceremony."[12]

The magical natural forces that Preuss describes among the Náayeri people have also been documented throughout Mesoamerica. For the Aztecs, the concept was referred to as *teotl*, or the "process, movement, and change" of a "world-in-motion."[13] Among the Maya the concept is referred to as *kinh*, "primordial reality, divine and without limit."[14] As the ancient

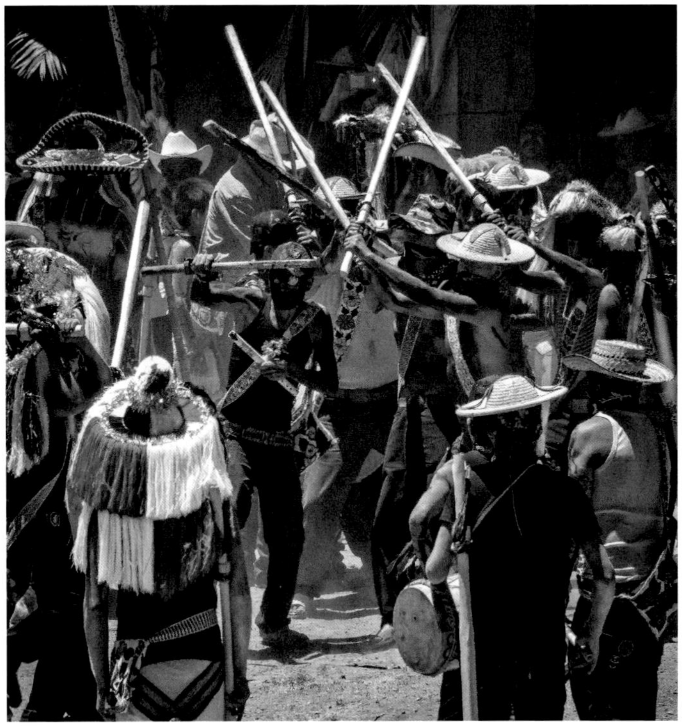

Ritual battles during Puáaxku jitsé, 2019

Aztecs saw it, these forces have cyclical and twisting characteristics because earthbound reality also has such characteristics. The sun rises at a marked point on the horizon and then moves on its eternal back-and-forth path each sunrise of the year. Smoke swirls upward from a pipe of tobacco and then seems to form into clouds. A twisting umbilical cord takes shape out of the cycles of menstruation and gestation, and a child emerges into the world.

Similarly, Náayeri people in Santa Teresa would speak of a kind of *fuerza* (force) or *electricidad* (electricity) that their ceremonial traditions—like the Puáaxku jitsé—are meant to harness and use for their own benefit, and for the benefit of the world as a whole. Ritual actors like the Xumuávika in Santa Teresa are assemblages or manifestations of these actually existing, universally pervasive magical forces, not just symbolic representations. Their power derives from their ceremonially arranged concentration of natural energy. Similarly, for Náayeri people, offerings left at churches and caves are not simply memorials or personal expressions of faith but magical acts that build up energy, even as it is borrowed away for use by people.

Anthropologist Maria Benciolini comes to similar conclusions, arguing that Náayeri ceremonial cycles create a flowering world in which teotl-like magical forces re-energize ceremonial places, like the town and people of Santa Teresa during the Puáaxku jitsé, or like beautiful flowers blooming on a hillside. For Benciolini, this magical force should be "conceptualized as the regenerative capacity of things and of the world, the same as is seen more strikingly in the case of flowers."[15] Thus, ancestors and other "gods" are not given at once in some distant past or far-off "supernatural" realm, "rather they are beings that exist and are refreshed in relation to humans."[16] Indeed, flowers are very similar to the Xumuávika—and other Náayari ritual actors and objects—in that they "appear in relation to the vital force that makes all things be born, as well as the gods themselves."[17]

Flowers are fundamental for understanding the Náayeri people, and in each of the ceremonies and in all of these cycles, a number of flowers are used. Their ongoing use throughout the year also shows that the Puáaxku jitsé cannot be understood outside of those larger cycles, which are themselves connected to the cycles of life and growth, as they exist in what is considered to be a flowering world of cyclical change.[18] This flowering world is built through relationships that combine realms that have been too often separated as either "natural" or "cultural." For the Náayeri people, flowers are not simply decorations or passive aspects of nature that are somehow separate from the world of humans; they are themselves animate beings with their own human-like subjectivity and agency whose appearance in the world indicates and manifests its ongoing life-force. The Puáaxku jitsé is one part of that living and flowering Náayeri world that combines nature and culture into a reality of emerging connections that, when they hold, maintain the health and well-being of people within a world of fruitfulness and abundance.

The much-photographed Xumuávika (the Borrados or Erased Ones) of the Puáaxku jitsé, then, are important because they are momentary emergences—or *seje'ereh* (appearances) of this moving, creative energy force field.[19] Their effect in the ritual is to remind participants of the existing presence of one's own life at a certain point in the ongoing fabric of being. Continuing to participate in Santa Teresa's Puáaxku jitsé provides metaphysical coherence and energetic force that protects a participant from disorder, decay, and, ultimately, illness and early death. All Náayeri ceremonies, including the Puáaxku jitsé, are attempts to harmonize people with reality—the natural forces of the universe—and so to connect people (who are themselves manifestations of them) in a beneficial way with those forces.

For Náayeri people, fasting is the basic way to harmonize people with reality and initiate and sustain any ritual period. This mental and physical preparation, along with the bringing together of the force-filled special elements needed for a ritual, are crucial for manifesting natural forces and so making them appear in the world of living people. As Margarita Valdovinos says, "a large part of the festival is spent in preparations."[20] These preparations take place "with the gourd bowl" (*nyatuxa'ara*) during five or more days prior to the culminating dances and rituals. The ritual period is activated, and the magical connection is launched by sprinkling a special variety of pure white maize into a gourd bowl of water collected from distant springs that are known for their energetic power and that mark the landscape corners of the wider Santa Teresa world. This is done by the main elder leading the ritual, who may be accompanied by others. This elder recites a prayer to the various beings who are called to attend and protect the ritual: the Sun, Nyitatáata, or "our father"; the Morning Star, Nyajá'ah xú'ura'abeh, or "our older brother"; the Maize, Nyitanáana, or "our mother"; and the impressive sacred lake of Santa Teresa, Nyiyáakwari, or "our grandmother." During this ritual period, people fast by not eating until noon (or longer), avoiding any kind of strong emotion, and denying themselves salt, alcohol, and sex, among other things. The goal is to focus people's hearts and minds into a purified and refined thought that acts as a kind of thread around which twisting energy manifests into a maize plant-like column of sacred connection with deceased ancestors—and, ultimately, with the ancient, foundational beings who continue to appear as stars, the moon, and the sun.

Fasting during ritual periods is directly related to the Náayeri concept of illness and "being well." The words *guá'ira'* and *tébi* both refer to the body, the former in its physical quality as "meat" and the latter to the person itself. During the period of gestation, the fetus is not properly considered the body of a person, but rather guá'ira', so a series of ritual actions are required to protect it and assure it develops a well-formed personal constitution.[21] Throughout the year, visits to sacred sites are connected to the well-being of people as individuals and as members of the community. When Náayeri people feel something outside what they would consider "being well," it is an indication of disease, which they argue cannot be seen. Rather it is "like an air that reaches you" and manifests in some part of the body. The heart (*juúrikame*) is considered a key point in the body from which thoughts and emotions originate, and these can cause illness.

Offerings serve as intermediaries in this process of connecting the body to sacred sites and, therefore, to the magical, natural forces of the universe. They also establish ties of kinship with other Náayeri people and with the saints themselves. Indeed, saints are considered to be relatives who can perform favors and intercede on behalf of people with yet higher divinities. As Eduardo Viveiros de Castro points out in his article, "Perspectival Anthropology and the Method of Controlled Equivocation,"[22] genealogical kinship among many Indigenous peoples is a result of these ritual acts, not the basis for them.

Each of the saints is guarded by a Mayordomo and a Tenanchi, who are responsible for cleaning them, decorating the church where they stay, and preparing special foods, while at the same time fasting. Through these acts, the saints hear the gratitude of the Mayordomos and Tenanchis. According to Náayeri people, the saints do not eat human food; they fast all the time. Similarly, the act of staying awake for long hours on various saint's days—as during any other special ceremonial period—is important for good health. It is an honest and irreducible effort that people must make in exchange for what they seek. It also is a way of expressing respect and even making their bodies analogous to the bodies of the saints. Alfred Gell refers to relationships like those that the Náayeri have with the saints as a kind of intersubjectivity in his book *Art and Agency: An Anthropological Theory*.[23] Images of the gods are human and humans also see themselves in the images of the saints; all are manifestations of the natural world of force. In other words, the relationship is comparable to relationships between human persons. Like human family, the saints must be protected, cared for, and fed. People say, "We are caught up with each other." If not cared for, the saint will release them "little by little," and consequently they will remain unprotected, causing illness in the family, starting with infants. Thus, this relationship must be maintained and recreated like any other social bond, all of which bring good health and community well-being.[24] During Holy Week, for example, people approach the Catholic images, particularly the image of Christ in his tomb, called the Santo Entierro. They ask for good health among the large family of saints that includes that image, really an intersubjective being that is part of an ancestral line of descent that expands back to the origins of the world. Recognizing this Náayeri understanding of themselves as part of reality helps us to appreciate the images of the Puáaxku jitsé rituals as they appear in the photographs presented here.

The Puáaxku jitsé celebration starts after a long series of pre-Lenten ceremonies called Las Pachitas. During this ceremonial season, a group of elders and musicians accompany a young girl called La Malinche as she visits houses around the cardinal points of the town, dancing exuberantly and providing a forum for young men and women to flirt. The Pachitas season ends with a final ceremony that involves literal bursts of color, as dyes are tossed over the participants who surround the young girl, whose costume accumulates more and more flowers and brightly colored decorations as the weeks go on. As the ceremony concludes, the Centurions, who will lead the black-and-white Xumuávika, make their first appearance. The Centurions are given ground maize,

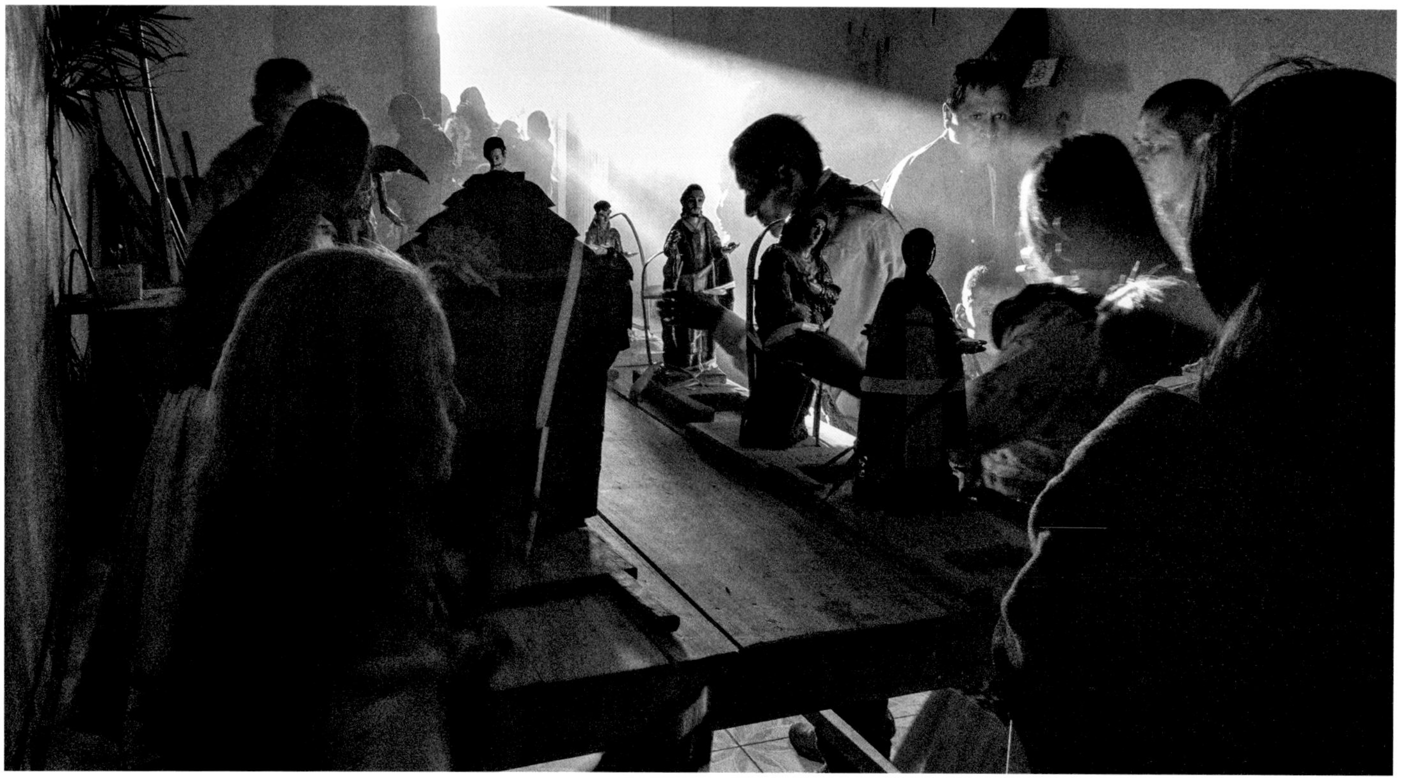

Carved wooden images of saints washed by the faithful inside the church, 2019

and they then begin to run inside the main plaza of the town. In the background, the Xumuávika begin to play their flutes. At the same time, La Malinche formally addresses the First Centurion: "Here I don't know if I did evil or good. But now you have been given over to us, so that you can fulfill what we attempted, so that you can move forward. I was wrong ... I couldn't do it. Now if you comply, it is your part to do the costumbre. Now you will comply." The First Centurion gravely replies, "Now I will follow."

During the ritual period of the Puáaxku jitsé celebration, men fill the following positions in a military-like organization: First Centurion, Second Centurion, Captains, Corporals, Dogs, Nazarene, Apostles, Pharisees, and Judíos. There are also male-female pairs of Mayordomos and Tenanchis, who perform various tasks for the ceremony, and throughout the ritual year as part of their cargo-service. Minors also take part, with young boys assuming the role of "the good boy," taking care of the Centurions' horses, and young girls assisting the female Tenanchis in various tasks. The Centurion—along with his junior partner, the Second Centurion, and other men who serve as Captains—places pinches of ground maize inside a gourd bowl filled with water brought from sacred springs. The Centurion makes a prayer to carry out the celebration in a satisfactory way during Holy Week. To make the prayer effective, these men all fast until the conclusion of the ceremony. During their fasts, the Centurion visits the important cosmologically oriented cardinal points immediately encircling the town until the forty days of Lent have concluded. As he does so, a different, alternate geography is superimposed on the everyday geography of the town, connecting it to unseen divinities and the magical forces of the universe.

The Centurions are dualistically opposed manifestations of the deceased ancestors of the town's living cargo-office-

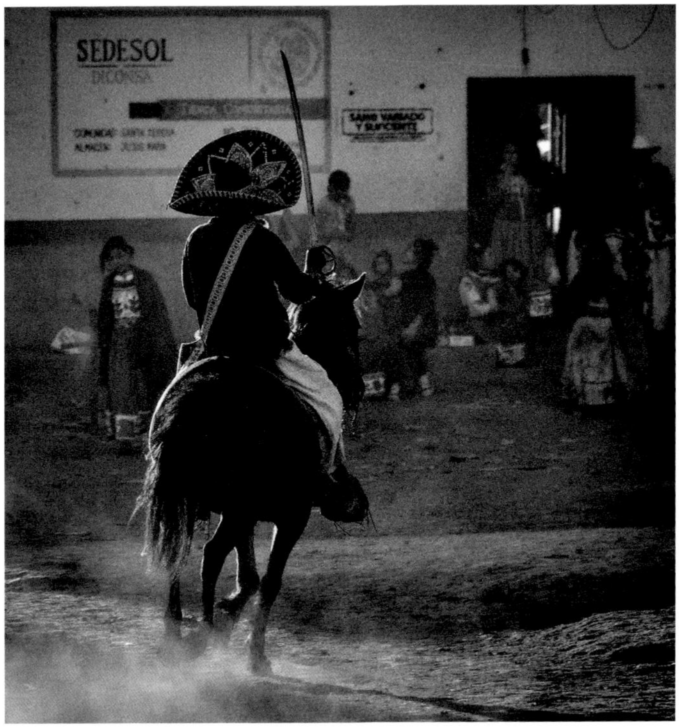

The Centurion riding out of the plaza in Santa Teresa, 2019

holding authorities. The horses that they ride connect them with the rainy season Santiago festival, when large groups of men ride horses around town making offerings at the cardinal points. These horsemen refer to the rain clouds of this season as their deceased ancestors (Tawósimua, literally "our elders"), and the dust raised by the horses' thundering hooves is a kind of cloud akin to tobacco smoke, which is crucial in Náayeri ceremonialism. A special homegrown type of very strong tobacco is smoked in special clay pipes similar to those excavated from ancient Mesoamerican archaeological sites on the adjacent coastal plains. The blowing of tobacco smoke from these pipes towards the cardinal points and onto people and ritual objects occurs in all ceremonies, as well as in private healing rituals for therapeutic purposes. It cleans and purifies spaces, objects, and participants, while protecting them from adversity.

Florentino, a resident of Santa Teresa who actively participates in the Puáaxku jitsé, explained that tobacco smoke is "like fog." He continued, "When there is fog you stop at thirty or forty meters, because you don't really see through it. That is protection. It hides you. That is what tobacco is for. You are in a mist; that tobacco becomes like a mist. That is its meaning." This protective cloudiness also emerges from the hoof beats of the horses ridden by the Centurions as they race through town, raising ocher dust from Santa Teresa's red earth. The dances and battles of the Xumuávika also raise clouds of this ocher dust, which surround the processions of saints as they are carried around the town, keeping them just slightly hidden and safe from the seen and unseen beings that prowl the place during Holy Week.

Early on Holy Thursday, men and boys go to the house of the Centurion, who provides them with the raw materials they will need to paint their bodies and "erase" themselves to become Xumuávika. These include white earth, taken from nearby streams, and dry grass, which is burned to make the black-colored body paint. Designs consist of horizontal and vertical stripes and circles that are painted on their arms, legs, abdomen, back, and face. On Good Friday, the black color is used to cover almost the entire body. On Saturday, they add red-colored aniline dye to the existing black and white pigments. The attire of the Xumuávika consists of white underwear or shorts with a *cotensia* (embroidered waist belt), along with a hat to which strips of crepe paper or brightly colored cloth are attached. According to the Náayeri, the hat has to be made by men, because a woman's touch would bring bad luck. They each carry a phallic wooden saber, which is used not only for battle during the ceremony

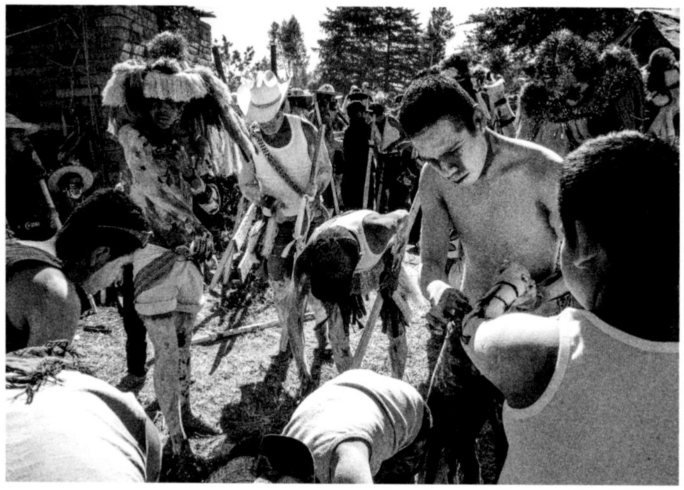

Men and boys applying white and black paint to become "erased," 2019

but also as a musical instrument that is struck on the ground to accompany the sound of the drums and phallic flutes. They also sing sexually oriented songs.

Body painting among the Xumuávika is a way of hiding or erasing their humanness, thus transforming them into other beings. They must comply with a series of proscriptions related to their altered mental and physical state. Fasting is fundamental, and this act of abstention is basic not only to this ceremony but to all Náayeri ceremonialism and ritual healing. Ricardo Ávila and Igor de la Garine point out that the purpose of such prohibitions is to demonstrate and enact the sanctity of the episodes and the purity of those who take part in them.[25] In other words, fasting harmonizes ritual participants with magical natural forces, bringing protection and healing. The men who participate should also not shower or go to streams, because, they say, water symbolizes the blood of Christ. They also do not eat red meat or salt, and they must obey the Centurion. Such orders are not always followed by the more disorderly rank-and-file Xumuávika or even by higher officers, like the Captains. However, if a Centurion is seen to break his fast by eating early in the day or drinking alcohol, it is considered a danger to everyone involved. Some years have seen a great deal of violence and chaos in the festival, which is attributed to the failure of the Centurions to maintain their fasts in the face of the chaotic Xumuávika, who engage in a series of dramatic and often injurious saber combats with each other in the plaza throughout the course of the festival.

An "erased" Náayeri boy's or man's intersubjective relationship with his Xumuávika alter ego is similar to that of a Mayordomo's or Tenanchi's with their saint. As one participant put it, "The three days of Holy Week are a way of acknowledging and thanking Christ. By participating in the festival, I feel very happy because I feel that we are honoring him. If you are protected by all the customs it is like it slows down the illness. It does not reach you as strongly. I do believe that the customs help me. They protect me a lot."

There is no set age for when a boy or man may begin the relationship, and many start young, either of their own free will or because they are easy prey for other participants who seek to recruit them into the group. This is how one Náayeri mother described it: "Jaimito asked me for permission to go see 'la Judea' in the plaza where they give out food. The Captains are in charge of inviting people to join, so that more people or children are part of them, but it could be said that they use a trap. They mainly offer a banana to the children, and since they don't know anything—because in this case, since Jaimito didn't know, he ate the banana and they painted it for me to indicate his commitment. Those who eat bananas must only participate by 'erasing' for five years. If they want to follow the Centurions later, then it is their own decision." The celebration ends on Easter Sunday, at which time all the black-and-white-painted Xumuávika head towards the nearest stream and remove their body paint—or, more precisely, return to their daily lives as people.

Women also follow restrictions during the Puáaxku jitsé. Like men, if women fail to adhere to their fasts, they also risk becoming ill or even dying because of their failure to live up to the intersubjective relationships with the family-like beings who manifest within the context of the festival. The restrictions for women during the festival include not eating red meat, not going to streams, not weaving or doing embroidery, and not braiding their hair. Some women even allow the Xumuávika to cut their braids as an offering to the Santo Entierro, which they consider a way of giving thanks or protecting themselves from adversity. The loose hair of the women is particularly striking during the processions in which the saints are carried around the cardinal points of the town on the heads of Mayordomos and Tenanchis. Surrounded by the Xumuávika, who carry long reed lances, the women huddle together behind the saints, their unbraided hair symbolizing the wild electricity in the air.

Women also do most of the crucial preparatory work for the festival and make the special foods that are necessary for its successful completion. As one resident of Santa Teresa put it, "It is impossible to think that women do not participate, because imagine a situation in which no woman takes on a vow to help, and no woman goes! They are the ones who fix up the church. That is a lot work, and it is always the Tenanchis who are asked to do more." Thus, on Holy Wednesday from early on, the Mayordomos and Tenanchis gather inside the church to create the elaborate Puáaxku jitsé decorations. Women from nearby ranches also join in this activity, coming of their own free will or for personal reasons.

Inside the church, a large staircase-like structure is constructed with an altar at the top that is covered with plants and flowers. Mayordomos and Tenanchis search throughout

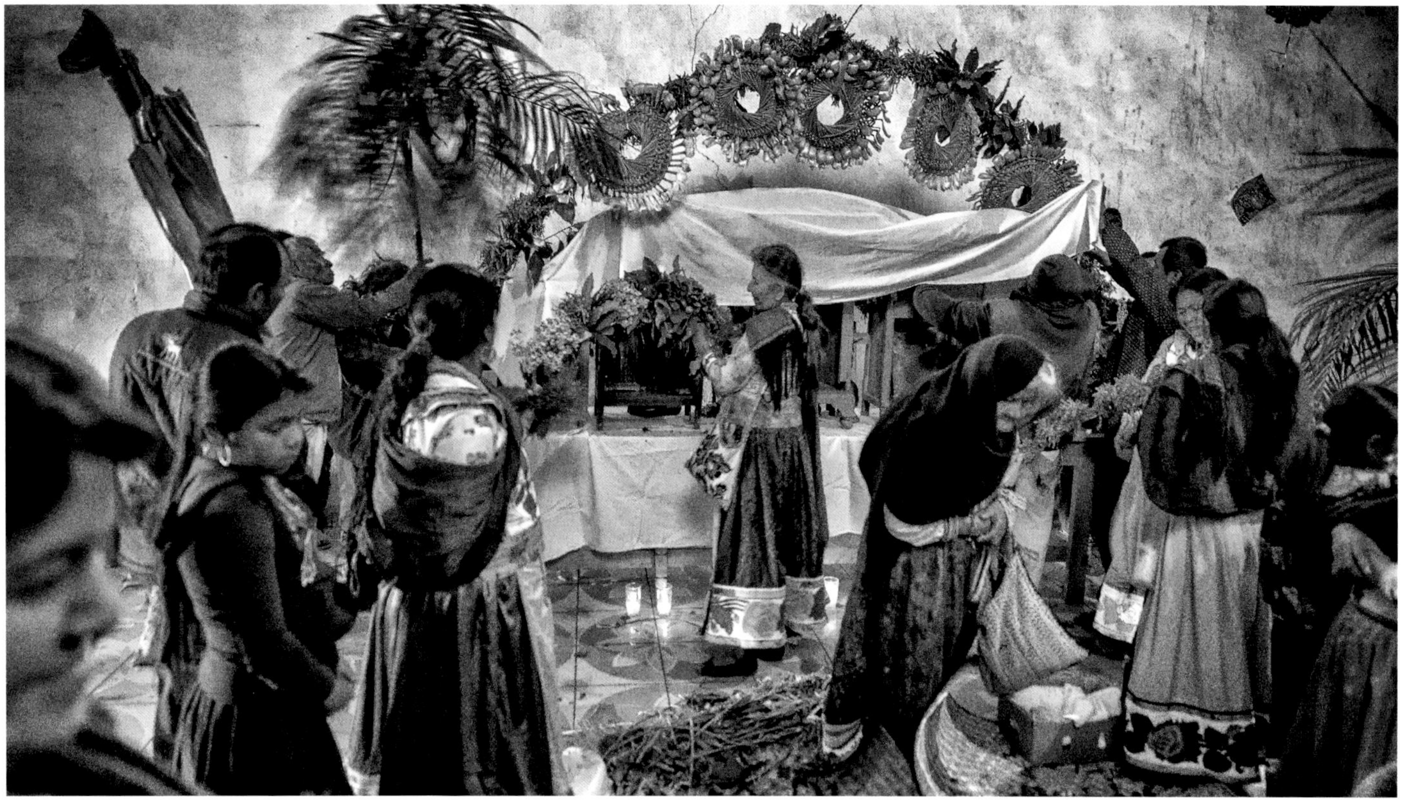

Flowers, palm fronds, and disks made from leaves of the sotol plant inside the church, 2019

the region for banana leaves, palms, and wild flowers, among them corpus leaves, and the saw-toothed sotol from which circular disks are woven that look like the sun. The effect is of the miraculous appearance of a stepped mountain, or even a Mesoamerican-style pyramid, inside the old Catholic church, which for the Náayeri people is also a womb-like cavern. The steps are built and decorated to manifest an ancestral line of connection and healing through the generations of life and death that extends upward to the east towards the Morning Star, and so to the rising sun. On Good Friday the Xumuávika penetrate the church and destroy the altar, its flowers, and woven sotol disks—along with the woven palm branches that people have brought with them. These palm branches are believed to be charged with renewed life-force energy, and are kept in homes for protection and good health. Many people also hang them in fruit trees to protect against a solar eclipse.

Within the overall annual ceremonial cycle, the figure of Jesus Christ in the church is opposed as the eastern Morning Star half of the dualistic star Venus. His younger brother, the western Evening Star—who is referred to as Sótari (the flower-cutter)—manifests along with the black-painted

Xumuávika. The fundamental drama of the festival is the regeneration of life through the reviving energy of the rising sun as it ascends its step-like pathway upward from the Morning Star–brightened horizon. That this renewal of life and refertilization of earth is activated by Xumuávika sexual energy in the context of a sacrificial, fratricidal murder—of even a dualistic self-immolation—taps into powerfully awesome and unknowable mysteries at the origins of reality itself.

Xúuxu'u (flowers) are undeniably a fundamental part of this continually manifesting reality, as Náayeri people understand it, and xúuxu'u may be used to refer to any offering that is deposited throughout the year at various sacred sites or in the church. When given to the saints, flowers also act as a kind of energizing non-human food. There is no specific flower for offerings, nor are some considered better than others, but their blooming across the landscape at distinct elevations and in ecologically distinct growing conditions varies based on time of year and their location in the mountainous region. During Holy Week, it is more difficult to find fresh flowers, which compels people to go deep into the mountains in search of them.

These remarkable efforts to find fresh, wild flowers show that making things pretty has a deeper meaning. Their presence implies a transformation of things.[26] Through decoration and delimitations, not only are territories transformed, but "other spaces" are also built.[27] We can see this change occur when the stepped altar is built within the church and also when the crosses that encircle the town are decorated with flowers. They mark limits while also indicating a special kind of interaction between humans and divinities as part of a connected flowering world of magical, natural forces. The Puáaxku jitsé is one key moment in a ceremonial year—and in the hundreds of ceremonial years that came before and should continue into the future—linking people through time with that emergent, flowering world in motion.

The role of flowers is not limited to their appearance across the landscape and in opening ritual spaces; they also have an essential place in the female mind. The Náayeri people have an appreciation for flowers as key elements in their ritual and daily life, and women, through their weaving and sewing, as well as through their decoration of ritual spaces, have special connections with these flowers. In fact, flowers are everywhere because people wear them as part of their clothing every day. In every instance they act as intermediaries, allowing people, especially women, to establish relationships of different types, which are themselves related to the different fields of their social, economic, and parental life with others, as well as to the natural forces of the universe, of which flowers are a particularly striking manifestation and access point for connection. Flower-covered clothing made by women circulates and transforms people at the individual level—marking the uniqueness of each person—while also protecting and healing them as members of a sacred lineage that goes back to the origins of the world. Through their clear thinking and dedicated work, Náayeri women are considered as crucial to ceremonies like the Puáaxku jitsé as they are to public life in the town more generally. The idea that they are constrained to the private domestic domain completely misrepresents the interdependence and interconnectedness of women and men in Náayeri life.

Weeks before the celebrations of Puáaxku jitsé, women make their own personal outfits: a *siiku̠'ri* (blouse), a *yuchi* (skirt), and *ka̠'ny* (shoulder bags), and design the waist belts worn by the Xumuávika. Women who are noted for their mental focus have developed the art of creating impressive floral designs, which are reflected in their outfits and in the distinctive shoulder bags that both women and men wear. The concentration required to make these weavings and clothes is analogous to the mental clarity that is considered a requirement for general wellness and good health. Indeed, at one of their first ceremonies as Náayeri people, young girls are given a spindle tied with twisted black and white wool threads. Boys, in contrast, are given a bow, referring to their roles as hunters and ritual singers. Both require fasting—and the resultant mental focus—to be successful. As with male hunters and ritual specialists, not everyone can bear the rigors of the difficult fasts that provide the powers of concentration required for connection to divine energy, and only a few women are able to successfully create the more complicated and innovative flower patterns for their weavings or embroidery.

The shoulder bags are an ethnically distinctive accessory for Náayeri men as well as women. The bags are created with embroidery with needle and thread on squared fabric, which has a weft of smaller squares whereon the stitch is worked. It takes six months to a year to make a single bag, and many different Náayeri women may work on a single bag. Men who will "erase" themselves as Xumuávika also pick designs and colors of the bag that they will wear, showing their desire to carry a bag with a unique and special floral design.

Women are also crucial in the Puáaxku jitsé celebration (as they are in every Náayeri celebration), because they are responsible for preparing, cooking, and offering food. These foods, like flowers, are gathered from different places across the Náayeri landscape. Foods from Santa Teresa, in the mountains, where corn and beans are grown, are combined with items from the lowland Náayeri areas, where the climate is warm and fish and bananas are found. Honey and eggs are also stockpiled in Náayeri villages over days and months for use in this festival. These foods have special importance because of their unique qualities of color, texture, sound, and taste. Ordinary foods are also combined with these ritual foods, with the overall result a complex logical system based on elements derived from the common Náayeri experience in their ancient homeland.

Obtaining the food also implies an interdependent division of labor between men and women. Men are usually the ones who get the foods, and the women are responsible for transforming them into Náayeri cuisine. These social functions highlight the Náayeri ideal of gender-based complementary and collaborative relationships within family groups. During a workshop on the Naayeri language from August 14 to October 24, 2020, Alicia Muñoz from Santa Teresa recounted to Frine Castillo, "My grandfather prepared for the festival in advance. We would bring fish and shrimp from the river. Eggs were collected when the hens laid them. I did get to go fishing with my grandfather. We fished at night. We stayed about eight days. I remember that my grandfather put a net in a place where the water looked deep, because that is where there are more fish, and he left the net down there all night. In the morning, we would go to see how many fish were stuck, at times there were about twenty. Sometimes my grandfather got up at night to go fishing. They were different fish. Any ones we happened to get!" All such excursions to obtain food end up returning to the hearth, where women prepare the ingredients and make the dishes ready for exchange with other community households in the festival.

At noon on Thursday of Holy Week, the families of the Mayordomos and Tenanchis, along with other families in the community, distribute various dishes to the Twelve Apostles, older men who fast in the church during the festival and who provide another complementary opposition to the Centurions as manifestations of the still-active deceased ancestors of living Náayeri people. These foods are fish broth, rice with cheese, beans, corn tortillas, eggs (which must be painted similarly to the bodies of the Xumuávika and which according to the Náayeri, bring special good luck), and bananas in honey. The giving and exchanging of these various dishes is often overlooked during the celebration, because it takes place as the Xumuávika stage spectacular battles that draw the attention of most spectators.

Women prepare these special dishes in their homes, taking extra care not to cook any red meat there at the same time. These foods are then exchanged with other women who come to the celebration from nearby ranches and towns. In addition, the Xumuávika ask for food in the houses arranged along the pathway connecting the cardinal points around the town, and it is an obligation to provide it. If the family refuses to do so, a family member could become ill. Providing food for them will in turn bring good health and luck. On Friday, the *guarache del Nazareno* (a sandal-shaped thick maize tortilla) is made in each home, and the Captains collect them from the women in each of the houses.

We can thus begin to imagine the complexity of all the gears in motion that revolve around the giving and sharing of food during this elaborate festival, which is only one of many during the ceremonial year. For example, between Saturday and Sunday, the Centurion distributes various dishes that his family has prepared to all of the Náayeri people of the town. These foods are then eaten in each of the different festivals during the year. In this way, they condense an entire annual festival cycle through a locally understood culinary code, which in turn relates to the sacred landscape from which the foods are obtained.

These foods include guá´ira´(meat), and through their consumption a bond is established with the landscape and with a kind of cosmological space and time that is literally incorporated into Náayeri bodies. They believe that without these rituals and eating the foods associated with them a person will become ill and die, their body rotting like uncooked meat. That is why there must be an order, a protection from adversity. It is for the well-being of the people, because food establishes social ties between individuals and with the world, based on offerings, sacrifices, and the ritual consumption of these special foods.[28] Náayeri celebrations (in this case, the Puáaxku jitsé) demonstrate successful communication with beings both seen and unseen and affirm in the participants a sense of belonging to the group. This only happens when the person actually takes part in these rituals with seriousness and purpose. Participants are reminded that the ceremonies are not a game, and few feel they are free to forget such heartfelt and wise advice.

It is difficult to capture the depth and meaning of Náayeri ceremonialism, but one thing is for sure: The Náayeri of Santa Teresa must be understood on their own staggeringly complicated and profound terms. That means that the Puáaxku jitsé celebration, as appealing and heavily documented as it has been, cannot be understood in isolation from the rest of Náayeri ceremonialism and their understanding of its importance for maintaining the flow of beneficial forces in and through their lives. William Frej's photographs, which were taken with permission by the traditional Náayeri authorities in Santa Teresa, help us to recognize that there are other ways of thinking and being in the world. They provide a window into the sense of profundity that comes from existing within a metaphysical reality that has been lost to most.

As anthropologists who have worked with the Náayeri people for years, and who have spent time with them at ceremonies and sacred sites across the landscape—while still only scratching the surface of understanding the depth and significance of those rituals and places—we see the photographs in this book as reflecting moments of connection.

They show people using ancient ceremonial traditions to weave their communities together and activate wellsprings of health and vitality for themselves, their families, and their world. It is about health and well-being in a world of abundance, taking responsibility, and working for the benefit of generations to come.

All people need connection to the natural forces of our earthbound reality. The Náayeri people believe they were given the tools to make these magical connections thousands of years ago. Only now are far too few of us learning to recognize and respect them. Let us, then, concentrate our thoughts and focus our minds on the images in this book, that we might open our hearts to the flowering world that is all around us, if only we can see it through the darkness.

NOTES

1. Joséph Antonio de Ortega, "Maravillosa reducción, y conquista de la Provincia de San Joseph del Gran Nayar, nuevo Reino de Toledo," in *Apostólicos afanes de la Compañía de Jesús en México, prólogo de Thomas Calvo y Jesús Jáuregui*, ed. Francisco Javier Fluviá (Ciudad de México: Centro de Estudios Mexicanos y Centroamericanos, Instituto Nacional Indigenista, 2018), 80–81.

2. Raquel Eréndira Güereca Durán, "Caciques, Lenguas' y Soldados Fronterizos: Actores indígenas en la conquista del Nayar (1721–1722)" (Tesis de Doctorado, Universidad Nacional Autónoma de México, 2018), 90.

3. Ibid., 496.

4. Rosa H. Yañez, "Procesos de contacto, conflicto y transculturación entre los grupos indígenas del occidente mesoamericano," *Revista Occidente*, vol. 4 (2015): 1–17.

5. Ibid., 6.

6. Jesús Jáuregui and Johannes Neurath "El pasado prehispánico y el presente indígena: Seler, Preuss y las culturas del Gran Nayar" in *Flechadores de estrellas. Nuevas aportaciones a la etnología de coras y huicholes*, Jesús Jáuregui y Johannes Neurath, coordinadores (Guadalajara: Universidad de Guadalajara, Instituto Nacional de Antropología e Historia, México, 2003), 19–33.

7. Konrad Teodor Preuss, "Más información acerca de las costum bres religiosas de los coras, especialmente sobre los portadores de falos en Semana Santa" in Fiesta, Literatura y Magia en el Nayarit: Ensayos sobre coras, huicholes y mexicaneros de Konrad Theodor Preuss, Jesús Jáuregui and Johannes Neurath, eds. (Ciudad de México: Centro Francés de Estudios Mexicanos y Centroamericanos, Instituto Nacional Indigenista, 1998), 133.

8. Ibid., 134.

9. Jesús Jáuregui, "La Judea de los coras: un drama astral de primavera" in México en movimiento, *La religión popular*, Hubertus Hermans, Dick Papousek and Catherine Raffi-Béroud, eds. (Gröningen: Centro de Estudios Mexicanos, University of Gröningen, 1998), 28–53.

10. Johannes Neurath, "La Semana Santa Cora de la Mesa del Nayar: Un Ritual Solar de Tradición Prehispánica," *Arqueología Mexicana* 52 (November–December 2001): 72–77.

11. Preuss, "Más información," 113–114.

12. Ibid.

13. James Maffie, *Aztec Philosophy: Understanding a World in Motion* (Louisville, CO: University Press of Colorado, 2014), 12.

14. Robert M. Carmack, Janine Gasco, and Gary H. Gossen, *The Legacy of Mesoamerica: History and Culture of a Native American Civilization*, second edition (New York: Routledge, 2007), 514.

15. Maria Benciolini, "Iridiscencias de un mundo florido: estudio sobre la relacionalidad y ritualidad cora" (Tesis de Doctorado, Universidad Nacional Autónoma de México, 2014), 81.

16. Ibid., 177.

17. Ibid., 313.

18. Ibid., 333.

19. Philip E. Coyle, *Náyari History, Politics, and Violence: From Flowers to Ash* (Tucson: University of Arizona Press, 2001), 242; and Margarita Valdovinos, *El Canto de la Chicharra y El Encantamiento del Mundo* (Ciudad de México: Universidad Nacional Autónoma de México, Instituto de Investigaciones Filológicas, 2019), 72.

20. Valdovinos, *El Canto de la Chicharra y El Encantamiento del Mundu*, 24.

21. Frine Castillo, "Náhue´ra´a, El concepto de cuerpo entre los coras de Santa Teresa del Nayar" (Tesis de Licenciatura, Escuela Nacional de Antropología e Historia, 2014).

22. Eduardo Viveiros de Castro, "Perspectival Anthropology and the Method of Controlled Equivocation," *Tipití: Journal of the Society for the Anthropology of Lowland South America* 2, no. 1 (2004): 1–20, https://digitalcommons.trinity.edu/tipiti/vol2/iss1/1/.

23. Alfred Gell, *Art and Agency: An Anthropological Theory* (Oxford: Oxford University Press, 1998), 137–138.

24. Frine Castillo, "El mundo artefactual de los náayeri: la subjetividad del mwátsi´ibi" (Tesis de Maestría, Universidad Nacional Autónoma de México, 2019).

25. Igor de la Garine and Ricardo Ávila, eds., "La dieta y la alimentaciónde los grupos humanos" in *Antropología de Alimentación: textos escogidoas de Igor de Garine* (Guadalajara: Universidad de Guadalajara, 2014): 31–71.

26. M. Benciolini, "Iridiscencias," 330.

27. Ibid., 102 and 105.

28. Ávila and Garine, "Antropología," 75.

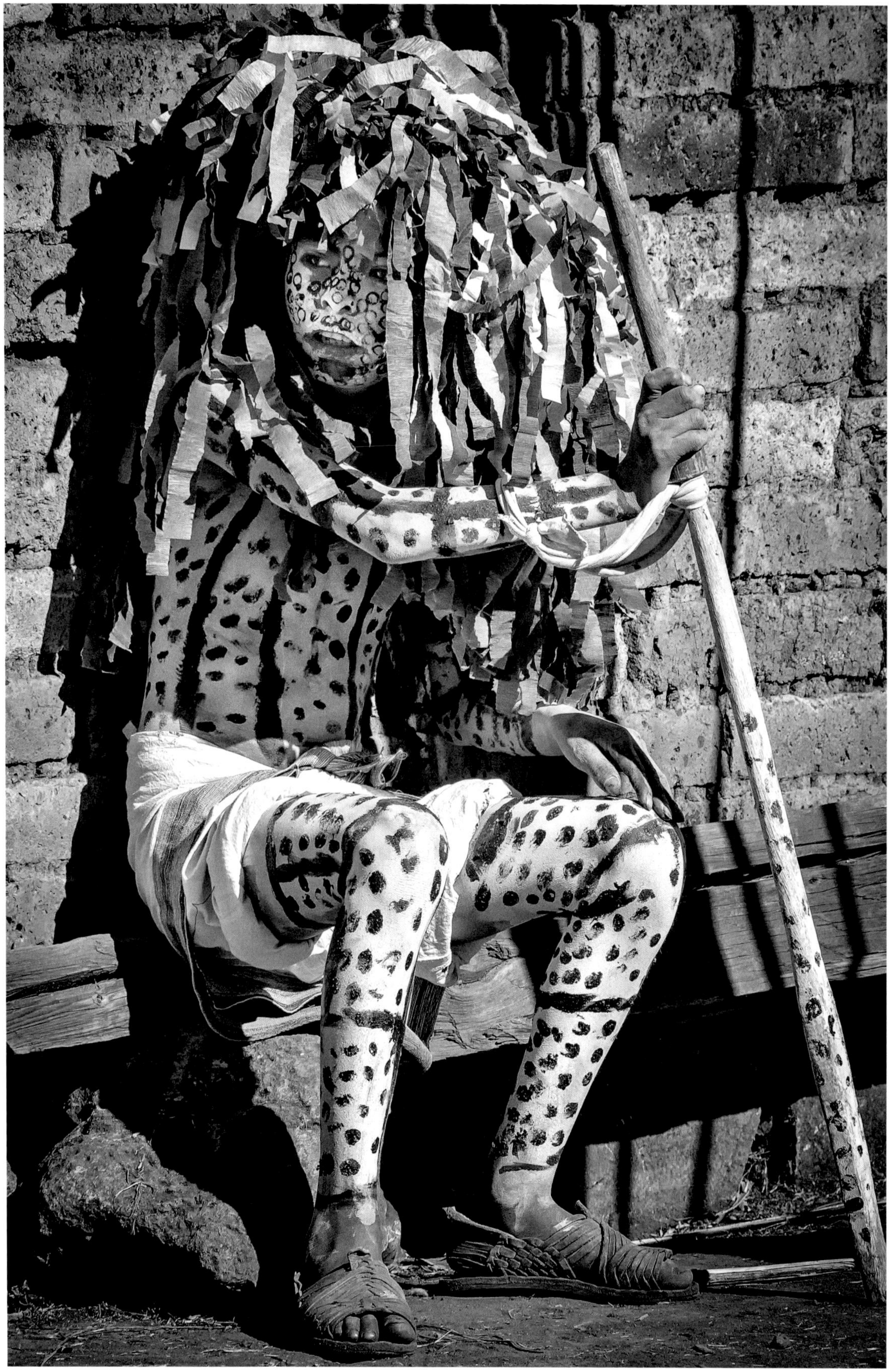

Puáaxku jitsé

March/April
Santa Teresa, Nayarit, Mexico

The Náayeri people live in the rugged Sierra del Nayar mountains in the Mexican state of Nayarit. In Santa Teresa, one of the most remote villages in the region, celebrations are held year-round. The most important is La Judea Cora, known to the local people as Puáaxku jitsé, which takes place during Holy Week before Easter. Although it coincides with an important Christian holiday, Puáaxku jitsé is much more than a celebration of the death and resurrection of Christ. It is a complex and multilayered event meant to harmonize and connect people with the natural forces of the universe.

A wide variety of roles are assumed by both men and women during the Puáaxku jitsé. For men, these include the First Centurion and his assistant, the Second Centurion, who ride in and out of the town center on horseback, as well as Captains, Corporals, and others. The highly visible black-and-white-painted men and boys called Xumuávika (the Blackened) in the Náayeri language are also known as Judíos (Jews), Borrados (Erased Ones), and Tiznados (the Ash-Covered) in Spanish. The Xumuávika ritually paint their bodies as a way of "erasing" their humanness. Like the other ritual actors, objects, and places, they are not mere symbolic representations but are believed to be manifestations of magical natural forces.

The celebrations begin in earnest on the Wednesday before Easter. Men with tall sticks run around the periphery of the town, which becomes a stage for sacred activities during the celebration. On Thursday, men and boys gather to paint themselves to become Xumuávika. The atmosphere is unruly, and there is much jostling in the lead-up to the onset of mock battles that occur over the next few days. On the morning of Good Friday, the town is quiet except for the background sounds of drums and flutes. Inside the church, women clean fresh flowers and decorate the church and the steps leading to the altar. At around noon, the Xumuávika storm into the church, and mayhem ensues as they strip the altar of its decorations and destroy the steps leading to it. Outside, the two Centurions ride into the plaza on their horses, men pick up their sticks, and mock battles begin, strengthening in intensity throughout the evening and night. On Saturday, the exhausted warriors continue to wage their ritual war, and the Xumuávika enter the church again and lie on the floor, writhing as if in pain. Soon they run out and chase young girls, lifting their skirts amid screams and laughter. At the end of the day, fireworks go off, the Centurions ride out of town, and the Puáaxku jitsé is over for another year.

opposite: A YOUNG XUMUÁVIKA, 2019

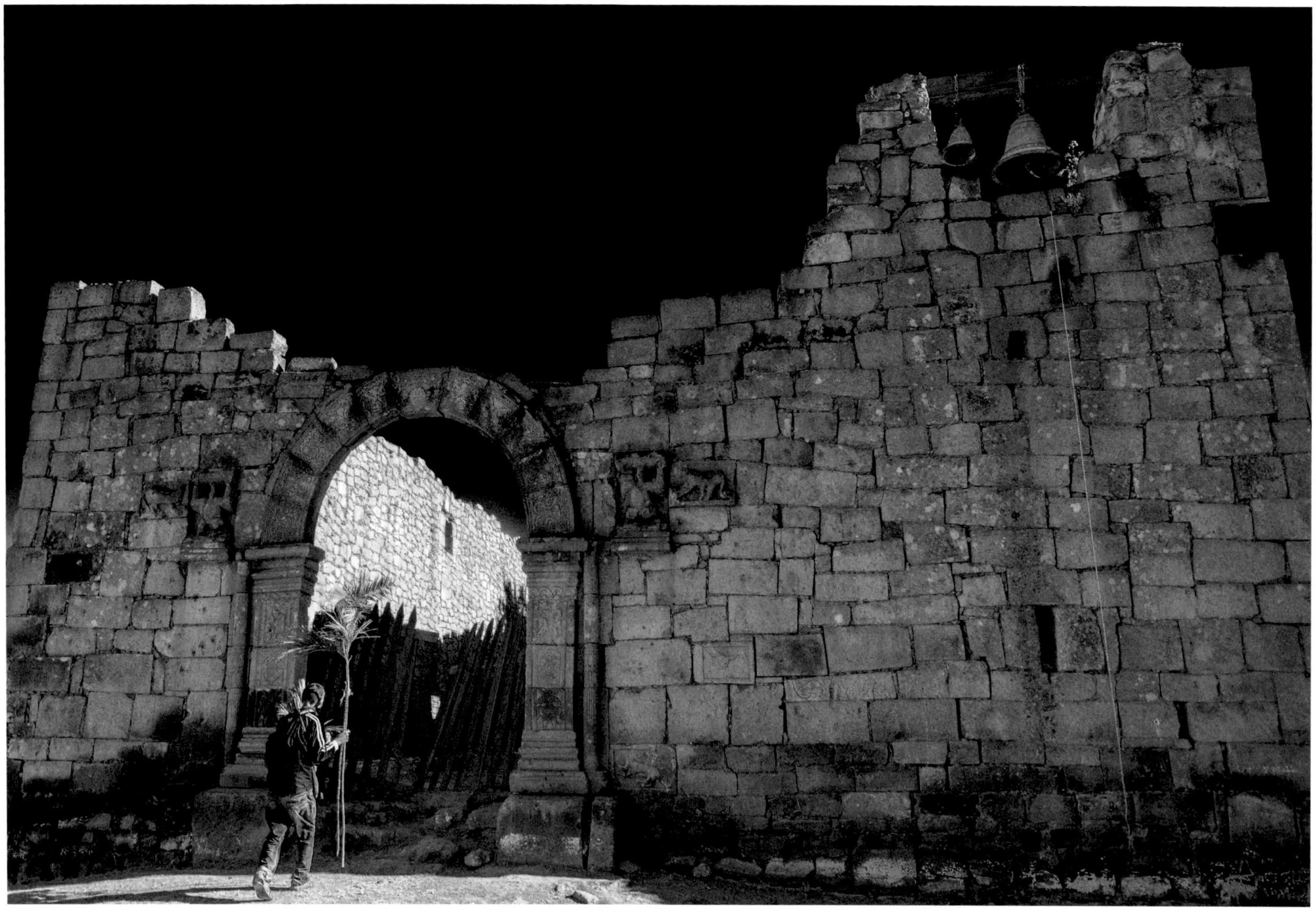

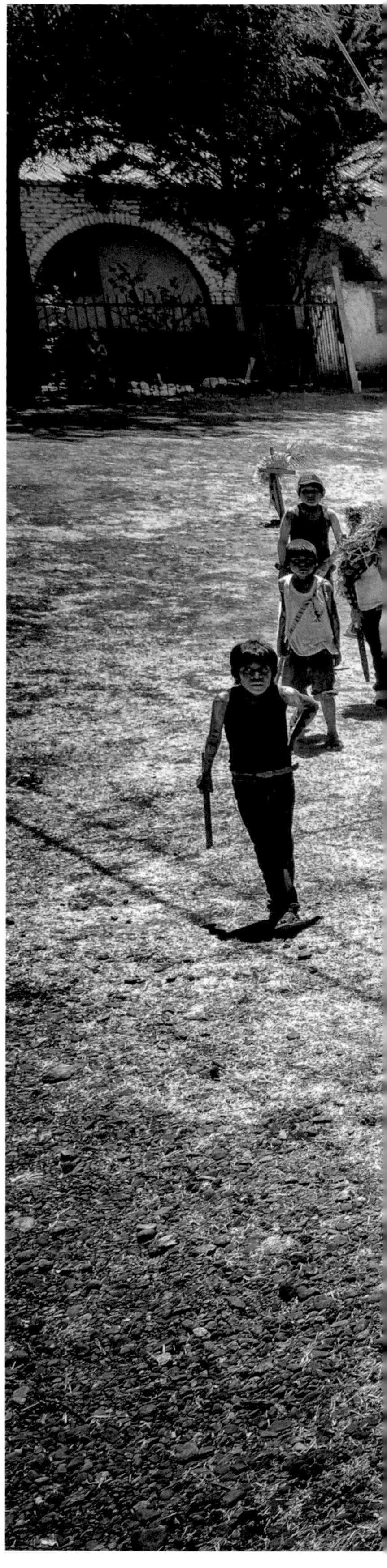

THE UNFINISHED JESUIT-INITIATED CHURCH, 2019

opposite: THE CENTURION LEADING THE XUMUÁVIKA OUT OF THE PLAZA, 2019

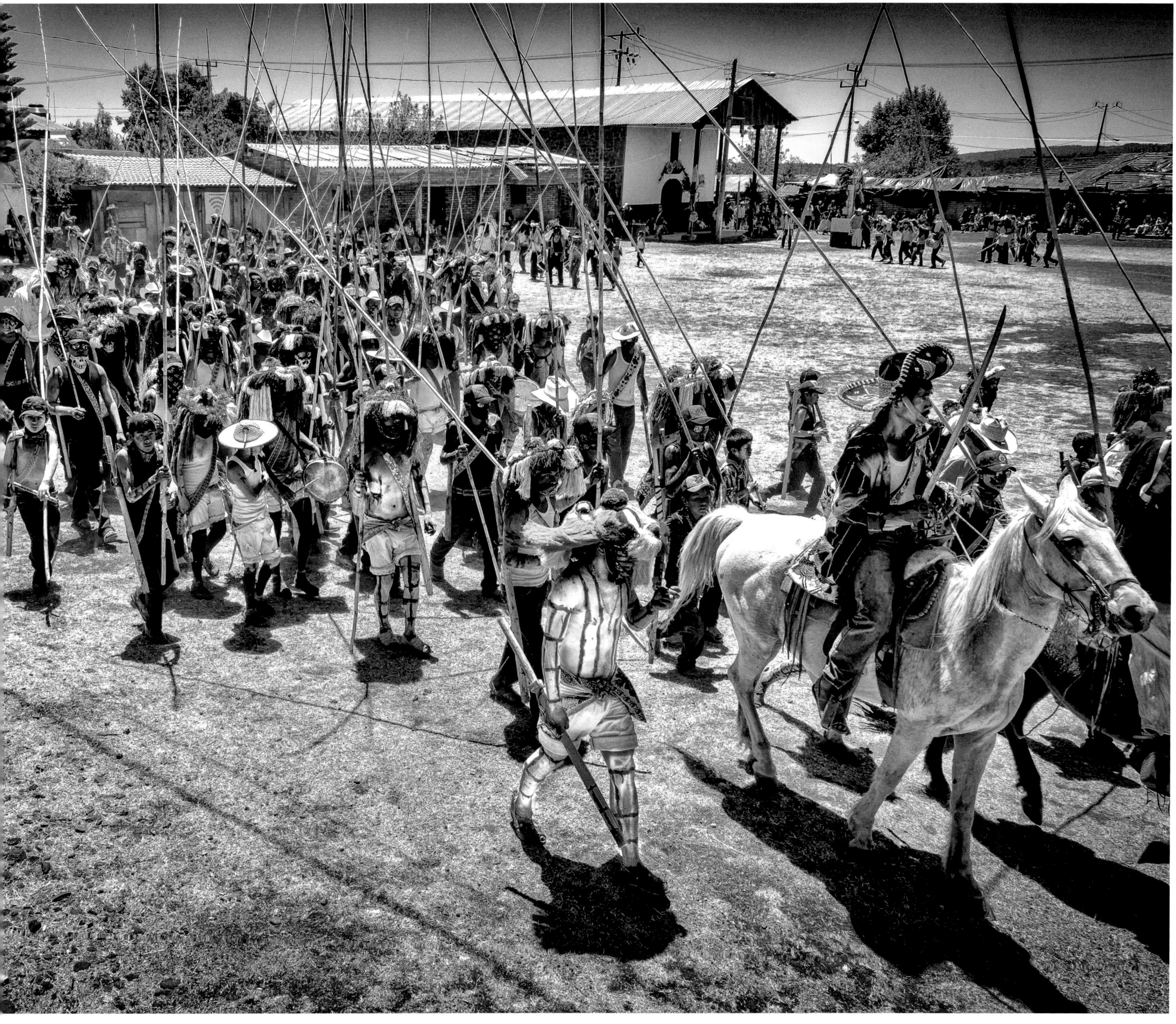

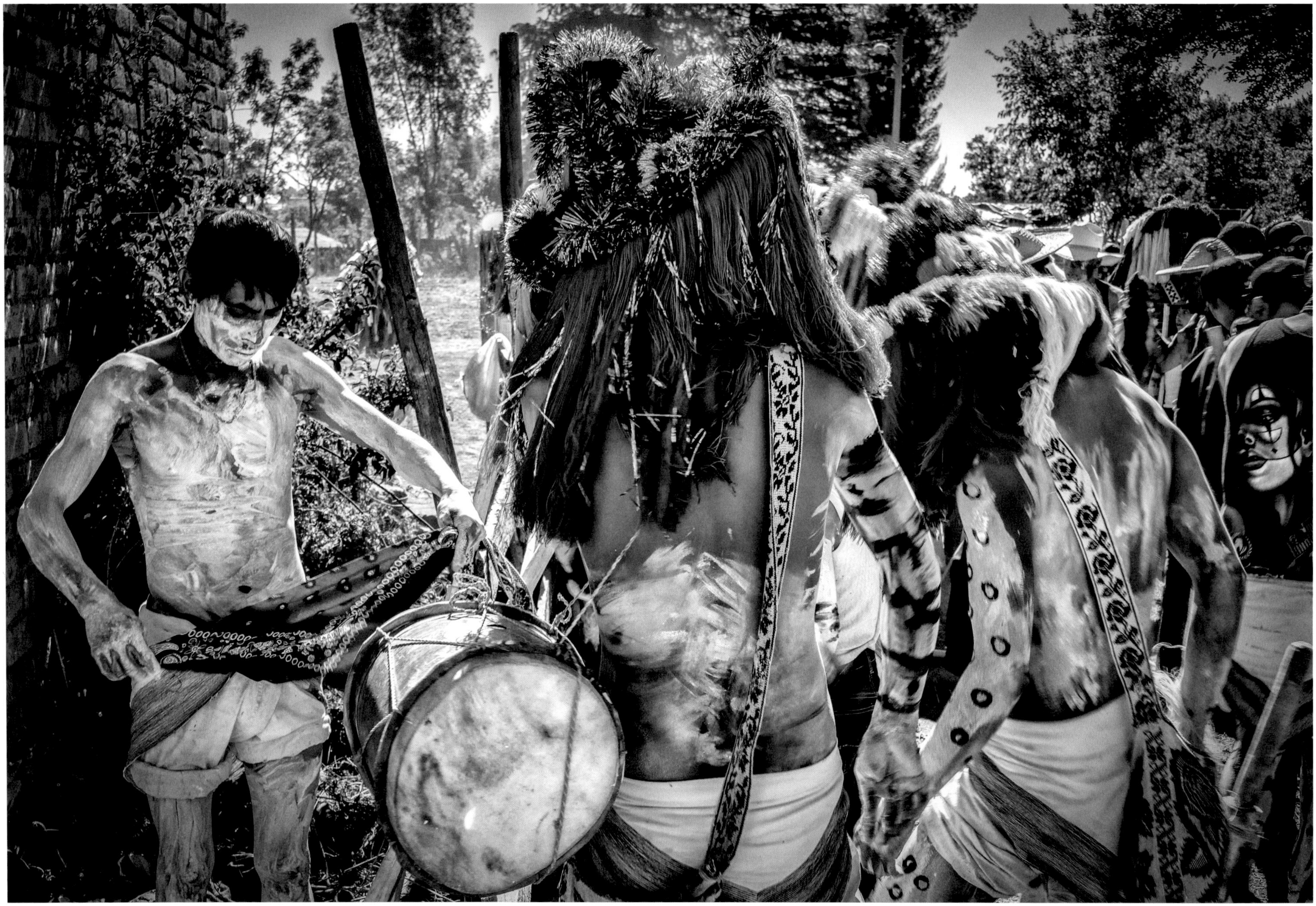

MEN AND BOYS PAINTING THEMSELVES BLACK AND WHITE ON HOLY WEDNESDAY, 2019

opposite: APPLYING BLACK AND WHITE PAINT, 2019 (ANNE FREJ)

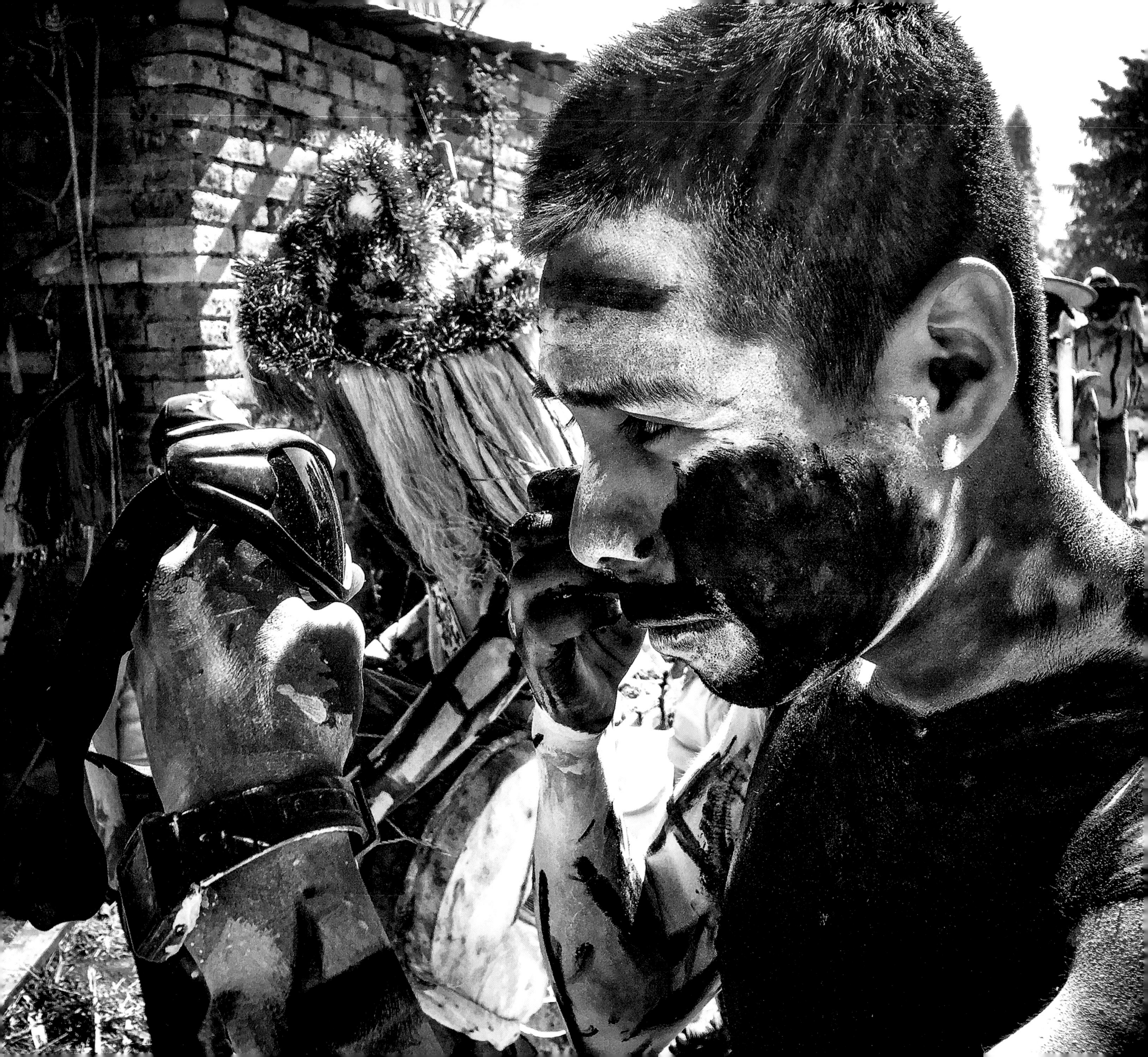

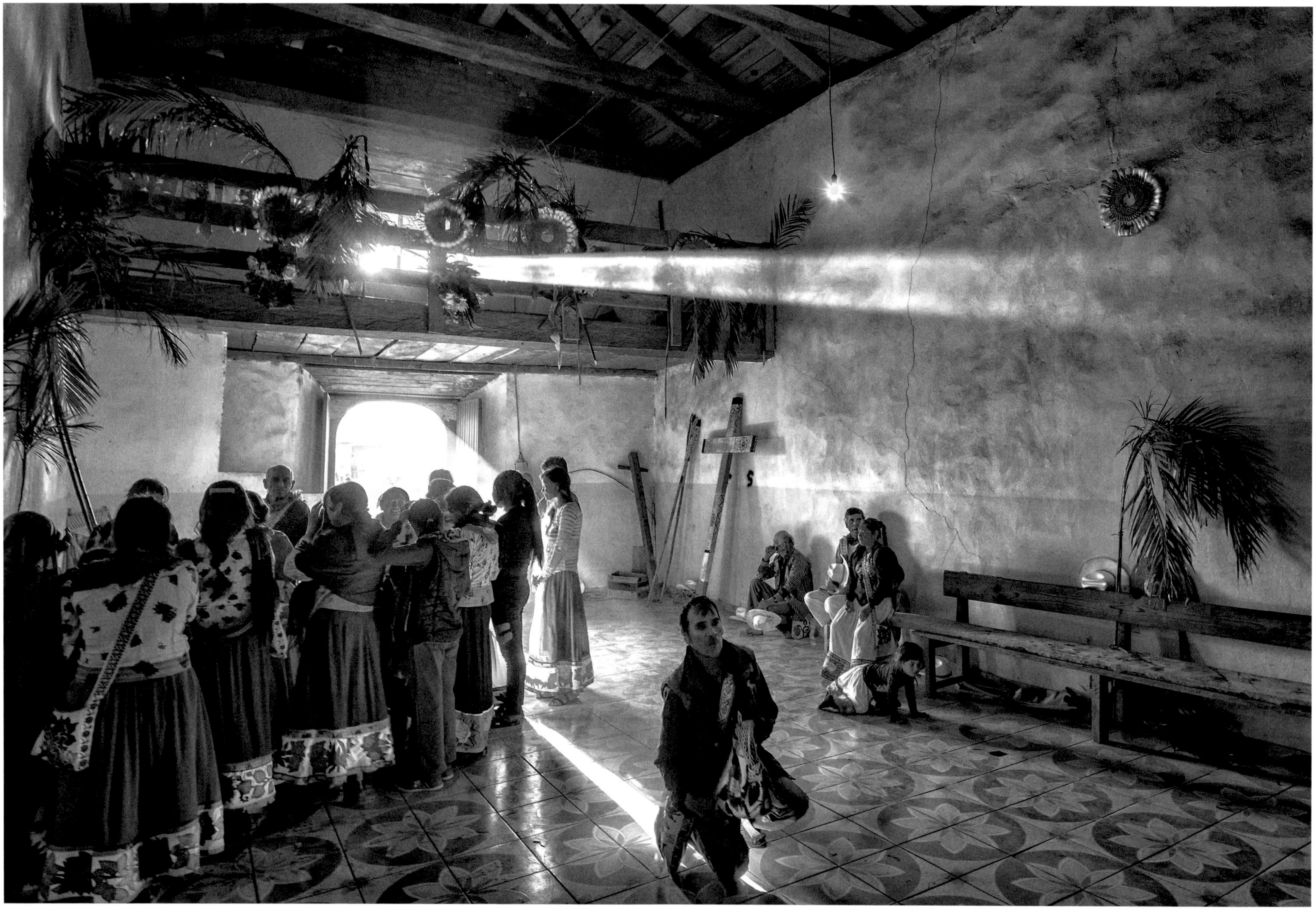

HOLY WEDNESDAY BLESSINGS IN THE VILLAGE CHURCH, 2019

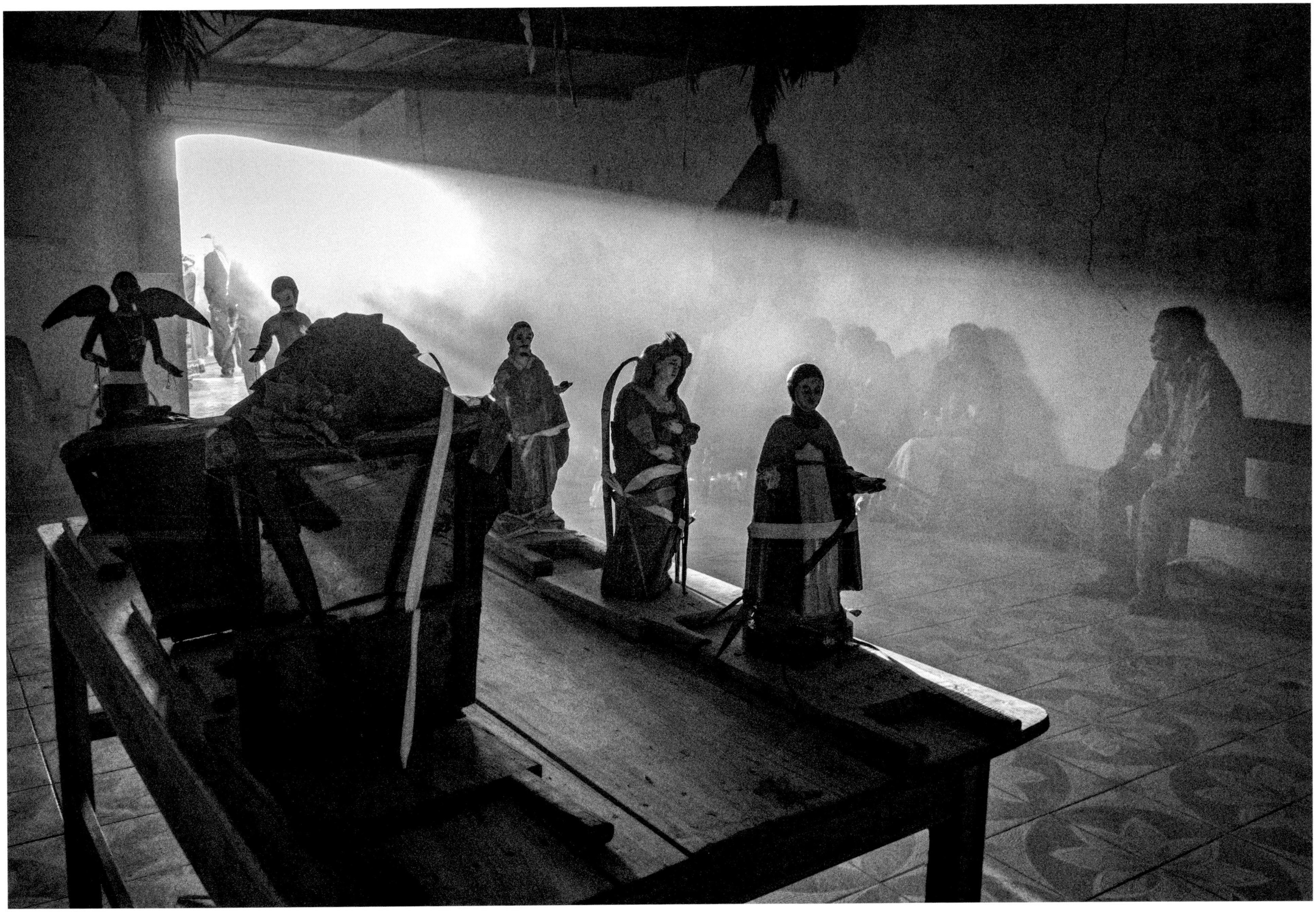

SAINTS RETURNED TO THEIR PLACES IN THE CHURCH AFTER A PROCESSION, 2019

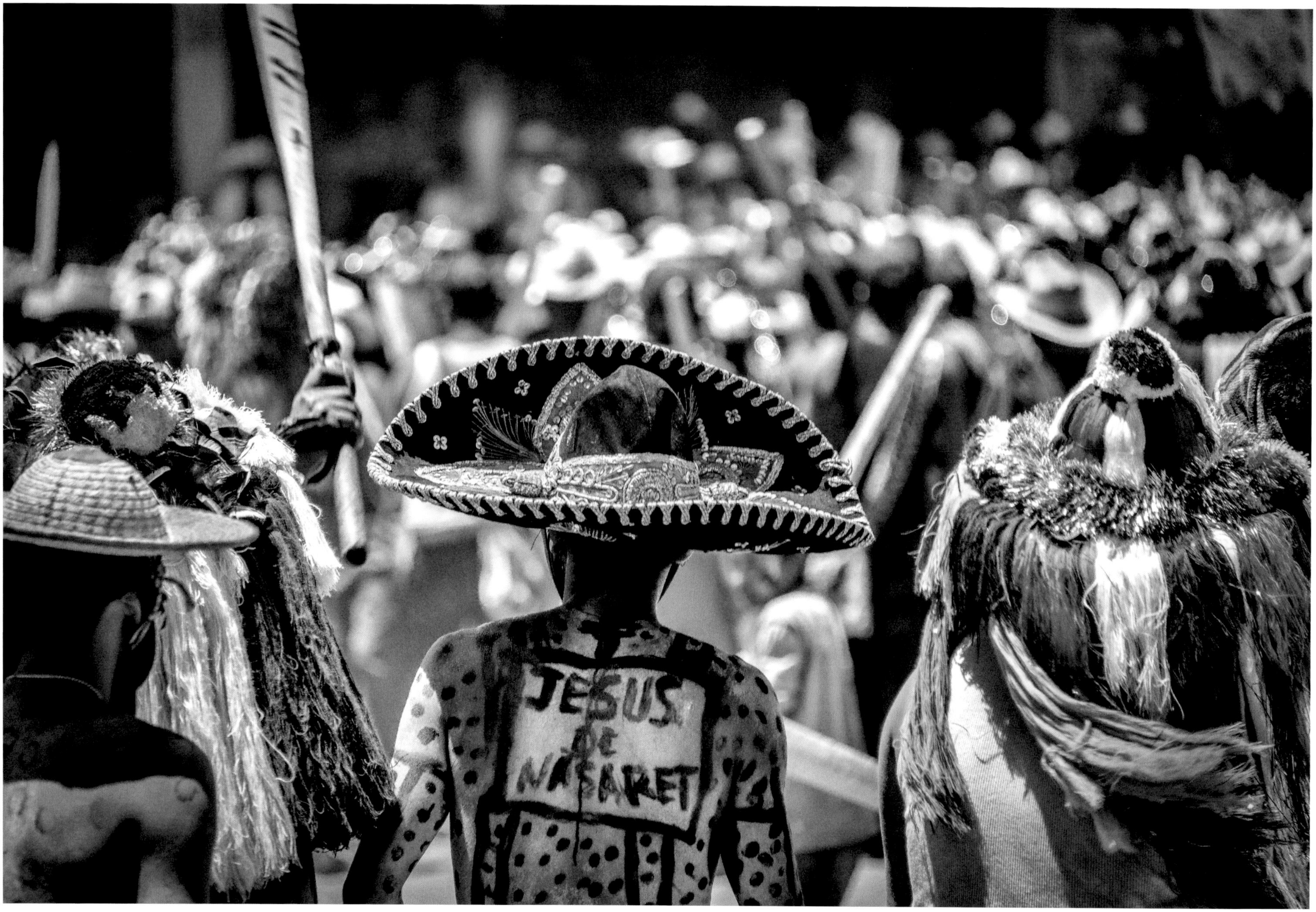

PROCESSIONS AROUND THE PERIMETER OF THE TOWN, 2019

opposite: PROCESSIONS AROUND THE PERIMETER OF THE TOWN, 2019 (ANNE FREJ)

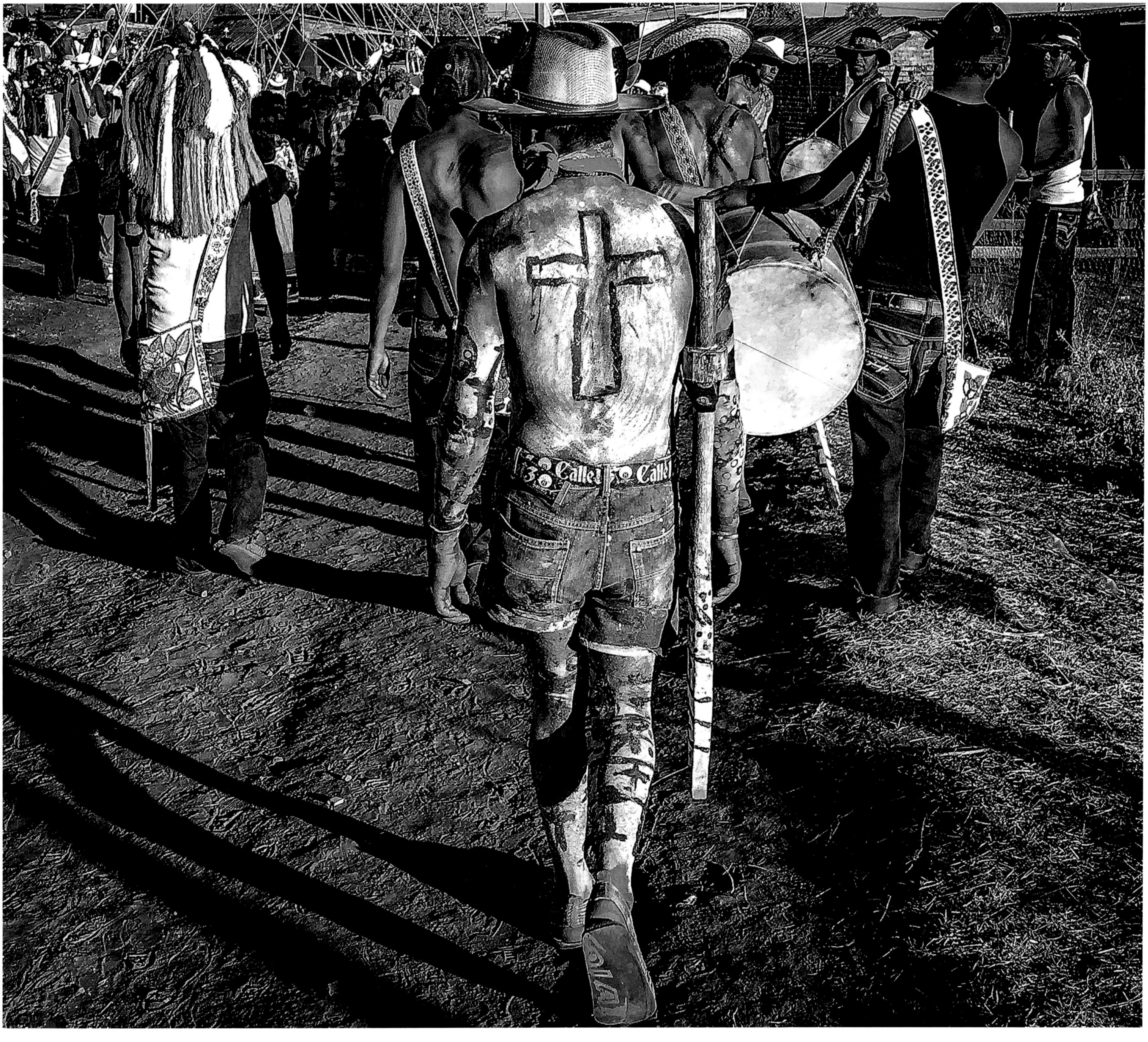

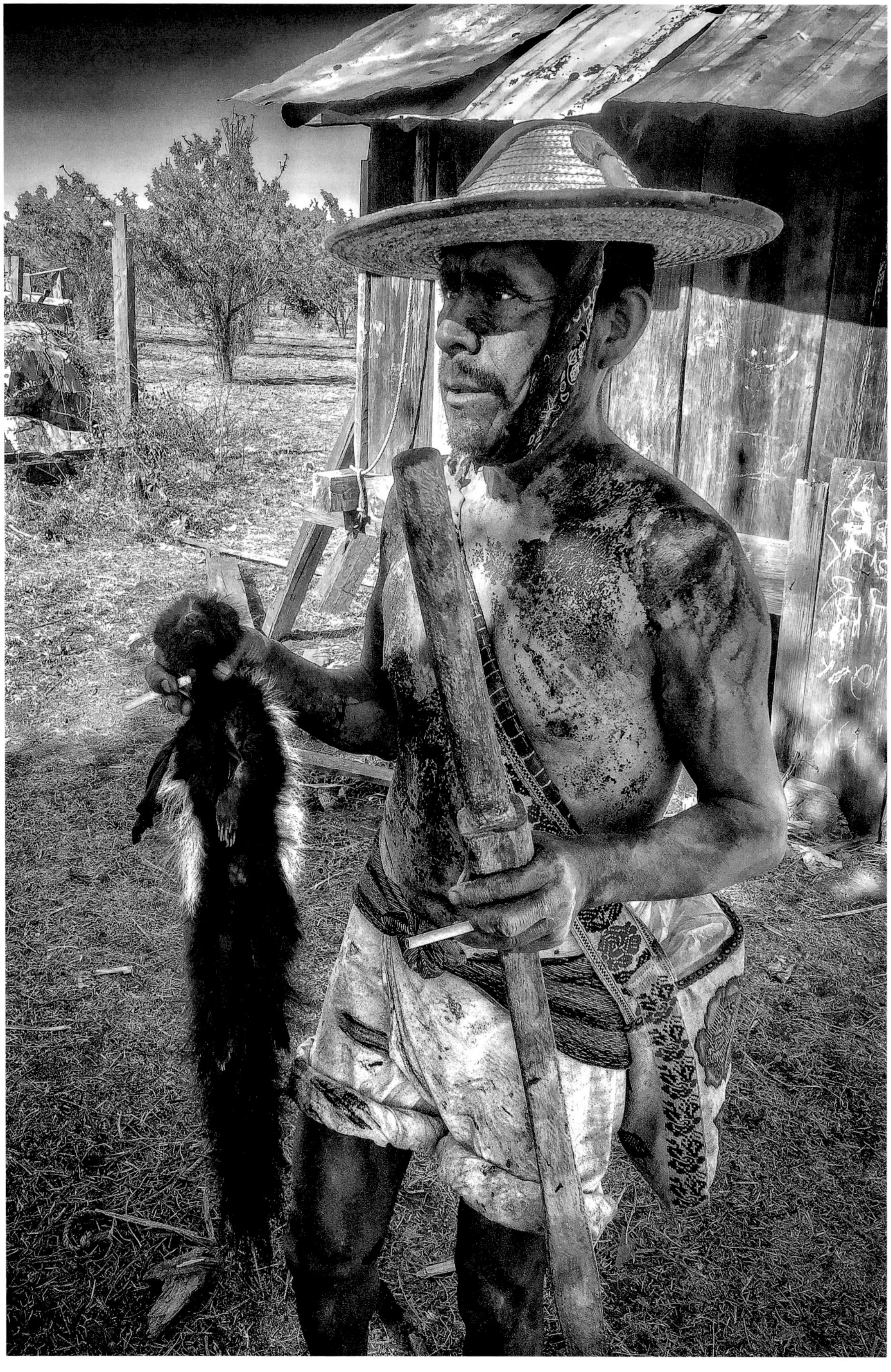

A XUMUÁVIKA WITH HIS STUFFED SKUNK, 2019 (ANNE FREJ)

opposite: THE FIRST PROCESSION OF PUÁAXKU JITSÉ LEAVING THE CHURCH WITH THE SAINTS, 2019

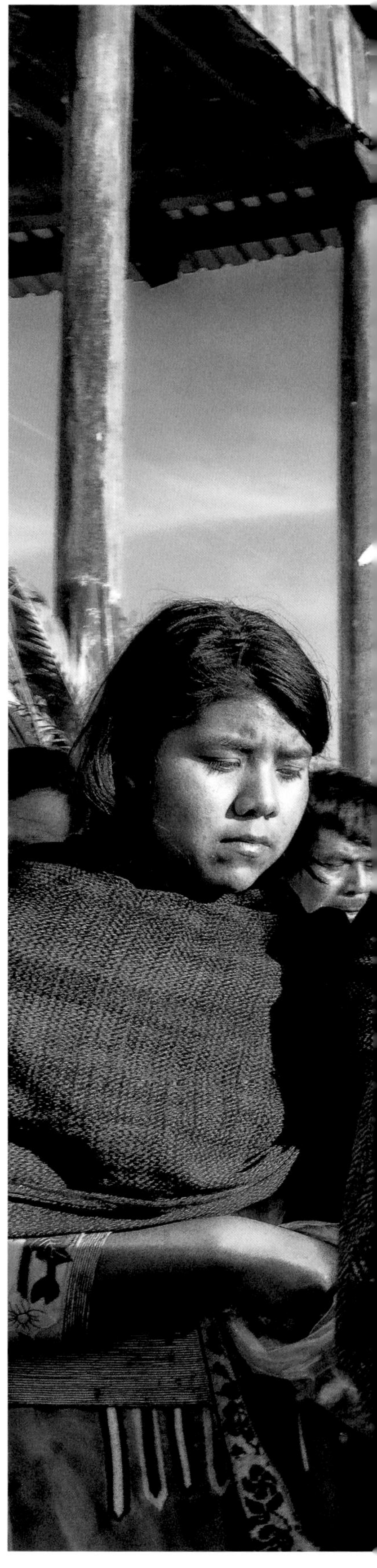

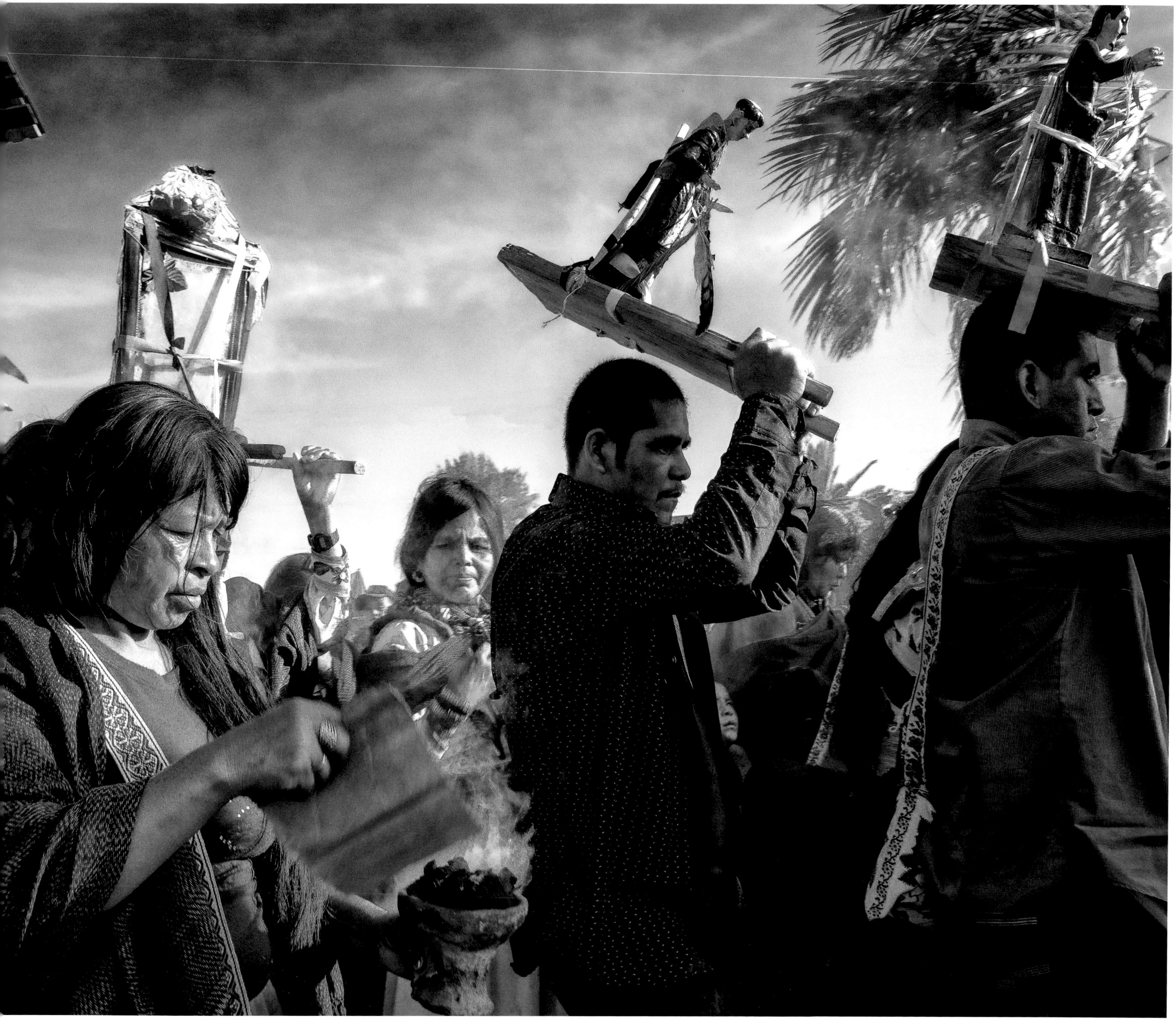

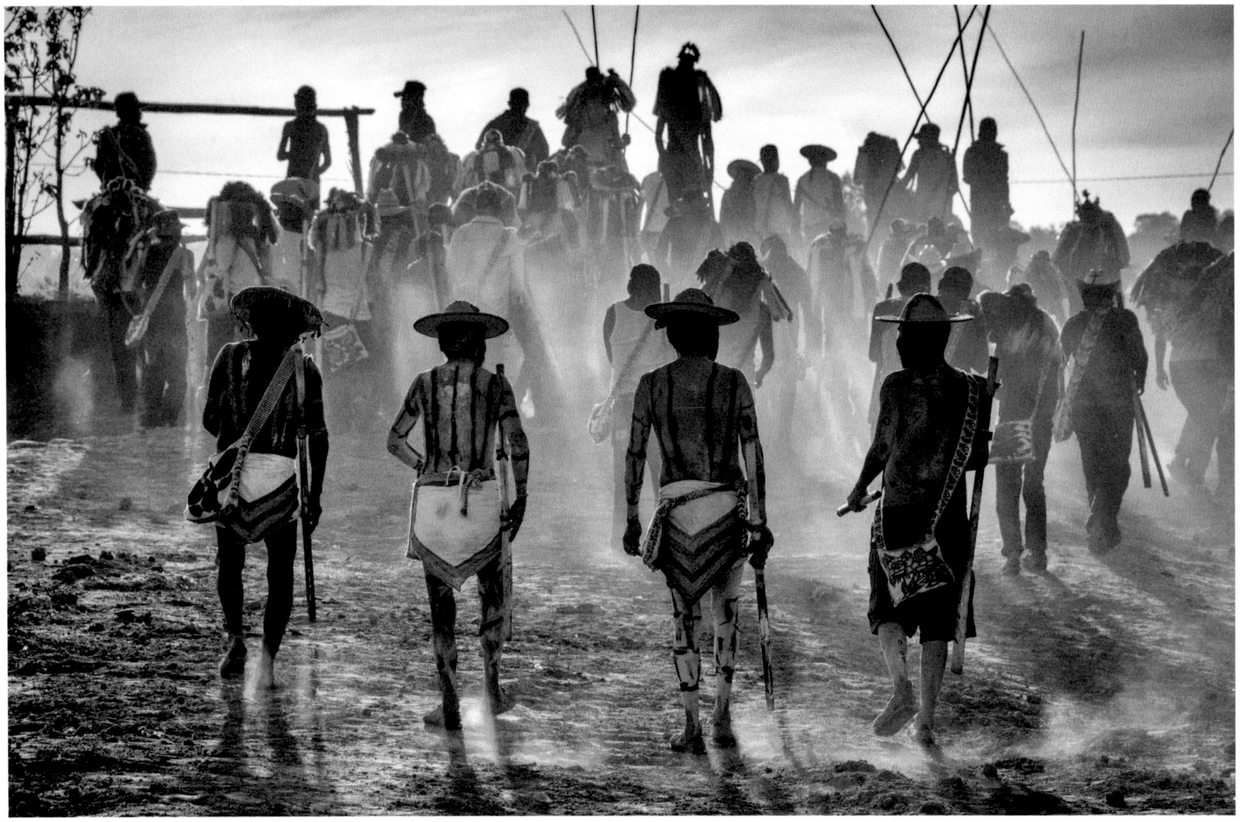

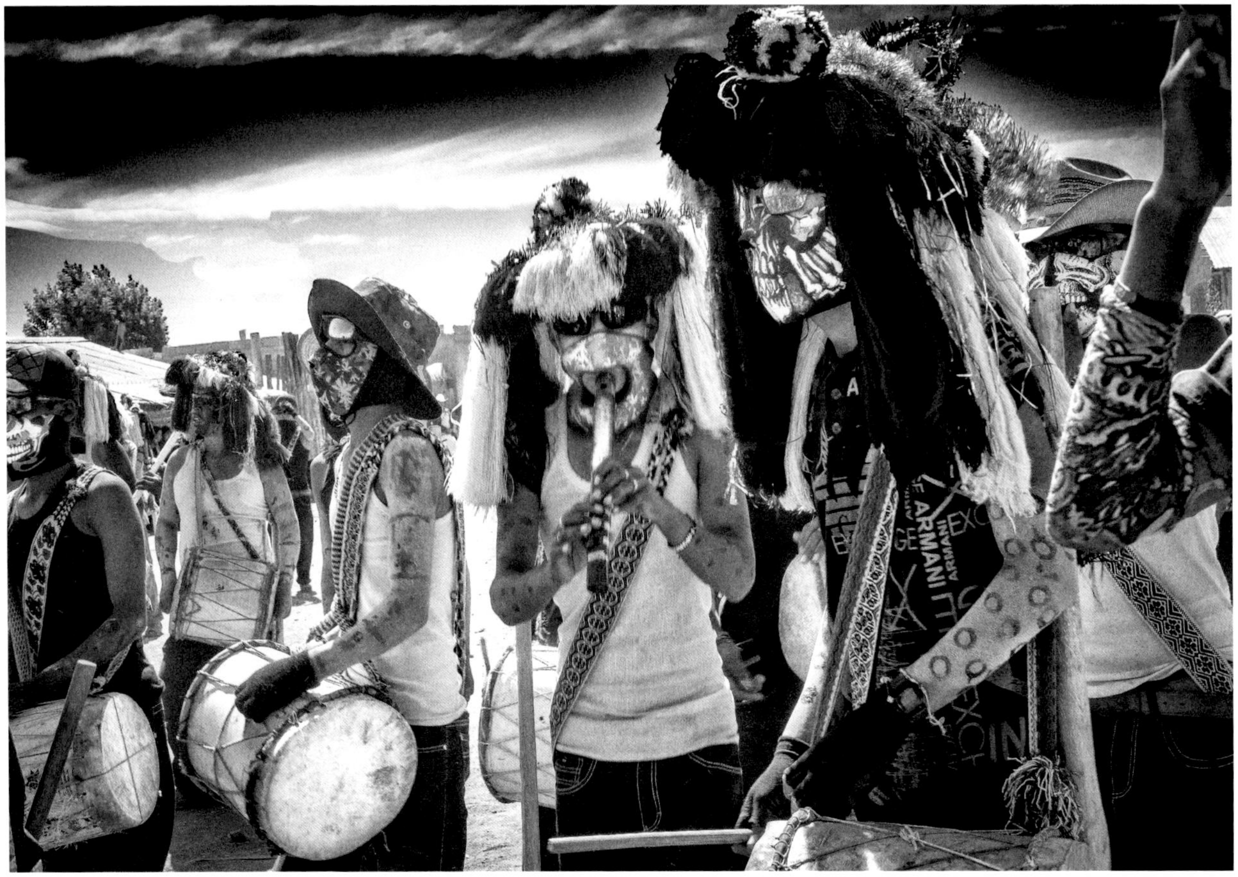

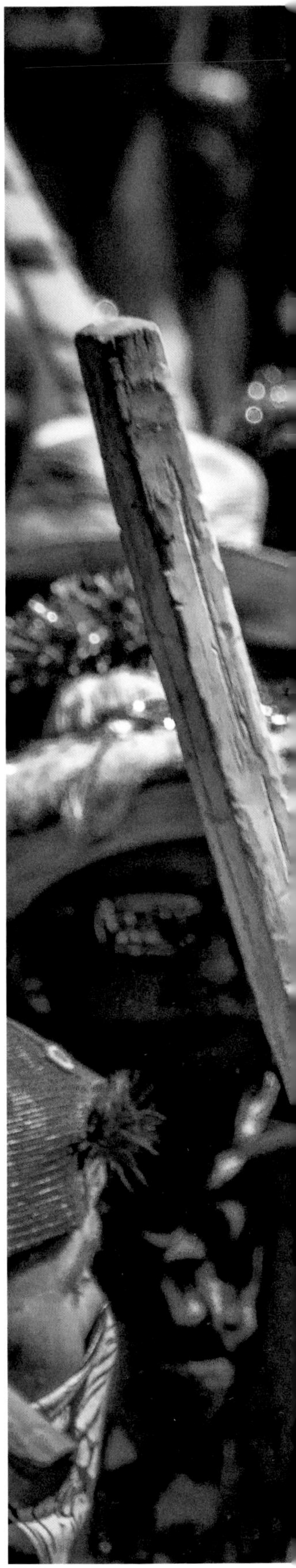

above: XUMUÁVIKA WITH SABERS GATHERING FOR A PROCESSION, 2019
below: FLUTE MUSIC AT THE START OF RITUAL BATTLES, 2019

opposite: RITUAL BATTLES, 2019

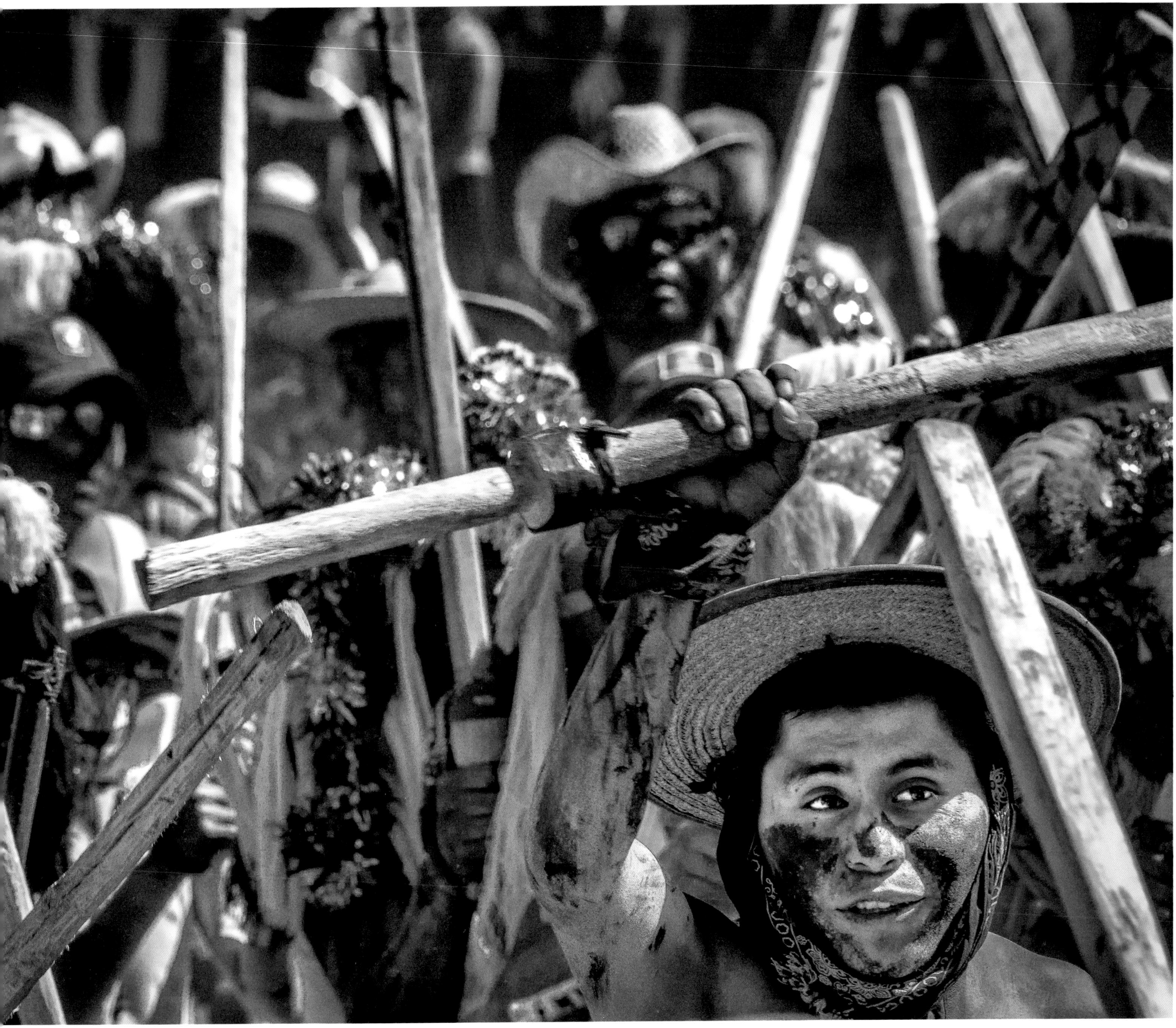

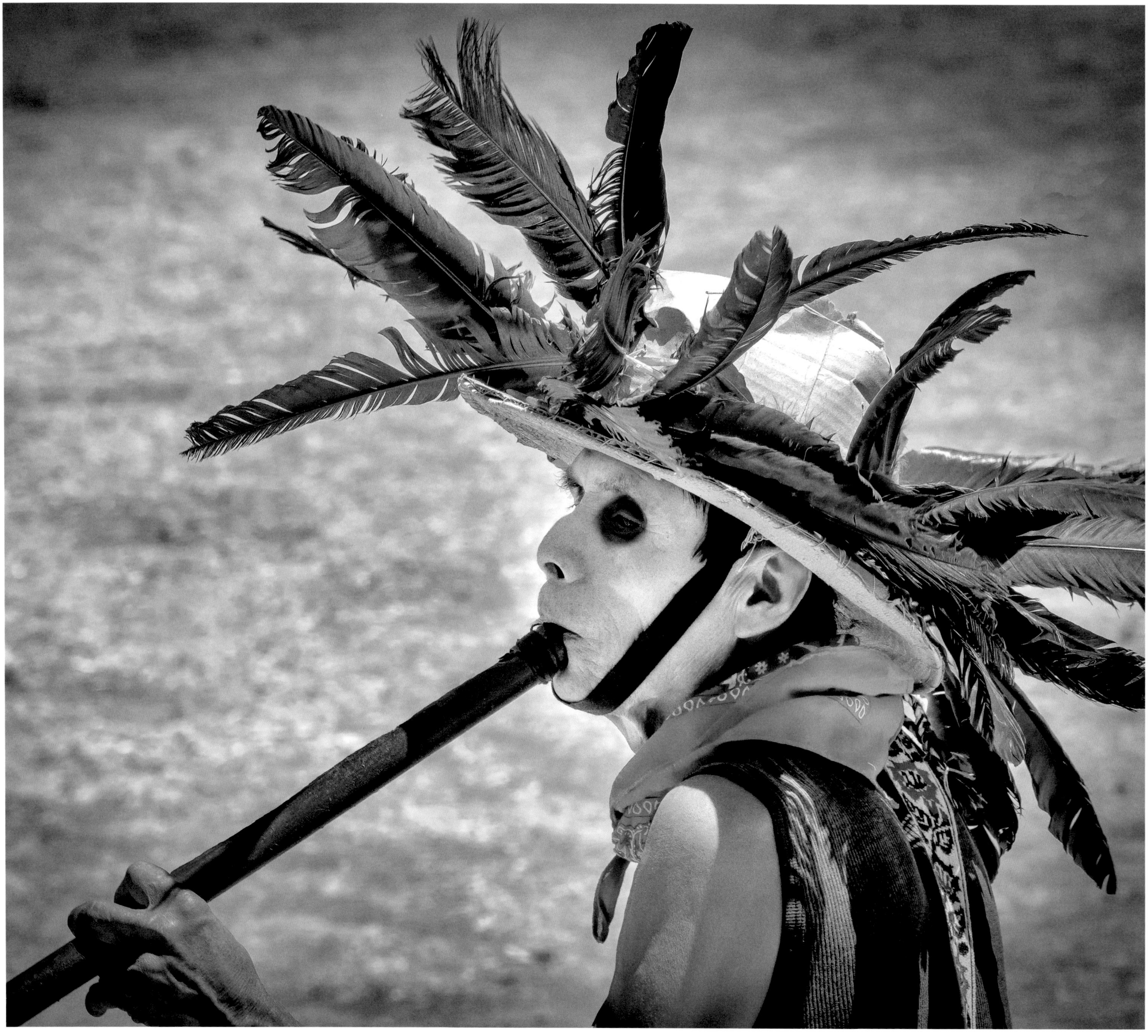

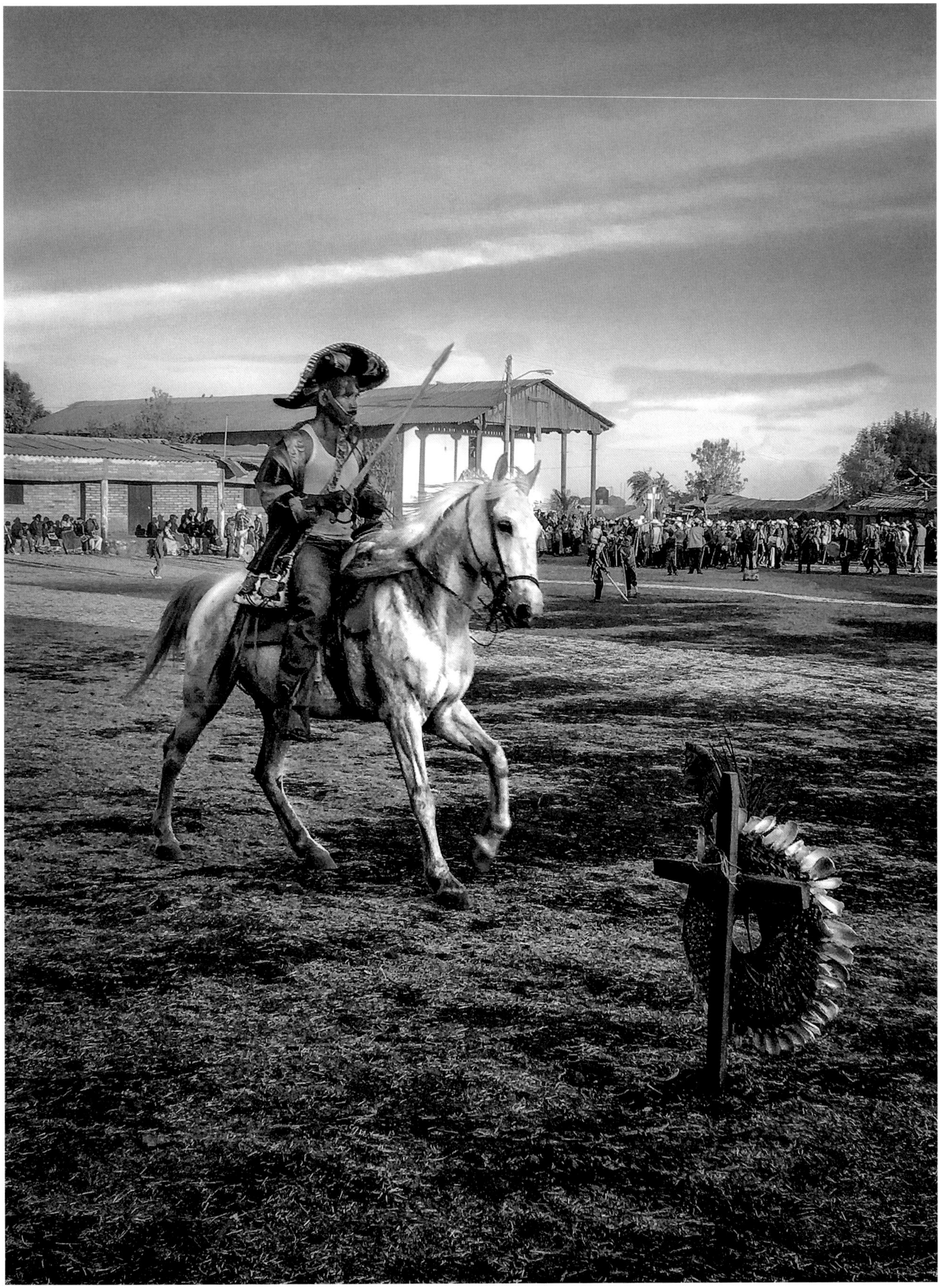

opposite: FLUTE PLAYER SIGNALING THE WARRIORS

THE CENTURION DEPARTING, 2019 (ANNE FREJ)

Fall

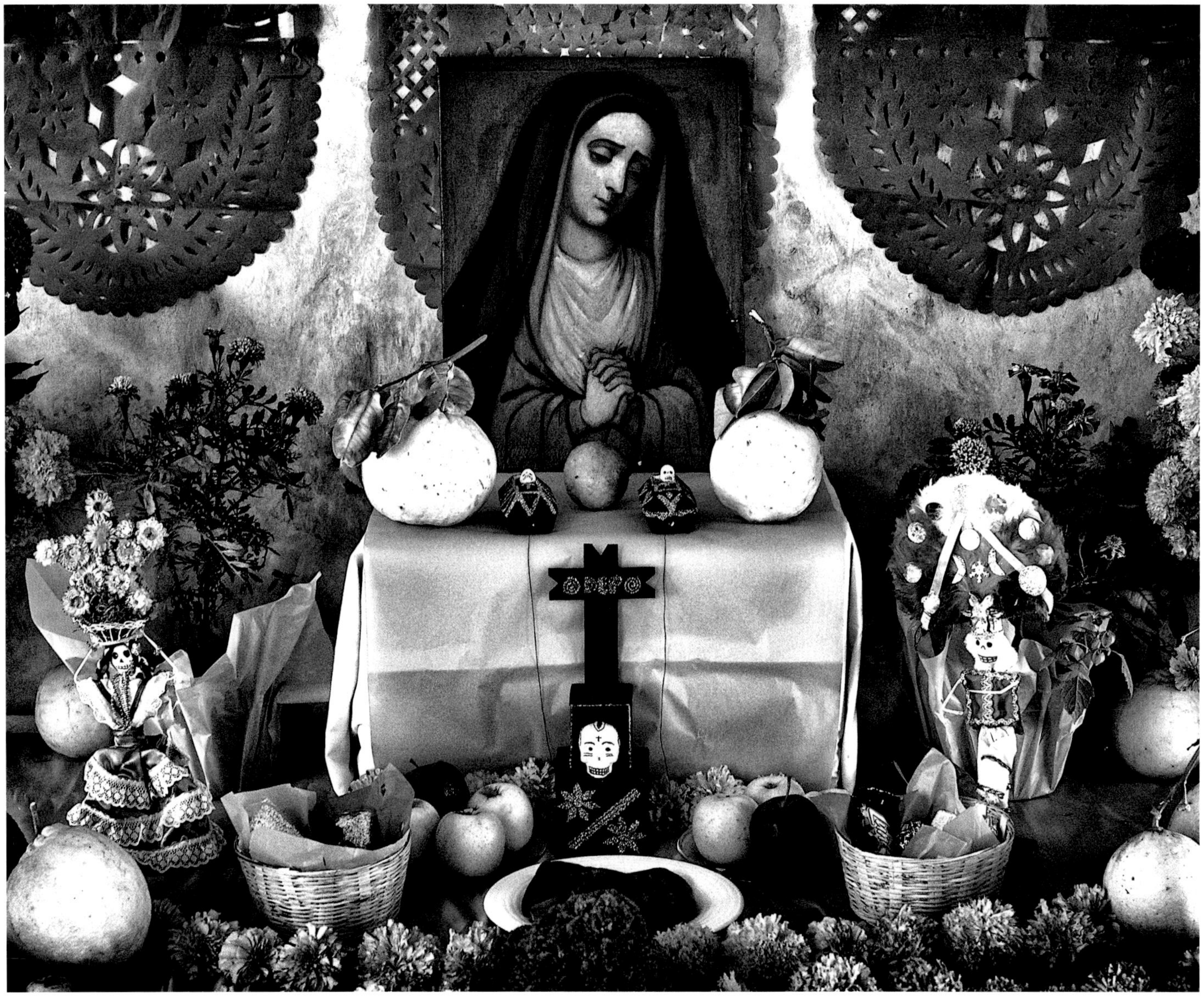

Altar adorned with flowers, food, and images of skeletons to celebrate Day of the Dead, Oaxaca, Mexico, 2013

Día de los Muertos: Honoring the Dead

NICOLASA CHÁVEZ

THROUGHOUT THE HISTORY OF HUMAN EXISTENCE, the peoples of the world have celebrated the cycles of life, which include ceremonies honoring death and resurrection. Life and death were viewed as opposite sides of the same coin; one could not exist without the other. Rituals of death and dying have been practiced by cultural groups from the ancient Sumerians to the ancient Egyptians to the Native peoples of the Americas. Many of these cultures did not consider death an ending but a new beginning; death represented the continuance of life but in a different form. These various belief systems and the rituals and ceremonies that were practiced helped individuals and communities make sense of the universe, and answer questions about the afterlife. More concretely, ceremonies and rituals honoring the dead or celebrating resurrection prepared an individual for his or her own eventual death, the one constant in life shared amongst all people.

Two of the most famous or widely known celebrations throughout the Indo-Hispano world are Semana Santa (Holy Week) and Día de los Muertos (Day of the Dead).[1] In the Northern Hemisphere, the former corresponds to spring, a time of rebirth and renewal, and the latter corresponds to the season of harvest, a time of death and the cutting of the grain. While on the surface these two celebrations appear to be entirely different and opposite from each other, both share many similarities, and one cannot exist without the other. Each shares symbols and ritualistic elements that are greatly influenced by ancient Native traditions in the Americas, as well as by the Christian calendar and Catholic religion brought by Spanish colonizers. Of the two, the more popular is perhaps Día de los Muertos in Mexico. Even though the holiday is celebrated throughout the Americas, including in Guatemala and farther south, Muertos ceremonies (as they are commonly known) in Mexico are most recognized, honored, and visited by outsiders. In Muertos ceremonies one experiences a perfect blending of pre-Columbian and Christian ritual and ceremony.

An outsider may experience these rituals in complete befuddlement, wondering how something so seemingly Christian can also appear to be entirely pre-Columbian in nature and a continuance of ancient ceremony and ritual. How did this cultural mixing and survival of ancient traditions come about under the rule of the Spanish Empire? In order to comprehend the cultural assimilation of ancient tribal elements in Christian religious ceremony, it is important to understand the world in which Christianity developed prior to the arrival of the Spanish in the Americas. One must also consider the power of the people and their ability to survive, adapt, and shape the present while honoring the past and, in the process, creating a new future.

During the early years of Roman expansion, the official religion of the empire was polytheistic. Christianity became the official religion under the Emperor Constantine, when he issued the Edict of Milan in 313 CE. Early Christianity existed side-by-side with earth-based religions in the Mediterranean world for hundreds of years. By the time Constantine declared Christianity the official religion, the ceremonies and rituals honoring Christ had been adapted to the earlier pagan cyclical traditions of the countryside. Various stages and themes in the life of Jesus Christ coincide with seasonal themes of earlier religions. On December 25 the Romans celebrated the Birth of the Unconquered Sun. Other ceremonies that honored a child of light also occurred near the winter solstice. It was 400 years after Christ's birth that his birthdate was placed in December near the solstice, at which time he also was celebrated as a child of light.

The earliest recorded official date for honoring the departed on the Roman Catholic calendar was established by Pope Boniface IV in 609 CE. He determined it should be May 13, which coincides with Eastern Orthodox celebrations of the Pentecost. This date was subsequently moved several times until finally landing permanently on November 1, per the decree of Pope Gregory III in the middle of the ninth century. In the Northern European part of the empire (present-day England, Scotland, and Ireland), the Romans encountered ancient Celtic and Saxon traditions honoring the dead or recently departed. The ceremonies associated with the festival Samhain coincided with the shortening days and the darker half of the year. The Celtic tribes celebrated the return of the departed by placing offerings of food and drink, and dead ancestors were remembered through storytelling and song. Soon a date was added to the Catholic calendar following All Saints' Day to honor the departed who had not entered sainthood. In the tenth century, Saint Odilo, the fifth Benedictine Abbot of Cluny, standardized the observance of All Souls' Day on November 2, which became the official date for the honoring ancestors and departed family members. In Europe, the Feast of All Souls involved visiting cemeteries to light candles and place flowers on the graves of the dead. In many places it was also common to leave bread and other earthly delights for those who had passed.

Spain had only recently united as a Christian nation by the time the Spanish arrived in the Americas. For nearly eight hundred years the Arabic cultures of North Africa ruled and controlled most of the Iberian Peninsula. The Iberian Peninsula itself was a loose group of individual kingdoms, and conflict and cultural assimilation coexisted while Christian people from the north attempted to gain control of the region. Elements of Arabic, Judaic, Celtic, and Visigoth culture imbued the daily lives of Spaniards. Cultural mixing within households and marriage between different cultures were common. By 1492 the kingdoms of Castilla and León were unified with the marriage of Ferdinand and Isabella, and the last Moorish stronghold in Spain, the Alhambra, in Granada, was defeated. The religious fervor and spreading of Christian doctrine that arrived with the Catholic monarchs came on the heels of, and was a continuance of, the European Crusades. The new Christian Spain had already experienced years of cultural mixing by the time Columbus was sent on his journey to cross the globe in search of a shorter route for the spice trade. While the rulers themselves were mostly culturally intolerant, the people who left for the Americas were less so and adapted to the customs and traditions of the new lands, mixing them with their own.

The cultural adaptation and mestizaje (mixing) that occurred between the Spanish colonizers and the Native people of the Americas varied by region and contributed to the unique ways in which different communities conducted sacred ceremonies and feast days. Outside onlookers are often fascinated by the fact that so many seemingly Christian feast days are celebrated via the modes of ancient Native traditions. How did the heritage of ritual practice survive colonialism and attempted conversion to Christianity? One answer lies in the northernmost frontier of the Viceroyalty of Nueva España (present-day New Mexico and Mexico), which was home to the first and only successful Native American revolt in history, referred as the Pueblo Revolt.

After the revolt, the Spanish retreated and then returned thirteen years later with lessons learned and new negotiations for the allowance of Native ritual practice and protection of Native lands under the land-grant system. In New Mexico the synthesis between Hispano and Native cultures became stronger after the Pueblo Revolt; indeed, this synthesis is evident in many parts of the Americas and the Philippines (also a former colony and a part of Nueva España). The European newcomers had to adjust to new people; a new environment that affected the availability of building materials, food, and water sources; and new, previously unknown ritual practices. Many found themselves as foreigners in a strange land, and they had to adapt.

Historian Thomas E. Chávez has noted: "Out of this New World expansion the people and culture changed from European to American."[2] Linguist and folklorist Enrique Lamadrid has commented: "The people who came here [to the Americas] changed."[3] These new mestizo Americans and their Native American cohabitants kept many of Spain's medieval traditions alive while maintaining Native ritual practices, creating their own Indo-Hispano traditions in the process. Even though the church set the official dates for the religious ceremonies of All Souls' Day and All Saints' Day, it was the people who transformed the traditions into the ceremonies that are cherished today. This is evident in complaints from church officials about colonial populations creating their own rituals and celebrations outside the church. Upon visiting northern Nueva España, church officials often complained of *hermandades* (brotherhoods organized by laymen) and of *penitentes* (penitents) who practiced their own Holy Week ceremonies and built their own houses of worship outside the church.[4]

Both Semana Santa and Día de los Muertos are celebrated within Latino communities around the globe. While the former concentrates more on the actual death of Jesus Christ and is more somber in nature, Muertos ceremonies are joyous occasions celebrating the seasonal return of ancestors and lost loved ones. Muertos time provides an occasion to eat, drink, and be merry, all the while honoring those who have passed and, indeed, spending time with them in spirit. Throughout the centuries, Día de los Muertos festivities have demonstrated how regional cultures turned a once-solemn ceremony into a joyous celebration of mestizo heritage. Even though both modes of celebration are practiced in the Americas and the Philippines, perhaps the most uniquely festive and colorful is the multi-day Muertos celebration in Mexico. Each region in the country observes the holiday with its own music, cuisine, costume, and lore, along with more widespread traditions dating back to precolonial times. The curious blending of Native and European traditions creates this special event, which is distinctive and widely popular.

By the time the Spanish arrived in Mexico, they were accustomed to celebrating the feast days of All Saints' and All Souls' Days (along with the Eve of All Saints, on October 31). Upon arrival in what is present-day Mexico, they witnessed Indigenous ceremonies honoring the dead. One of the earliest historical written records of events honoring the dead is that of Fray Diego Durán at the end of the sixteenth century.[5] He described the first night of celebrations during the ninth month of the Aztec calendar, writing: "The festival celebrated at the beginning of this month was performed with great rejoicing. It was called Micailhuitontli, which is a diminutive and means Feast of the Little Dead. According to my information, it was the commemoration of innocent dead children, and that is why the diminutive was used."

He went on to describe the use of the diminutive "little," because the feast was in preparation or anticipation of the subsequent celebration: "the Great Feast of the Dead, where adults were to be remembered."[6] These celebrations were perhaps descended from some of the oldest in the world (paralleling those of the ancient Egyptians and Celtic cultures). The original Aztec calendar was based on a 260-day year, and their original festivities took began around our present-day August 8. The Feast of the Little Dead lasted close to twenty days, after which the Great Feast of the Dead commenced, near our present-day August 28. Durán suspected that part of the reason for the August dates was to celebrate before the first frost and to have all the crops brought in, and to prepare "offerings, oblations, and sacrifices." Later he noted seeing similar rituals and offerings of food conducted at the same time as All Saints' Day and All Souls' Day ("All Hallows" and "the Day of Faithful Departed," in his words).[7] It was the ceremony and ritual of the people that would overshadow the more solemn religious ceremony, resulting in the festivals of today. A special mass may be given at the local church, but the bulk of planning, arrangement, and execution of the festivities are left to the people who create elaborate altars within the home and adorn the gravesites of the departed.

The most common ingredient of all Muertos ceremonies, past and present, is the cuisine. Durán noted: "On the first [Little Feast] I saw people offering chocolate, candles, fowl, fruit, great quantities of seed, and food. On the next day I saw the same being done."[8] Today, as in the past, family and friends share in the cooking and the preparation of food for feasting with the departed and for leaving offerings on beautifully decorated altars called *ofrendas*. Special favorite foods of lost loved ones are set out to entice them back home during the festivities. Once the home altars are completed, families then move to the cemeteries, bringing with them more foodstuffs, as well as candles and decorations. The cuisine of Muertos festivities represents the perfect synthesis of Native and Spanish cultures, due to the Columbian exchange.[9] Considered the first mestizaje of the Americas, the Columbian exchange altered the way the world eats and forever changed what was considered traditional around the globe. (Imagine Italian food without the tomato or Irish food without the potato.) It also influenced the regional cuisine of Muertos celebrations in Mexico.

Original celebratory items left for and shared with the dead include tamales, chocolate, and *calaveras*, edible skulls shaped from seeds and grain, such as amaranth. Of these foodstuffs, chocolate may be the most ancient, with the tamale a close second. The earliest known use of chocolate dates to 3000–3600 BCE in the upper Amazon basin (present-day Ecuador), where archaeological evidence of chocolate-making implements was found. Human populations expanded the range of where chocolate trees grew, and chocolate moved into areas of present-day Mexico, where production flourished.[10]

The original chocolate drink was thick and frothy, bitter and spicy. The only sweetener would have been locally harvested honey. Chocolate was known for its powers of spiritual transformation (what we might refer to today as a "chocolate high") and its sustenance. Both Maya and Aztec warriors were known to take along solid blocks of chocolate when waging war. Upon arriving in Mexico, the Spanish noticed the ritual use of chocolate.

The Spanish introduction of new items such as fruits, vegetables, sugar, flour, and livestock added to the array of new foods coming to the Americas. Columbus brought sugar cane from the Canary Islands to the Caribbean on his first journey westward. The first sugar mill was established in Hispaniola in 1516, and by 1531 Cortés possessed three mills that produced a very fine sugar. By the middle of the century, sugar was exported to Peru and back to Spain.[11] The addition of sugar in hot drinking chocolate was further enhanced with almonds (a tradition dating to the Arabic period in Spain) and milk and cream, which arrived with the first Spanish livestock. These ingredients, along with local spices and pre-Columbian chile, resulted in a perfect frothy drink that soon became used not only by the ruling elite but by inhabitants of every town and village. The drink was highly revered and continued to be used in sacred ceremonies and community festivities. On a local ofrenda, foodstuffs may differ depending on the favorite items of the departed, but chocolate was and is the constant and necessary item to attract and entice those from the spirit world.

The introduction of wheat also contributed to another seasonal favorite food of Día de los Muertos. Wheat was introduced as early as 1493, during Columbus' second voyage, and the Spanish brought with them the tradition of baking bread and other goods made from flour. Within fifteen years of colonization, by 1535, Mexican-grown wheat was exported on a regular basis to the Antilles. Culinary traditions that were celebrated in Northern Spain during All Saints' Day and All Souls' Day included an offering of soul cakes for the departed. As old European traditions merged with the newly discovered ceremonies honoring the dead, *pan de los muertos* (bread of the dead) became a mainstay, as did Native *tamales de maíz* (cornflour tamales). The bread today is made in the shape of a skull and also as a round loaf with crossed bones placed over the top. Pan de los muertos has crossed national borders and today

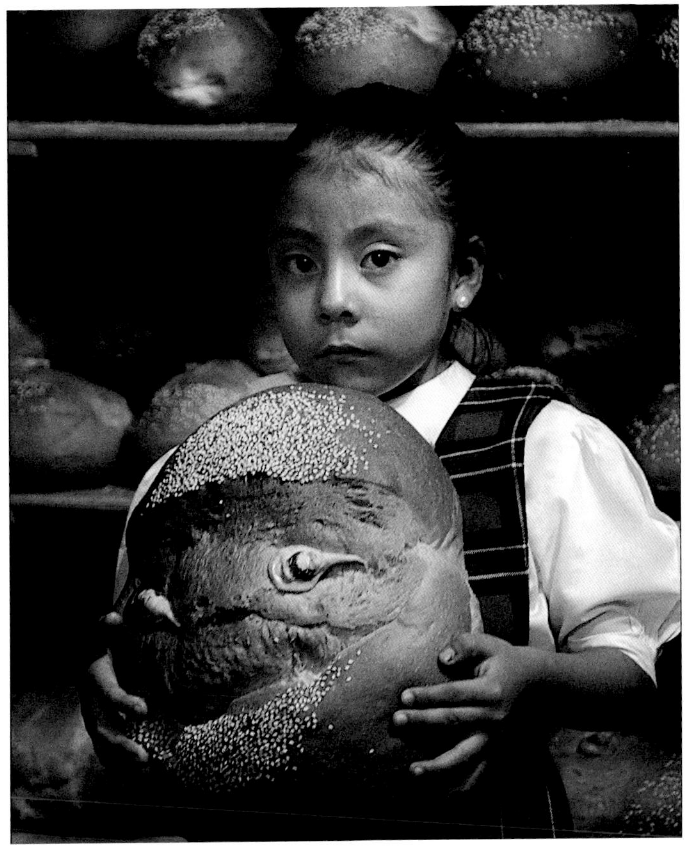

A young girl holding a loaf of the sweet bread popular during Day of the Dead, Oaxaca, Mexico, 2013

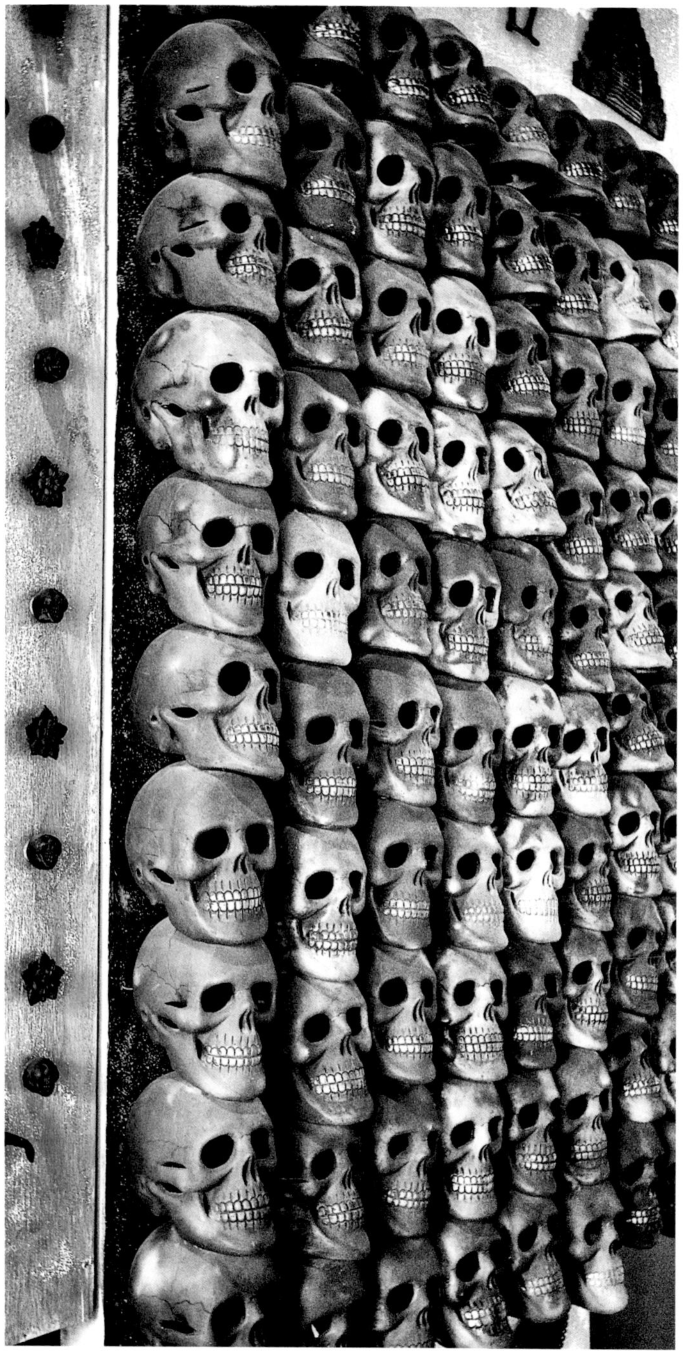

Skulls, which are found everywhere during Day of the Dead celebrations, Oaxaca, Mexico, 2013

is baked in Mexican *panaderías* (bakeries) all over the United States for celebrations among expatriate communities.

The sugar skull is another popular food item associated with Día de los Muertos. Earlier the *calavera* (skull) was made of seeds and grain such as amaranth, but with prolific sugar production during the colonial period, the sweetener eventually became the main ingredient in the sugar skull. Later colored decoration was added, and the names of the departed were written onto these edible sculptures. Today sugar skulls are, along with pan de los muertos, the most recognizable of the seasonal foods associated with Día de los Muertos.

Although the sugar skull is a relative newcomer in the long history of rituals for the dead, the use of the skull itself has its origins in both ancient Native practice and the medieval European Christian tradition. Catholic use of skulls or skeletons has a long history. Many saints are depicted with a skull in hand or nearby. In contemporary society the skull is associated with death and is viewed as frightening. In the world of medieval Catholics, however, the skull was a symbol of mortality that reminded the faithful to lead a good life and to do good deeds, for it is action during life that determines fate after death. The European tradition of a skeleton representing death made its way to the Americas, where it took on a new form in the colonies. In northern Nueva España, the character La Muerte (also referred to as Doña Sebastiana) makes her appearance during the Good Friday processions of Holy Week. She rides upon a *carreta* (two-wheeled cart carved from wood) and points a bow and arrow to indicate to onlookers that death is always at the door. She reminds us all that we are mortal.

For Indigenous cultures in Mexico, the skull or skeleton symbolized the continuance of the life cycle. Whether dead or alive, all beings were skeletons underneath their clothing and underneath their skin. La Santa Muerte makes an appearance in the regions of Nueva España that make up present-day Mexico. Looking very much like a female Grim Reaper, with black robe and scythe in hand, she may be frightening to see at first glance. She symbolizes the very personification of death itself, which is considered a natural part of the life cycle, universal to all beings no matter their status in life. She does not represent a particular individual and does not serve as a personal warning, but instead represents a commonality that binds all humans together. Indeed, she is considered a folk saint, lifted up to sainthood by the will and reverence of the people. Once a year she reminds communities it is time to reconnect with deceased friends and relatives in a spirit of celebration and remembrance.[12]

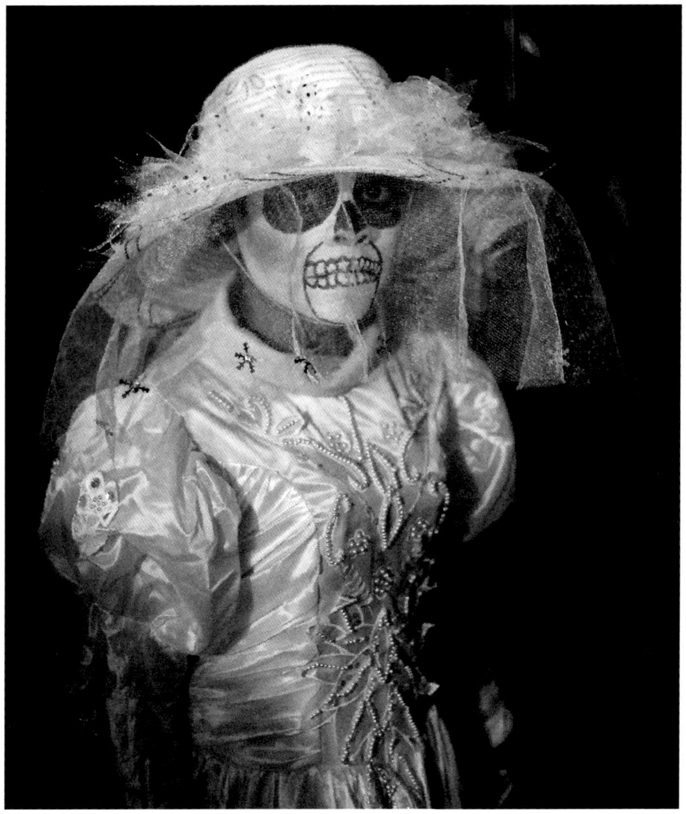

A girl dressed and made up as Catrina, a favored image associated with Day of the Dead, Oaxaca, Mexico, 2013

Our more contemporary eye is accustomed to the widely popular figure of La Calavera Catrina (or La Katrina, as she is sometimes called in the United States). A more recent incarnation, dating to the beginning of the twentieth century, she is now perhaps the most internationally famous of all Muertos symbols and traditions. The original image was created by the Mexican artist and illustrator José Guadalupe Posada. His 1910 etching portrayed La Calavera Catrina as a satirical drawing to mock the elite classes of early twentieth-century Mexico. Posada's image bore a likeness to Carmen Romero Rubio, the second wife of Mexican President Porfirio Díaz. Díaz's presidency was one of the main targets in many of Posada's satirical works, which were widely popular during and following the Mexican Revolution. The historical symbolism of the skeleton as representing the continuation of life and the popularity of La Calavera Catrina became widely used in Día de los Muertos celebrations. In areas both rural and urban, Catrina's image showed that death comes to each and every human being, no matter their status in life. Townspeople and urban dwellers alike have continued the historic tradition of painting their faces as calaveras, although the elegant Catrina has replaced older and more traditional images. Today she graces thousands, if not millions, of faces during the festivities. Mexican-American tradition-bearer and face-painter Judith Bautista explained that when people are doing themselves up for Día de los Muertos, "odds are you're not doing sugar skull makeup; you're actually painting your face like a Catrina."[13] Even so, in various regions throughout the country, millions of variants of calavera face paint can be witnessed among the participants of the local comparsas (impromptu groups of musicians and revelers who travel in joyous processions from the home to the cemetery). The ritual face paint is not only for costume and decoration; it also connects to an earlier time when participants truly transformed spiritually into a skeleton in order to commune on the same level as the departed. Along with music, dance, and sacred foodstuffs, ritual calavera face painting brings participants into a space that was without time—no present nor past, only the here and now, a space in which to simply coexist with the spirits of the departed.

Catrina, the contemporary image of the calavera, also includes items from the ancient Mesoamerican heritage. Atop her brightly colored calavera face paint lies a headband or garland of bright orange and yellow flowers and sometimes a monarch butterfly. Aside from the elaborately painted faces and lively comparsas marching in the streets, these are the two symbols that most beautifully illustrate Muertos celebrations. They are also entirely Mexican. The marigold and monarch butterfly are among the most ancient and historical components of Día de los Muertos decor and adornment, and each has been featured in rituals honoring the dead long before the arrival of the Spanish. The *cempasúchitl* (*zempoalxochitl* in Nahuatl), the marigold, is often referred to as *flor de muerto* (flower of the dead). Native to central Mexico, it grows abundantly in the wild but was also cultivated by the Aztecs. It blooms naturally at the end of the rainy season just in time for the late-October and early-November ceremonies. The bright orange and yellow colors of the petals are said to represent the sun, which, according to Aztec mythology, guides spirits on their way to the underworld. Much in the manner of evergreen garlands, trees, and wreaths at Christmastime in the United States and parts of Europe, marigolds adorn ofrendas, doorways, and gravesites. Their pungent scent fills the air, and it is believed that the strong aroma, coupled with the enticing scents of chocolate and home-baked goods, attracts the spirits and helps them find their way home.

In Mexican tradition, flowers also represent the fragility and impermanence of life, since they are at their fullest and most colorful immediately before they die. Their brilliant display of golden orange is further enhanced by the majestic annual return of migrating monarch butterflies to Mexico. Local mythology posits that the souls of the departed are carried home on their wings. Use of the marigold and images of the monarch butterfly are so greatly intertwined with the season and celebration that many intricately painted calavera faces also include an array of floral designs. Whether celebrations lean more toward the Indigenous or toward the European, none is complete without the brilliant display of orange from Mother Nature, an element that makes these ceremonies uniquely Mexican.

The ritual ceremonies of Semana Santa and Día de los Muertos honor a multicultural past that is still evident today in both Spain and the Americas. Present-day celebrations show that heritage is a continuum that moves toward the future while always including the past; they express a new world, a new society, a new people, and the people of today. They reflect the present while nodding to an ancient heritage. This temporal blending and the preservation of a rich cultural heritage are two elements that perhaps make Día de los Muertos so widely accepted in the minds of non-Mexicans around the globe. The various traditions of the Mexican Día de los Muertos have now reached the popular imagination of celebrants in the United States and among expatriate communities elsewhere around the globe. The universal theme of celebrating death is one impetus for the popularity of Día de los Muertos today. After years of living among cultures that are trained to fear death, people are hungry for a way to honor this most natural of passages. Día de los Muertos provides comfort, solace, and a celebration that occupies a shared space—in person, virtually, or simply by practicing at the same time as others around the globe. Inside and outside Mexico, it is the people who continue to honor the dead with food, music, color, and fanfare, keeping their traditional rituals alive now and into the future.

NOTES

1. The celebrations are also referred to in the plural as Días de los Muertos, or Days of the Dead, because the festivities last over a three-day period. Throughout this article the full title of the festivities is abbreviated to "Muertos."

2. Fray Angélico Chávez, *My Penitente Land: Reflections of Spanish New Mexico* (Albuquerque: University of New Mexico Press, 1974), 1.

3. Enrique Lamadrid, interview on December 10, 2020.

4. Ramón A. Gutierrez, "The Genízaro Origins of the Hermanos Penitentes," in *Nación Genízara: Ethnologies, Place and Identity in New Mexico*, Moises Gonzales and Enrique Lamadrid, eds. (Albuquerque: University of New Mexico Press, 2019), 108–109. See also John L. Kessel, *Kiva, Cross, and Crown: The Pecos Indians and New Mexico, 1540–1840* (Albuquerque: University of New Mexico Press, 1987).

5. Fray Diego Durán, *Book of the Gods and Rites and the Ancient Calendar*, Doris Heyden and Fernando Horcasitas, trans. and eds. (Norman, OK: University of Oklahoma Press, 1971), 441.

6. Ibid.

7. Ibid.

8. Ibid., 442–443 and 444–446.

9. For an in-depth and delicious history of the Columbian exchange, see Raymond Sokolov, *Why We Eat What We Eat: How Columbus Changed the Way the World Eats* (New York: Touchstone Books, 1991).

10. For a readable and in-depth history of the sacred uses of chocolate in Mesoamerica, see Fray Diego Durán, *Book of the Gods and Rites and the Ancient Calendar*, trans. and ed. Doris Heyden and Fernando Horcasitas (Norman, OK: University of Oklahoma Press, 1971). For another concise history of chocolate from its origins in Mesoamerican times to our present-day uses, see Michael D. Coe and Sophie D. Coe, *The True History of Chocolate* (New York: Thames and Hudson, 1986). For a brief early history, see Franz Lidz, "The Delicious, Ancient History of Chocolate and Vanilla," *Smithsonian Magazine*, July 11, 2019, https://www.smithsonianmag.com/history/delicious-ancient-history-chocolate vanilla-180972551.

11. Eric Williams, *From Columbus to Castro: The History of the Caribbean*, 1492–1969 (New York: Vintage Books, 1970), 26–29.

12. R. Andrew Chestnut, "Holy Death: Santa Muerte, Day of the Dead, and La Catrina," *Huffington Post*, October 15, 2016, https://www.huffingtonpost.com/r-andrew-chestnut/holy-death-santa-muerte-d_b_8305040.html.

13. Meirav Devash, "5 Things to Know Before Doing Day of the Dead Makeup," *Allure* magazine, October 12, 2016.

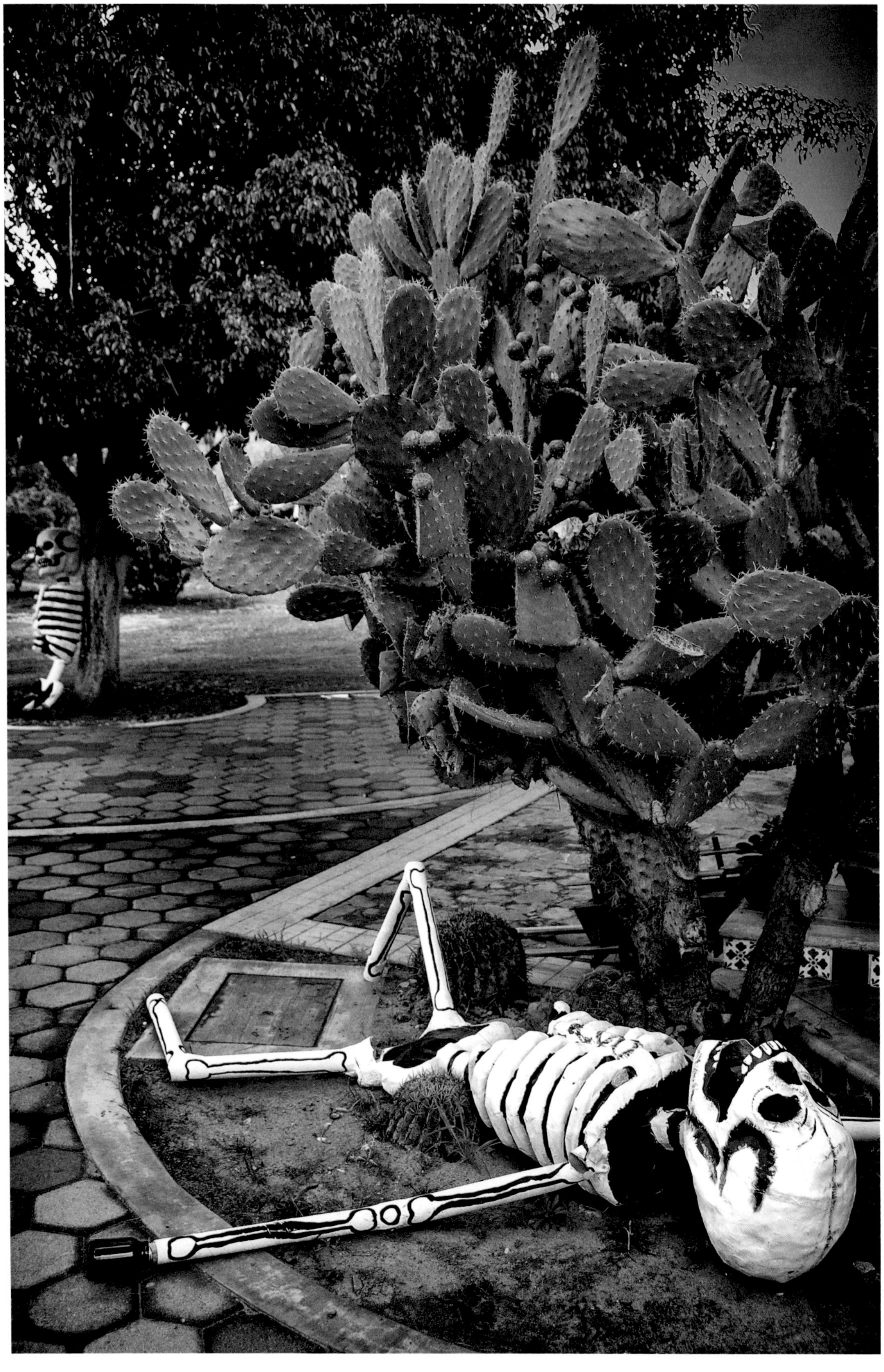

Day of the Dead/ Día de los Muertos

October/November
Oaxaca, Mexico

Day of the Dead takes place officially on November 1 and 2, but is celebrated in Latin communities around the world for several days around these dates. This celebration blends Christian practices brought to the New World by Spanish colonizers with Indigenous rituals honoring the dead that harked back to ancient times. The festivities that take place in Oaxaca, Mexico, and outlying towns during this holiday are among the most colorful anywhere. For three days the streets of the city are filled with successive processions of men, women, and children, all in costume and with painted faces. Homes and shopfronts exhibit richly adorned altars known as *ofrendas*, which pay homage to deceased family members and friends and offer treats to entice them briefly back to the world of the living. In the town's cemeteries, families gather and decorate gravesites with flowers and candles.

opposite: SYMBOLS OF DAY OF THE DEAD AT SANTA CRUZ XOXOCOTLÁN, OUTSIDE OAXACA, 2013

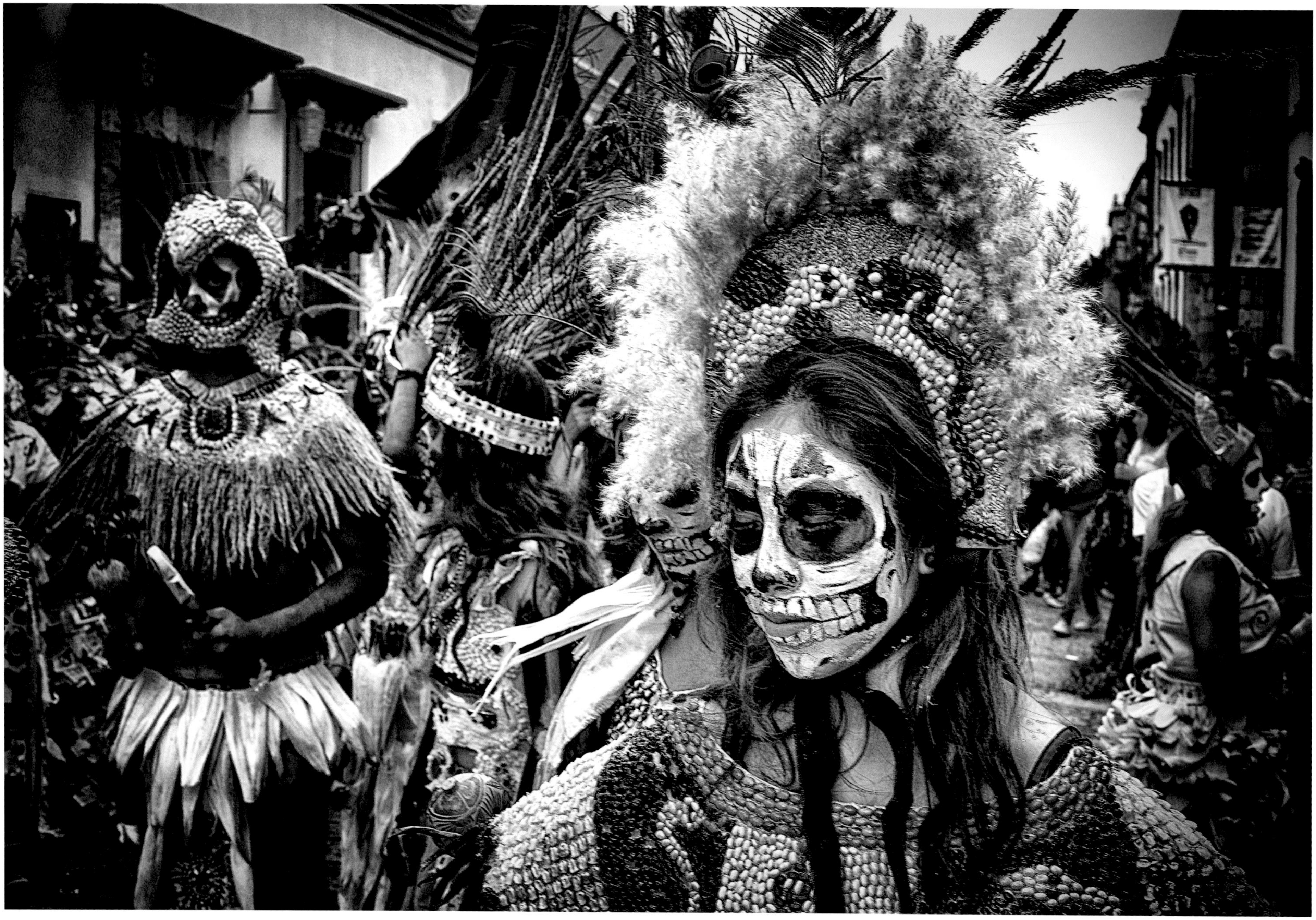

PROCESSION THROUGH THE STREETS OF OAXACA, 2013

opposite: DAY OF THE DEAD PROCESSION, 2013

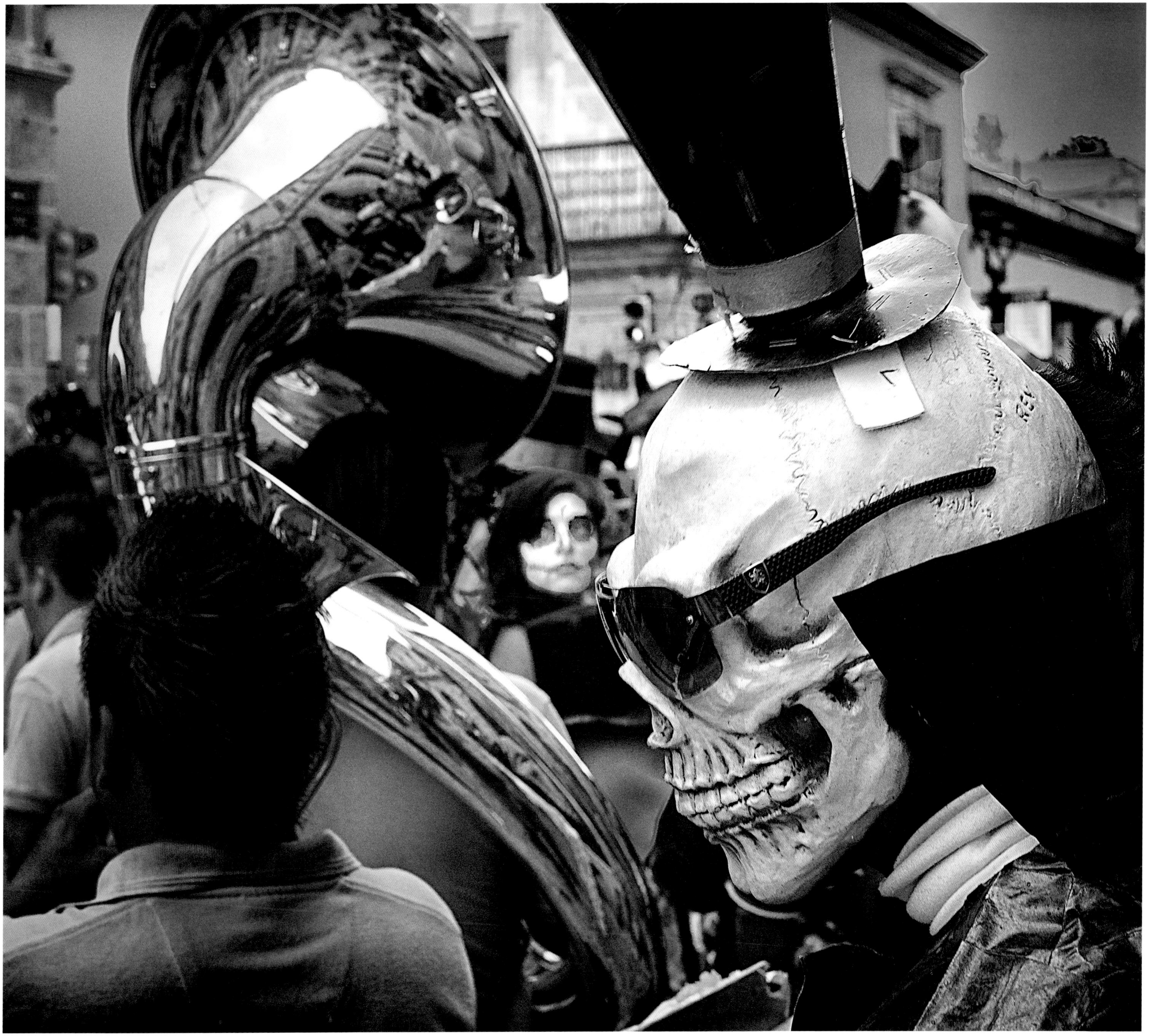

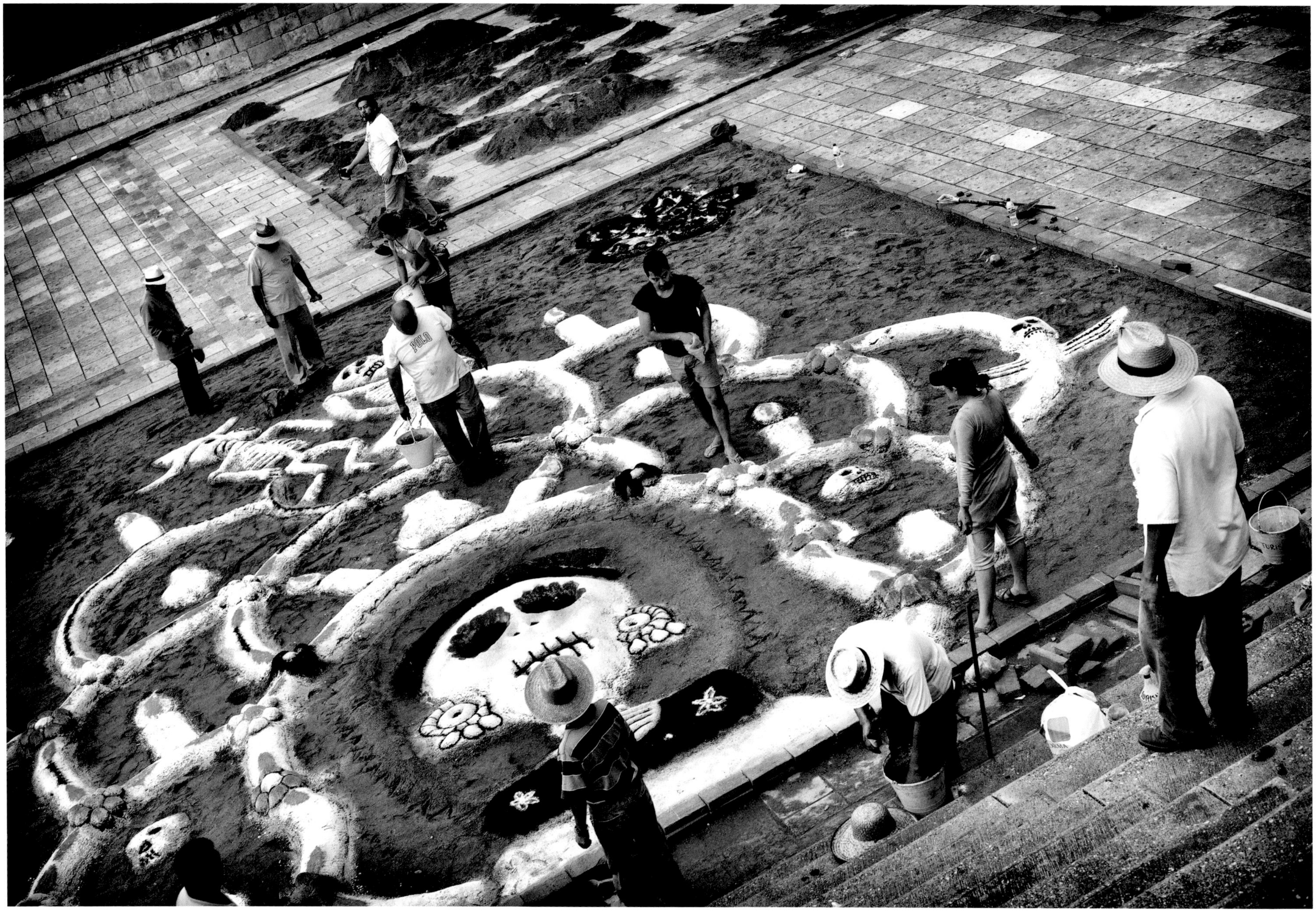

SAND PAINTING AT THE BASILICA OF OUR LADY OF SORROWS, 2013

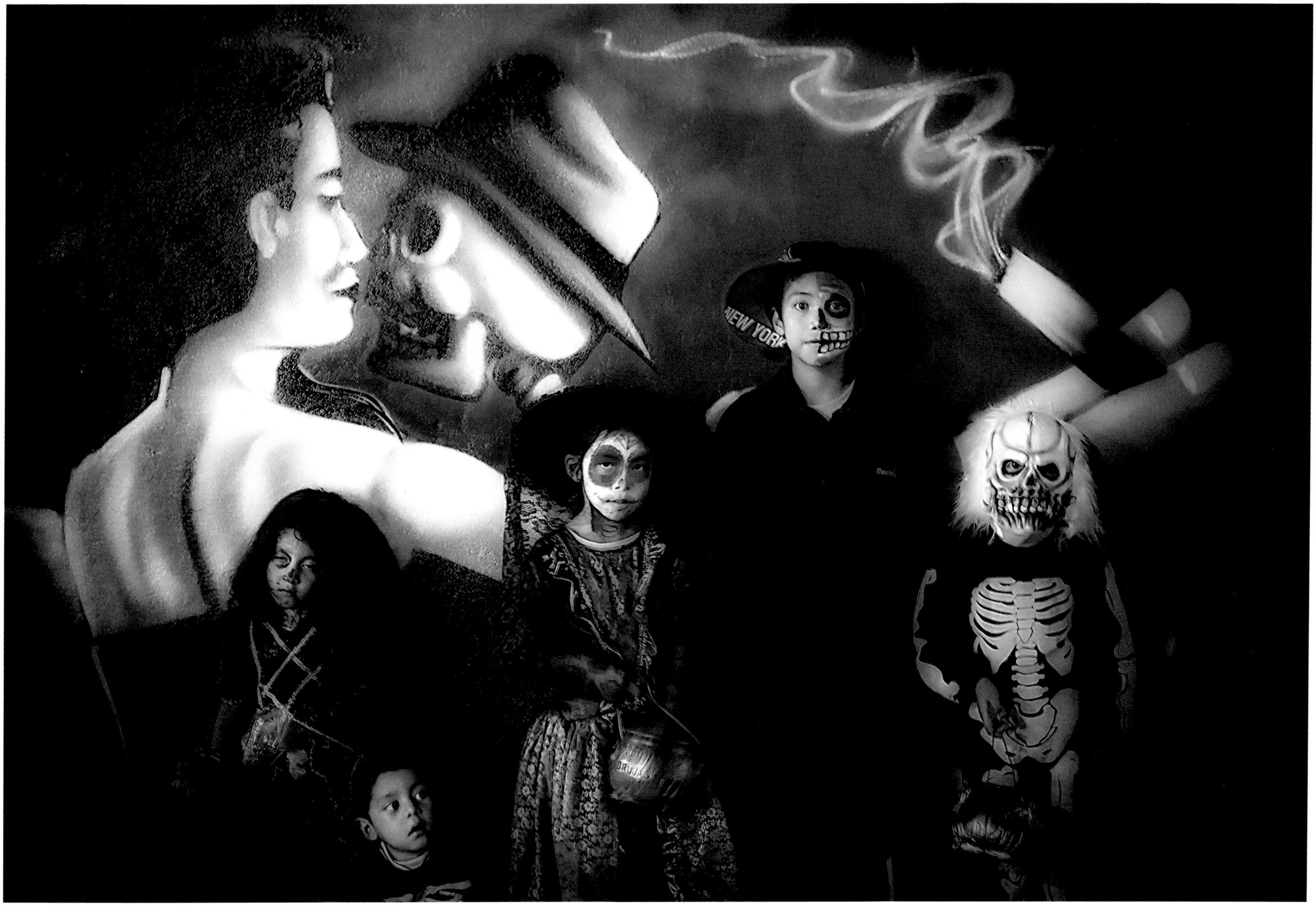

CHILDREN OUTSIDE THE CEMETERY IN SANTA CRUZ XOXOCOTLÁN ON OCTOBER 31, 2013

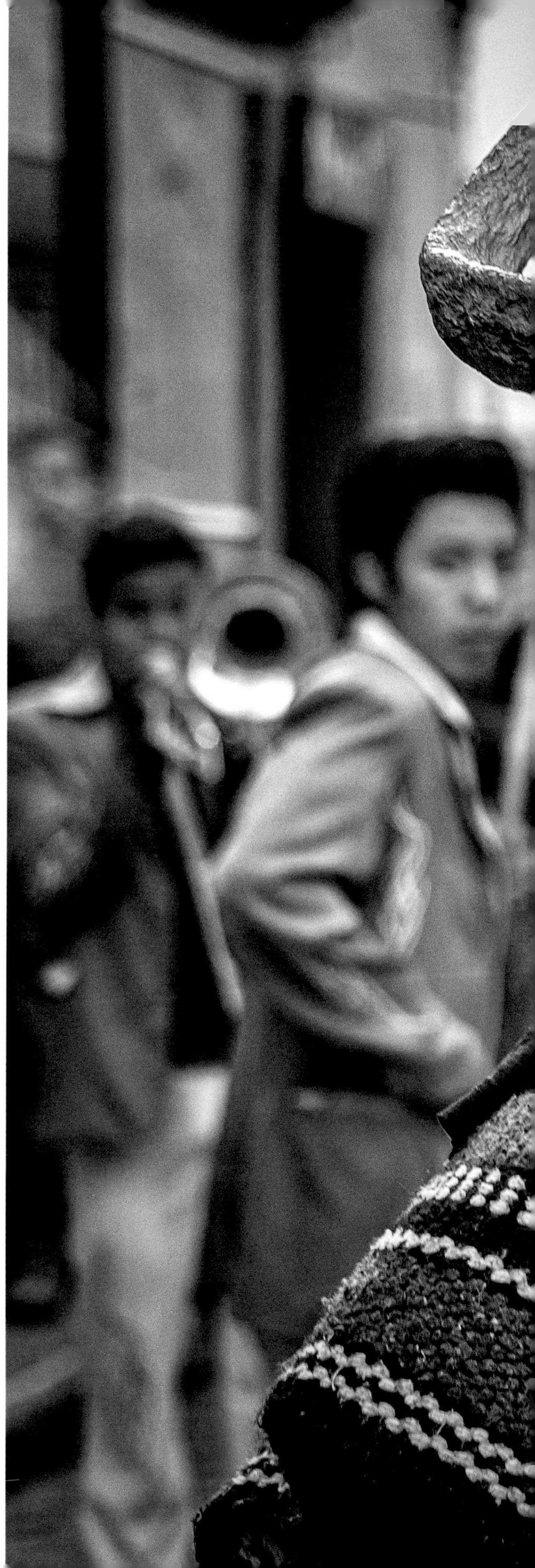

DANCE OF THE DEVILS IN OAXACA, 2014

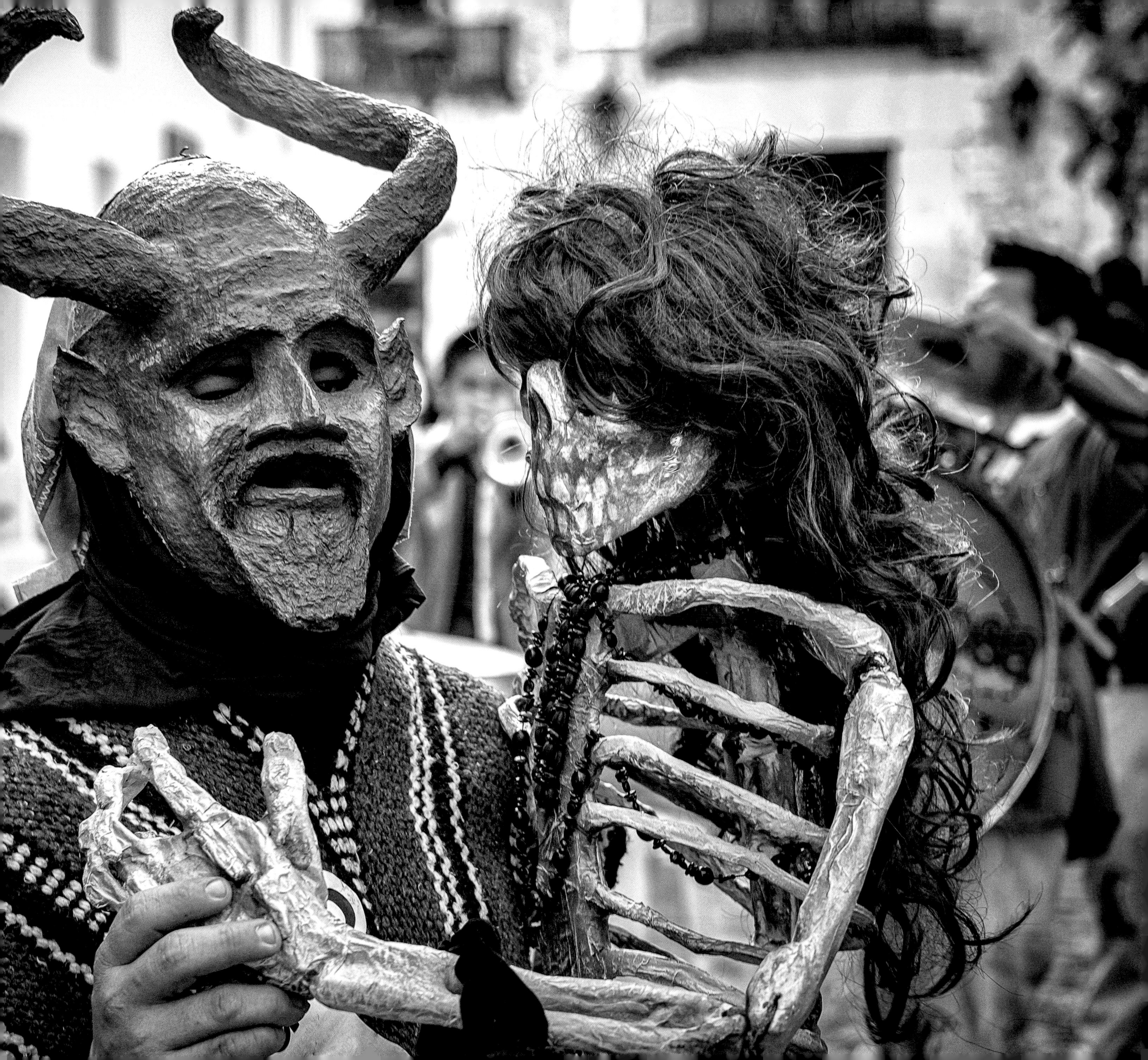

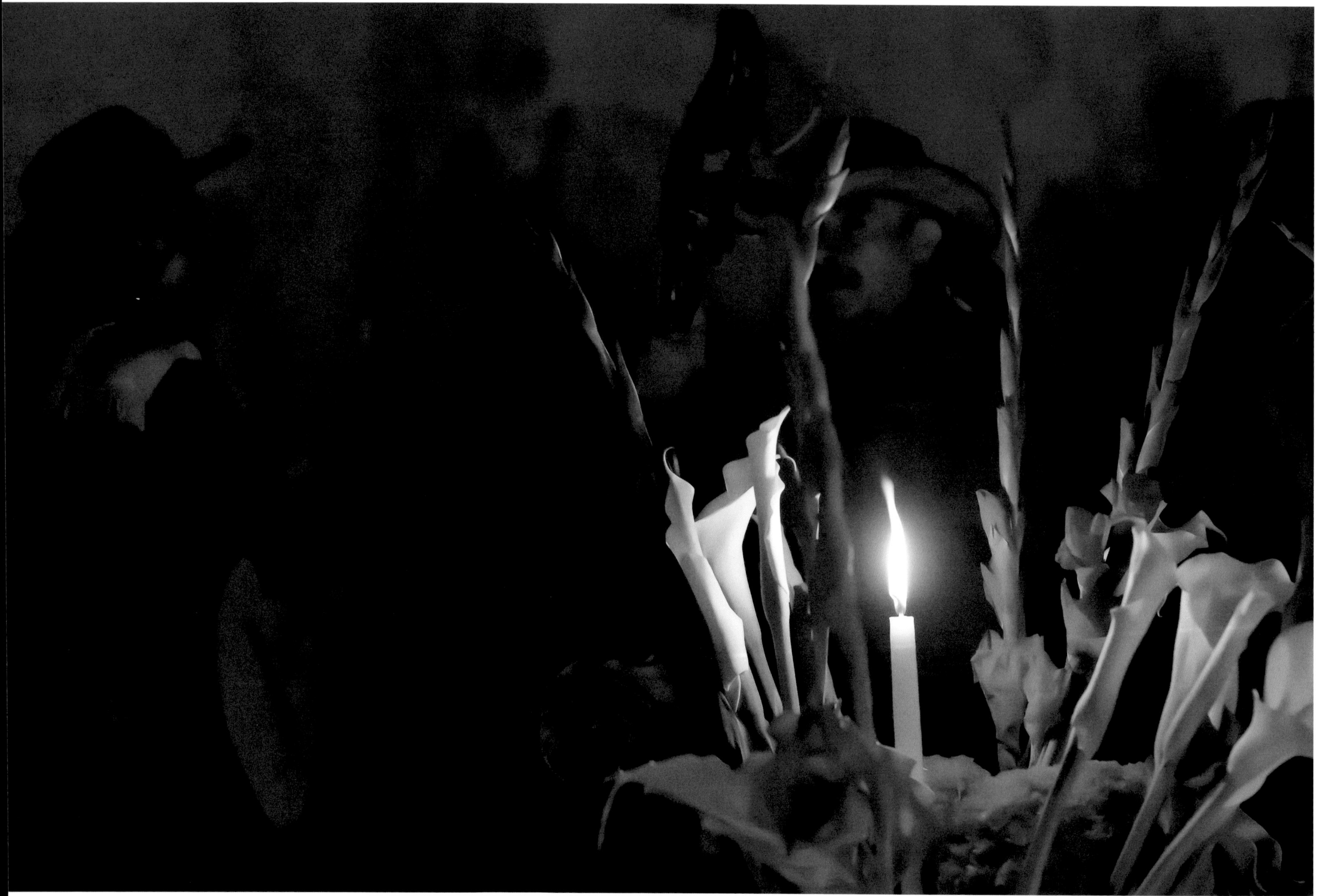

MARIACHI MUSICIANS IN SANTA CRUZ XOXOCOTLÁN CEMETERY, 2013

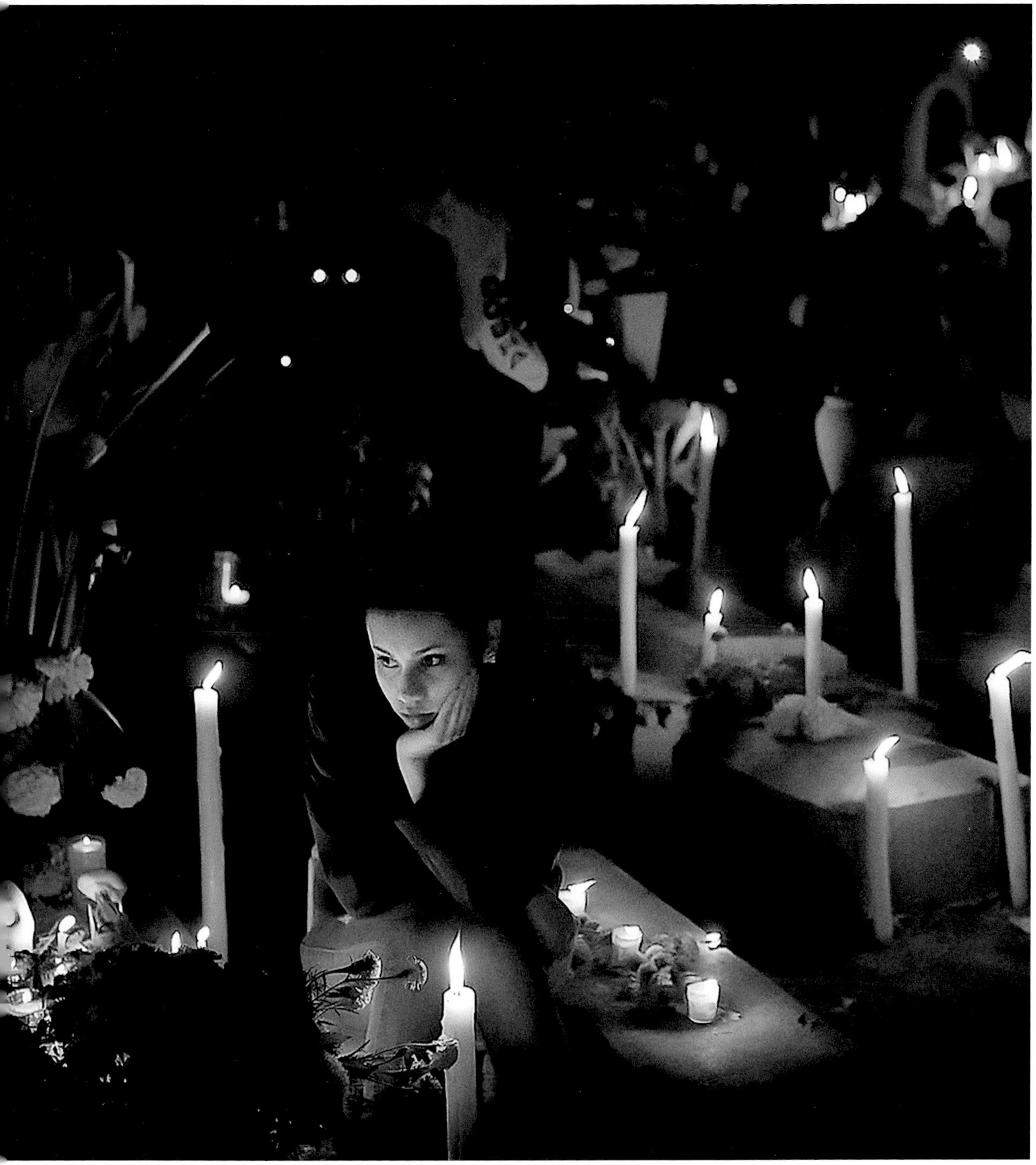

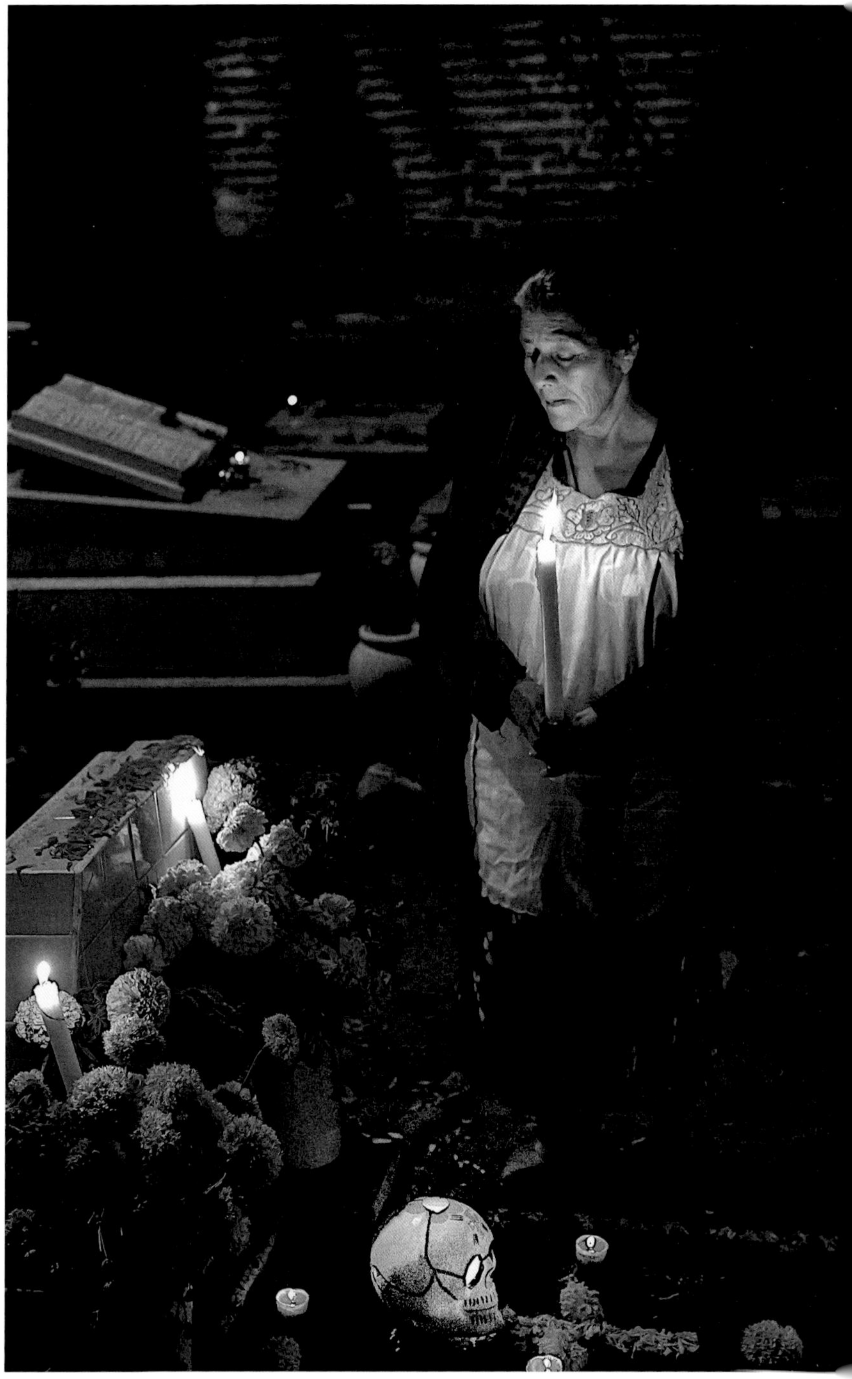

center: IN PANTEÓN VIEJO, THE OLD CEMETERY, 2013
right: PRAYERS FOR DECEASED LOVED ONES IN THE SANTA CRUZ XOXOCOTLÁN CEMETERY, 2013

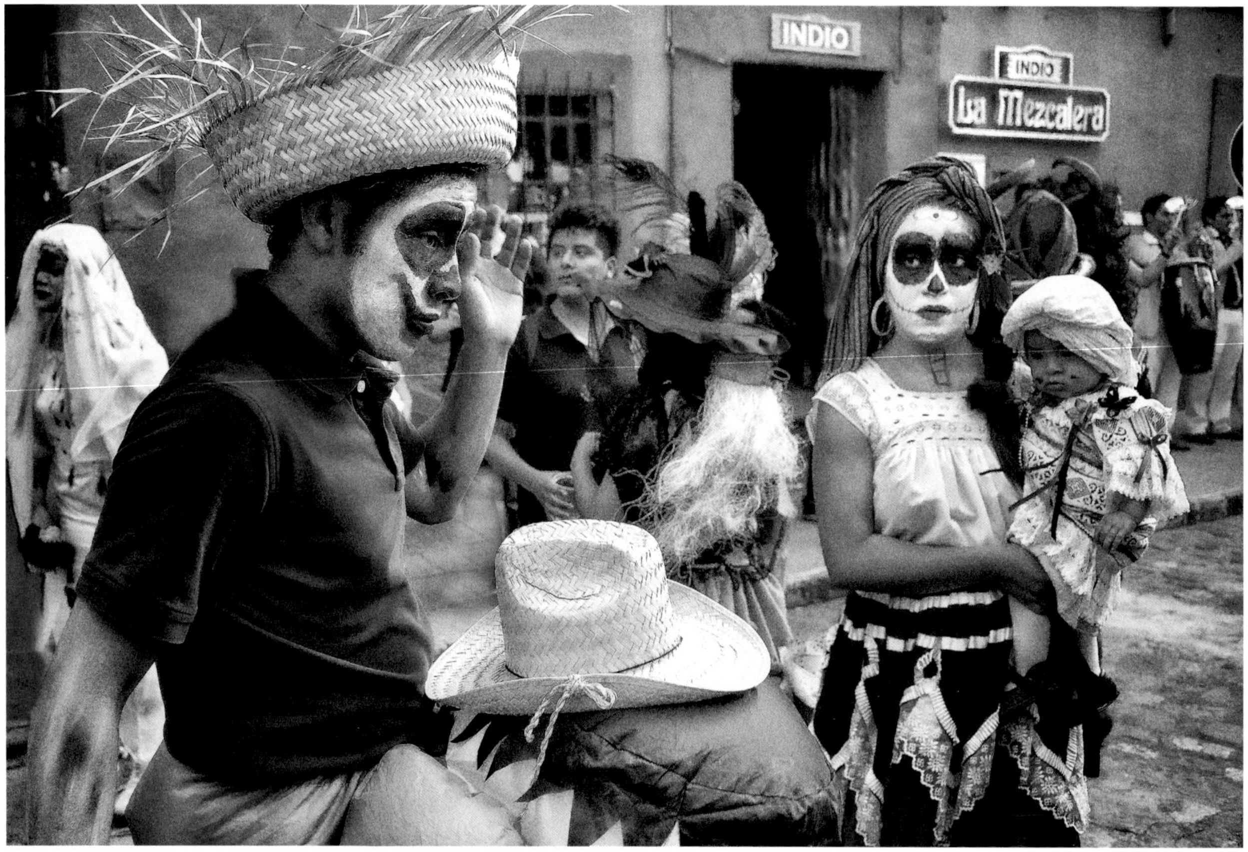

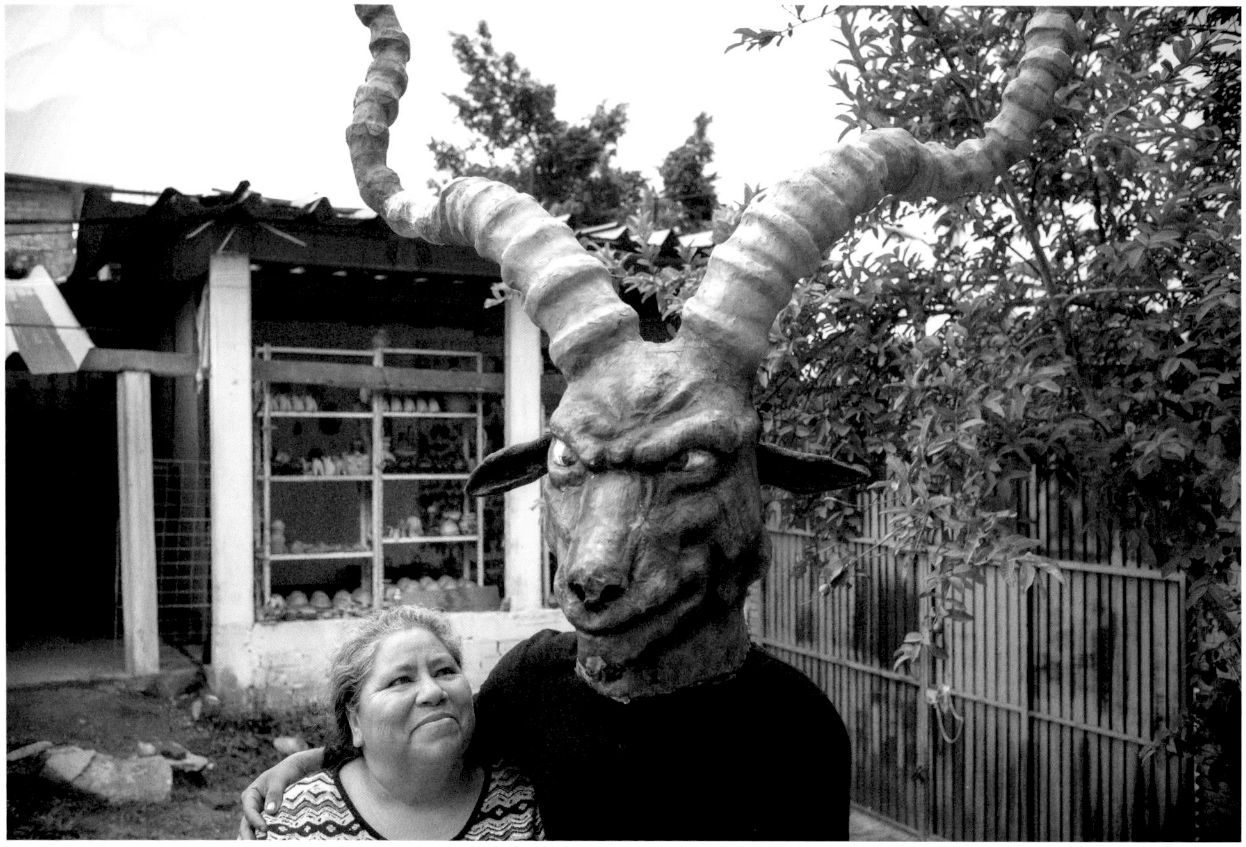

above: FAMILIES JOINING A PROCESSION, 2014
below: MOTHER AND SON IN SANTA MARÍA ATZOMPA, 2013

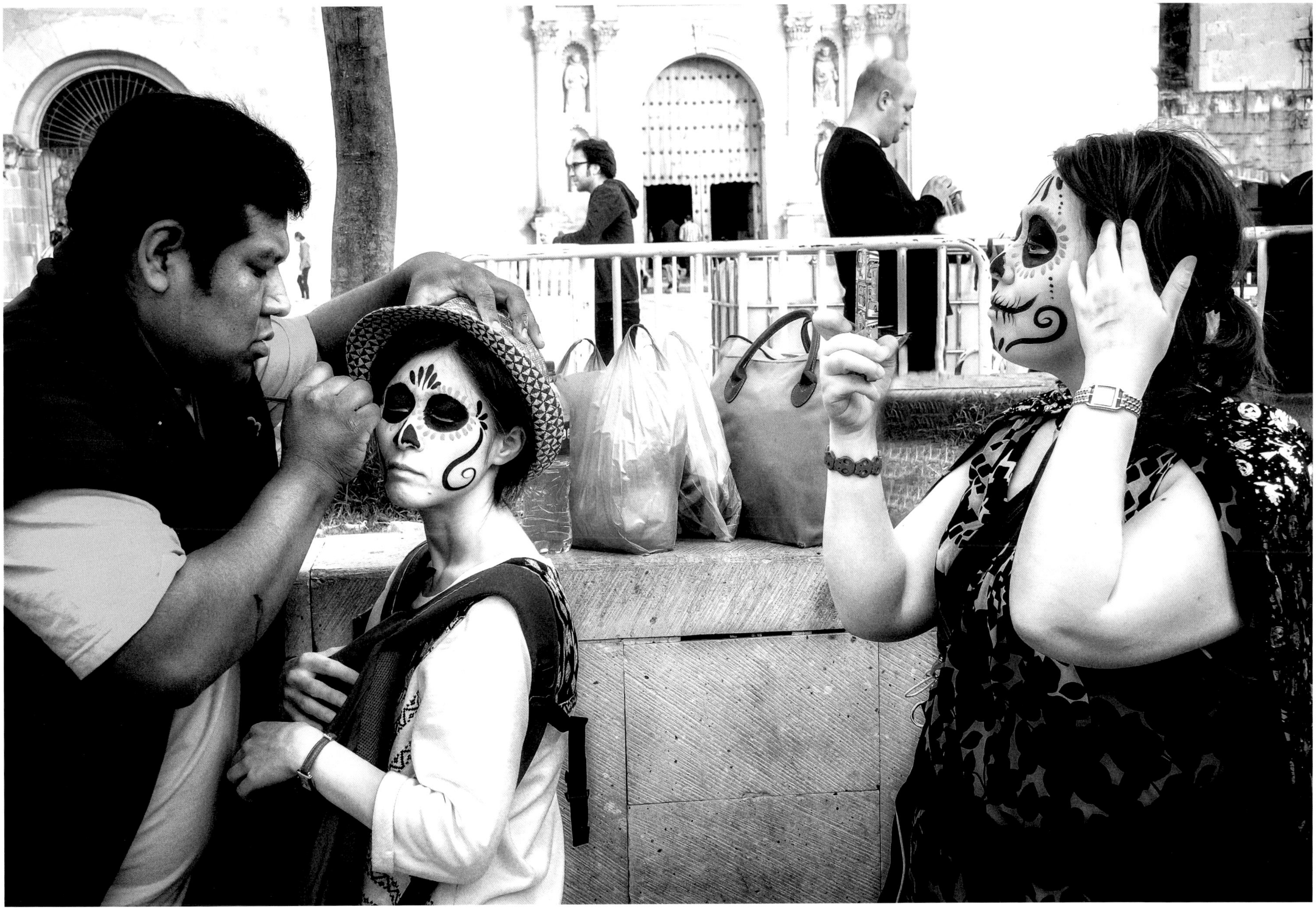

PREPARING FOR THE NEXT PROCESSION AT THE OUR LADY OF ASSUMPTION CATHEDRAL, 2014

following spread, left: THE WALKING DEAD, 2014
right: A GHOSTLY MAIDEN WANDERING THE STREETS, 2014

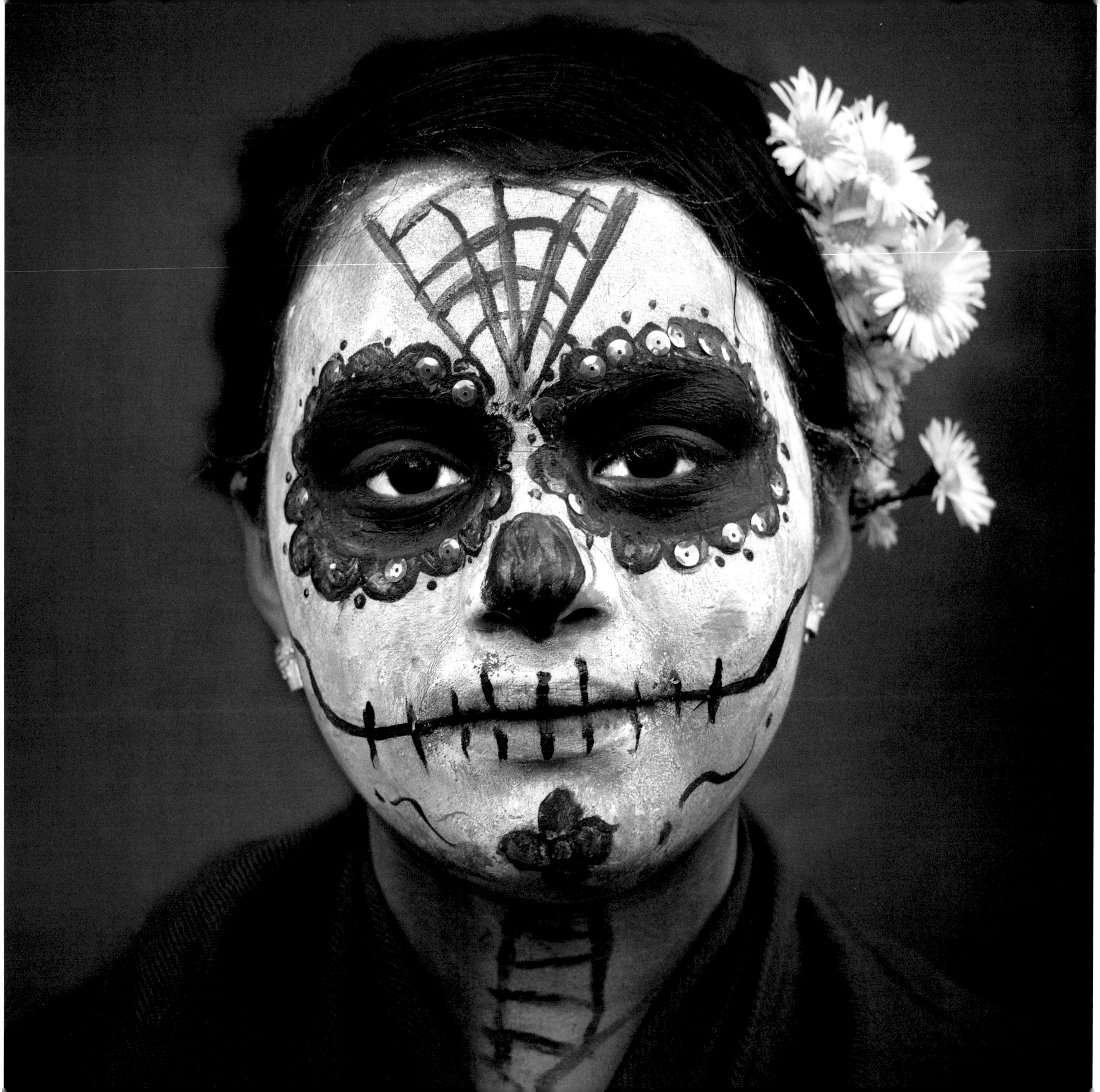

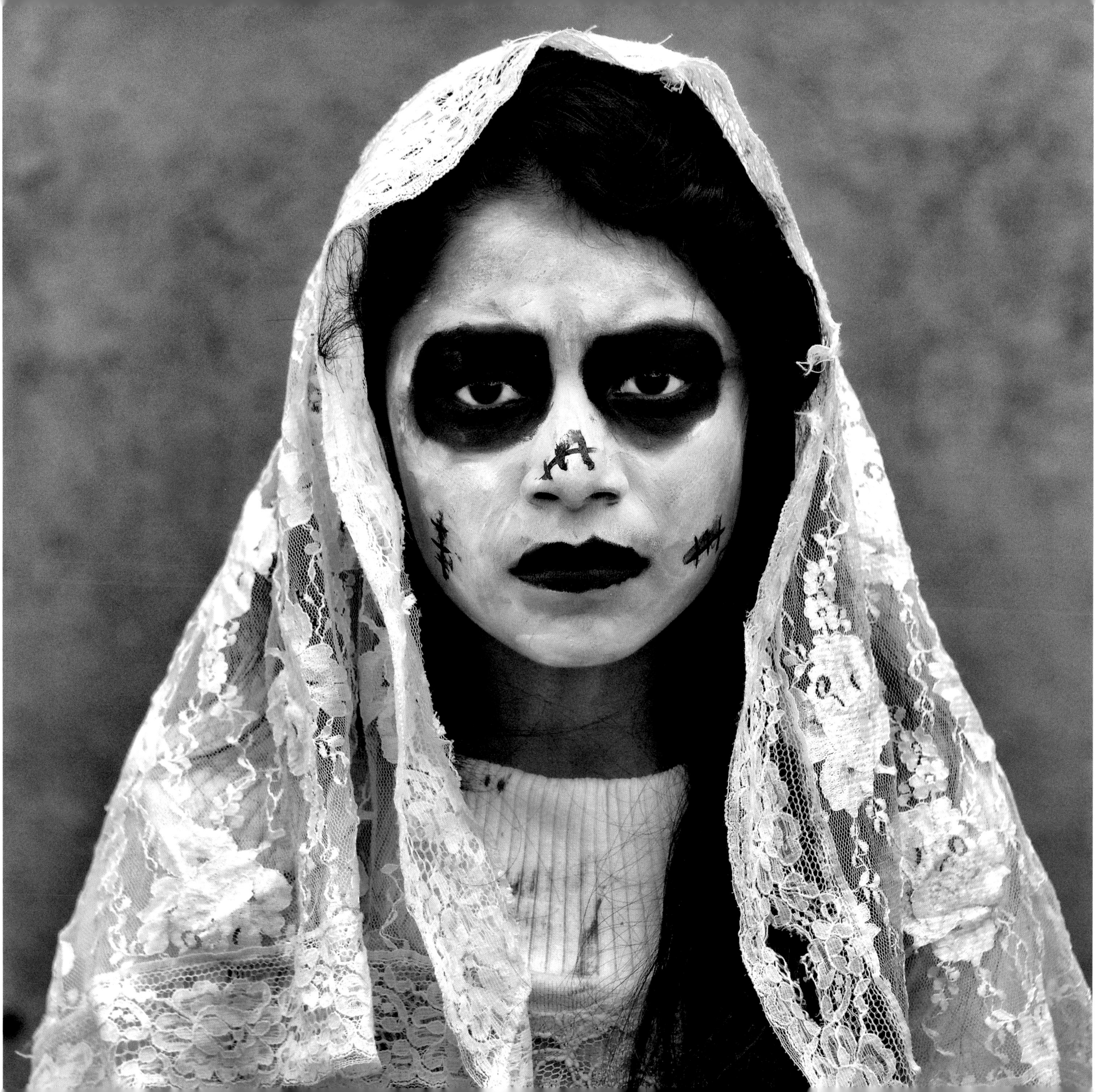

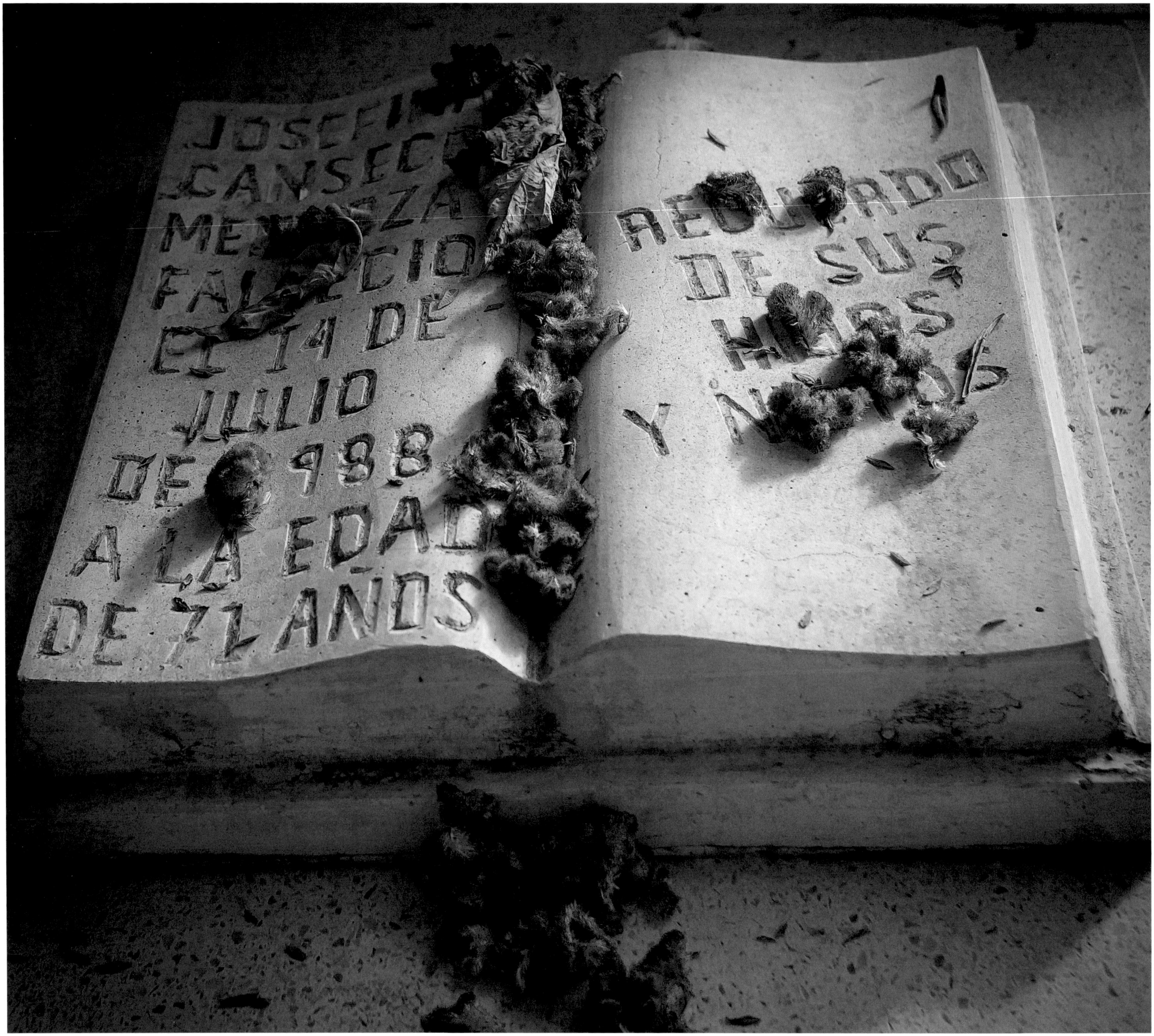
EL 14 DE
JULIO
A LA EDAD
DE SUS

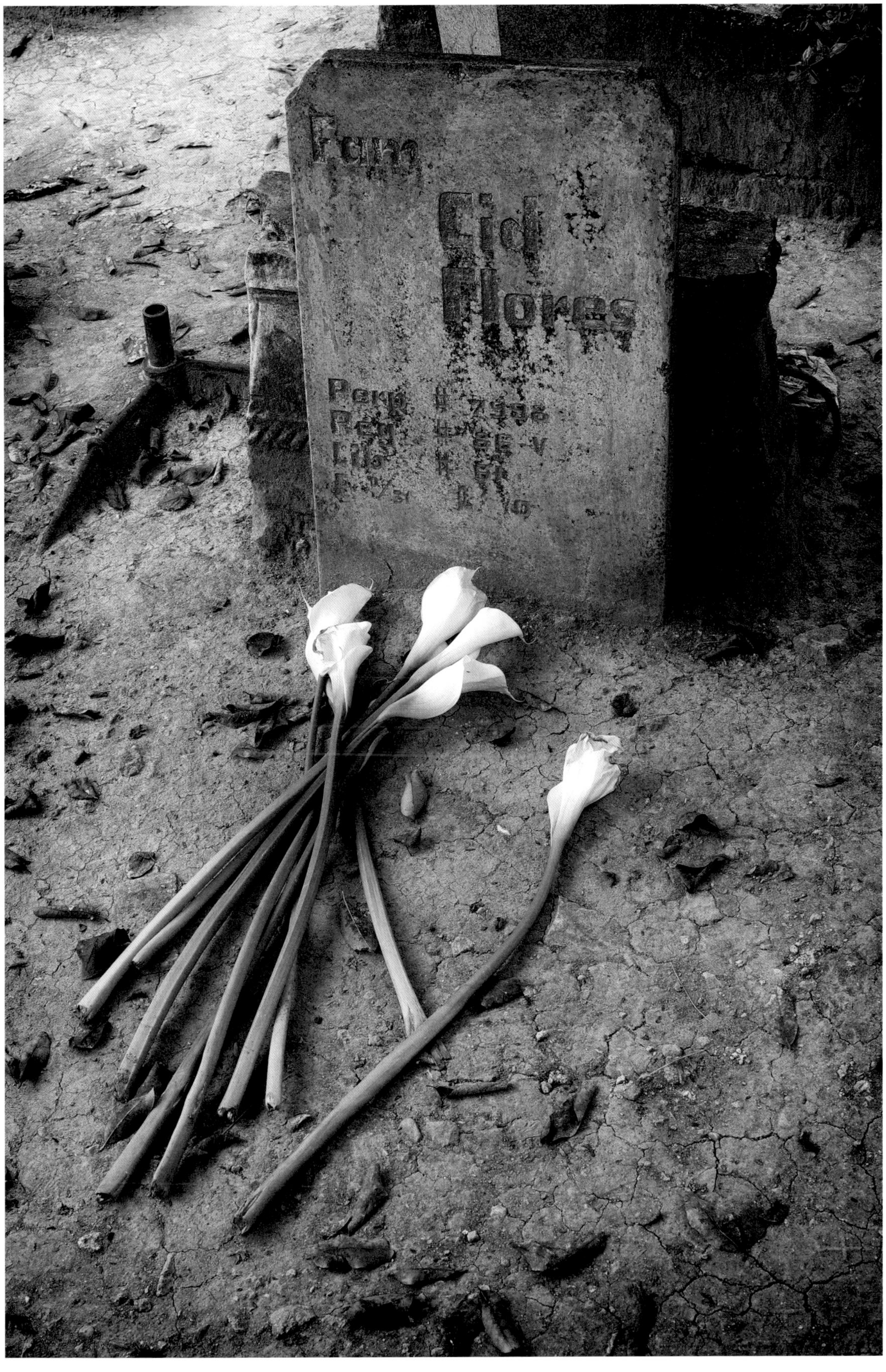

opposite: IN PANTEÓN VIEJO, THE OLD CEMETERY, 2013

HONORING LOST LOVED ONES IN
SANTA CRUZ XOXOCOTLÁN CEMETERY, 2014

following spread: A TRIBUTE TO FAMILY MEMBERS IN OAXACA, 2014

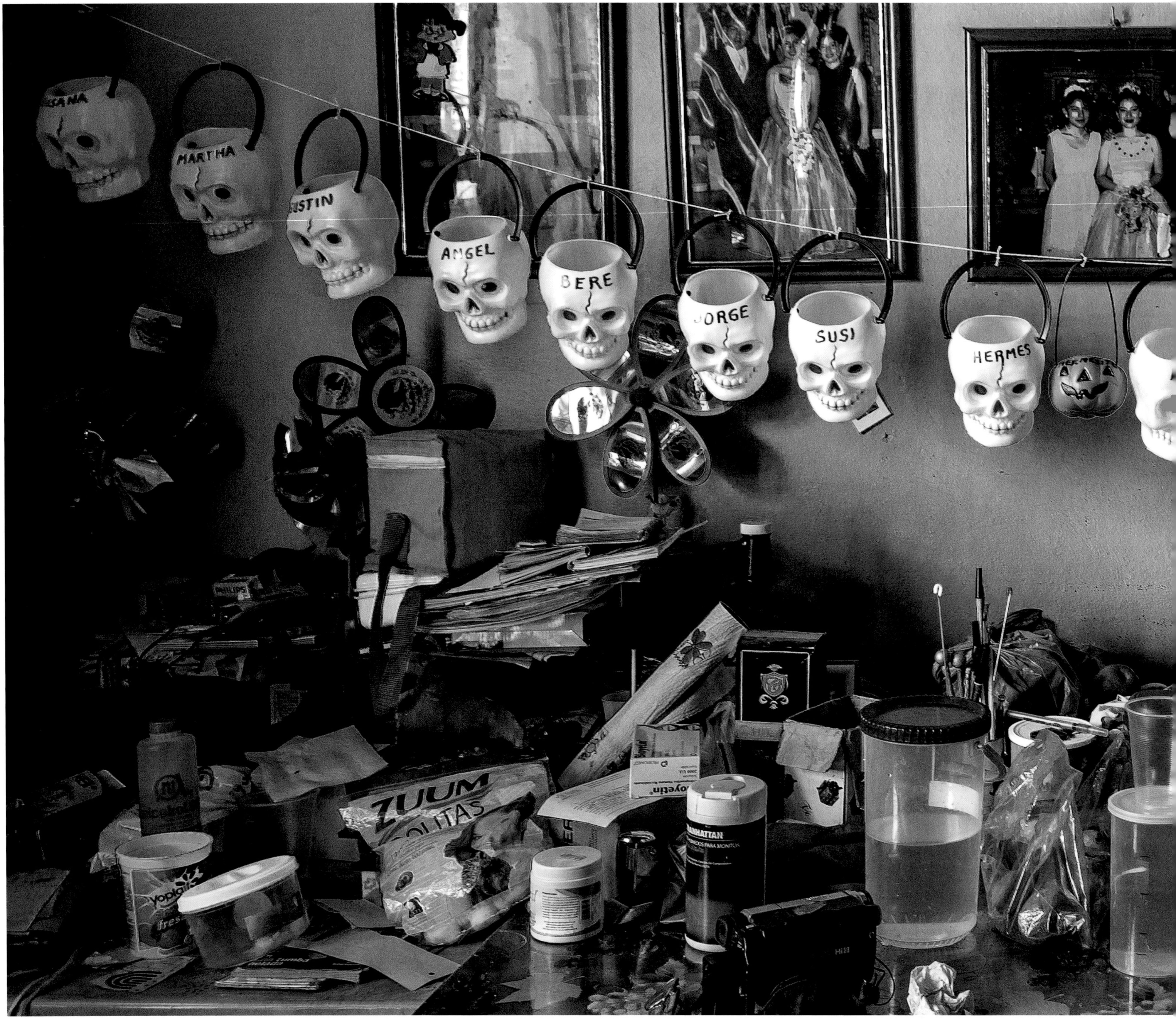
MARTHA
ANGEL
BERE
JORGE
SUSI
HERMES
ZUUM
yoplait

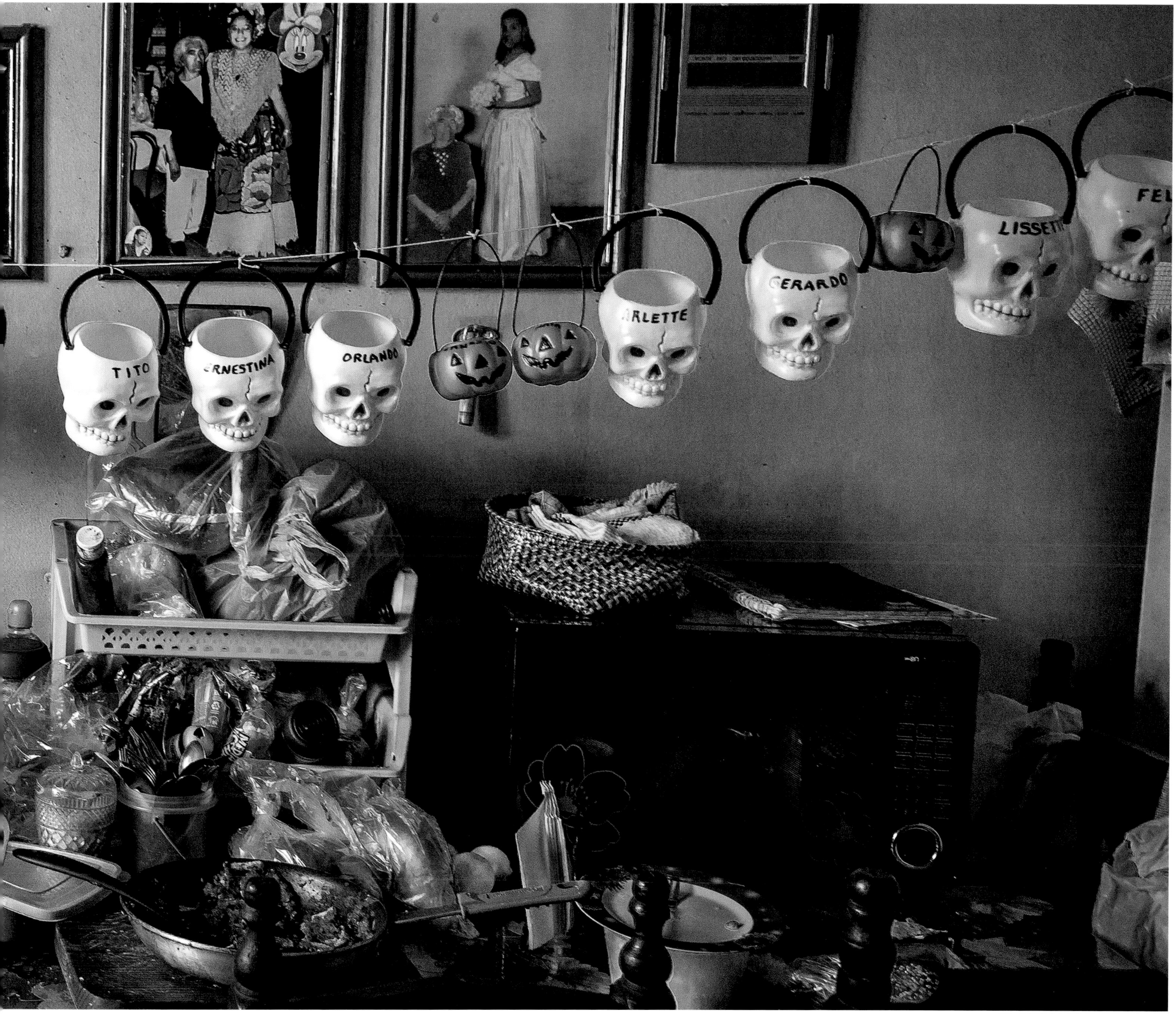
TITO
ERNESTINA
ORLANDO
ARLETTE
GERARDO

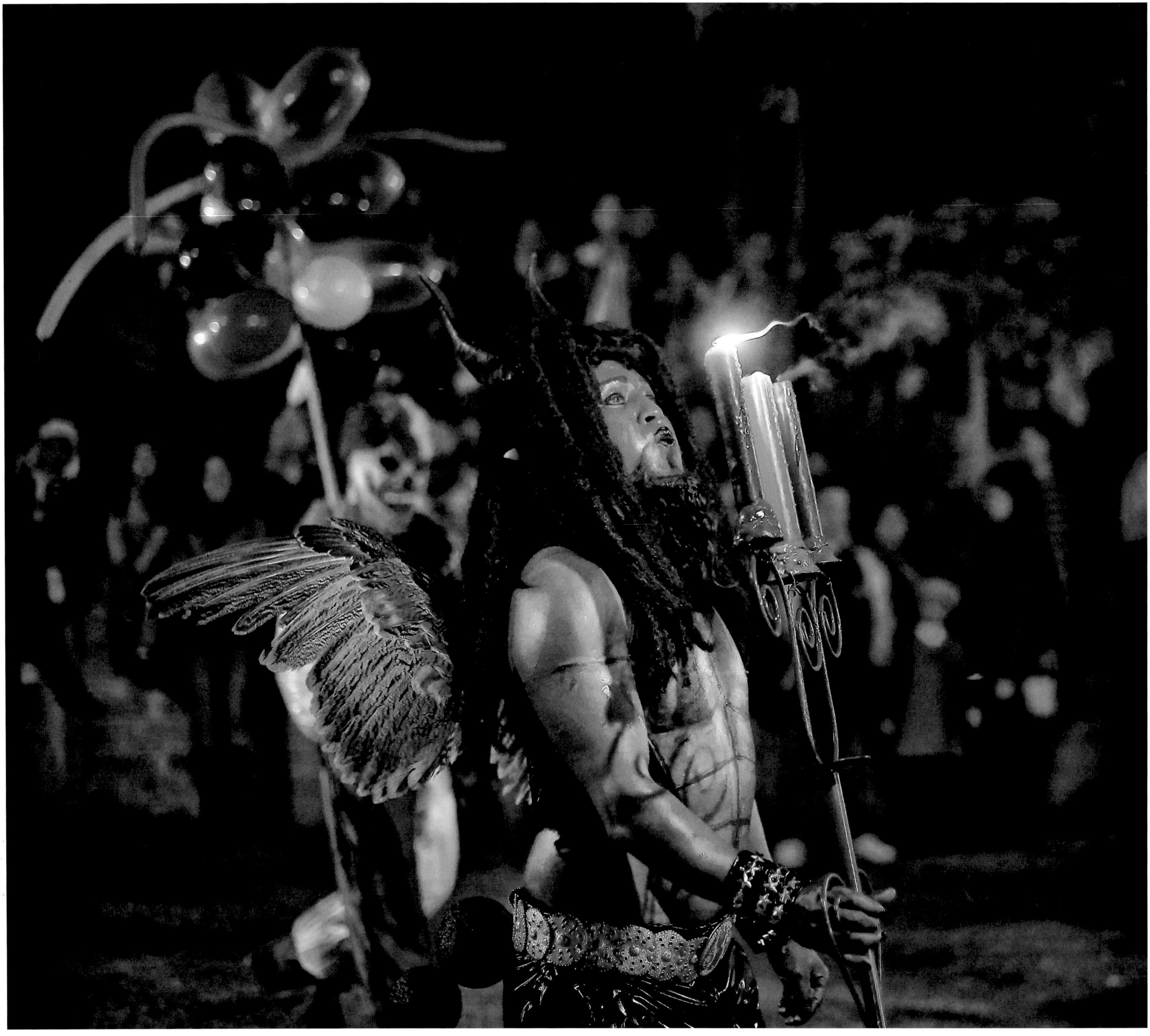

Comparsa of Día de los Muertos

San Agustín Etla, Oaxaca, Mexico

In San Agustín Etla, a small town located outside the city of Oaxaca, the most dramatic and raucous events associated with Día de los Muertos are the *comparsas*—groups of costumed men or women who dance and carouse to the accompaniment of loud music from evening until morning. After a procession through the town, the men's comparsa is staged within a fenced area at the edge of the town, where it is difficult but not impossible for onlookers to gain entry and join the celebration, which is a blur of grotesque masks and fantastic costumes. Sequins, baubles and even blinking lights adorn the dancers. The women's comparsa, staged separately several days later, also features masks, ghoulish makeup, and intricately designed costumes, but is slightly more restrained.

opposite: THE COMPARSA IN SAN AGUSTÍN ETLA, BEGINNING WITH A PROCESSION, 2013

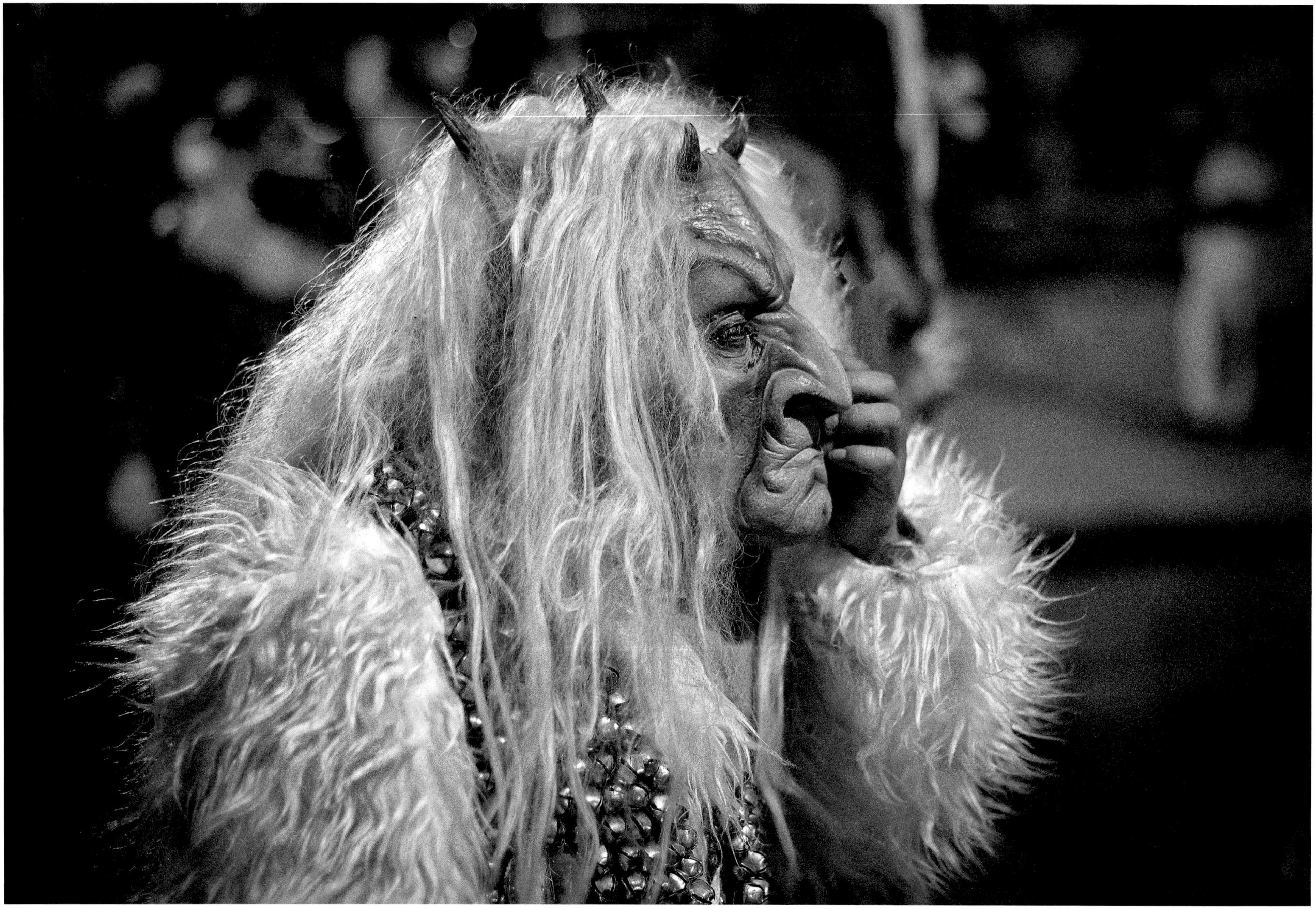

DANCER IN DEVIL MASK, 2013

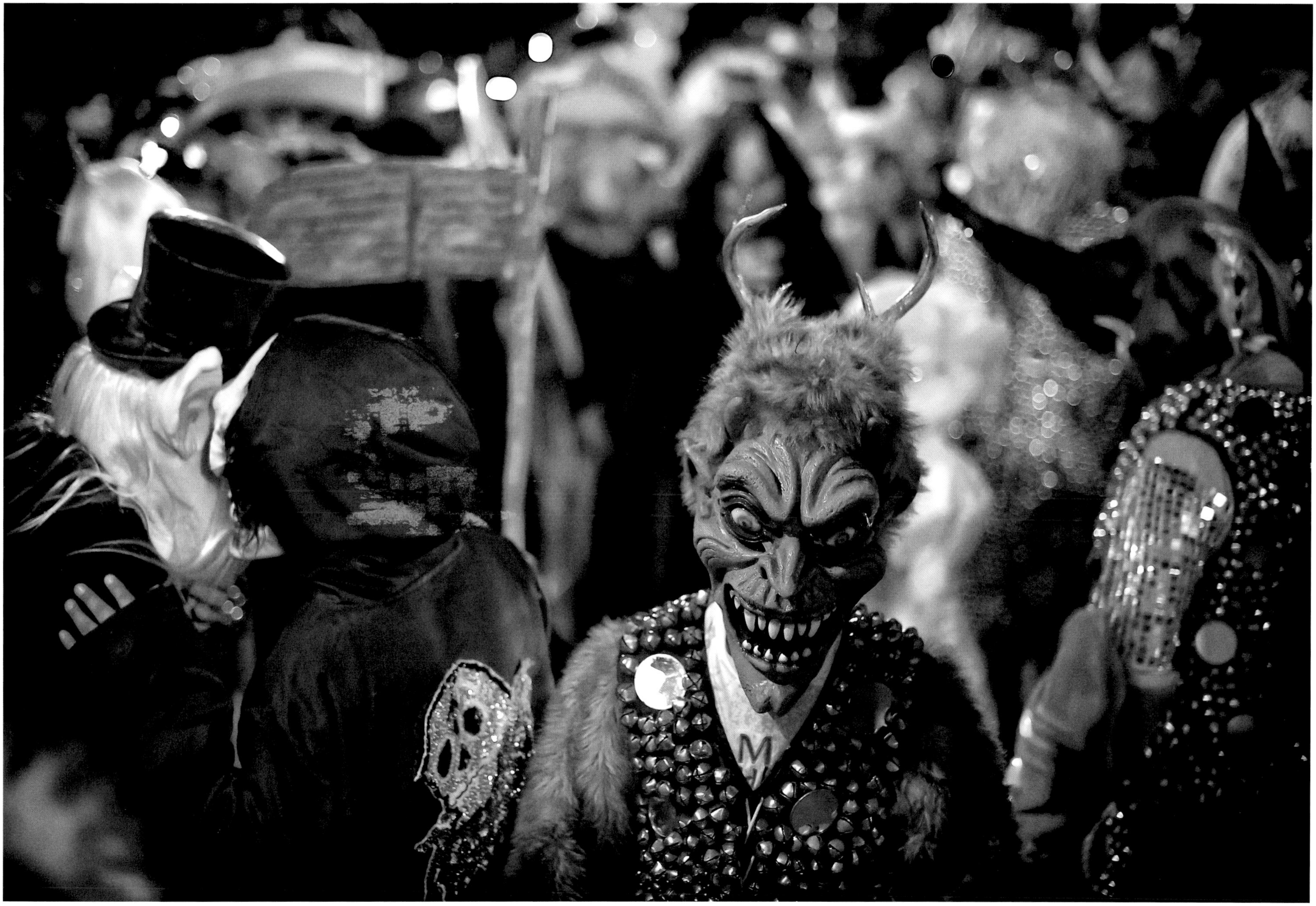

DANCER IN DEVIL MASK, 2013

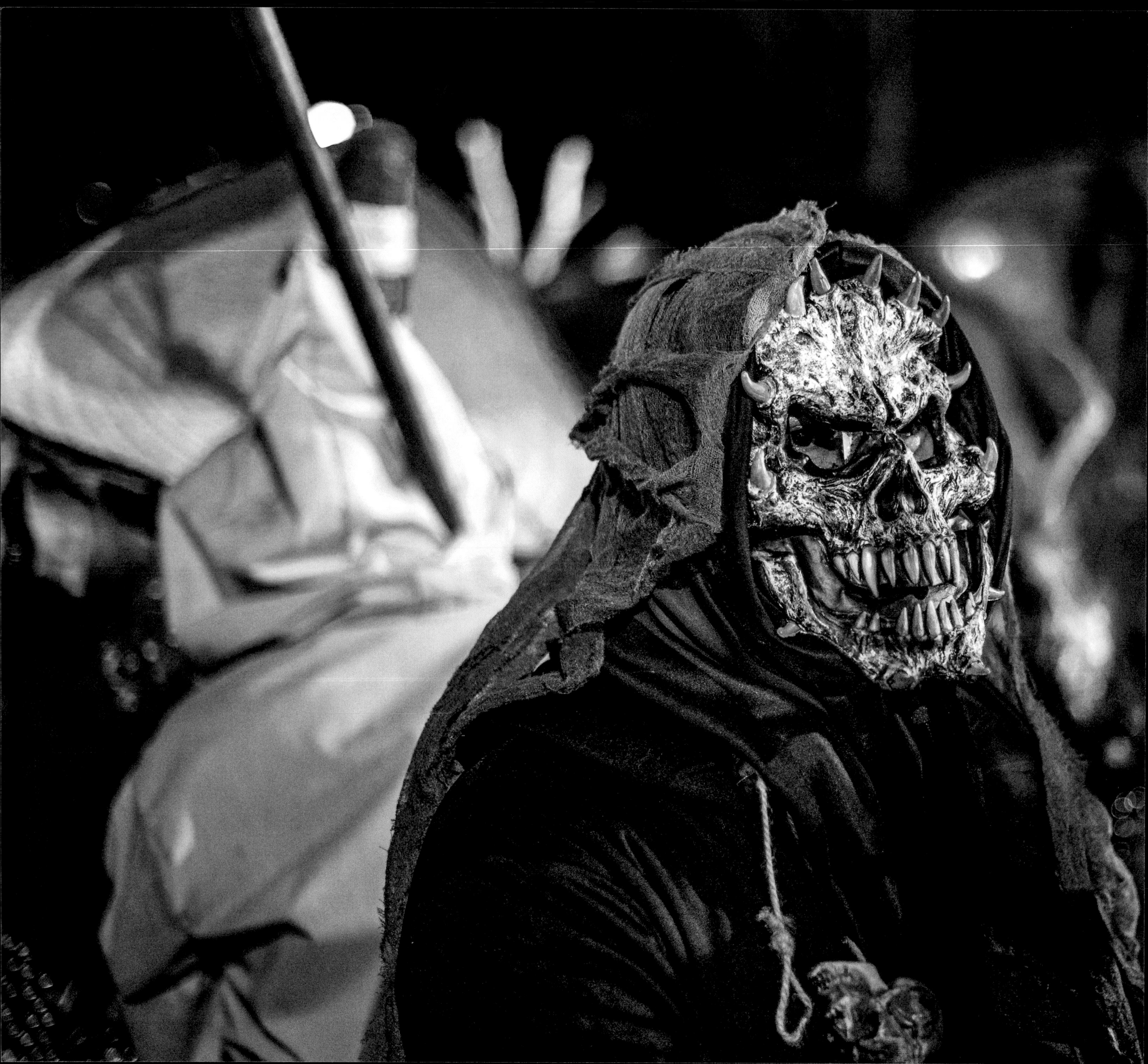

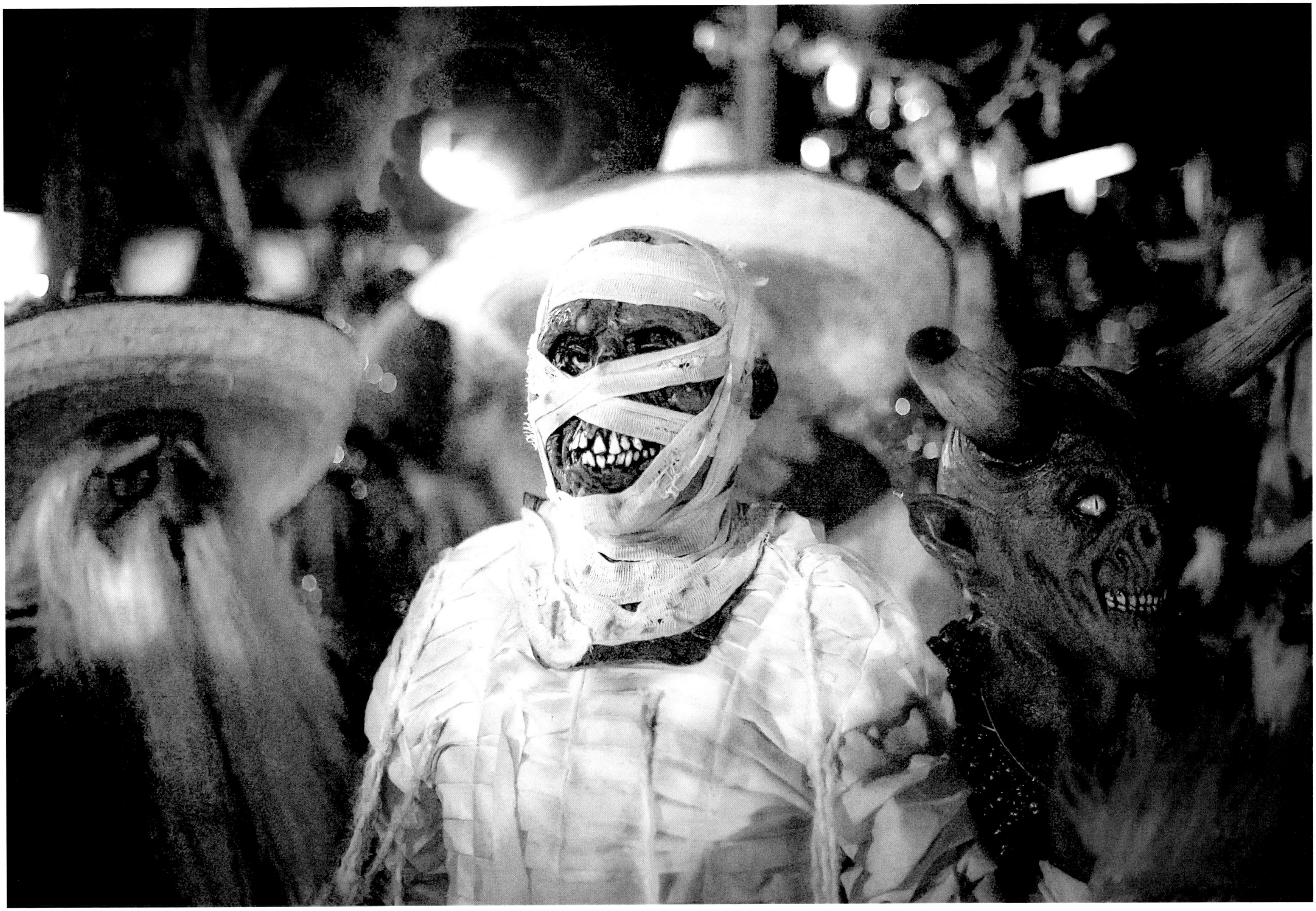

COMPARSA DANCERS, 2013

following spread: THE WOMEN'S COMPARSA, 2014

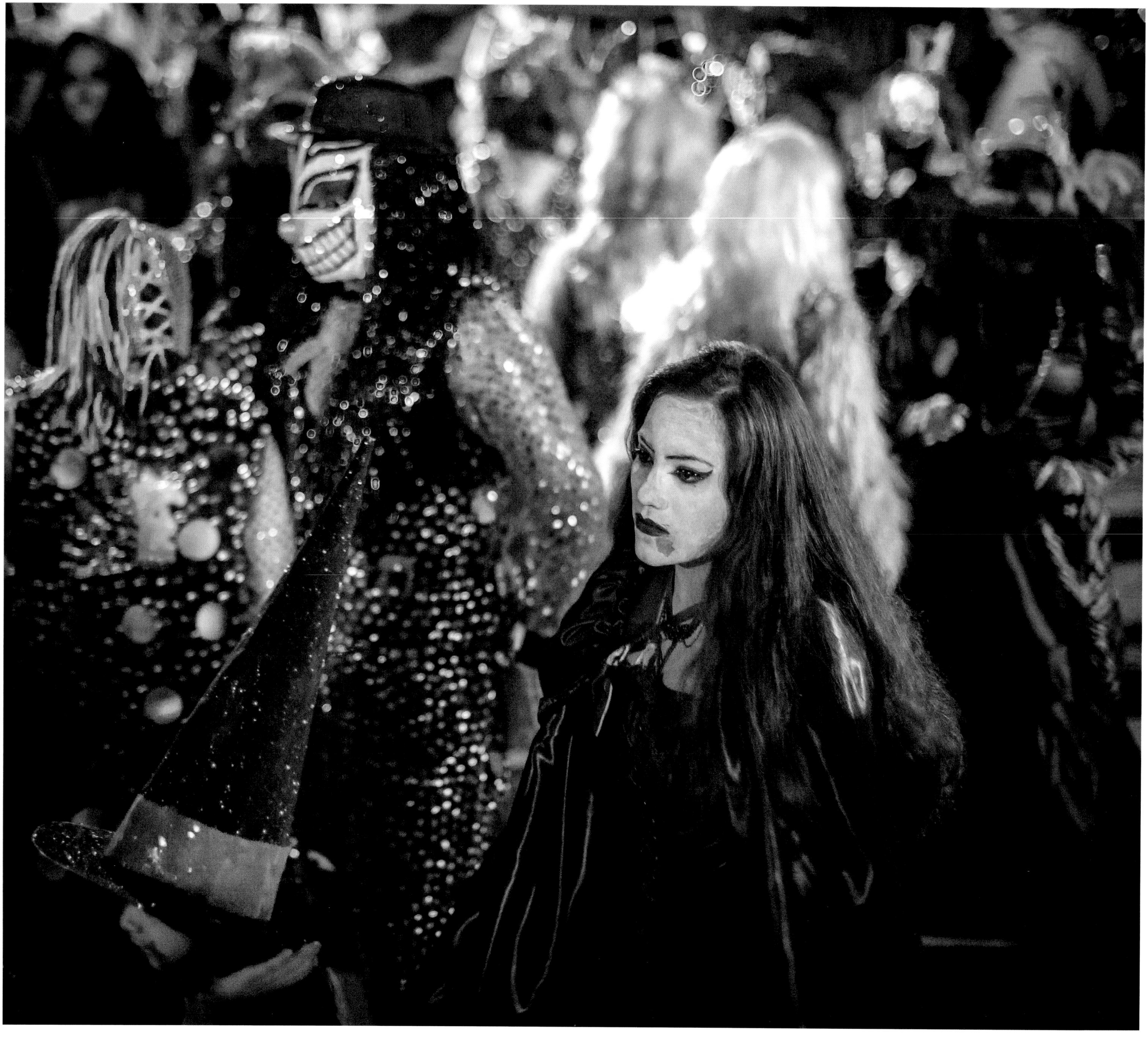

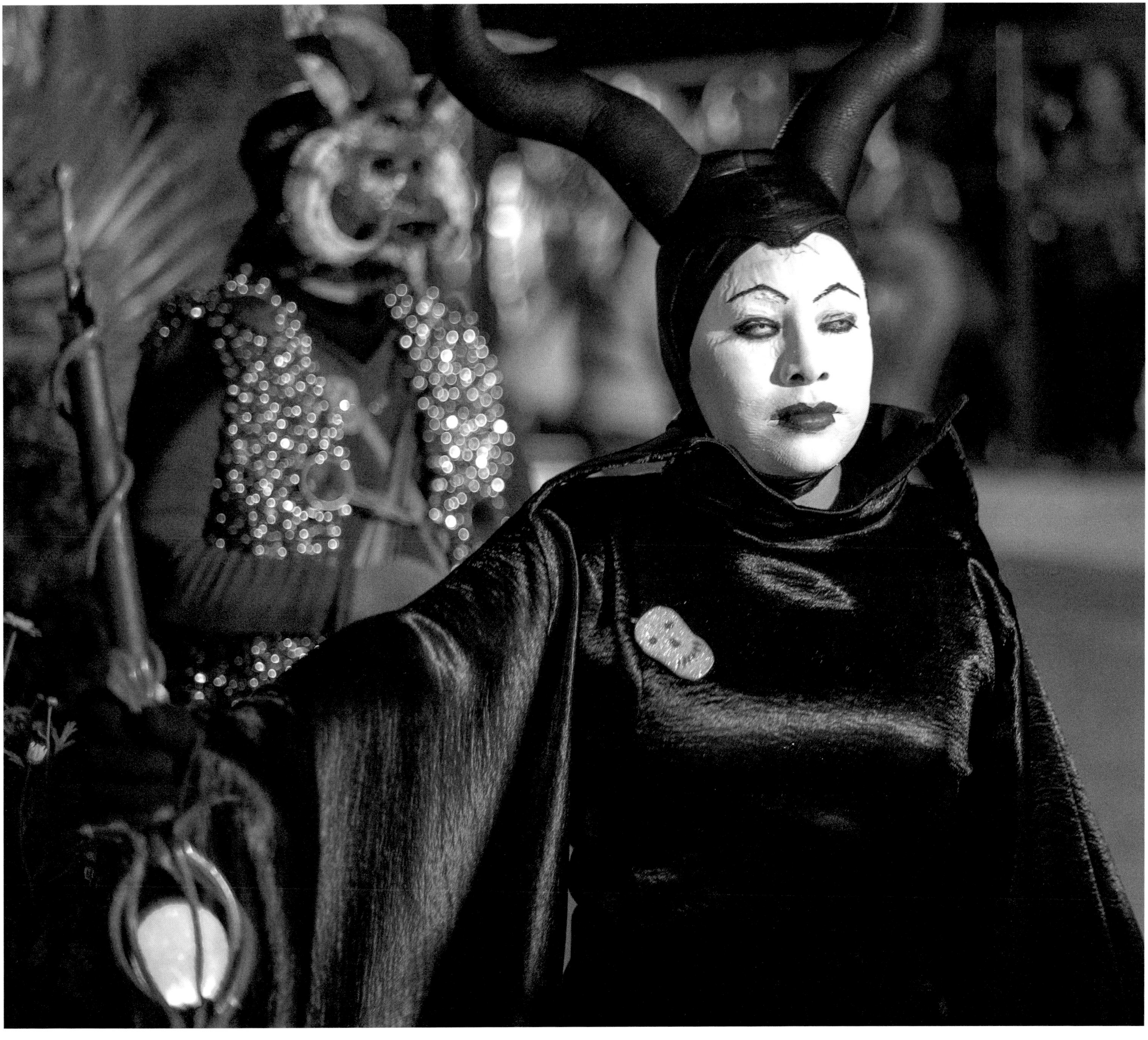

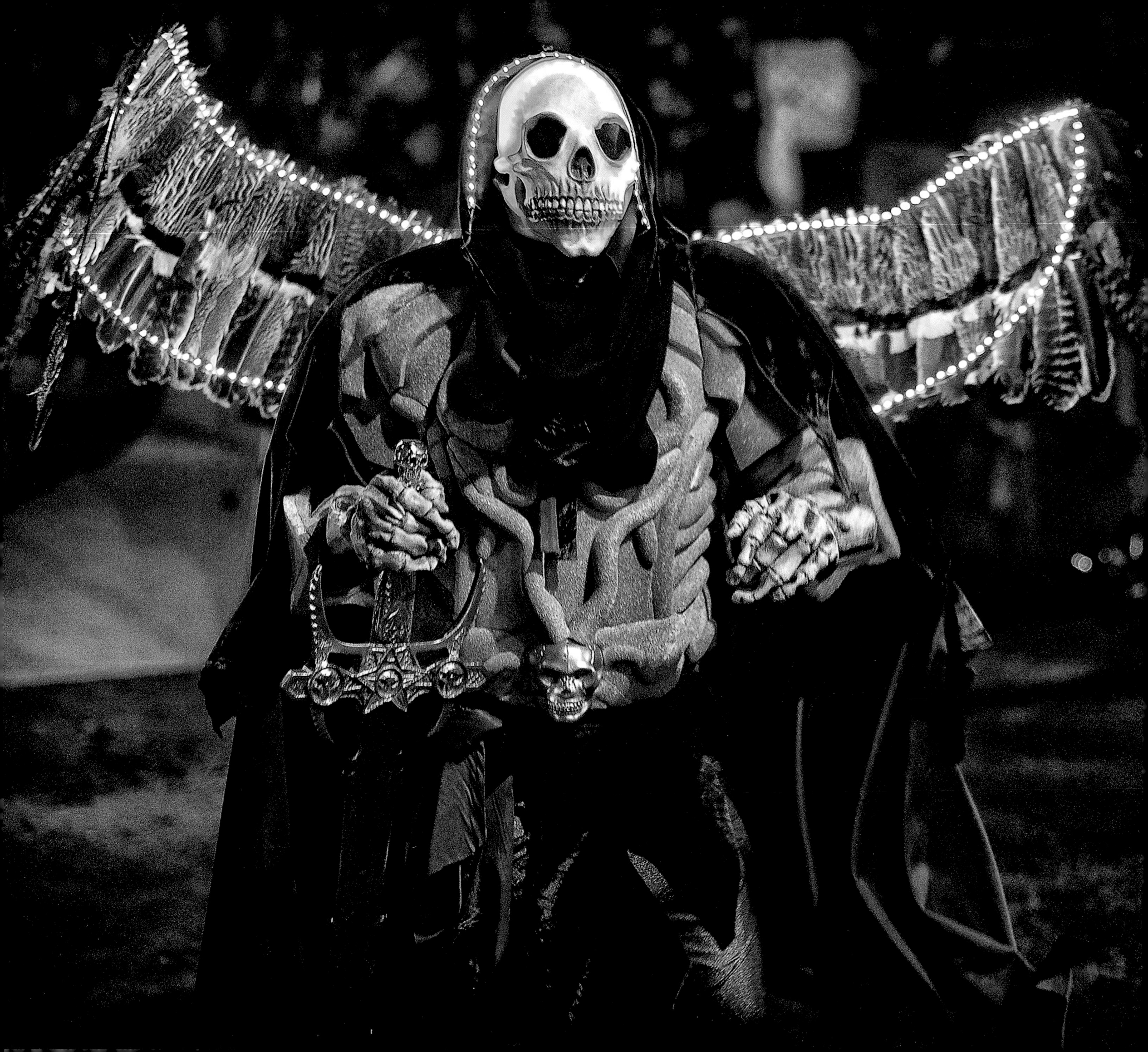

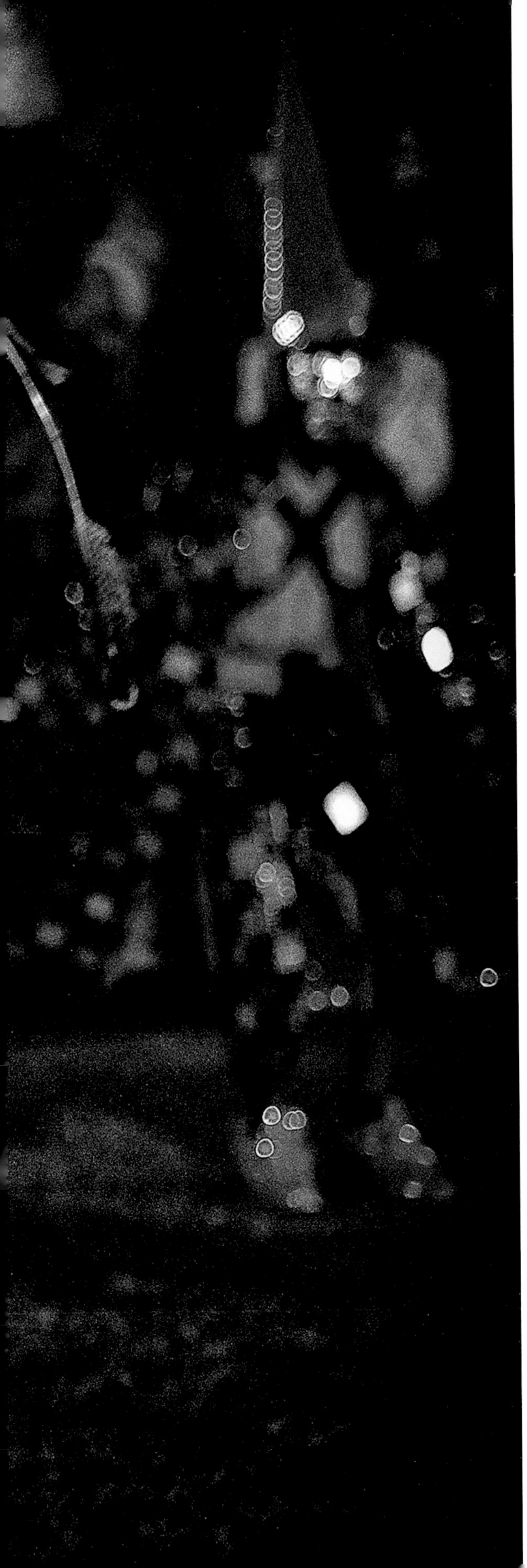

COMPARSA DANCER, 2013

Acknowledgments

I AM GRATEFUL TO THE PEOPLE of Santa Teresa, Oaxaca, San Agustín Etla, San Juan Chamula, Tenejapa, Huixtán, Izamal, Zinacantán, Dzitnup, Rabinal, and Antigua, who welcomed my wife, Anne, and me into their communities and festivals. We hope the photographs here portray not only the deep significance of these celebrations but also the tremendous amount of joy and fun that is involved. I also thank the local authorities and traditional leaders of these communities for their permission to photograph these events.

Two photographers and chroniclers of life in Mexico and Guatemala, Antonio Turok and Santiago Albert, deserve my heartfelt thanks for creating inspirational black and white imagery that influenced my work within this volume. Thank you to Gary H. Gossen, Frine Castillo Badillo, Philip E. Coyle, and Nicolasa Chávez, whose thoughtful and perceptive essays help convey the significance of the rites and rituals portrayed in the photographs. Special thanks also to Dr. Marina Aguirre, who introduced Anne and me to the captivating beauty and fascinating cultures of Chiapas and Nayarit, in Mexico, and to Hugo Mayans, a brilliant Guatemalan guide and good friend, who opened doors for us to places both ancient and contemporary throughout his country.

I would like to acknowledge David Skolkin for his creativity and adept book design skills and Joanna Hurley, whose insights were valuable in framing the direction of this volume. Anna Gallegos, director of the Museum of New Mexico Press, and Lisa Pacheco, editorial director, deserve special appreciation for embracing this project and publishing it. Finally, I wish to recognize my wife, Anne Frej, for her advice, guidance, and editing skills—and, most of all, for her companionship as we visited these and other celebrations together.

About the Author and Contributors

THE AUTHOR

William Frej, an award-wnning photographer, has been photographing Indigenous people for more than forty years, while traveling in remote mountainous regions of Asia and while living and working in Indonesia, Poland, Kazakhstan, and Afghanistan as a career diplomat with the United States Agency for International Development (USAID). Frej's photographic work has been featured in a variety of exhibitions at galleries and museums in the United States and Mexico, including the Museum of Spanish Colonial Art, Peters Projects Gallery, Edition One Gallery, and Peyton Wright Gallery, all in Santa Fe, New Mexico; as well as the Tucson Art Center; Eye Gallery, in San Francisco; the San Francisco Arts Festival; and Galería La Eskalera, in Mérida, Mexico. His photography is represented in private collections and in the collections of several universities, including University of California at Berkeley, University of Notre Dame, University of New Mexico, Columbia, Duke, Stanford, and Yale. He has a bachelor's degree in architecture from the University of Arizona and a master's degree in city and regional planning from the University of California at Berkeley. His first book, *Maya Ruins Revisited: In the Footsteps of Teobert Maler*, was published in 2020 by Peyton Wright Gallery Press in Santa Fe to wide acclaim. It was awarded the Best Photography Book of the Year by the Independent Press Award and the National Indie Excellence Awards in 2021 and is available from the University of Oklahoma Press.

CONTRIBUTORS

Anne Frej is an urban planner whose career has focused on market feasibility studies and design concepts for real estate development projects in the United States, Indonesia, Central Europe, and Central Asia. At the Urban Land Institute (ULI) in Washington, DC, she was the project director and primary contributor to *Green Office Buildings: A Practical Guide* (2005), *Just-in-Time Real Estate* (2004), and *Professional Real Estate Development: The ULI Guide to the Business* (2003). While living in Jakarta, Indonesia, she served as the Asia editor of *Urban Land* magazine. She has a master's degree in urban planning from the George Washington University.

Gary H. Gossen is the author of several books about the Maya community of San Juan Chamula in Chiapas, Mexico. Among them are *Chamulas in the World of the Sun: Time and Space in a Maya Oral Tradition* (Harvard University Press, 1974), *Telling Maya Tales: Tzotzil Identities in Modern Mexico* (Routledge, 1999), and *Four Creations: An Epic Story of the Chiapas Mayas* (University of Oklahoma Press, 2002). He is the co-author, with Robert M. Carmack and Janine L. Gasco, of *The Legacy of Mesoamerica: History and Culture of a Native American Civilization* (Prentice Hall, 1996), which has become a standard college textbook in Mesoamerican Studies. Gossen is retired from a long teaching and research career at the State University of New York at Albany, where he holds the title of Distinguished Professor Emeritus of Anthropology and Latin American Studies.

Frine Castillo Badillo has a bachelor's degree in ethnography from the National School of Anthropology and History in Mexico and a master's degree in Mesoamerican Studies from the National Autonomous University of Mexico. Since 2011 she has carried out fieldwork in the Sierra Madre Occidental region of western Mexico, specifically the rugged Gran Nayar area in Nayarit state. Since 2013 she has focused on themes of corporality, rituals, artifacts, and technological processes in the Náayeri town of Santa Teresa and neighboring ranches.

Philip E. Coyle is a cultural anthropologist and folklorist, who has published widely on the history, politics, and public ceremonial traditions of the Náayeri people in the Mexican state of Nayarit. The former editor of the *North Carolina Folklore Journal*, he also has published articles on the folklore of Irish traditional music in North Carolina and completed research on the people traditionally associated with national parks in the Southern Appalachian region, including Indigenous people as well as Euro-American descendants and African-Americans. Coyle has a bachelor's degree from San Francisco State University and a PhD from the University of Arizona, and is a professor in the Department of Anthropology and Sociology at Western Carolina University, in Cullowhee, North Carolina. His book, *Náyari History, Politics, and Violence: From Flowers to Ash* was published by the University of Arizona Press in 2001.

Nicolasa Chávez is the Deputy State Historian of New Mexico. A fourteenth-generation New Mexican, she was previously Curator of Latino/Hispano/Spanish Colonial Collections at the Museum of International Folk Art (MOIFA), in Santa Fe, New Mexico. Chávez is also a performer and educator who lectures and conducts demonstrations on flamenco and Argentine tango, combining the music and dance with its history. She received her master's degree in history at the University of New Mexico. She has curated and co-curated numerous exhibitions at MOIFA including *Música Buena: Hispano Folk Music of New Mexico* (2019–2021), *Flamenco: From Spain to New Mexico* (2015–2017), *The Red that Colored the World* (2015), *New World Cuisine: The Histories of Chocolate, Mate y Más* (2012–2014), and *A Century of Masters* (2009–2011), for which her accompanying publication won a New Mexico/Arizona Book Award in 2010. She is the author of *The Spirit of Flamenco: From Spain to New Mexico* (Museum of New Mexico Press, 2015).

Further Reading

Artes de México, Número 85, *Arte Antiguo: Cora y Huichol.* Ciudad de México: Artes de México México y Mundo, S.A. de C.V., August 2007.

Brading, David. *Mexican Phoenix: Our Lady of Guadalupe: Image and Tradition Across Five Centuries.* Cambridge and New York: Cambridge University Press, 2002.

Broyles, Bill, Ann Christine Eek, Phyllis La Farge, Richard Laugharn, and Eugenia Macías Guzmán. *Among Unknown Tribes: Rediscovering the Photographs of Explorer Carl Lumholtz.* Austin: University of Texas Press, 2014.

Carmack, Robert M., Janine Gasco, and Gary H. Gossen. *The Legacy of Mesoamerica: History and Culture of a Native American Civilization*, second edition. New York: Routledge, 2007.

Coyle, Philip E. *Náyari History, Politics, and Violence: From Flower to Ash*. Tucson: University of Arizona Press, 2001.

Doníz, Rafael, *Náyari Cora*. Ciudad de México: Universidad Autónoma Metropolitana/Artes de México y Mundo, S.A. de C.V., 2014.

Gallembo, Phyllis. *Mexico/Masks/Rituals*. Santa Fe: Radius Books, 2019.

Gell, Alfred. *Art and Agency: An Anthropological Theory*. Oxford: Oxford University Press, 1998.

Gossen, Gary H., ed. *South and Meso-American Native Spirituality: From the Cult of the Feathered Serpent to the Theology of Liberation*. New York: The Crossroad Publishing Company, 1997.

Gossen, Gary H., ed. *Symbol and Meaning Beyond the Closed Community: Essays in Mesoamerican Ideas*. Albany: Institute for Mesoamerican Studies, State University of New York, 1986.

Gossen, Gary H. *Telling Maya Tales: Tzotzil Identities in Modern Mexico*. New York and London: Routledge, 1999.

Murdy, Ann. *On the Path of Marigolds: Living Traditions of México's Day of the Dead*. Staunton, VA: George F. Thompson Publishing, 2019.

Norget, Kristin. *Days of Death, Days of Life: Ritual in the Popular Culture of Oaxaca*. New York: Columbia University Press, 2006.

Tedlock, Dennis. *Rabinal Achi: A Mayan Drama of War and Sacrifice*. Oxford: Oxford University Press, 2005.

Director: Anna Gallegos
Editorial Director: Lisa Pacheco
Art Director and book designer: David Skolkin
Project Manager: Anne Frej
Editorial Advisor: Joanna Hurley, HurleyMedia, LLC

Composition: Set in Granjon and Legacy
Printed in Verona, Italy by EBS Editoriale Bortolazzi Stei on acid-free paper.

10 9 8 7 6 5 4 3 2 1

Library of Congress Control Number: 2021940451

ISBN: 978-0-89013-668-3 hardcover

Museum of New Mexico Press
PO Box 2087
Santa Fe, NM 87504
mnmpress.org